BIRDS *of* OREGON

Roger Burrows
Jeff Gilligan

with contributions from Andy Bezener and Chris Fisher

LONE PINE

Lone Pine Publishing International

Distributed by: Lone Pine Publishing
1808 B Street NW, Suite 140
Auburn, WA, USA 98001

Website: www.lonepinepublishing.com

National Library of Canada Cataloguing in Publication Data

Burrows, Roger, 1942–
    Birds of Oregon / Roger Burrows and Jeff Gilligan.

    Includes bibliographical references and index.
    ISBN-13: 978-1-55105-374-5
    ISBN-10: 1-55105-374-8

    1. Birds—Oregon—Identification.   I. Gilligan, Jeff.   II. Title.
QL684.O6B87 2003   598'.09795   C2003-910903-8

Editorial Director: Nancy Foulds
Project Editor: Volker Bodegom
Editorial: Volker Bodegom, Gary Whyte, Genevieve Boyer
Illustrations Coordinator: Carol Woo
Production Manager: Gene Longson
Layout & Production: Elliot Engley, Ian Dawe
Cover Design: Gerry Dotto
Cover Illustration: Great Blue Heron by Gary Ross
Illustrations: Gary Ross, Ted Nordhagen
Maps: Volker Bodegom, Elliot Engley, Ian Dawe
Separations & Film: Elite Lithographers Co.

PC: P13

CONTENTS

ACKNOWLEDGEMENTS

Thanks are extended to the growing family of ornithologists and dedicated birders who have offered their inspiration and expertise to help build Lone Pine's expanding library of field guides. Thanks also go to John Acorn, Chris Fisher, Andy Bezener and Eloise Pulos for their contributions to previous books in this series. In addition, thank you to Gary Ross and Ted Nordhagen, whose skilled illustrations have brought each page to life. Thanks also to Gerald and Rose Gilligan and Dori Jones.

Red-throated Loon
size 25 in • p. 34

Pacific Loon
size 26 in• p. 35

Common Loon
size 31 in • p. 36

Pied-billed Grebe
size 13 in • p. 37

Horned Grebe
size 13 in • p. 38

Red-necked Grebe
size 19 in • p. 39

Eared Grebe
size 13 in • p. 40

Western Grebe
size 22 in • p. 41

Clark's Grebe
size 21 in • p. 42

Black-footed Albatross
size 28 in • p. 43

Northern Fulmar
size 18 in • p. 44

Sooty Shearwater
size 17 in • p. 45

Fork-tailed Storm-Petrel
size 8 in • p. 46

Leach's Storm-Petrel
size 8 in • p. 47

American White Pelican
size 60 in • p. 48

Brown Pelican
size 45 in • p. 49

Brandt's Cormorant
size 33 in • p. 50

Double-crested Cormorant
size 29 in • p. 51

Pelagic Cormorant
size 26 in • p. 52

American Bittern
size 25 in • p. 53

Least Bittern
size 13 in • p. 54

Great Blue Heron
size 52 in • p. 55

Great Egret
size 39 in • p. 56

Snowy Egret
size 24 in • p. 57

Cattle Egret
size 20 in • p. 58

Green Heron
size 18 in • p. 59

HERONLIKE BIRDS

Black-crowned Night-Heron
size 24 in • p. 60

White-faced Ibis
size 22 in • p. 61

Turkey Vulture
size 29 in • p. 62

WATERFOWL

Greater White-fronted Goose
size 30 in • p. 63

Snow Goose
size 30 in • p. 64

Ross's Goose
size 23 in • p. 65

Canada Goose
size 35 in • p. 66

Brant
size 25 in • p. 67

Trumpeter Swan
size 60 in • p. 68

Tundra Swan
size 52 in • p. 69

Wood Duck
size 19 in • p. 70

Gadwall
size 20 in • p. 71

Eurasian Wigeon
size 19 in • p. 72

American Wigeon
size 20 in • p. 73

Mallard
size 24 in • p. 74

Blue-winged Teal
size 15 in • p. 75

Cinnamon Teal
size 16 in • p. 76

Northern Shoveler
size 19 in • p. 77

Northern Pintail
size 24 in • p. 78

Green-winged Teal
size 14 in • p. 79

Canvasback
size 20 in • p. 80

Redhead
size 20 in • p. 81

Ring-necked Duck
size 16 in • p. 82

Greater Scaup
size 18 in • p. 83

Lesser Scaup
size 16 in • p. 84

Harlequin Duck
size 16 in • p. 85

Surf Scoter
size 19 in • p. 86

WATERFOWL

White-winged Scoter
size 21 in • p. 87

Black Scoter
size 19 in • p. 88

Long-tailed Duck
size 18 in • p. 89

Bufflehead
size 14 in • p. 90

Common Goldeneye
size 18 in • p. 91

Barrow's Goldeneye
size 18 in • p. 92

Hooded Merganser
size 17 in • p. 93

Common Merganser
size 24 in • p. 94

Red-breasted Merganser
size 22 in • p. 95

Ruddy Duck
size 15 in • p. 96

BIRDS OF PREY

Osprey
size 23 in • p. 97

White-tailed Kite
size 16 in • p. 98

Bald Eagle
size 36 in • p. 99

Northern Harrier
size 20 in • p. 100

Sharp-shinned Hawk
size 12 in • p. 101

Cooper's Hawk
size 17 in • p. 102

Northern Goshawk
size 23 in • p. 103

Red-shouldered Hawk
size 18 in • p. 104

Swainson's Hawk
size 20 in • p. 105

Red-tailed Hawk
size 21 in • p. 106

Ferruginous Hawk
size 24 in • p. 107

Rough-legged Hawk
size 21 in • p. 108

Golden Eagle
size 35 in • p. 109

American Kestrel
size 8 in • p. 110

Merlin
size 11 in • p. 111

Peregrine Falcon
size 17 in • p. 112

Prairie Falcon
size 16 in • p. 113

REFERENCE GUIDE

Chukar
size 13 in • p. 114

Gray Partridge
size 12 in • p. 115

Ring-necked Pheasant
size 30 in • p. 116

Ruffed Grouse
size 17 in • p. 117

Greater Sage-Grouse
size 26 in • p. 118

Spruce Grouse
size 15 in • p. 119

Blue Grouse
size 19 in • p. 120

Wild Turkey
size 43 in • p. 121

Mountain Quail
size 11 in • p. 122

California Quail
size 10 in • p. 123

Yellow Rail
size 7 in • p. 124

Virginia Rail
size 10 in • p. 125

Sora
size 9 in • p. 126

American Coot
size 14 in • p. 127

Sandhill Crane
size 45 in • p. 128

Black-bellied Plover
size 12 in • p. 129

American Golden-Plover
size 12 in • p. 130

Pacific Golden-Plover
size 10 in • p. 131

Snowy Plover
size 6 in • p. 132

Semipalmated Plover
size 7 in • p. 133

Killdeer
size 10 in • p. 134

Black Oystercatcher
size 17 in • p. 135

Black-necked Stilt
size 14 in • p. 136

American Avocet
size 17 in • p. 137

Greater Yellowlegs
size 14 in • p. 138

Lesser Yellowlegs
size 10 in • p. 139

Solitary Sandpiper
size 8 in • p. 140

Willet
size 15 in • p. 141

Wandering Tattler
size 10 in • p. 142

Spotted Sandpiper
size 7 in • p. 143

Whimbrel
size 17 in • p. 144

Long-billed Curlew
size 23 in • p. 145

Marbled Godwit
size 18 in • p. 146

Ruddy Turnstone
size 9 in • p. 147

Black Turnstone
size 9 in • p. 148

Surfbird
size 9 in • p. 149

Red Knot
size 10 in • p. 150

Sanderling
size 7 in • p. 151

Western Sandpiper
size 6 in • p. 152

Least Sandpiper
size 6 in • p. 153

Baird's Sandpiper
size 7 in • p. 154

Pectoral Sandpiper
size 7 in • p. 155

Sharp-tailed Sandpiper
size 8 in • p. 156

Rock Sandpiper
size 9 in • p. 157

Dunlin
size 8 in • p. 158

Short-billed Dowitcher
size 11 in • p. 159

Long-billed Dowitcher
size 11 in • p. 160

Wilson's Snipe
size 11 in • p. 161

Wilson's Phalarope
size 8 in • p. 162

Red-necked Phalarope
size 7 in • p. 163

Red Phalarope
size 8 in • p. 164

Pomarine Jaeger
size 20 in • p. 165

Parasitic Jaeger
size 18 in • p. 166

Franklin's Gull
size 14 in • p. 167

Bonaparte's Gull
size 13 in • p. 168

Heermann's Gull
size 17 in • p. 169

Mew Gull
size 16 in • p. 170

Ring-billed Gull
size 19 in • p. 171

California Gull
size 19 in • p. 172

Herring Gull
size 24 in • p. 173

Thayer's Gull
size 23 in • p. 174

Western Gull
size 25 in • p. 175

Glaucous-winged Gull
size 25 in • p. 176

Sabine's Gull
size 13 in • p. 177

Black-legged Kittiwake
size 17 in • p. 178

Caspian Tern
size 21 in • p. 179

Common Tern
size 13 in • p. 180

Arctic Tern
size 15 in • p. 181

Forster's Tern
size 14 in • p. 182

Black Tern
size 9 in • p. 183

Common Murre
size 17 in • p. 184

Pigeon Guillemot
size 13 in • p. 185

Marbled Murrelet
size 9 in • p. 186

Ancient Murrelet
size 9 in • p. 187

Cassin's Auklet
size 8 in • p. 188

Rhinoceros Auklet
size 15 in • p. 189

Tufted Puffin
size 15 in • p. 190

Rock Dove
size 13 in • p. 191

Band-tailed Pigeon
size 14 in • p. 192

Mourning Dove
size 12 in • p. 193

Barn Owl
size 14 in • p. 194

Flammulated Owl
size 6 in • p. 195

Western Screech-Owl
size 9 in • p. 196

Great Horned Owl
size 21 in • p. 197

Snowy Owl
size 23 in • p. 198

Northern Pygmy-Owl
size 7 in • p. 199

Burrowing Owl
size 8 in • p. 200

Spotted Owl
size 18 in • p. 201

Barred Owl
size 20 in • p. 202

Great Gray Owl
size 29 in • p. 203

OWLS

Long-eared Owl
size 14 in • p. 204

Short-eared Owl
size 15 in • p. 205

Boreal Owl
size 10 in • p. 206

Northern Saw-whet Owl
size 8 in • p. 207

NIGHTJARS, SWIFTS & HUMMINGBIRDS

Common Nighthawk
size 9 in • p. 208

Common Poorwill
size 7 in • p. 209

Black Swift
size 7 in • p. 210

Vaux's Swift
size 5 in • p. 211

White-throated Swift
size 6 in • p. 212

Black-chinned Hummingbird
size 3 in • p. 213

Anna's Hummingbird
size 3 in • p. 214

Calliope Hummingbird
size 3 in • p. 215

Rufous Hummingbird
size 3 in • p. 216

Allen's Hummingbird
size 3 in • p. 217

Belted Kingfisher
size 12 in • p. 218

WOODPECKERS

Lewis's Woodpecker
size 11 in • p. 219

Acorn Woodpecker
size 9 in • p. 220

Williamson's Sapsucker
size 9 in • p. 221

Red-naped Sapsucker
size 8 in • p. 222

Red-breasted Sapsucker
size 8 in • p. 223

Downy Woodpecker
size 6 in • p. 224

Hairy Woodpecker
size 8 in • p. 225

White-headed Woodpecker
size 9 in • p. 226

Three-toed Woodpecker
size 8 in • p. 227

11

WOODPECKERS

Black-backed Woodpecker
size 9 in • p. 228

Northern Flicker
size 12 in • p. 229

Pileated Woodpecker
size 17 in • p. 230

FLYCATCHERS

Olive-sided Flycatcher
size 7 in • p. 232

Western Wood-Pewee
size 5 in • p. 233

Willow Flycatcher
size 5 in • p. 234

Hammond's Flycatcher
size 5 in • p. 235

Gray Flycatcher
size 5 in • p. 236

Dusky Flycatcher
size 5 in • p. 237

Pacific-slope Flycatcher
size 5 in • p. 238

Cordilleran Flycatcher
size 5 in • p. 239

Black Phoebe
size 7 in • p. 240

Say's Phoebe
size 7 in • p. 241

Ash-throated Flycatcher
size 8 in • p. 242

Western Kingbird
size 8 in • p. 243

Eastern Kingbird
size 8 in • p. 244

SHRIKES & VIREOS

Loggerhead Shrike
size 9 in • p. 245

Northern Shrike
size 10 in • p. 246

Cassin's Vireo
size 5 in • p. 247

Hutton's Vireo
size 4 in • p. 248

Warbling Vireo
size 5 in • p. 249

Red-eyed Vireo
size 6 in • p. 250

JAYS & CROWS

Gray Jay
size 11 in • p. 251

Steller's Jay
size 11 in • p. 252

Western Scrub-Jay
size 11 in • p. 253

Pinyon Jay
size 10 in • p. 254

Clark's Nutcracker
size 12 in • p. 255

Black-billed Magpie
size 20 in • p. 256

American Crow
size 19 in • p. 257

Common Raven
size 24 in • p. 258

LARKS & SWALLOWS

Horned Lark
size 7 in • p. 259

Purple Martin
size 7 in • p. 260

Tree Swallow
size 5 in • p. 261

Violet-green Swallow
size 5 in • p. 262

Northern Rough-winged Swallow
size 5 in • p. 263

Bank Swallow
size 5 in • p. 264

Cliff Swallow
size 5 in • p. 265

Barn Swallow
size 6 in • p. 266

CHICKADEES, WRENS & NUTHATCHES

Black-capped Chickadee
size 5 in • p. 267

Mountain Chickadee
size 5 in • p. 268

Chestnut-backed Chickadee
size 5 in • p. 269

Oak Titmouse
size 5 in • p. 270

Juniper Titmouse
size 5 in • p. 271

Bushtit
size 4 in • p. 272

Red-breasted Nuthatch
size 4 in • p. 273

White-breasted Nuthatch
size 6 in • p. 274

Pygmy Nuthatch
size 4 in • p. 275

Brown Creeper
size 5 in • p. 276

Rock Wren
size 6 in • p. 277

Canyon Wren
size 5 in • p. 278

Bewick's Wren
size 5 in • p. 279

CHICKADEES, WRENS & NUTHATCHES

House Wren
size 4 in • p. 280

Winter Wren
size 4 in • p. 281

Marsh Wren
size 5 in • p. 282

American Dipper
size 7 in • p. 283

KINGLETS, BLUEBIRDS & THRUSHES

Golden-crowned Kinglet
size 4 in • p. 284

Ruby-crowned Kinglet
size 4 in • p. 285

Blue-gray Gnatcatcher
size 4 in • p. 286

Western Bluebird
size 7 in • p. 287

Mountain Bluebird
size 7 in • p. 288

Townsend's Solitare
size 8 in • p. 289

Veery
size 7 in • p. 290

Swainson's Thrush
size 7 in • p. 291

Hermit Thrush
size 6 in • p. 292

American Robin
size 10 in • p. 293

Varied Thrush
size 9 in • p. 294

Wrentit
size 6 in • p. 295

MIMICS, STARLINGS & WAXWINGS

Gray Catbird
size 8 in • p. 296

Northern Mockingbird
size 10 in • p. 297

Sage Thrasher
size 8 in • p. 298

European Starling
size 8 in • p. 299

American Pipit
size 6 in • p. 300

Bohemian Waxwing
size 8 in • p. 301

Cedar Waxwing
size 7 in • p. 302

WOOD-WARBLERS & TANAGERS

Orange-crowned Warbler
size 5 in • p. 303

Nashville Warbler
size 4 in • p. 304

Yellow Warbler
size 5 in • p. 305

Yellow-rumped Warbler
size 5 in • p. 306

Black-throated Gray Warbler
size 5 in • p. 307

Townsend's Warbler
size 5 in • p. 308

Hermit Warbler
size 5 in • p. 309

Palm Warbler
size 5 in • p. 310

American Redstart
size 5 in • p. 311

Northern Waterthrush
size 6 in • p. 312

MacGillivray's Warbler
size 5 in • p. 313

Common Yellowthroat
size 5 in • p. 314

Wilson's Warbler
size 4 in • p. 315

Yellow-breasted Chat
size 7 in • p. 316

Western Tanager
size 7 in • p. 317

Green-tailed Towhee
size 7 in • p. 318

Spotted Towhee
size 7 in • p. 319

California Towhee
size 9 in • p. 320

American Tree Sparrow
size 6 in • p. 321

Chipping Sparrow
size 5 in • p. 322

Brewer's Sparrow
size 5 in • p. 323

Vesper Sparrow
size 6 in • p. 324

Lark Sparrow
size 6 in • p. 325

Black-throated Sparrow
size 5 in • p. 326

Sage Sparrow
size 5 in • p. 327

Savannah Sparrow
size 5 in • p. 328

Grasshopper Sparrow
size 4 in • p. 329

Fox Sparrow
size 7 in • p. 330

Song Sparrow
size 5 in • p. 331

Lincoln's Sparrow
size 5 in • p. 332

Swamp Sparrow
size 5 in • p. 333

SPARROWS, GROSBEAKS & BUNTINGS

White-throated Sparrow
size 6 in • p. 334

White-crowned Sparrow
size 7 in • p. 335

Golden-crowned Sparrow
size 7 in • p. 336

Dark-eyed Junco
size 6 in • p. 337

Lapland Longspur
size 6 in • p. 338

Snow Bunting
size 6 in • p. 339

Black-headed Grosbeak
size 7 in • p. 340

Lazuli Bunting
size 5 in • p. 341

BLACKBIRDS & ORIOLES

Bobolink
size 7 in • p. 342

Red-winged Blackbird
size 8 in • p. 343

Tricolored Blackbird
size 8 in • p. 344

Western Meadowlark
size 9 in • p. 345

Yellow-headed Blackbird
size 9 in • p. 346

Brewer's Blackbird
size 8 in • p. 347

Brown-headed Cowbird
size 7 in • p. 348

Bullock's Oriole
size 8 in • p. 349

FINCHLIKE BIRDS

Gray-crowned Rosy-Finch
size 6 in • p. 350

Black Rosy-Finch
size 6 in • p. 351

Pine Grosbeak
size 8 in • p. 352

Purple Finch
size 5 in • p. 353

Cassin's Finch
size 6 in • p. 354

House Finch
size 5 in • p. 355

Red Crossbill
size 5 in • p. 356

Common Redpoll
size 5 in • p. 357

Pine Siskin
size 4 in • p. 358

Lesser Goldfinch
size 4 in • p. 359

American Goldfinch
size 5 in • p. 360

Evening Grosbeak
size 7 in • p. 361

House Sparrow
size 6 in • p. 362

INTRODUCTION

BIRDWATCHING IN OREGON

In recent decades, birdwatching has evolved from an eccentric pursuit practiced by a few dedicated individuals to a continent-wide activity that boasts millions of professional and amateur participants. There are many good reasons why birdwatching has become so popular. Many people find it simple and relaxing, whereas others enjoy the outdoor exercise that it affords. Some enjoy the challenges of bird identification, and others enjoy listing species seen, a non-acquisitive form of collecting. Some see it as a rewarding learning experience, an opportunity to socialize with like-minded people and a way to monitor the health of the local environment. Still others watch birds to reconnect with nature. These days, a visit to any of Oregon's premier birding locations, such as Clatsop Spit at the mouth of the Columbia River, Sauvie Island near Portland, Fern Ridge near Eugene and Malheur National Wildlife Refuge, would doubtless uncover still more reasons why people watch birds.

We are truly blessed by the geographical and biological diversity of our state. Because the Pacific Ocean and Cascade Range modify the climate, and the south of the state has the same latitude as Northern California, Oregon has a great variety of birds and many birds remain in Oregon during the winter months. In addition to supporting a wide range of breeding birds and year-round residents, Oregon hosts a large number of spring and fall migrants that move between breeding and wintering grounds. In all, 477 bird species have been seen and recorded in Oregon, and more than 357 species make annual appearances.

Yellow Warbler

Oregon also has a long tradition of friendly birdwatching. In general, Oregon birders and bird clubs are willing to help beginners and involve novices in their projects. Christmas bird counts, breeding bird surveys, beached bird censuses, the Pacific Shorebird Project, field trips, pelagic trips, the Eugene Bluebird Trail Nest Box Program and birdwatching lectures and workshops all provide a chance for novice, intermediate and expert birdwatchers to interact and share the splendor of birds. So, whatever your level, there is ample opportunity for you to get involved!

BEGINNING TO LEARN THE BIRDS

Birdwatching (also known as "birding") can be extremely challenging and getting started is often the most difficult part. Although any standard North American field guide will help you identify local birds, such guides can be daunting, because they cover the entire continent and present an overwhelming number of species. By focusing specifically on the bird life of Oregon, we hope to ease the beginner's difficulty.

TECHNIQUES OF BIRDWATCHING

Being in the right place at the right time to see birds in action involves both skill and luck. The more you know about a bird—its range, preferred habitat, food preferences and hours and seasons of activity—the better your chances will be of seeing it.

Generally, spring and fall are the busiest birding times. Temperatures are moderate then, and a great number of birds are on the move, often cramming themselves into small patches of habitat before moving on. Male songbirds are easy to identify on spring mornings as they belt out their courtship songs. Throughout much of the year, diurnal birds are most visible in the early morning hours when they are foraging, but during winter they are often more active later in the day, when milder temperatures prevail. Timing is crucial, but because summer foliage often conceals birds and cold weather drives many species south of Oregon for winter, birdwatching also involves a great deal of luck.

Barred Owl

BIRDING BY EAR

Recognizing birds by their songs and calls can greatly enhance your birding experience. When experienced birders conduct breeding bird surveys each June, they rely more on their ears than their eyes. There are numerous tapes and CDs that can help you learn bird songs, and a portable player with headphones can let you quickly compare a live bird with a recording.

The old-fashioned way to remember bird songs is to make up words for them. We have given you some of the classic renderings in the species accounts that follow, such as *Who cooks for you? Who cooks for you-all?* for the Barred Owl, as well as some nonsense syllables, such as *tsik* or *te* for the Hermit Warbler.

WATCHING BIRD BEHAVIOR

Once you can confidently identify birds and remember their common names, you can begin to appreciate their behavior. Studying birds involves keeping notes and records. The timing of bird migrations is an easy thing to record, as are details of feeding, courtship and nesting behavior if you are willing to be patient.

Birding, for most people, is a peaceful, nondestructive recreational activity. One of the best ways to watch bird behavior is to look for a spot rich with avian life and then sit back and relax. If you become part of the scenery, the birds, at first startled by your approach, will soon resume their activities and invite you into their world.

BIRDING BY HABITAT

Oregon can be separated into seven biophysical regions or "bioregions": they are Coast Range/Western Cascades; Blue, Wallowa and Ochoco Mountains; Siskiyou Mountains; East Slope Cascades; Western Oregon Interior Valleys; Great Basin/Columbia Basin and Coastal Littoral. Each bioregion is composed of a number of different habitats, such as open salt water, saltmarshes, freshwater wetlands, grasslands, agricultural lands, arid scrubland and sagebush, chaparral, pine-juniper woodlands, riparian woodlands, oak and other deciduous woodlands, coniferous forests, subalpine tundra and urban areas. Each habitat is a community of plants and animals supported by the infrastructure of water and soil and regulated by the constraints of topography, climate and elevation.

Simply put, a bird's habitat is the place in which it normally lives. Some birds prefer the open water, some birds are found in cattail marshes, others like mature coniferous forest, and still others prefer abandoned agricultural fields overgrown with tall grass and shrubs. Knowledge of a bird's habitat increases the chances of identifying the bird correctly. If you are birding in freshwater wetlands, you will not be identifying woodpeckers or warblers; if you are wandering among the conifers of high-elevation forests, do not expect to meet nesting ducks or rails.

BIRD LISTING

Many birders list the species they have seen during excursions or at home. It is up to you to decide what kind of list—systematic or casual—you will keep, and you may choose not to make lists at all. However, a list may prove rewarding in unexpected ways. By reviewing it, you can recall memories and details that may otherwise be forgotten.

There are computer programs available for listing birds, but many naturalists simply keep records in field notebooks. Waterproof books and waterproof pens work well on rainy days, although many birders prefer to use a pocket recorder in the field and to transcribe the observations into a dry notebook at home.

BIRDWATCHING ACTIVITIES

Birdwatching Groups

It is a good idea to join in on such activities as Christmas bird counts, birding festivals and the meetings of your local birding or natural history club. Meeting other people with the same interests can make birding even more pleasurable, and there is always something to be learned when birders of all levels gather. If you are interested in bird conservation and environmental issues, natural history groups and conscientious birdwatching stores can keep you informed about the situation in your area and what you can do to help. Bird hotlines provide up-to-date information on the sightings of rarities, which are often easier to relocate than you might think.

American Kestrel

Organizations

American Bird Conservancy
P.O. Box 249
The Plains, VA 20198
Phone: (540) 253-5780
Website: www.abcbirds.org

Oregon Field Ornithologists (OFO)
P.O. Box 10373
Eugene, OR 97440
Website: www.oregonbirds.org
(OFO publishes the *Oregon Birds* quarterly)

Audubon Society of Portland
5151 N.W. Cornell Rd.
Portland, OR 97210
Phone: (503) 292-6855
Nature Store: (503) 292-9453
Website: www.audubonportland.org

National Audubon Society
700 Broadway
New York, NY 10003
Phone: (212) 979-3000
Website: www.audubon.org
To locate local Oregon chapters of the Audubon Society, including those in Eugene, Salem, Medford, Bend, Corvallis and others, phone the national office or go to the following website: www.audubon.org/states/or

Bird Hotlines

Portland Audubon Society (statewide hotline): (503) 292-0661
Klamath Basin Hotline: (541) 850-3805
Northern Idaho, Eastern Washington and Northeastern Oregon Hotline: (208) 882-6195

Internet e-mail List

Oregon Birders Online (OBOL)
To subscribe to an e-mail list for discussions with other birders, go to the Lyris webpage: www.lists.oregonstate.edu and enter the list name "OBOL."

Bird Conservation

Oregon is a good place to watch birds. After all, there are still large areas of wilderness here, including national and state parks, national wildlife refuges and management areas and national forests. Nevertheless, forestry and development for housing are threatening viable bird habitat throughout the state. It is hoped that more people will learn to appreciate nature through birding, and that those people will do their best to protect the nature that remains. Many bird enthusiasts support groups such as Ducks Unlimited, which helps waterbirds by buying and managing tracts of good habitat, and the American Bird Conservancy, which is dedicated exclusively to the conservation of birds.

Landscaping your own property to provide native plant cover and natural foods for birds is an immediate way to ensure the conservation of bird habitat. The cumulative effects of such urban "nature-scaping" can be significant. If your yard is to become a bird sanctuary, you may want to keep the neighborhood cats out; every year, millions of birds are killed by cats. Check with the local Humane Society for methods of protecting both your feline friends and wild birds. Ultimately, cats are best kept indoors.

Anna's Hummingbird

Bird Feeding

Many people set up a backyard birdfeeder to attract birds to their yard, especially in winter. It is possible to attract specific birds by choosing the right kind of food. If you have a feeder, keep it stocked through late spring. The weather may be balmy, but birds have a hard time finding food before flowers bloom, seeds develop and insects hatch. In summer, hummingbirds can be attracted to your yard with a special feeder filled with artificial nectar (a simple sugar solution of three to four parts water and one part white sugar). Be sure to follow the feeder's cleaning instructions.

Birdbaths will also bring birds to your yard, and heated birdbaths are particularly effective in winter. Avoid birdbaths that have exposed metal parts, because wet birds can accidentally freeze to them. In general, feeding birds is good, especially if you provide food in the form of native berry- or seed-producing plants grown in your backyard. Contrary to popular opinion, birds do not become dependent on feeders, nor do they subsequently forget to forage naturally. However, if you feed hummingbirds, keep doing so as long as you have birds coming to your feeder. Anna's Hummingbirds, which are nonmigratory, depend on feeders in the winter. Many good books are available about feeding birds and landscaping your yard to provide natural foods and nest sites.

Nest Boxes

Another popular way to attract birds is to set out nest boxes, especially for wrens, bluebirds and swallows. Not all birds will use nest boxes: only species that normally use cavities in trees are comfortable in such confined spaces. Larger nest boxes can attract kestrels, owls and cavity-nesting ducks.

OREGON'S TOP BIRDING SITES

There are hundreds, if not thousands, of good birding areas throughout the state. The following areas have been selected to represent a broad range of bird communities and habitats, with an emphasis on accessibility. Common birds are included in these accounts, as well as exciting rarities.

Fort Stevens State Park

The trail that winds around Coffenbury Lake is best birded early in the morning for breeding birds and migrants. Nesting waterbirds include Pied-billed Grebes, Green Herons, Wood Ducks and Hooded Mergansers, and the brushy growth on the east side usually harbors Wrentits year-round. Clatsop Spit attracts an occasional wintering Gyrfalcon or Snowy Owl as well as errant songbird migrants. The South Jetty extends west of Clatsop Spit from a parking lot and observation tower, from which waterfowl and shorebirds can easily be seen. Most shorebirds gather just below the parking lot, and gulls and terns are usually seen just to the west on the ocean side. Loons, grebes, shearwaters, alcids and all three jaegers can be seen from the jetty in fall. The Jetty Lagoon east of Clatsop Spit is a good place to look for wintering Brant and any Bald Eagles or Peregrine Falcons. Haystack Rock at Cannon Beach, 25 miles to the south, has a large colony of Tufted Puffins.

Green Heron

Yaquina Bay and Newport

Yaquina Bay is a productive site at any time of year and is easily accessible by road. The South Jetty area attracts thousands of scoters of all three species from September to early May, and there are usually a few Harlequin Ducks and Long-tailed Ducks. All three common loons, all three cormorants and a good number of grebes, Brant and diving ducks can be seen, as well as Brown Pelicans and Heermann's Gulls. Parasitic Jaegers often pursue the gulls and terns gathered by the jetty. Nearby Yaquina Head to the north of Newport is the best place to watch alcids and rock-loving shorebirds.

The Mark O. Hatfield Marine Science Center's nature trail east of the Yaquina Bay Bridge is the best place to look for shorebirds at high tide, with Whimbrels and Willets joining the usual wintering species. A few Eurasian Wigeons can be expected among the American Wigeon flocks both here and in the Sally's Bend area of Yaquina

Brown Pelican

Bay. Yaquina Bay is also known for its migrant gulls and terns. Shrubby growth alongside the Marine Science Center trail attracts migrant songbirds, including fairly regular Palm Warblers.

Coos Bay

Coos Bay offers a variety of habitats, from open sandy beaches, rocky headlands, tidal mudflats and coastal salt marshes to dense coniferous forest, open meadows and residential areas. North of the Coos Bay Bridge, a road to the west passes through a mudflat section of the Oregon Dunes, where Great Egrets are particularly common, along with a few Snowy Egrets. Both here and at Pony Slough by the North Bend airport, ducks and shorebirds are very common from August through winter. Simpson Park, at the south end of the Coos Bay Bridge, attracts a good variety of nesting passerines and is especially productive during migration and in winter.

The Charleston area is good for viewing loons, grebes, cormorants, Brown Pelicans, sea ducks and gulls during migration and in winter. The Oregon Institute of Marine Biology feeders attract hummingbirds, as does the Botanical Gardens at Shore Acres State Park. A nature trail beyond the Coos Head Naval Facility is the best place to look for nesting passerines.

Coquille River Estuary

The mouth of the Coquille River has been the site of some of Oregon's most exceptional rare shorebird sightings. The best viewing on the mudflats off River Road is at low tide, whereas good viewing north of Coquille Point and the Coquille River Lighthouse is at high tide. Whimbrels, Marbled Godwits and Short-billed Dowitchers are all regular visitors. Coquille Point provides a viewpoint for offshore seabird colonies, including Tufted Puffins.

Sauvie Island

This large island at the confluence of the Columbia and Willamette Rivers is an important migration and wintering sanctuary for waterfowl, especially several races of Canada Geese and Sandhill Cranes. Access is limited, especially during the winter hunting season, but roads reach most parts of the sanctuary, and trails provide access to Oak Island, Coon Point and Rentenaar Road, where many of the waterfowl and migrant shorebirds can be seen. Sauvie Island is an excellent site for wintering sparrows. Bald Eagles, Northern Harriers, Red-tailed Hawks and a variety of other raptors are regular in winter. A fall or winter visit to Scappoose Bottoms to the north of Multnomah Channel is equally worthwhile. Summer birding is much less productive but provides a variety of nesting species, especially from the trail that goes around Virginia Lake.

Bald Eagle

Portland

Portland's park system offers a number of natural reserves that provide a cross-section of birdlife. The Audubon Society of Portland's Pittock Bird Sanctuary is mainly dense coniferous forest in a steep ravine. Trails crisscross the property and the visitor center is a model for any society to copy. Forest Park in the northwest of the city, one of the largest city parks in the United States, is best known for its spring and early summer nighttime owling. Oaks Bottom Wildlife Refuge in southeastern Portland consists mainly of marshy wooded river bottoms and brushy areas. Great Blue Herons and Green Herons nest alongside Wood Ducks in the wetter areas, and the woodlots contain plenty of migrant songbirds. Winter raptor and sparrow searches often turn up rare species. Crystal Springs Rhododendron Garden to the east is the best place to study wintering waterfowl at close range and provides a chance to see wintering warblers.

Hermit Warbler

Larch Mountain

Located 45 miles east of Portland, Larch Mountain is the closest site for observing mountain birds. Densely forested with Douglas-fir, western redcedar, western hemlock, and both grand fir and subalpine fir, Larch Mountain is best visited from May to mid-June, when Hermit Warblers are in full song. Gray Jays are widespread, and both Calliope Hummingbirds and Townsend's Solitaires have been seen at the summit viewpoint. Logging activity can restrict movement, but lower forests and clear-cuts attract Mountain Quail, Band-tailed Pigeons and a few territorial Dusky Flycatchers.

Forest Grove

The former Forest Grove Sewage Ponds are now a dedicated bird reserve, the Fern Hill Wetlands, and birders no longer need to ask for access to the area. Gadwalls, Blue-winged Teals, Cinnamon Teals, Ruddy Ducks, American Bitterns, Virginia Rails and Soras are occasionally joined by Wilson's Phalaropes in summer, and migration periods are notable for large numbers of shorebirds, gulls and terns. Winter brings many Tundra Swans and Canada Geese, as well as loons, grebes, cormorants, and occasionally Trumpeter Swans, ducks and other geese. Brush patches alongside Geiger Road harbor large numbers of wintering sparrows and finches, including Lesser Goldfinches and some rare sparrows, thereby attracting raptors and Northern Shrikes. Pacific University's oak trees house a colony of Acorn Woodpeckers, and the university campus is also good for White-breasted Nuthatches.

Ankeny National Wildlife Refuge

Ankeny was founded in the 1960s as one of three Oregon preserves for the Dusky race of Canada Goose. A parking lot off Wintel Road provides access to a year-round boardwalk trail that is good for viewing nesting birds, including Acorn Woodpeckers and Lesser Goldfinches. Another parking lot off Buena Vista Road provides an excellent view of one of the ponds where grebes, geese and ducks gather in large numbers. This is a good place to look for geese and Eurasian Wigeons in winter. Raptors are also common in winter, and Dunlins typically gather at the refuge in late afternoon in one enormous flock to roost.

Fern Ridge Reservoir and Eugene

When water levels are high, Fern Ridge Reservoir offers many of the typical habitats of the Willamette Valley wetlands. The main birding attractions are wintering waterfowl and raptors, and migrant shorebirds and gulls. The Krugur Park and Richardson Park areas off Clear Lake Road are especially productive for shorebirds and wintering herons and egrets. Raptors can also be expected anywhere in the area, with Red-shouldered Hawks and Black-shouldered Kites both regular. Migrant passerines are more common in the wooded areas north of Highway 126 and wintering sparrow flocks often attract rarities. A visit to Fern Ridge Reservoir can be combined with visits to several birding sites in Eugene itself. Spencer Butte and Skinner Butte provide excellent places to enjoy woodland birds, especially during migration periods.

Northern Pygmy-Owl

Whitehorse County Park

Just west of Grants Pass, Whitehorse County Park requires a willingness to find your own trails through the riparian woodlands where Wrentits can be found. The upland mixed woodland by the park entrance has Hutton's Vireos, and the wetter lowland areas also attract Oak Titmice and Black Phoebes. Sandbars east of the park where the Applegate River joins the Rogue River may have migrant ducks, shorebirds and other waterbirds. Great Egrets are common in winter, and open fields attract Western Kingbirds, Lazuli Buntings and Lesser Goldfinches in summer.

Mountain Lakes Resort Area

Both Hyatt and Howard Prairie Reservoirs are artificial lakes in the high mountains east of Ashland. A few Great Gray Owls still occupy this area. The area's forests also support Blue Grouse, Northern Goshawks, Three-toed Woodpeckers, Black-backed Woodpeckers, Mountain Bluebirds, Cassin's Vireos and Hermit Warblers.

Sisters Campgrounds

Two campgrounds, Cold Springs and Indian Ford, situated northwest of Sisters, are located in ponderosa pine forests known for nesting White-headed Woodpeckers and sapsuckers. Three sapsucker species occur in the pines, with the Williamson's and Red-naped joined by an occasional Red-breasted. Pygmy Nuthatches and Red-breasted Nuthatches are common in the dry pine–sage–juniper areas, where Gray Flycatchers may be seen as well as the more widespread Dusky Flycatchers and Hammond's Flycatchers. Vireos and warblers are also common in summer, and Indian Ford Creek is a good place to listen for Northern Pygmy-Owls.

Bend

Bend is located in the juniper uplands and offers a variety of birding opportunities. Sawyer Park and Tumalo State Park have riparian species in summer, including Vaux's Swifts, Northern Rough-winged Swallows, Rufous, Calliope and Anna's hummingbirds and Warbling Vireos, plus a number of flycatcher species in migration. Mirror Pond in Bend attracts migrant waterfowl, including Wood Ducks, Gadwalls, Redheads, Ruddy Ducks and Hooded Mergansers, which may remain through winter. Hatfield Lake to the east of Bend is known for its shorebirds, gulls, terns and waterfowl. Access to the ponds is limited but birders are welcome as long as they check in at the wastewater treatment plant. Most shorebird species, including rarities, use the ponds between July and late September, when loons, grebes, cormorants and geese are joined by ducks and

Peregrine Falcon

marsh birds. Peregrines prey on the shorebirds and ducks and often create a commotion among the migrant gulls and terns.

Cascade Lakes Highway (National Forest Road 46)

Located in the Deschutes National Forest southwest of Bend, this route links a series of more than a dozen lakes and varied habitats. The smaller, northern lakes and conifer forests offer high-elevation bird species, including Gray Jays and Hermit Warblers, as well as the more widespread Northern Goshawks, Vaux's Swifts, Dusky Flycatchers, Western Tanagers and Red Crossbills. Lodgepole pine stands have nesting Three-toed Woodpeckers and Black-backed Woodpeckers, whereas Lava Lake Campground has fairly regular Northern Pygmy-Owls and occasional Pine Grosbeaks.

The larger, southern lakes and riparian woodlands have small numbers of nesting Bald Eagles and Ospreys, as well as migrant waterbirds, especially at Wickiup Reservoir. Davis Lake, the last in the chain of lakes, is the best birding site for nesting Western Grebes, Eared Grebes, rails, Wilson's Phalaropes, Forster's Terns, Black Terns, plus several summering ducks. The northern end of the lake is blocked by a lava flow where

Common Poorwills, Rock Wrens, Mountain Bluebirds, Clark's Nutcrackers and Brewer's Sparrows nest. The pine forests are also worth checking for several local species, including White-headed Woodpeckers, Nashville Warblers and Green-tailed Towhees.

Upper Klamath Lake

The large lake north of Klamath Falls has both Horned Grebes and Red-necked Grebes nesting in the same areas as Western Grebes and Clark's Grebes. American White Pelicans and Double-crested Cormorants also have nesting colonies in the area, and Caspian Terns join the Forster's Terns and Black Terns in summer. Upper Klamath National Wildlife Refuge's wet marshland is hard to explore, so a rented canoe may be the best way to look for Least Bitterns and Red-necked Grebes. The bordering ponderosa pine forest has White-headed Woodpeckers, Pygmy Nuthatches, Mountain Chickadees, Mountain Bluebirds, Western Bluebirds, Dusky Flycatchers and Green-tailed Towhees. Agency Lake to the east, which offers the same nesting waterbirds, is best reached from Henzel Park west of Highway 97.

Mountain Chickadee

Lower Klamath Area

Miller Island, between the Klamath River and Highway 97, is managed as a migration resting area for waterfowl and is best visited from late February to late April, when large numbers of Ross's Geese join flocks of Canada, Snow and Greater White-fronted geese and Tundra Swans. Tricolored Blackbirds are also conspicuous at this time, with shorebirds following through May, and Black-necked Stilts, American Avocets and Wilson's Phalaropes staying to nest. Lower Klamath Lake Road has migrant waterfowl and Sandhill Cranes, as well as Tricolored Blackbirds.

To the south, straddling the California border, Lower Klamath National Wildlife Refuge offers a number of self-guided auto tours. State Line Road passes through dry upland habitats, marshes and alkaline ponds. Black-necked Stilts, Cinnamon Teals, Snowy Egrets and Long-billed Curlews can be found in the wetlands, with Sage Thrashers, Western Meadowlarks and Sage Sparrows in the dry sage areas. White Lake to the east has nesting Snowy Plovers at times, and migratory shorebirds usually visit. In winter, Lapland Longspur flocks should be checked for the presence of Chestnut-collared Longspurs and McCown's Longspurs.

Ladd Creek Area

Just south of the Interstate 84 overpass in La Grande, the sewage ponds have nesting American Avocets and Wilson's Phalaropes as well as Blue-winged Teals and Cinnamon Teals, and there are often Long-billed Curlews and Gray Partridges in the farm fields. Gulls and terns gather on the ponds, which are also popular with grebes, waterfowl and shorebirds in migration. The grasslands on either side of Route 203 have raptors most of the year and a few Barn Owls and Burrowing Owls that are losing ground to grazing cattle. The marshy mouth of Ladd Creek includes a Great Blue Heron rookery, and the willows and cottonwoods often have raptors hunting from them. Shorebirds are also regular in this area, along with the occasional White-faced Ibis.

Upper Wallowa Valley

The Enterprise–Joseph area is one of eastern Oregon's best birding areas year-round. Just west of Enterprise, the Wallowa Fish Hatchery and Enterprise Wildlife Management Area is best known for its variety of migrant and wintering waterfowl and nesting Western Screech-Owls. The marshy areas have nesting rails and warblers, and the brushy juniper woodland has large wintering flocks of California Quail and Ring-necked Pheasants. Pete's Pond, a former mill pond that has been converted into a water-fowl pond, attracts migrant waterfowl. The spruces at the county courthouse in Enterprise and area bird feeders are good places to look for Pine Grosbeaks, White-winged Crossbills and Common Redpolls in winter finch years. Farmlands south of Enterprise have a small colony of Bobolinks and the forests south of it attract Northern Pygmy-Owls, Townsend's Solitaires, winter finches and sparrows.

Starr Campground

Situated 14 miles south of John Day in Malheur National Forest, Starr Campground is a first-class location for an avian overview of the southern Blue Mountains. White-headed Woodpeckers and Pileated Woodpeckers nest in the campground area, along with Williamson's Sapsuckers. Black-backed Woodpeckers and Three-toed Woodpeckers also nest in the area, and Flammulated Owls are present from late May to early August. Rufous Hummingbirds, Calliope Hummingbirds, Dusky Flycatchers, Hammond's Flycatchers and Cassin's Vireos also nest in the lodge-pole pine woodlands.

Malheur National Wildlife Refuge

Malheur is best known for its migrant geese and ducks, including thousands of Ross's Geese and a nesting population of about 20 Trumpeter Swans. Sandhill Cranes also stage in huge numbers, and another major attraction is several active Greater Sage-Grouse leks. Other regularly seen species include American White Pelicans, White-faced Ibises, Ferruginous Hawks, Chukars, Burrowing Owls, Common Poorwills, Black-throated Sparrows and Sage Sparrows.

The best habitats for songbirds are around the refuge headquarters, especially during migration, from early April to late May and from September to October. Many eastern species have been reported more than once, including many rare warblers, and the flowers attract migrant hummingbirds, such as Black-chinned Hummingbirds. The Narrows area between Malheur and Mud Lakes has marsh birds, shorebirds and gulls from April to October, and usually some Clark's Grebes and American White Pelicans when water levels are high.

Trumpeter Swan

OREGON'S TOP BIRDING SITES

North Coast
1. Ft. Stevens SP/Clatsop Spit
2. Ecola SP/Cannon Beach
3. Nehalem Meadows
4. Northern Tillamook Bay
5. Bayocean Spit
6. Cape Meares SP
7. Siletz Bay
8. Boiler Bay State Park
9. Yaquina Head
10. Yaquina Bay/Newport
11. Seal Rock SP

South Coast
12. Siuslaw River Estuary
13. Coos Bay
14. Coquille River Estuary
15. Cape Blanco SP
16. Chetco River/Brookings

Willamette Valley/Western Cascades
17. Scappoose Bottoms
18. Sauvie Island
19. Portland
20. Lower Sandy River
21. Larch Mountain
22. Scoggins Valley Park
23. Forest Grove/Fern Hill Wetlands
24. Timothy Lake
25. Ankeny NWR
26. Salem
27. Detroit Reservoir/Santiam Flats
28. W.L. Finley NWR
29. Foster Reservoir
30. Fern Ridge Reservoir
31. Eugene
32. Salt Creek/Waldo Lake

Southwestern Oregon
33. Merlin Rest Area
34. Whitehorse Park
35. Lake Selmac County Park
36. Lower Table Rock
37. Mountain Lakes Resort Area

North-central Oregon
38. White River WMA
39. Deschutes River SRA
40. Santiam Pass Area
41. Sisters Campgrounds
42. Smith Rock SP
43. Ochoco Mountains
44. Prineville Reservoir
45. Bend
46. Cascade Lakes Highway
47. John Day Fossil Beds NM

South-central Oregon
48. Crater Lake NP
49. Klamath Marsh NWR
50. Fort Klamath Area
51. Upper Klamath Lake
52. Lower Klamath Area
53. Fort Rock Area
54. Summer Lake
55. Abert Lake and Rim
56. Lakeview
57. Warner Valley Lakes
58. Hart Mountain National Antelope Refuge

Northeastern Oregon
59. Umatilla NWR
60. McNary
61. Cold Springs NWR
62. McKay Creek NWR
63. Tollgate Area
64. Spring Creek Road
65. Grande Ronde River Area
66. Ladd Creek Area
67. Grande Ronde Valley
68. Moss Springs Guard Station
69. Upper Wallowa Valley
70. Crow Creek
71. Wallowa Lake SP
72. Imnaha Area
73. Eagle Cap Wilderness Area
74. Thief Valley Reservoir
75. Virtue Flat
76. Powder River Area
77. Anthony Lakes Ski Area
78. Clyde Holliday State Wayside
79. Starr Campground
80. Logan Valley

Southeastern Oregon
81. Idlewild Campground
82. Burns–Hines Area
83. Diamond Area
84. Malheur NWR
85. Page Springs Campground
86. Steens Mountain Recreation Area
87. Alvord Basin
88. Ontario Area
89. Succor Creek SP

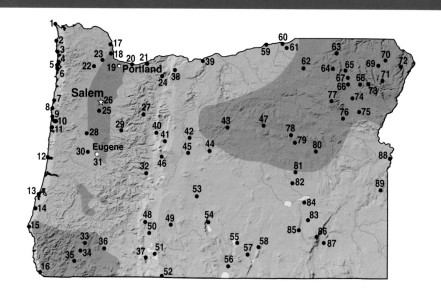

 Coastal Littoral

 East Slope Cascades

 **Coast Range/
Western Cascades**

 **Great Basin/
Columbia Basin**

Western Interior Valleys

**Blue, Wallowa and
Ochoco Mountains**

 Siskiyou Mountains

BEST SITES ABBREVIATIONS

NM = National Monument
NP = National Park
NWR = National Wildlife Refuge
SP = State Park
SRA = State Recreation Area
WMA = Wildlife Management Area

ABOUT THE SPECIES ACCOUNTS

This book gives detailed accounts of the 328 species of birds that can be expected on an annual basis. Twenty-eight occasional species and species of special note are briefly mentioned in the appendix. These species are likely to be seen again because of anticipated range expansion, migration or well-documented wandering tendencies. The order of the birds and their common and scientific names follow the American Ornithologists' Union's Check-list of North American Birds (7th edition, July 1998) and its supplements.

As well as discussing the identifying features of the birds, each species account also attempts to bring the birds to life by describing their various character traits. Personifying a bird helps us relate to it, but the characterizations presented should not be mistaken for scientific propositions. Given humans' limited understanding of non-human creatures, our interpretations and our assumptions most likely fall short of truly defining birds. Nevertheless, we hope that a lively, engaging text will communicate scientific knowledge as smoothly and effectively as possible.

One of the challenges of birdwatching is that many species look different in spring and summer than they do in fall and winter. Many birds have what are generally called breeding and nonbreeding plumages, and immature birds often look different from their parents. This book does not try to describe or illustrate all the plumages of a species; instead, it focuses on the forms that are most likely to be seen in our area. Most illustrations are of adult birds.

Mountain Bluebird

ID: It is difficult to describe the features of a bird without being able to visualize it, so this section is best used in combination with the illustrations. Where appropriate, the description is subdivided to highlight the differences between male and female birds, breeding and nonbreeding birds and immature and adult birds. The descriptions use as few technical terms as possible, and favor easily understood language. Birds may not have "eyebrows," "cheeks" or "chins," but these and other terms are easily understood by all readers, in spite of their scientific inaccuracy. Some of the most common features of birds are pointed out in the Glossary illustration (p. 368).

Size: The size measurement, an average length of the bird's body from bill to tail, is an approximate measurement of the bird as it is seen in nature. The size of larger birds is often given as a range, because there is variation among individuals. In addition, wingspan (from wing tip to wing tip) is given. Please note that birds with long tails often have large measurements that do not necessarily reflect "body" size.

Status: A general comment, such as "common," "uncommon" or "rare," is usually sufficient to describe the relative abundance of a species. Situations are bound to differ somewhat because migratory pulses, seasonal changes and centers of activity tend to concentrate or disperse birds.

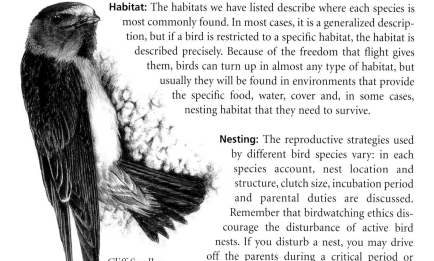

Habitat: The habitats we have listed describe where each species is most commonly found. In most cases, it is a generalized description, but if a bird is restricted to a specific habitat, the habitat is described precisely. Because of the freedom that flight gives them, birds can turn up in almost any type of habitat, but usually they will be found in environments that provide the specific food, water, cover and, in some cases, nesting habitat that they need to survive.

Nesting: The reproductive strategies used by different bird species vary: in each species account, nest location and structure, clutch size, incubation period and parental duties are discussed. Remember that birdwatching ethics discourage the disturbance of active bird nests. If you disturb a nest, you may drive off the parents during a critical period or expose defenseless young to predators. The nesting behavior of birds that do not nest in Oregon is not described.

Cliff Swallow

Feeding: Birds spend a great deal of time foraging for food. If you know what a bird eats and where the food is found, you will have a good chance of meeting the bird you are looking for. Birds are frequently encountered while they are foraging; we hope that our description of their feeding styles and diets provides valuable identifying characteristics, as well as interesting dietary facts.

Voice: You will hear many birds, particularly songbirds, which may remain hidden from view. Memorable paraphrases of distinctive sounds will aid you in identifying a species by ear. These paraphrases only loosely resemble the call, song or sound produced by the bird. Should one of our paraphrases not work for you, feel free to make up your own—the creative exercise will reinforce your memory of the bird's sound.

Similar Species: Easily confused species are discussed briefly. If you concentrate on the most relevant field marks, the subtle differences between species can be reduced to easily identifiable traits. You might find it useful to consult this section when finalizing your identification; knowing the most relevant field marks will shortcut the identification process. Even experienced birders can mistake one species for another.

Cedar Waxwing

Best Sites: If you are looking for a particular bird in Oregon, you will have more luck in some places than in others, even within the range shown on the range map. We have listed places that, besides providing a good chance of seeing a species, are easily accessible. As a result, conservation areas and state and national parks are often mentioned.

Range Maps: The range map for each species represents the overall range of the species in Oregon in an average year. Most birds will confine their annual movements to this range, though each year some birds wander beyond their traditional boundaries. These maps do not show differences in abundance within the range—areas of a range with good habitat will support a denser population than areas with poorer habitat. These maps also cannot show small pockets within the range where the species may actually be absent, or how the range may change from year to year.

Unlike most other field guides, we have attempted to show migratory pathways—areas of the state where birds may appear while en route to nesting or winter habitat. Many of these migratory routes are "best guesses," which will no doubt be refined as new discoveries are made. The representations of the pathways do not distinguish high-use migration corridors from areas that are seldom used.

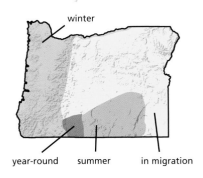

winter

year-round   summer   in migration

Harlequin Duck

NONPASSERINES

Nonpasserine birds represent 17 of the 18 orders of birds found in Oregon, but only about 57 percent of the species in our region. They are grouped together and called "nonpasserines" because, with few exceptions, they are easily distinguished from the "passerines," or "perching birds," which make up the 18th order. Being from 17 different orders, however, means that our nonpasserines vary considerably in their appearance and habits—they include everything from the 5-foot-tall Great Blue Heron to the 3-inch-long Calliope Hummingbird.

Generally speaking, nonpasserines do not "sing." Instead, their vocalizations are referred to as "calls." There are also other morphological differences. For example, the muscles and tendons in the legs of passerines are adapted to grip a perch, and the toes of passerines are never webbed. Many nonpasserines are large, so they are among our most notable birds. Waterfowl, raptors, gulls, shorebirds and wood-peckers are easily identified by most people. Some of the smaller nonpasserines, such as doves, swifts and hummingbirds, are frequently thought of as passerines by novice birders and can cause those beginners some identification problems. With a little practice, however, they will become recognizable as non-passerines. By learning to distinguish nonpasserines from passerines at a glance, birders effectively reduce by half the number of possible species when trying to identify a bird.

Barn Owl

Tufted Puffin

33

RED-THROATED LOON

Gavia stellata

The Red-throated Loon is our smallest and lightest loon. It is the only member of its family that can take off from smaller ponds or, in an emergency, from land. • The Red-throat is a common migrant along the Oregon coast, but it only occasionally occurs inland. Migrants begin to appear in late August, with numbers building to a peak in late October and November. Most birds migrate through the region to winter southward, but others remain in estuaries and more sheltered inshore ocean waters until the first northbound migrants reappear in late March. Only a few birds linger into June, and occasionally beyond. • Red-throats are reliable meteorologists: they often become very noisy before the onset of foul weather, possibly sensing changes in barometric pressure. • The scientific name *stellata* refers to the white, starlike speckles on this bird's back in its nonbreeding plumage.

breeding

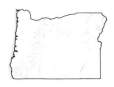

ID: small, slim bill points upward. *Breeding:* deep reddish throat; gray head; plain dark back. *Nonbreeding:* light underparts; dark gray upperparts; small white spots on upper back; eye surrounded narrowly by white.
Size: *L* 24–27 in; *W* 3½–3¾ ft.
Status: common spring and fall migrant, uncommon winter resident and rare in summer along the coast; rare to uncommon winter resident and spring migrant in western Oregon and along Columbia R.; rare fall migrant at larger lakes in eastern Oregon.
Habitat: primarily inshore coastal waters, including river mouths, bays and estuaries; larger bodies of water inland.

Nesting: does not nest in Oregon.
Feeding: dives for small fish and aquatic invertebrates in shallower water than other loons.
Voice: Mallard-like *kwuk-kwuk-kwuk-kwuk* in flight; loud *gayorwork* distraction call; mournful, gull-like wail during courtship; spring pair duets seldom heard here.
Similar Species: *Common Loon* (p. 36): much heavier, straighter bill; much darker; all-dark back in nonbreeding plumage; immature can be finely barred. *Pacific Loon* (p. 35): bill held level; eye indistinct on all-dark face; nonbreeding plumage uniform dark gray above, often with dark "chin strap."
Best Sites: inshore coastal waters and Columbia R. west from Sherman Co. to the Pacific Ocean; larger bodies of water inland, mainly in fall and early winter.

PACIFIC LOON

Gavia pacifica

Pacific Loons migrate in huge numbers within sight of land in both spring and fall. These movements, which take place from October to mid-November and from mid-April to mid-June, can involve large, open flocks that sometimes stretch for a mile or more. Small numbers migrate before and after these peak periods. • Sporting twin white racing stripes across the shoulders, a blackish throat and a lustrous, gray head and nape, this loon is easily recognized in breeding plumage, but more somberly attired fall migrants are much less easily detected. • Pacific Loons generally avoid upper-estuarine waters used by Red-throated Loons and inshore waters favored by Common Loons, preferring to raft on the open ocean beyond the surf line, often in the immediate shelter of a headland or jetty.

breeding

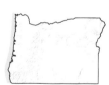

ID: slender body; thin, straight bill is held level; high, smoothly rounded crown. *Breeding:* gleaming, silver gray crown and nape; finely white-streaked, blackish throat; dark back with large, bold white spots. *Nonbreeding:* dark gray above; white below; dark face; thin, black trim at sides of neck; often has very thin, dark "chin strap."
Size: *L* 23–29 in; *W* 3½–4 ft.
Status: abundant spring and fall migrant, uncommon winter resident and summer lingerer along the coast; rare migrant and winter visitor to western inland Oregon; rare east of the Cascades.
Habitat: coastal ocean waters, including harbors and bays; occasionally larger inland water bodies.

Nesting: does not nest in Oregon.
Feeding: dives deeply for small fish; summer diet includes aquatic invertebrates and some plant material.
Voice: largely silent away from breeding sites; sharp *kwao* flight call.
Similar Species: *Common Loon* (p. 36): larger; heavier bill; regular rows of white spots on underparts and more extensive white-on-black spotting on upperparts in breeding plumage; pale ring around eye in nonbreeding plumage. *Red-throated Loon* (p. 34): smaller head; slimmer, upward-tilted bill; plain upperparts and reddish throat in breeding plumage; fine, white spotting on back and more distinct white around eye in nonbreeding plumage; faster, deeper wingbeats in flight.
Best Sites: inshore waters, usually beyond the surf line, and estuaries.

COMMON LOON

Gavia immer

Common Loons are a regular sight on water near the coast from late August until May, remaining into summer in very small numbers. They may summer at mountain lakes, but there is no recent evidence of nesting, and most inland sightings are of migrants and wintering birds. • Loons are well adapted to their diving lifestyle: solid bones make them less buoyant (most birds have hollow bones), and their feet are placed well back on their bodies for effective propulsion. • The word "loon" is derived from the Scandinavian *lom*, meaning "clumsy," perhaps referring to this bird's awkwardness on land. However, many people would say that "loony" is also a good description of the weird wails and actions at loon breeding sites.

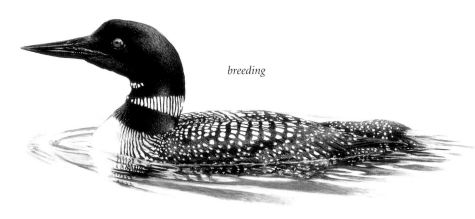

breeding

ID: heavy, daggerlike bill; full or partial white "collar." *Breeding:* green-glossed black head; stout, black bill; black-and-white striped "necklace"; white-spotted dark upperparts; white underparts mottled and striped with black on sides and flanks; red eyes. *Nonbreeding:* much duller plumage; dark, unmarked gray above; white below; dark eyes; pale eye-arcs.

Size: *L* 28–35 in; *W* 4–4¾ ft.

Status: common migrant and resident along the coast from late August to May, with scattered birds irregularly summering, usually in nonbreeding plumage; uncommon migrant and winter resident on inland lakes and reservoirs; very rare summer visitor at mountain lakes.

Habitat: mainly open ocean close to shore, estuaries and freshwater lakes.

Nesting: not known to nest in Oregon.

Feeding: pursues fish underwater to depths of 180 ft; occasionally eats aquatic invertebrates and amphibians.

Voice: quavering tremolo alarm call often called "loon laughter"; long but simple wailing note contact call; male's summer territorial call is an undulating, complex yodel.

Similar Species: *Pacific Loon* (p. 35): smaller; slimmer bill; more rounded crown; no white "collar"; distinctive, silver gray head and nape in breeding plumage; eye is indistinct against dark face in nonbreeding plumage; dark "chin strap" is usual in nonbreeding plumage.

Best Sites: suitable habitats throughout Oregon.

PIED-BILLED GREBE
Podilymbus podiceps

The Pied-billed Grebe is the most widespread grebe species in North America, yet it is not always easy to find. Shy and retiring by nature, this grebe most often hides behind shady, protective cover in its marshland habitat. Its exuberant call is sometimes the only clue to its presence. • In breeding season, the male is bold, aggressively chasing off any intruders, even those that are much larger. At other times of the year, when frightened by an intruder, this grebe will slide noiselessly under the water's surface, with only its bill and eyes exposed. • Pied-billed Grebes breed throughout Oregon and are year-round residents in western Oregon, with numbers increasing toward winter. They prefer fresh water but do use brackish upper estuaries somewhat.

breeding

ID: short tail; oversized head and stubby, laterally compressed, pale bill; individually lobed toes.
Breeding: black throat and forehead; black ring neatly divides bill; dark eyes; narrow, white eye ring. *Nonbreeding:* rich brown plumage; yellowish bill; white "chin" and "cheek" markings. *Juvenile:* darker stripes on side of head
Size: *L* 12–15 in; *W* 22–25 in.
Status: common summer resident and breeder; common migrant and winter resident in western Oregon; rare to uncommon in eastern Oregon until freeze-up.
Habitat: *Breeding:* marshy ponds and sloughs; freshwater lakes and reservoirs with dense aquatic vegetation.
Nonbreeding: various open and semi-open fresh and estuarine waters, rarely salt water or eelgrass beds.

Nesting: in the densely vegetated margin of a lake or marsh; platform with a shallow saucer of wet and decaying plants is anchored to emergent vegetation; pair incubates 3–10 bluish or greenish white eggs for 23–27 days and raises young together until late summer.
Feeding: opportunistic feeder; dives in pursuit of fish, amphibians, invertebrates and water plants; gleans seeds and insects from the water's surface.
Voice: loud, whooping *kuk-kuk-kuk cow cow cow cowp cowp cowp* call begins quickly then slows down; other calls are short and rail-like.
Similar Species: *Other small grebes* (pp. 38–42): slender bills; underparts very dark in breeding plumage and white in winter; varied amount of white on wings; more white on bellies.
Best Sites: *Summer:* marsh-edged fresh water with emergent vegetation. *In migration* and *early winter:* open fresh and brackish water.

HORNED GREBE

Podiceps auritus

Horned Grebes are unmistakable in their breeding finery, with their bright rufous underparts and golden head ornaments. As soon as this striking plumage fades, however, they become very nondescript until they attain their contrasting black-and-white winter plumage. • These grebes breed inland on fresh water. Outside the breeding season, Horned Grebes commonly patrol harbors, industrial waterfronts and shipping channels for underwater food, which places them at risk from oil spills and surface pollution. • Like loons, grebes appear hunch-backed in flight, with hastily beating wings, head held low and feet trailing behind the stubby tail. • Grebes migrate mainly at night to avoid detection by predators. • The scientific name *auritus* refers to the golden feather tufts, or "horns," acquired in breeding plumage.

nonbreeding

ID: small, stubby, whitish-tipped dark bill; red eyes; flat crown; stubby tail; white underparts. *Breeding:* rufous neck and flanks; black "cheek" and forehead; golden "ear" tufts; white shoulder patch. *Nonbreeding:* well-defined dark crown, hindneck and upperparts; pale spot ahead of eye. *Juvenile:* brownish tinge, especially on throat; dark-smudged "cheeks."
Size: *L* 12–15 in; *W* 23–25 in.
Status: common migrant and uncommon in winter along the coast; uncommon migrant and rare winter resident in interior valleys; irregular summer resident and breeder in the Cascades and eastward; state-listed as sensitive.
Habitat: *Breeding:* shallow, well-vegetated wetlands and marshes with some open

water. *Nonbreeding:* inshore ocean waters, brackish estuaries and open fresh water.
Nesting: singly or in small, loose colonies; in thick vegetation along the water's edge; platform of wet plant material, usually attached to emergent vegetation; pair incubates 4–7 brown-stained white eggs for 23–24 days; pair raises young.
Feeding: makes shallow dives and gleans the water's surface for aquatic invertebrates, small fish and amphibians.
Voice: usually quiet outside the breeding season; during courtship, a loud series of croaks and shrieking notes and a also sharp *keark keark;* shrill *kowee* alarm call.
Similar Species: *Eared Grebe* (p. 40): smaller head; finer, all-dark bill; black neck in breeding plumage; black "cheek" and whitish ear patch in nonbreeding plumage.
Best Sites: *Summer:* Malheur NWR; Upper Klamath L.; Downie L., Wallowa Co.; Sycan L., Lake Co. *In migration:* any open water. *Winter:* Columbia R.; western valleys.

RED-NECKED GREBE
Podiceps grisegena

S parsely scattered among more sharply patterned diving birds at harbor entrances and estuaries, obscurely marked and generally unobtrusive Red-necked Grebes in nonbreeding plumage might go unrecognized. Only when pre-breeding or post-breeding birds in showy colors return to the coast do Red-necked Grebes become readily identifiable. Most birds breed and winter well to the north of our state, but a few pairs nest in Oregon. • Very few birds stray inland in migration or in winter, preferring salt water up to ¼ mile from shore. • The scientific name *grisegena* means "gray cheek"—a distinctive field mark of this bird's nonbreeding plumage.

nonbreeding

ID: thick, yellowish bill; long neck. *Breeding:* red neck; white "cheek"; black crown; bright yellow bill; dark eyes. *Nonbreeding:* dingy neck; dusky gray "cheek"; dull yellow bill; white underparts. *In flight:* 2 white wing patches; feet extend beyond tail.
Size: *L* 17–22 in; *W* 30–33 in.
Status: uncommon migrant on the coast from late August to November and from late March to early June; rare to uncommon winter resident on the coast; local and irregular inland in winter; rare and local summering and breeding species; state-listed as sensitive.
Habitat: *Breeding:* emergent vegetation zone of larger lakes and ponds.
Nonbreeding: protected bays, estuaries and harbors.

Nesting: singly, or in small, loose colonies; floating platform of aquatic vegetation is anchored to submerged plants; pair incubates 4–5 light blue to chalky white, usually stained eggs for 25–35 days.
Feeding: dives and gleans the water's surface for small fish and crustaceans and other invertebrates.
Voice: usually silent away from breeding sites; often-repeated, laughlike, excited *ah-ooo ah-ooo ah-ooo ah-ah-ah-ah-ah;* calls include ducklike quacks and grunts.
Similar Species: *Western Grebe* (p. 41) and *Clark's Grebe* (p. 42): black and white year-round; slender, bright yellow or yellowish orange bill. *Horned Grebe* (p. 38): smaller; shorter, darker bill with white tip; golden "ear" tufts and rufous flanks in breeding plumage; white foreneck and all-white lower face in nonbreeding plumage.
Best Sites: *Summer:* Upper Klamath L.; Howard Prairie Reservoir. *In migration and winter:* protected coastal salt water; locally on large freshwater lakes and rivers.

EARED GREBE

Podiceps nigricollis

Common summer residents of marshes east of the Cascades, Eared Grebes arrive at interior ponds and marshes in their black-and-rufous breeding plumage, adorned with bright golden "ears." Much more distinctive than their dingy dark-and-light nonbreeding plumage, this color pattern makes the many colonial breeding pairs easy to pick out among the cattails of their nesting ponds and marshes. • The molting process leaves some nonbreeding birds flightless for much of the year, and even breeding adults are grounded for three to four months. • Like all grebes, Eared Grebes consume feathers to aid in digestion and to protect the stomach lining and intestines from sharp fish bones. • The scientific name *nigricollis* refers to the black neck of the breeding plumage.

breeding

ID: thin, all-dark bill; small, rounded head; red eyes; fluffy white undertail. *Breeding:* thin, black neck; black face and forehead with golden-plumed "ear" tufts; black back; rufous flanks. *Nonbreeding:* neck usually dusky, with white on foreneck and "chin" and behind ear.
Size: *L* 12–14 in; *W* 22–23 in.
Status: locally common breeder in south-central and southeastern Oregon; common migrant and rare winter resident east of the Cascades; uncommon on the coast and rare in interior valleys from September to early May; rare in summer west of the Cascades.
Habitat: *Breeding:* freshwater or slightly alkaline shallow lakes and wetlands with floating or emergent vegetation. *Nonbreeding:* coastal and interior water bodies.

Nesting: strongly colonial; in thick vegetation of lake edge, pond or marsh; pair builds a shallow, flimsy platform of floating wet and decaying plants; pair incubates 4–7 bluish white, often brownish-stained eggs for 20–23 days.
Feeding: makes shallow dives and gleans the water's surface for aquatic invertebrates, small fish and amphibians.
Voice: usually silent away from breeding sites; loud, chirping *kowee* threat call; mellow *poo-eee-chk* during courtship.
Similar Species: *Horned Grebe* (p. 38): straighter, chunkier bill with small, whitish tip; rufous neck and denser golden "ear" tufts in breeding plumage; white "cheek" and foreneck, and pale spot in front of eye in nonbreeding plumage. *Pied-billed Grebe* (p. 37): thicker bill; browner plumage; dark eyes.
Best Sites: *Summer:* lakes in Harney, Lake and Klamath Counties. *In migration:* Malheur NWR; L. Albert.

WESTERN GREBE
Aechmophorus occidentalis

On open water, a medium-sized, long-necked, black-and-white diving bird with a long, daggerlike, yellow bill could be either a Western Grebe or its recently split-off sibling species, the Clark's Grebe. Both grebes exhibit a spectacular courtship display in which participants posture with bits of water plants in their bills, then arise from the surface to patter frantically on parallel courses, heads held high, ultimately dropping back into the water or diving below the surface. • Western Grebes are more likely than Clark's to be seen on estuaries and lagoons much of the year, but most of them move to freshwater lakes and marshes to breed. • *Aechmophorus* is derived from Greek words that mean "spear bearer."

ID: long, slender neck with broad, dark stripe on hindneck; long, daggerlike, yellowish bill; dark crown extends below red eye; black upperparts; white underparts. *In flight:* long, pointed body and wings; inconspicuous white wing stripe.
Size: *L* 20–24 in; *W* 30–40 in.
Status: common along the coast in winter, from mid-September to October and from late March to early May, but uncommon in summer; locally common summer resident east of the Cascades; locally common inland in migration and uncommon in winter.
Habitat: *Breeding:* large freshwater lakes with dense areas of emergent vegetation or thick mats of floating aquatic plants. *Nonbreeding:* any large, open water body, fresh or salt.

Nesting: colonial; pair builds floating nest of wet or decaying vegetation anchored to submerged plants; pair incubates 2–4 pale, bluish white, brown-stained eggs for about 24 days.
Feeding: dives for small fish, invertebrates and other small, aquatic or marine prey; sometimes eats small birds and salamanders.
Voice: often heard at both breeding and wintering sites; shrill, brief, 2-note *kreee-krreeet* or *krrrik krrrikk;* female's calls are reminiscent of Killdeer's.
Similar Species: *Clark's Grebe* (p. 42): brighter, orange yellow bill; white around eye and to base of bill; narrower hindneck stripe; different calls. *Red-necked Grebe* (p. 39): shorter neck; duller yellow bill; red neck and white "cheeks" in breeding plumage; grayer, dingier neck and grayish white "cheeks" in nonbreeding plumage.
Best Sites: *Summer:* Malheur NWR; other freshwater lakes in Harney, Lake, Klamath, Deschutes, Morrow and Umatilla Counties. *In migration* and *winter:* open water bodies.

41

CLARK'S GREBE
Aechmophorus clarkii

For some time, ornithologists had recognized that Western Grebes came in two varieties: those with duller yellow bills and red eyes on a black background, and those with bright yellowish orange bills and red eyes clearly visible below the black crown on a white face. What they eventually realized—something the grebes had known all along—was that there are two separate species. We now know the less widespread, paler-faced birds with paler downy young as Clark's Grebes, but, particularly in winter, identification remains an intriguing challenge. For the most part, the two species remain reproductively isolated even when both share a breeding site, although some individuals do choose mates of the other species. • Clark's Grebe was named in honor of John Henry Clark, a mathematician, surveyor and successful bird collector who procured the first scientific specimen in 1858.

ID: long, slender neck with slender black stripe on hindneck; long, dagger-like, yellowish orange bill, noticeably longer on male; white on face extends to surround red eyes; black upperparts; white underparts. *In flight:* long, pointed body and wings; conspicuous white wing stripe.
Size: *L* 20–23 in; *W* 31–38 in.
Status: locally common summer resident and breeder east of the Cascades; rare fall migrant and winter visitor west of the Cascades.
Habitat: *Breeding:* large lakes with dense areas of emergent vegetation or thick mats of floating aquatic plants. *Nonbreeding:* sizable water bodies, including sluggish rivers and lagoons, and open coast up to a mile offshore, often with Western Grebes.
Nesting: colonial; floating nest of wet or decaying vegetation anchored to submerged plants; pair incubates 2–4 bluish white eggs for about 24 days.
Feeding: dives for small fish, invertebrates and other small aquatic or marine prey.
Voice: similar to the call of the Western Grebe, but generally higher pitched.
Similar Species: *Western Grebe* (p. 41): duller yellow bill; black on face extends beyond eye; broader black hindneck stripe; different calls. *Other grebes* (pp. 37–40): smaller; shorter, less daggerlike bills.
Best Sites: Klamath Co. and Lake Co., especially Upper Klamath L. and Goose L.; less common in Harney Co. and Malheur Co., notably Malheur NWR.

BLACK-FOOTED ALBATROSS

Phoebastria nigripes

Albatrosses are the ultimate ocean wanderers, logging thousands of miles and enduring the toughest storms the oceans have to offer even before they reach breeding age. Black-footed Albatrosses visit offshore Oregon waters year-round in varying numbers. From April until October, when most adults return to Pacific islands to nest, Black-footeds in our area are most common from 10 miles offshore to the edge of the continental shelf. Small numbers, probably nonbreeding immature birds, remain through the winter months. • Like other albatrosses, Black-footeds have a well-developed sense of smell and are often attracted to fishing vessels. • With extremely long, slender wings designed to take advantage of strong ocean wind currents, these large birds can fly for long periods of time without flapping, needing only an occasional deep dip of the wings to stay aloft. • In calm conditions, or when loafing, birds will gather together on the water in flocks of up to two dozen birds.

ID: ashy brown overall; heavy, dark bill; white on face at base of bill and under eye; white crescent at base of tail in all but immature plumage; undertail coverts may be white; becomes paler overall with age. *In Flight:* long, narrow wings; black feet extend beyond tail.

Size: L 27–29 in; W 6¼–7 ft.

Status: common offshore from April to October and uncommon in winter; rare within sight of land.

Habitat: open ocean, except during breeding; prefers continental shelf waters.

Nesting: does not nest in Oregon.

Feeding: snatches fish, flying-fish eggs, squid, crustaceans, natural marine oils and carrion from water's surface; plunges to just below the surface; follows fishing vessels, consuming remains of discarded fish and other marine creatures caught in fishing nets.

Voice: generally silent, but will sometimes groan, shriek or squawk, especially in feeding flocks.

Similar Species: *Laysan Albatross:* dark back; white underparts; dark-tipped yellow bill. *Short-tailed Albatross:* larger; heavier, pale bill; black-and-white plumage; immature has pale pink bill, pale legs and more white in tail and wings.

Best Sites: open ocean from 10 mi offshore to the edge of the continental shelf, especially where vessels are actively fishing.

43

NORTHERN FULMAR

Fulmarus glacialis

Northern Fulmars are the only mid-sized tubenoses that breed in the North Pacific and spend all their lives north of the equator. Regularly found well out to sea, Northern Fulmars follow fishing vessels and sometimes enter bays and harbors in search of food scraps and refuse, so they are likely to be seen from land, often in winter. • Relatively slim-winged but thick-necked and bull-headed, the Northern Fulmar shares many physical attributes—except for its stubby, greenish yellow bill—with the closely related shearwaters. • Northern Fulmar color morphs range from all-dark to all-pale, with darker morphs predominating in Oregon waters. • Fulmars are among the longest-lived birds, and some have been known to breed for 40 or more years. • "Fulmar" is derived from the Old Norse words meaning "foul gull," a derivation obvious to anyone who has approached one of these birds too closely and received a shot of foul-smelling fish oil.

light morph

dark morph

ID: short, pale yellow, tubed bill; dark eyes; thick neck; stubby, rounded tail. *Light morph:* whitish head and underparts; bluish gray upper-parts. *Dark morph:* deep bluish gray throughout, except for paler flight feathers (many birds are intermediate).
Size: *L* 17–20 in; *W* 3½ ft.
Status: common offshore in winter and until early April; rare to uncommon in spring and summer; uncommon from late July through October; occasionally driven inshore by gales.
Habitat: open ocean waters over upwellings and along the outer continental shelf; rarely approaches coastlines or bays.

Nesting: does not nest in Oregon.
Feeding: seizes almost any edible item when swimming, including fish, squid, invertebrates and carrion; makes shallow plunges beneath water's surface; cannot feed in flight.
Voice: generally silent; possible low quacking call when competing for food.
Similar Species: *Shearwaters* (p. 45): narrower wings; more slender bills; less heavy heads and necks; less fluttery flight. *Albatrosses* (p. 43): much larger; longer, heavier bills; more leisurely flight. *Gulls* (pp. 167-78): slimmer neck and body; bill not tubed.
Best Sites: open ocean waters, far from land; comes close to land during westerly storms in fall and winter, especially at Cape Meares SP, Boiler Bay SP and Yaquina Head.

SOOTY SHEARWATER

Puffinus griseus

Each summer, shearwaters arrive from breeding islands in the Southern Hemisphere in numbers beyond estimation. One of the world's commonest birds, the Sooty Shearwater dominates the tens of thousands of birds spread out on the open ocean. Any boat trip between May and September will reveal scattered individuals or huge flocks. Because these shearwaters are the most numerous birds in most mixed-seabird foraging flocks on the continental shelf, it is often easiest to identify other shearwater species by their differences from Sooties. • The Sooty is one of the few shearwater species that prefers the waters close to land. Large concentrations of fish often draw it there and into competition with other seabirds, including pelicans, cormorants and gulls. Using a telescope, you may well find some Sooties without even venturing out to sea.

ID: mostly sooty brown body; grayer "chin" and throat; pale underparts; long, slender, black bill; blackish, rounded tail; black to gray legs and feet. *In flight:* possible silvery flash in underwings; feet extend just beyond tail; strong, direct flight with several deep flaps followed by long glide.

Size: *L* 16–18 in; *W* 3–3½ ft.

Status: common to abundant postbreeding visitor from May to October—often seen from shore in large concentrations from early July onward; rare to very uncommon in winter.

Habitat: open ocean, especially at upwellings and within a few miles of shore; some birds enter larger estuaries.

Nesting: does not nest in Oregon.

Feeding: gleans the water's surface or snatches prey from below in a shallow dive or plunge; eats mostly fish, squid and crustaceans; gathers in large concentrations around fishing vessels but ignores other ships.

Voice: usually silent; occasionally utters quarrelsome calls when competing for food.

Similar Species: *Short-tailed Shearwater:* slightly smaller; smaller bill; sometimes has pale "chin" and throat; more uniformly colored underwings; toes project just beyond tail. *Flesh-footed Shearwater:* larger; black-tipped pinkish bill; pale pinkish legs and feet; uniformly dark underwings; slower wingbeats.

Best Sites: off headlands of the north coast, including Clatsop Spit, Cape Meares SP, Boiler Bay SP and Yaquina Head.

FORK-TAILED STORM-PETREL

Oceanodroma furcata

The Fork-tailed Storm-Petrel's secretive nesting strategy typifies the breeding habits of the smaller tubenoses. To minimize predation, a pair will place its single egg at the end of an underground burrow. The adults maintain a strictly nocturnal schedule of incubation shift changes and make nightly visits with food for the growing nestling. Foraging miles from the nest during the day, members of the colony disperse over the open ocean to feed in colder water over banks on the continental shelf. • Although they sometimes fly alongside ships, Fork-tails are usually attracted only by fishing vessels discarding fish oil and small waste items. • These storm-petrels can appear inshore (but very rarely inland), closely approaching beaches, jetties and piers, in April and May. They may also be seen inshore when ocean temperatures rise in late summer or if driven there by westerly gales in late fall.

ID: bluish gray upperparts; dark eye patch; pale gray underparts; bluish gray wing tips; deeply forked tail. *In flight:* flutters low across the ocean's surface with rapid, shallow wingbeats interspersed with brief glides.

Size: *L* 8–9 in; *W* 18 in.

Status: locally uncommon breeder on offshore rocky islets; uncommon year-round at least 10 mi from shore; rare inshore from spring to late fall; state-listed as sensitive.

Habitat: cold, open ocean waters from near shore to beyond the continental shelf; occasionally visits bays and estuaries; often found in large Leach's Storm-Petrel colonies.

Nesting: colonial; on vegetated offshore islet; self-excavated burrow, rock crevice or old burrow excavated by other species; burrow can have many side channels with additional nest chambers; pair incubates 1 white egg with dark terminal dots for 37 or more days; pair takes turns at night feeding the nestling.

Feeding: skims or snatches small fish, crustaceans and floating natural oils from the surface while hovering; will drop briefly onto the water or glean and pick while swimming.

Voice: usually silent away from breeding sites; low-pitched trilling calls at the nest.

Similar Species: *Leach's Storm-Petrel* (p. 47): much darker; white rump; dark wing linings; flight erratic and bouncy.

Best Sites: most birds are seen at least 10 mi from land; colonies found at Haystack Rock near Ecola SP, Cape Blanco SP and Goat I., Curry Co.

LEACH'S STORM-PETREL

Oceanodroma leucorhoa

Leach's Storm-Petrel is familiar to many coastal residents, because storms can force it inshore and occasionally inland. One of the more widespread small storm-petrels, Leach's appears longer-winged than most of them. Its buoyant and graceful, weaving flight incorporates deep, ternlike wingbeats and short, shearwater-like glides on bowed wings for an overall effect like that of a nighthawk. • Sometimes called "Sea Swallows" because of their tiny size and erratic flight, storm-petrels owe their name to mariners who believed that their presence foretold an approaching storm. Mariners also likened the habit some storm-petrels have of dangling their feet to patter on the water's surface to St. Peter's water-walking attempt. • Colonies can be extremely large, but the birds are almost entirely nocturnal close to breeding sites and are rarely seen nearby.

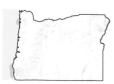

ID: dark brown head and underparts; whitish rump with gray center line; conspicuous lighter diagonal band separates brown and blackish parts of upperwings; slender, black bill; black legs. *In flight:* deeply forked tail (not always visible); occasionally hangs motionless with wings raised slightly and feet pattering on the water's surface.

Size: *L* 8–9 in; *W* 18–19 in.

Status: common to locally abundant in summer at breeding colonies; uncommon to common year-round over the continental shelf and beyond; rare inshore in spring and fall; occasionally blown inshore and inland in fall and early winter.

Habitat: warmer waters at least 75 mi from shore.

Nesting: strongly colonial; on an offshore island or islet; uses a rock crevice or an old burrow excavated by another species, or male excavates a burrow; pair incubates 1 white egg, with lilac or burgundy dots at the larger end, for 37–50 days; pair feeds the nestling at night.

Feeding: skims or snatches small fish, squids, crustaceans, jellyfish and floating natural oils from the water's surface while hovering; rarely picks and gleans while swimming.

Voice: commonly gives purring, chattering and trilling nocturnal notes at the nest site; otherwise usually silent.

Similar Species: *Fork-tailed Storm-Petrel* (p. 46): paler gray; contrasting dark wing linings; no white on rump; more direct flight. *Sooty* (p. 45), *Short-tailed* and *Flesh-footed shearwaters:* larger; all-dark rumps; strong, direct flight; short flaps and long glides.

Best Sites: colonies in Curry Co., at Haystack Rock near Ecola SP and Cape Blanco SP.

AMERICAN WHITE PELICAN
Pelecanus erythrorhynchos

American White Pelicans swim through schools of small fish, plunging their bills beneath the surface to scoop out one or several fish. Before swallowing their prey, the pelicans lift their bills from the water, keeping the fish within their flexible pouches as they drain the water out. These huge birds sometimes work alone, but typically they work together in flocks to herd schools of fish into shallows, where each bird then earns the reward of teamwork. • Unlike Brown Pelicans, White Pelicans breed in colonies on undisturbed, barren, rocky islands in large lakes and freshwater marshes; they are rarely seen with their cousins on saltwater estuaries. • The true grace of the White Pelican is appreciated when a flock is seen gliding and soaring effortlessly in thermals.

nonbreeding

ID: huge; white overall; massive, yellowish orange bill; orange throat patch; extensive black in wings; short, white tail; naked, orange skin patch around eyes. *Breeding:* small, keeled, upright plate develops on upper mandible; pale yellow crest on back of head. *In flight:* black-tipped white wings; S-shaped neck.

Size: *L* 4–6 ft; *W* 9–12 ft.

Status: locally common breeder and migrant in south-central and southeastern Oregon; otherwise very rare; state-listed as sensitive.

Habitat: *Breeding:* large interior lakes with islands largely or totally devoid of vegetation. *In migration* and *winter:* lakes, rivers and large ponds.

Nesting: colonial; on a bare, low-lying, rocky island; nest scrape is rimmed with gravel soil and nearby material and may be lined with pebbles; pair incubates 2 chalky white eggs for 30–33 days; 1st-hatched nestling is always fed first with regurgitated food.

Feeding: dips along the surface for small fish, amphibians and sluggish bottomfeeders; small groups often herd fish cooperatively; sometimes steals fish from other birds.

Voice: generally silent; brief, low grunts at colony site; loud squawks and begging calls by young.

Similar Species: *Brown Pelican* (p. 49): much darker; dusky bill; coastal. *Snow Goose* (p. 64): much smaller; smaller bill; neck extended in flight; steady wingbeats without flap-and-glide. *Tundra Swan* (p. 69) and *Trumpeter Swan* (p. 68): longer, thinner necks held straight in flight; smaller, dark bills; no black in wings; steady, measured wingbeats.

Best Sites: *Summer:* Malheur NWR; Warner Valley; Upper Klamath L. and other large freshwater lakes; wider parts of Columbia R. east of the Cascades. *In migration:* Fern Ridge Reservoir; Lane Co.

BROWN PELICAN

Pelecanus occidentalis

Where numerous, Brown Pelicans are among the most conspicuous waterbirds. Often seen perched on rocks or pilings, lined up on the water or flying past in single file, they will tolerate close inspection. Their easy grace in flight and tumbling dives elicit admiration from even the most blasé observer. • Numbers have recovered following a DDT-related decline in California's nesting population in the 1950s and 1960s, increasing the post-breeding dispersal into Oregon, but these birds are still considered endangered. • Some of Oregon's Brown Pelicans arrive from Mexico as early as late April, spending summer and fall in estuaries, at river mouths and along the open seacoast, but the general northward movement is in July and August. More and more birds are lingering beyond October, but most are gone by the end of November.

breeding

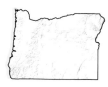

ID: grayish brown upperparts; dark brown underparts; very large, dusky bill; relatively short tail. *Nonbreeding:* white neck; yellow wash on head; pale yellowish pouch. *Breeding:* yellow head; white foreneck; dark, rufous brown hindneck and lower neck patch; red pouch. *Immature:* light feet; dusky head; pale belly.

Size: L 3½–4 ft; W 6½–7 ft.

Status: common spring, summer and fall migrant and resident along the coast; most common from July to early November; a few pairs have recently bred at Columbia R. mouth; extremely rare away from marine and intertidal zones; federal- and state-listed as endangered.

Habitat: coastal and estuarine waters within a mile of shore; visits offshore islands; roosts on islets, sea stacks, sandbars, piers and jetties.

Nesting: colonial; on an island, on the ground or on a cliff, possibly in a low tree; nests in a scrape or pile of sticks or debris gathered by the male and arranged by the female; pair incubates 2–4 nest-stained white eggs for 28–30 days; young leave the nest at 5–9 weeks.

Feeding: forages almost exclusively for fish, caught by diving headfirst into water from heights of up to 60 ft; holds fish in its flexible pouch until the water has drained out; flocks here tend to be relatively small, even around large schools of fish.

Voice: usually silent; a startled bird may utter a heronlike alarm call.

Similar Species: *American White Pelican* (p. 48): all-white body; extensive black on wings; yellow bill and legs; dips for fish.

Best Sites: any marine coast or large estuary with available feeding and roosting areas.

BRANDT'S CORMORANT
Phalacrocorax penicillatus

The Brandt's Cormorant is the largest of the three species of cormorants found year-round along Oregon's coast. The two commonest species, the Brandt's and the Pelagic, often nest and forage in close proximity. Brandt's Cormorants nest in expansive colonies on flat or sloping ground on top of rocky islets and stacks, whereas Pelagic Cormorants occupy small ledges and shallow nooks on cliffs and steep pinnacles. • Brandt's colonies are often isolated from each other, with breeding adults scattering widely to feed anywhere from within the surf zone to several miles offshore. Flocks sometimes assemble in and around harbor entrances and in the sheltered waters of headlands and jetties. • The species is named for J.F. Brandt, who distinguished the first specimen in the St. Petersburg Academy of Sciences collection in Russia.

breeding

ID: blackish plumage; pale brown on throat below blue throat patch; heavy, hooked bill; blue green eyes. *Breeding:* bright blue throat patch; purplish green gloss on plumage; long, white plumes extend from neck and upper back. *Nonbreeding:* dull gray plumage; faint greenish gloss on head and rump. *In flight:* shorter wings and tail than other cormorants; flies with neck out straight.

Size: *L* 32–35 in; *W* 3¾–4 ft.

Status: locally common breeder and common year-round coastal resident and migrant.

Habitat: sandy and rocky underwater substrates for feeding, offshore during migration but close to shore in winter; roosts on offshore reefs, rocks and breakwaters.

Nesting: colonial; barren area on offshore island, islet or sea stack or protected headland; pair builds nest of sticks and seaweed lined with eelgrass or seaweed and cemented by droppings; pair incubates 3–4 pale blue to whitish, nest-stained eggs on their webbed feet for 29–31 days.

Feeding: forages underwater, diving more than 150 ft below the surface for fish; also takes some crabs and shrimp and occasionally squid and other invertebrates.

Voice: deep, low grunts and croaks at the nesting colony.

Similar Species: *Double-crested Cormorant* (p. 51): longer wings and tail; flies with bent neck; conspicuous yellowish or yellowish orange throat region; immature is brown above and usually much paler below; more vocal.

Best Sites: Bird Rocks, Lane Co. has the largest colony, with more than 1500 nests; additional colonies in Lincoln, Clatsop, Tillamook and Curry Counties.

DOUBLE-CRESTED CORMORANT

Phalacrocorax auritus

Double-crested Cormorants are a familiar sight at most large bodies of water and are easy to recognize, whether they are swimming, diving, loafing and drying their wings atop pilings or in trees, or flying past in loose formation. Unlike Oregon's other two cormorant species, this one is equally at home on the coast or inland, and coastal birds will go far up rivers and onto freshwater lakes for foraging and feeding. • Cormorants, unlike most waterbirds, cannot waterproof their feathers and must partially spread their wings to dry the flight feathers. Waterlogged feathers (decreasing buoyancy), rudderlike tails, sealed nostrils and excellent underwater vision all enhance their underwater abilities. • The common and scientific names refer to the crest of short, whitish "eyebrow" plumes of the breeding plumage.

breeding

ID: blackish overall, sometimes with greenish gloss; black-scaled coppery brown back; yellowish throat; thin, hook-tipped bill; long neck and tail; green eyes. *Breeding:* intensified throat-pouch color; fine, whitish "eyebrow" plumes (darkening in late summer). *In flight:* long wings; short tail; noticeable neck bend.
Size: *L* 26–32 in; *W* 4–4½ ft.
Status: common year-round resident along the coast; uncommon inland along the Columbia R. and west of the Cascades; common in summer east of the Cascades at breeding colonies and rare at other times of the year.
Habitat: *Summer:* interior wetlands, lakes, reservoirs and rivers; offshore islands, sea stacks and various coastal habitats. *In migration* and *winter:* lowland and near-coastal waters.

Nesting: colonial, often with other species; on a low-lying island, in an extensive marsh, high in a tree, or on a sea stack; mass of sticks, vegetation and debris is cemented into the platform with guano; pair incubates 3–4 pale blue, nest-stained eggs for 25–28 days.
Feeding: makes long underwater dives of up to 30 ft to catch fish and, less often, amphibians and invertebrates.
Voice: generally quiet; possible piglike grunts or croaks, especially near nest colonies.
Similar Species: *Brandt's Cormorant* (p. 50): all-black bill; bluish green eyes; shorter tail; bluish throat patch with buffy edges in breeding plumage; flies with neck straight; immature is darker below with whitish "V" patch. *Pelagic Cormorant* (p. 52): slender, all-black bill; white flank patches and small, red throat patch in breeding plumage; immature is uniformly brown.
Best Sites: Upper Klamath L.; Malheur NWR; Lower Klamath NWR; Summer L.; coastal headlands, estuaries and offshore rocks.

PELAGIC CORMORANT
Phalacrocorax pelagicus

Despite its name, the Pelagic Cormorant prefers the nearshore zone, leaving offshore waters to the Brandt's Cormorant. • It is the smallest of Oregon's three cormorant species. • The Pelagic Cormorant is an almost reptilian-looking bird, sleek and black with a subtle iridescent green and purplish blue gloss at close range. Its long, slender neck and slender bill can be twisted and turned at will. This bird appears particularly elegant in its breeding plumage. • Cormorants have a naked, extensible throat patch and powerful, fully webbed feet that aid swimming and diving. The throat patch is used in a panting behavior known as "gular fluttering," perhaps to cool the body by bringing air across the blood vessels of the throat. • Pelagic Cormorants are less colonial than other cormorants and less sociable, almost never forming feeding flocks or flying in formation.

breeding

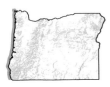

ID: greenish-glossed dark plumage; small head and slender neck. *Breeding:* white flank patches; 2 scruffy head crests; small, red throat patch (visible at close range).

Size: *L* 25–28 in; *W* 3–3¼ ft.

Status: common year-round along the coast.

Habitat: *Breeding:* along the coast and on offshore islands and sea stacks. *Foraging:* open ocean within 1 mi of shore and lower reaches of estuaries and harbors but never fresh water.

Nesting: loosely colonial; on a narrow cliff ledge or flat area; pair builds a nest of grass, seaweed and moss, together with sticks, and reuses it each year; pair incubates 3–5 greenish white eggs for 25–33 days.

Feeding: forages by swimming underwater, up to 120 ft below the surface, to catch mainly fish, but also shrimp, crabs, amphipods, marine worms and some algae.

Voice: generally silent; sometimes utters low groans at the nest site.

Similar Species: *Brandt's Cormorant* (p. 50): larger; heavier bill; immature has pale V-shaped area on breast. *Double-crested Cormorant* (p. 51): larger; heavier bill; larger head; conspicuous pale yellow or yellowish orange throat patch; immature has white on underparts.

Best Sites: Barview Jetty; Cape Meares SP; Newport South Jetty; Umpqua Lighthouse SP; Coquille Point.

AMERICAN BITTERN

Botaurus lentiginosus

The American Bittern's deep, booming call is as characteristic of a spring marsh as the sounds of croaking frogs. • When approached by an intruder, this bird's first reaction is to freeze. It points its bill skyward, and, to enhance the illusion of invisibility, an American Bittern will always keep its streaked breast toward danger, swaying in time with the surrounding stems. An American Bittern will instinctively adopt this frozen stance even if completely in the open, apparently unaware that a lack of cover betrays its presence! • The American Bittern might look similar to an immature night-heron, but it is a daylight feeder. Its camouflage also helps it forage—it relies on stealth to hunt in its freshwater habitat. • When the male calls, watch the accompanying strange, contorted movements of his head and neck.

ID: large and stocky; pale buff underparts with brown streaking from "chin" down through breast and flanks; straight, straw-colored bill; noticeable black "whisker"; yellowish green legs and feet; conspicuous white patch visible on shoulders when bird is calling. *In flight:* faster wingbeats than other herons; neck held tucked in except if being harassed by other birds.

Size: *L* 23–27 in; *W* 3½ ft.

Status: common summer resident and breeder throughout Oregon; very rare to rare in winter.

Habitat: freshwater and brackish marshes with tall, dense emergent vegetation; migrants can visit almost any body of water, including ditches, wet fields and urban ponds.

Nesting: above the waterline in a dense cattail or bulrush marsh; nest platform is made of grass, sedges and dead reeds; nest often has separate entrance and exit paths; female incubates 4–5 plain buffy eggs for 24–28 days and feeds young by regurgitation.

Feeding: stand-and-wait predator; stabs for small fish, amphibians, aquatic insects and crustaceans; occasionally takes small mammals and snakes; active during the day, but more so in deep twilight.

Voice: deep, slow, resonant, repetitive *pomp-er-lunk* or *onk-a-blonk*; most often heard in the evening or at night.

Similar Species: *Least Bittern* (p. 54): much smaller; black crown. *Immature Green Heron* (p. 59): smaller; more heavily marked; different facial markings. *Immature night-herons* (p. 60): grayer overall; white-spotted upperparts; different facial markings; more active at night.

Best Sites: suitable habitats in Harney, Lake and Klamath Counties.

LEAST BITTERN

Ixobrychus exilis

The tiny Least Bittern normally remains concealed in tall, impenetrable stands of cattails that hide its movements. It moves about with ease, its slender body passing freely and unnoticed through dense marshland habitat without getting its feet wet. This expert climber learns soon after hatching to wrap its long toes around stems 3 feet or so above water. • Extremely rare in most of western North America, the Least Bittern reaches its northernmost limits in southern Oregon, but its secretive behavior and solitary lifestyle make sightings infrequent even where it may be most common, in the Klamath Basin. In flood or drought conditions, it will not always breed, and, with its minimal tolerance to chilly nights, it is rarely seen after the evenings turn cold.

ID: buff flanks and sides; buff-streaked fore-neck; white underparts; pale yellow bill with brown top; short tail; orangy buff wings with blackish brown tips. *Male:* black crown and back. *Female:* chestnut brown crown and purplish brown back.

Size: *L* 12–14 in; *W* 17 in.

Status: rare summer resident and irregular breeder in southern Oregon; vagrant elsewhere; *hesperis* ssp. is a federal species of concern and is state-listed as sensitive.

Habitat: freshwater marshes with cattails and other dense emergent vegetation, often interspersed with woody vegetation and open water.

Nesting: nest site is well concealed and partially covered within dense vegetation; male builds a platform of dry plant stalks on top of bent marsh vegetation and female completes the nest; pair incubates 4–5 pale green or blue eggs for 17–20 days and feeds young by regurgitation.

Feeding: stabs small prey, mostly fish, with its bill; also takes large insects, especially dragonflies, tadpoles, frogs, small snakes, leeches and crayfish; sometimes builds hunting platforms at good sites.

Voice: quite vocal at breeding sites, with a guttural *uh-uh-uh-oo-oo-oo-ooah* by the male and ticking reply by the female; low *tut-tut* flight call; sharper *koh* or short, flat *gik* alarm call; relatively loud hissing and shrieking notes on the nest or if agitated.

Similar Species: *American Bittern* (p. 53): much larger; boldly brown-streaked underparts; dark whisker stripe; upperwings dark and light brown, not buff. *Green Heron* (p. 59): darker plumage; somewhat larger; immature has dark brown upperparts and dense, dark streaking below.

Best Sites: Malheur NWR; Upper Klamath L.

GREAT BLUE HERON

Ardea herodias

Great Blue Herons can appear in even the smallest and most isolated patches of suitable habitat. Because they frequent rivers, lakeshores, beaches, sand flats and piers visited by people, they are seen more often at close range than any other heron. • Although these herons appear clumsy when taking off, once airborne, their slow, steady progress enables them to travel long distances with ease. • Slow-motion movements and a lack of fluffy, bunched feathers hanging over the tail distinguish these herons from cranes. Also, Great Blues fly with their necks held in a shallow "S" (unless being harassed by another heron or a raptor), whereas cranes keep their necks straight. • In large colonies, the adults may recognize their offspring by the constant rhythmic sounds they make.

ID: blue gray overall; long, dark-striped gray neck; long, straight, dagger-like, dark-topped yellow bill; long, dark legs with chestnut thighs. *Breeding:* intensified colors; thin, pointed plumes extend from crown and throat. *In flight:* head and upper neck held in "S"; legs and feet extend well beyond tail; chestnut stripe on leading edge of underwing.
Size: *L* 4¼–4½ ft; *W* 6 ft.
Status: common year-round resident and breeder west of the Cascades; uncommon to locally common summer resident and breeder and uncommon winter visitor east of the Cascades.
Habitat: almost any freshwater habitat or calm-water intertidal habitat, including farmlands and occasionally urban areas.

Nesting: colonial; in a tree, snag, tall bush or marsh vegetation; stick-and-twig platform nest up to 4 ft in diameter is lined with pine needles, moss, reeds and dry grass; may be refurbished for reuse; pair incubates 3–5 pale blue eggs for 27–29 days; pair feeds young by regurgitation.
Feeding: stand-and-wait predator or slowly stalks prey in shallow water or grass; impales fish, amphibians, reptiles, invertebrates, small mammals and birds with its bill; occasionally scavenges carrion, including discarded fish remains and domestic animal carcasses in winter.
Voice: usually quiet away from the nest; occasionally gives a deep, harsh *fwaark* call at takeoff.
Similar Species: *Sandhill Crane* (p. 128): tall; pale gray, often rust tinged; red "cap" extends below eye; almost always seen in pairs or social flocks.
Best Sites: almost any wetland.

GREAT EGRET

Ardea alba

G reat Egrets are the largest of a nearly worldwide group of generally white, small to medium-large herons. • Foraging individually over a wide area by day, Great Egrets gather at sunset to return to communal nighttime roosting sites in undisturbed stands of trees or, in summer, to their nests. • During the breeding season, egrets develop their characteristic ornamental plumes, and the color of face and leg skin intensifies. • In the 1800s, Great Egrets and many other showy, colonial-nesting waterbirds were nearly extirpated in North America because their plumes were used to decorate women's hats. Outrage over the destruction of adults and the starvation of orphaned nestlings helped change public opinion and start the National Audubon Society (with the Great Egret as its symbol). Great Egrets are now widespread in Oregon, nesting in several locations.

breeding

nonbreeding

ID: white plumage; long, all-black legs and feet; yellow bill; short tail. *Breeding:* white plumes trail from throat and rump; orangy yellow bill. *In flight:* black feet extend well beyond tail.
Size: *L* 3–3½ ft; *W* 4¼ ft.
Status: common summer resident and breeder in south-central Oregon, but rare in winter and rare elsewhere east of the Cascades; common on the south coast in late summer and fall; locally common inland west of the Cascades from late summer through winter; can be a wanderer or migrant anywhere.
Habitat: almost any open or semi-open wetland habitat; favors expansive shallows, marshes and rushy lakeshores; regularly found on inner estuarine tidal flats.

Nesting: colonial; in a tree, shrub or thicket; pair builds a stick platform and incubates 3–4 pale bluish green eggs for 23–26 days; both adults feed young by regurgitation.
Feeding: stand-and-wait predator or actively forages in shallow water; eats mostly fish, but also takes aquatic and intertidal invertebrates, amphibians, reptiles, rodents and small birds.
Voice: rapid, low-pitched, loud *kuk-kuk-kuk*, usually only when flushed or alarmed.
Similar Species: *Snowy Egret* (p. 57): smaller; spikelike, black bill; yellow or red patch between bill and eyes; black legs with "golden slippers"; immature has pale greenish legs and feet. *Cattle Egret* (p. 58): smaller and stockier; shorter, yellow or reddish orange bill; yellow or purplish patch above bill; dusky red legs and feet; buff plumes in breeding plumage.
Best Sites: *Summer:* Malheur NWR; Upper Klamath L.; Pelican L.; Summer L. *Winter:* inner estuarine flats; Willamette Valley.

SNOWY EGRET

Egretta thula

A Snowy Egret in breeding plumage is truly glamorous, and this species is the subject of more photos than any other North American waterbird. • Although quite widespread in Oregon, the Snowy is not as common as the larger Great Egret, nor is it inclined to remain past fall in any numbers. • As with many other egrets, Snowy Egret populations were greatly affected by the commercial demand for "aigrettes" in the 1800s, and the birds disappeared from many colony sites. Protective legislation ended the slaughter, and Snowies have recolonized many of their former sites in North America and spread northward on both coasts. In Oregon, the Malheur Lake population became reestablished in the 1940s. Although still very rare, Snowies began to reappear regularly west of the Cascades in the 1970s.

breeding

nonbreeding

ID: all-white plumage; straight, slender, black bill; rounded head; dark legs; yellow feet. *Breeding:* elegant plumes extend from head, neck and back; crown feathers can be raised in crest; orange red on lores; bright yellowish orange feet. *Nonbreeding:* duller yellow lores and feet. *Juvenile:* greenish yellow lores and legs.
Size: *L* 22–26 in; *W* 3½ ft.
Status: uncommon summer resident and breeder in Harney Basin and locally in Lake Co.; rare to uncommon from spring to fall in Klamath Basin and Rogue Valley; summer vagrant elsewhere east of the Cascades; rare from midsummer to April on the south coast; state-listed as sensitive.
Habitat: standing or slow-moving shallow fresh water of lakes and floodplains,

marshes and tidal flats of inner estuaries. *In migration:* reservoirs and narrow river corridors.
Nesting: colonial; in an undisturbed stand of trees or shrubs or in a marsh; platform of twigs is lined with finer plant materials; pair incubates 3–5 pale greenish blue eggs for 22–24 days and feeds young for 50–56 days.
Feeding: walks and runs to stab aquatic invertebrates, fish, amphibians and reptiles or shuffles a foot underwater in a shake-and-stir technique.
Voice: low croaks; bouncy *wulla-wulla-wulla* on breeding grounds.
Similar Species: *Great Egret* (p. 56): larger; yellow bill; black feet. *Cattle Egret* (p. 58): chunkier; yellowish orange bill; yellowish feet; yellow or dark legs; orange legs and rusty patches in breeding plumage.
Best Sites: *Summer:* Malheur NWR; Lower Klamath NWR; Summer L. *Winter:* notably Coos Bay.

CATTLE EGRET

Bubulcus ibis

Through the ages, herons have evolved to exploit a variety of foraging niches, ranging from dense marshes to open mudflats and from riverside tangles to kelp beds. Among the herons, Cattle Egrets are the least tied to wetland habitats. They originated on the semi-arid savannas of the Old World, where herds of large herbivores constantly stirred up insects as they foraged through the grass. Cattle Egrets appeared in South America in the first half of the 20th century. By the 1940s, they had reached Florida and then quickly spread throughout North America. With large herds of wild ungulates no longer roaming the land here, Cattle Egrets readily took to following domestic cattle. Although most Cattle Egrets do follow cattle, a few will hang around other domestic animals, particularly goats and horses.

nonbreeding

breeding

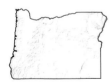

ID: short bill with partly feathered lower mandible. *Breeding:* orangy buff crown, back and foreneck; long plumes on throat and rump; orangy red bill and legs; lores can become purple. *Nonbreeding:* all-white plumage; yellowish or dark legs and feet; yellowish orange bill.

Size: *L* 19–21 in; *W* 3 ft.

Status: rare late fall and early winter migrant on the coast and very rare in western interior valleys; rare local summer resident and breeder in Harney Basin; rare spring and summer visitor to Klamath Basin; vagrant elsewhere.

Habitat: forages among grazing cattle, and sometimes other herbivores, in lowland pastures; also hunts in brackish marshes, pond margins or croplands.

Nesting: colonial; female uses materials gathered by the male to build a stick platform in a tree or shrub; pair incubates 3–4 pale blue eggs for 21–26 days and feeds young by regurgitation.

Feeding: captures insects, spiders and ticks flushed by movements of grazing animals; also takes snakes, frogs, nestling birds, eggs, earthworms and crayfish and rarely fish.

Voice: generally silent; feeding groups may utter nasal quacks or grunts.

Similar Species: *Snowy Egret* (p. 57): slender, black bill; black legs; yellow feet. *Great Egret* (p. 56): larger; slender; long neck; long bill; black legs and feet.

Best Sites: *Summer:* Harney Basin; Klamath Basin. *Fall* and *winter:* coast; Nehalem Meadows; Tillamook pasturelands; along Coquille R. valley east of Coos Bay.

GREEN HERON

Butorides virescens

Green Herons favor shrubby stream meanders, the backwaters of sluggish rivers, undisturbed pond margins and protected estuarine shallows, where they can feed without being discovered. While foraging, these small, colorful herons move furtively within easy flight distance of sheltering vegetation. However, they will risk exposed stream outflows, rushy tidal channels, breakwaters, disused piers and sheltered mudflats, often using the cover of logs and branches, to get closer to their prey. Green Herons are also known for the feathers, leaves and other small objects that they drop onto the water's surface to lure small fish within striking distance. • Green Herons arrive earlier in spring than most other herons and leave later in fall, with the main migrations taking place in April and October. • The scientific name *virescens* is Latin for "becoming green," referring to the transition from a streaky brown juvenile to a greenish adult.

ID: greenish black crown; chestnut face and neck; white-streaked throat and underparts; bluish gray with iridescent green on back and wings; short, yellow legs; dark-topped, greenish bill; short tail. *Breeding male:* bright orange legs. *Immature:* heavily streaked underparts; dull brown upperparts; greenish legs; dusky bill. *In flight:* contrasting feet extend past tail.
Size: *L* 15–22 in; *W* 26 in.
Status: uncommon summer resident and breeder in western Oregon; rare elsewhere in summer; seldom seen after October.
Habitat: freshwater and tidal shores, ponds, streamside willows, mudflat edges and similar sheltered or semi-wooded situations.
Nesting: singly or in small, loose groups; male constructs a stick platform in a tree or shrub, very close to water; pair incubates 3–5 pale green to bluish, brown-stained eggs for 19–21 days and feeds young by regurgitation for 30–35 days.
Feeding: stabs prey with bill after slowly stalking or while standing and waiting; adult occasionally plunges into deeper water; eats mostly small fish, frogs, tadpoles, crustaceans and aquatic insects.
Voice: generally silent except when startled; loud *kowp*, *kyow* or *skow* alarm and flight calls; harsh *raah* in aggression.
Similar Species: *Least Bittern* (p. 54): small; bold, buffy upperwing patches; secretive nature. *American Bittern* (p. 53): larger; buff neck and breast with heavy, brown streaks; noticeable black "whisker."
Best Sites: Rogue, Umpqua, Willamette and Tualatin Rivers; Cannon Beach sewage ponds; Yaquina Bay; Coos Bay; Fern Ridge Reservoir.

BLACK-CROWNED NIGHT-HERON
Nycticorax nycticorax

Herons offer a very obvious example of successful diversification. All have relatively large, pointed bills with which they spear prey, but they can be large or tiny, brilliantly colored or drab, reclusive or highly social, and diurnal or nocturnal. Black-crowned Night-Herons hunt in a variety of settings and occupy the mid-range in other characteristics. They disperse widely, mostly by night, into almost any habitat offering aquatic or estuarine prey. With their large, light-sensitive eyes, they can feed in much lower light situations than other herons and egrets, thus avoiding competition. • Adults are boldly patterned, yet their counter-shading and relative lack of movement render them inconspicuous in the dappled shadows of their daytime hangouts. The streaked plumage of immatures also provides excellent camouflage among tree branches and in marsh vegetation.

breeding

nonbreeding

ID: stout, black bill; black "cap" and back; large, red eyes; gray wings; dull yellow legs. *Breeding:* 2 long, white plumes trail from crown. *Immature:* white-spotted gray upperwings; gray underwings; streaked, brown-and-white head and underparts; dark-topped pale bill. *In flight:* "lazy" wingstrokes; stubby neck; little foot extension.
Size: *L* 23–26 in; *W* 3½ ft.
Status: locally common near breeding colonies but rare elsewhere in both summer and migration; winters locally at Klamath Falls and in western Oregon.
Habitat: *Foraging:* marshes, mudflats, cropland, ponds and slow-moving streams. *Breeding:* dense stands of trees and brush, often in seclusion.

Nesting: colonial; female uses material gathered by the male for a loose stick nest lined with roots and grass; pair incubates 3–5 greenish eggs for 23–26 days.
Feeding: chiefly at night, but also by day; stalks or waits quietly for fish, amphibians, reptiles, invertebrates, such as mollusks, and small birds and mammals.
Voice: deep, guttural *quark* or *wok*, often on takeoff.
Similar Species: *American Bittern* (p. 53): much larger; lightly mottled brown back; rarely sits hunched in waterside shrubbery. *Great Blue Heron* (p. 55): much larger; longer, more heavily marked neck; longer legs.
Best Sites: *Summer* and *in migration:* Malheur NWR, as well as sites in Lake Co. and Klamath Co., especially Ladd Marsh WMA and Link Canal (Klamath Falls).

WHITE-FACED IBIS
Plegadis chihi

Revered in various parts of the world, ibises are slender, long-legged, highly social wading birds. White-faced Ibises have a preference for flooded croplands and the expansive reedbeds and muddy shallows of federal wildlife refuges. Requiring high-quality marshes for nesting, ibises will abandon and relocate breeding sites to ensure optimal conditions. • Long legs, slender toes and a remarkable downcurved bill all contribute to the success of the White-faced Ibis in extracting food items from soft or semi-fluid soil. • White-faces fly rapidly, easily traversing the miles between secluded nesting colonies and outlying feeding locations. • Migrating ibises use traditional flyways, so this species can be a familiar sight in some areas and scarcely known a few miles away. • Highly iridescent at close range or in excellent light, this bird's plumage appears entirely dark brown at a distance.

breeding

nonbreeding

ID: dark red eyes; long, downcurved pale bill; long, dark legs. *Breeding:* rich red legs and facial patch; eyes bordered by white facial skin; green iridescence on back. *Nonbreeding:* brown with less distinct greenish gloss; pinkish bare skin in front of eye.
Size: *L* 19–26 in; *W* 3 ft.
Status: common local summer resident and breeder in south-central and southeastern Oregon; increasing stray throughout Oregon; federal species of concern.
Habitat: marshes, lake edges, mudflats, wet pastures and irrigation ditches.

Nesting: colonial; in bulrushes or other emergent vegetation; deep cup nest of coarse materials is lined with fine plant matter; pair incubates 3–4 bluish green eggs for about 22 days.
Feeding: probes and gleans soil and shallow water for aquatic invertebrates, amphibians and other small vertebrates; feeds in large flocks or individually.
Voice: generally quiet; occasionally gives a series of low, ducklike quacks.
Similar Species: *Herons* and *egrets* (pp. 53-60): straight bill. *Long-billed Curlew* (p. 145): rich buffy brown; cinnamon underwing linings; uniformly thin, longer bill.
Best Sites: regular nesting colonies at Malheur NWR, Harney L. and Summer L.; new colonies in Lake Co.; regular in Burns–Hines area; migrant and visitor in Klamath Co.

TURKEY VULTURE

Cathartes aura

Turkey Vultures are among North America's greatest wanderers, literally "following their noses." Their advanced sense of smell, coupled with a large wing area relative to their weight, have enabled Turkey Vultures to patrol broad stretches of countryside for dead animals, moving from one bubble of warm, rising air to another. The long wings and tail are spread to the fullest extent as these accomplished soarers aim to tease the greatest performance possible with minimal energy expenditure. • Often maligned by the general public, Turkey Vultures perform a valuable service by locating and disposing of smelly carcasses. These vultures are dependent on carrion, and their bills and feet are not designed to kill or crush living animals. The naked head, like that of some carrion-eating storks, is an adaptation to deter bacteria and parasites.

ID: very large; mostly dark brown; small, featherless red head; dark "collar." *Immature:* gray head. *In flight:* silvery gray flight feathers; black wing linings; wings held in shallow "V"; tilts when soaring; head seems hunched between shoulders.

Size: *L* 26–32 in; *W* 5¾–6 ft.

Status: common summer resident and breeder throughout Oregon but less regular in the northeast; common migrant, with birds moving between mid-February and April and from August to mid-October; very rare and local in winter.

Habitat: cruises over almost all terrestrial and shoreline habitats but favors valley edges and foothills for regular thermals;

roosts, sometimes colonially, in large trees, especially cottonwoods.

Nesting: on bare ground, among boulders, in a hollow tree or on the forest floor; no nest material is used; pair incubates 2–3 dull or creamy white eggs for 30–40 days; nestlings are fed by regurgitation.

Feeding: scavenger; eats carrion of nearly any type, including mammals, reptiles and beached fish.

Voice: generally silent; occasionally hisses or grunts if threatened.

Similar Species: *Golden Eagle* (p. 109): generally brown plumage, lighter on head; wings appear flat or slightly uptilted in profile; does not rock in flight; darker flight feathers; brown wing linings. *Hawks* (pp. 100-109): generally smaller; shorter, broader wings usually flat when soaring; many have distinctive tail color or pattern.

Best Sites: foothills; along mountain ridges.

GREATER WHITE-FRONTED GOOSE
Anser albifrons

Wild geese have come to mean many things to many people. We flatter them with the attributes of pair devotion, family tenacity and vigor—all traits prized and praised by humans—yet hunting continues to be an obstacle to their survival. White-fronted Geese endure many other rigors in their annual cycle: breeding may be delayed or threatened by late spring ice at their arctic breeding sites, and traditional wetland staging and feeding areas are often encroached on or taken over for development. Fortunately, any geese visiting Oregon are presented with a mosaic of national wildlife refuges and local sanctuaries that offer both shelter and food crops. • White-fronts often travel with Canada Geese and Snow Geese and sometimes join flocks of domestic or feral geese and ducks at park and farm ponds.

ID: brownish gray plumage; blackish speckling or barring across whitish lower breast and belly; orangy pink bill; bright orange legs and feet; white patch across bill and forehead; white hindquarters. *Tule White-front* (from Cook Inlet, Alaska): somewhat larger; dark brown head; blackish back. *Immature:* mottled, brown-and-white belly; dark around and above bill; yellow bill until mid-fall.
Size: *L* 27–33 in; *W* 4½–4¾ ft.
Status: common throughout Oregon from August to November and from February to early May; locally uncommon winter resident along the coast, in the Willamette Valley and at Sauvie I.

Habitat: extensive marsh-dotted lakes and reservoirs and crop stubble; roosts on open water, shorelines, ice and sometimes plowed fields. *In migration:* nearly anywhere.
Nesting: does not nest in Oregon.
Feeding: forages on land by stripping and gleaning plant material, including grasses, sedges, seeds and crop wastes; submerges head or tips up in water for submerged and emergent vegetation.
Voice: contact and flight call in flocks is a distinctive series of far-carrying falsetto notes likened to laughing or yelping; *gig-gog* alarm call, usually given on the ground.
Similar Species: *Canada Goose* (p. 66): dark head and neck with distinctive white "chin strap"; heavier body and wings; more cackling or honking calls.
Best Sites: Sauvie I.; Umatilla NWR; Malheur NWR; Summer L.; Klamath Basin; Warner Valley.

SNOW GOOSE
Chen caerulescens

Along the Pacific Flyway, Snow Geese are seen mainly in the managed wetland ecosystems of the national wildlife refuges and local wildlife management areas. Clannish by nature, and perhaps the noisiest of geese, they prefer their own company but will travel with both Greater White-fronted Geese and Canada Geese. Flocks are composed of family groups that stay together for winter and assemble in highly localized groups at their wintering grounds. • The establishment of refuges has helped stabilize numbers on wintering grounds and in migration to the extent that fragile tundra nesting habitat is being put under pressure to support the increasing number of geese. Many of the Snow Geese wintering in Oregon breed in northeastern Siberia and cross the Bering Strait twice each year in migration.

white morph

ID: pink feet; stubby, pink bill with thin, black "grinning patch" along mandible edges. *White morph:* all white, except for black wing tips and occasional light rusty or buffy orange staining on head. *Dark morph (Blue Goose):* bluish gray to brown body; white head, upper neck and sometimes belly. *In flight:* flocks often in large, loose "V"s.
Size: *L* 28–33 in; *W* 4¾–5 ft.
Status: widespread, uncommon to locally abundant spring and fall migrant; locally uncommon winter resident, mainly in Klamath Co. and in the northwest, especially on Sauvie I.; dark morph is extremely rare in Oregon.

Habitat: shallow freshwater lakes and wetlands, grain fields and croplands; some birds appear at coastal lowlands, parks, reservoirs and golf courses.
Nesting: does not nest in Oregon.
Feeding: gleans from land, in marshes or in shallows; eats seeds, stems, leaves and most other parts of aquatic vegetation, as well as berries, grains, leafy stems of crops and horsetail stems; bill is adapted to gripping and stripping vegetation.
Voice: loud, nasal, constant *houk-houk* in flight; flocks can be heard from a great distance.
Similar Species: *Ross's Goose* (p. 65): smaller; more triangular bill; no black "grinning patch"; slightly shorter neck; more smoothly rounded head; sometimes hybridizes with Snow Goose, producing birds with intermediate characteristics.
Best Sites: *Winter:* Sauvie I. *In migration:* Summer L.; Malheur NWR; Klamath Basin; Harney Basin.

ROSS'S GOOSE

Chen rossii

Ross's Goose nests in the Canadian Arctic and migrates through southeastern Oregon, arriving in mid-October and leaving for California wintering sites by early December. Spring migration tends to be more leisurely, with flocks returning in late February and early March and remaining until late April before heading northeast. • Ross's Geese are rarely seen away from their favored staging sites, but single birds and small numbers sometimes join larger flocks of Snow Geese or Cackling Geese in areas outside their normal routes. • The particularly handsome but very rare dark-morph Ross's Goose may have originated from occasional hybridization between white-morph Ross's Geese and dark-morph Snow Geese.

white morph

Habitat: shallow freshwater wetlands, lakes and farm fields; rarely in tidal marshes, estuaries and urban lakes.
Nesting: does not nest in Oregon.
Feeding: eats most parts of crop wastes, grasses and sedges; often digs for roots; swims or wades in shallows to eat aquatic vegetation.
Voice: flight call is a high-pitched *kug, kek* or *ke-gak.*
Similar Species: *Snow Goose* (p. 64): larger; prominent black "grinning patch" on more angular, rounder-based bill; slightly longer neck; head may be stained orange or rusty; dark-morph bird is darker on head and body; noisier.
Best Sites: Malheur NWR; Klamath Basin; Summer L.; Miller I. WMA.

ID: smallest North American goose; white overall; black wing tips; small, triangular, deep pink bill; pink legs and feet. *White morph:* like miniature Snow Goose. *Dark morph:* white head; blackish nape, back and body; white wing coverts.
Size: *L* 21–26 in; *W* 4¼ ft.
Status: locally common migrant and rare in winter in much of eastern and south-central Oregon; vagrant in migration elsewhere.

CANADA GOOSE

Branta canadensis

Of the many Canada Goose subspecies, eight occur here. The two largest, *B.c. maxima* and *B.c. moffitti*, are breeding residents. *B.c. minima*, distinguished by its cackling calls, extremely small size, stubby neck and short bill, arrives in mid-October; most shortly depart again, but a few winter in Oregon. *B.c. leucopareia* is a rare fall migrant and local winter resident along the coast. The most widespread and abundant subspecies, *B.c. taverneri* and *B.c. occidentalis*, arrive in October and leave by mid-April. Except for *B.c. maxima*, which was introduced to Oregon, and *B.c. moffitti*, which breeds throughout the western states, all of these subspecies nest in Alaska or the Aleutian Islands. • Each subspecies shows a high degree of individuality in behavior such as habitat selection, winter mixing and roosting, leading many ornithologists to suggest that some subspecies may merit full species status.

ID: long, black neck; rounded, white "chin strap" encircling throat; black bill and legs; light brown underparts; dark brown upperparts; white rump and undertail coverts; short, black tail.

Size: *L* 25–45 in; *W* 4¼–5¾ ft.

Status: locally common breeding resident; common migrant and winter resident; *leucopareia* ssp. federal-listed as threatened and state-listed as endangered.

Habitat: along water bodies, parks, marshes and croplands.

Nesting: on the ground on an islet, shoreline point or cliff, or in an old eagle or Osprey nest close to water; female builds a nest of grass and other vegetation and lines it with feather down; male guards the nest and female incubates 4–7 white eggs for 25–30 days; both adults raise the young.

Voice: familiar, loud *ah-honk;* smaller ssp. have a higher-pitched cackling call.

Similar Species: *Brant* (p. 67): same size as smaller Canada Geese; no "chin strap"; more coastal.

Best Sites: *B.c. moffitti:* Harney Basin. *B.c. maxima:* Clatsop Co. *B.c. minima:* Columbia R.; Willamette Valley; Klamath Co.; Lake Co. *B.c. taverneri:* Umatilla NWR; Cold Springs NWR; McKay Creek NWR; Sauvie I.; Willamette Valley. *B.c. occidentalis:* Sauvie I.; Willamette Valley; northern coast. *B.c. leucopareia:* Nestucca NWR.

BRANT

Branta bernicla

Most of its larger cousins prefer the interior, but the Brant, which is coastal by nature, stays largely along the coast as it migrates between Siberia or Alaska and California or Mexico. • Brant are among the later-arriving fall migrants, appearing from mid-November to December and wintering in small numbers. They are conspicuous and recognizable at a great distance as they skim close to the surf line in undulating skeins. • Brant rely to a great extent on eelgrass, a submergent plant that has greatly suffered from human abuses of estuaries and harbors. Consequently, Brant are only locally common, staging for weeks at favored sites before migrating. • The northward movement along the coast begins in late February, with most birds on the move in March and the first part of April, but some birds remain into early May. A few birds appear in inland locations with other waterfowl, and some may summer along the coast.

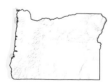

ID: deep brown overall; black head, neck and breast; broken white "collar"; stubby, dark bill; dark legs; barred, gray-and-white sides; extensive white tail coverts; belly usually dark but sometimes light or intermediate. *Immature:* like adult, but has uniform belly color; no "collar."
Size: *L* 25 in; *W* 3¾ ft.
Status: common migrant and locally common winter resident along the coast; rare migrant and winter resident inland.
Habitat: tidal estuaries, river mouths and large, shallow coastal lagoons with eelgrass; occasionally found in farm fields with other grazing and gleaning waterfowl.
Nesting: does not nest in Oregon.
Feeding: tips up and gleans for submergent vegetation over tidal shallows; prefers aquatic plants and algae, especially eelgrass.
Voice: deep, prolonged croak on the ground; soft clucking in flight.
Similar Species: *Small ssp. Canada Goose* (p. 66): paler brown bellies; conspicuous "chin strap"; rarely seen on coast. *Ross's Goose* (p. 65): dark morph has pale foreneck and face; pink bill and legs; more black in tail in flight.
Best Sites: *In migration:* most of coast. *Winter:* Tillamook Bay; Bayocean Spit; Netarts Bay; Yaquina Bay; Coos Bay.

TRUMPETER SWAN

Cygnus buccinator

The majestic Trumpeter Swan was hunted nearly to extinction for its meat and feathers during the early 1900s. Breeding populations in Alaska and Alberta were the only ones that survived. This swan was probably a rare migrant and winter resident in Oregon for several decades, until a total of 137 birds from captive breeding flocks in Montana were transplanted to Malheur National Wildlife Refuge between 1939 and 1958. • Malheur birds remain through winter, but the species is rare elsewhere east of the Cascades. In western Oregon, small numbers winter close to the lower Columbia River and in Polk County. • Both the common and scientific species names refer to the loud, bugling voice created by the long windpipe.

ID: all-white plumage; large, all-black bill; black skin from bill to eyes; sloping head; black legs and feet; long neck. *Immature:* grayish brown plumage; grayish pink bill. *In flight:* straight neck; flies in family groups.

Size: *L* 4¾–5¼ ft; *W* 9½ ft.

Status: rare winter visitor to northwestern and eastern Oregon; reintroduced breeding resident at Malheur NWR.

Habitat: shallow areas of large lakes and wetlands, spring-fed rivers, farm fields and flooded pastures; rarely on mudflats and salt marshes.

Nesting: on an island, often on a beaver or muskrat house, or along a freshwater shoreline; pair builds a large mound of vegetation and lines it with down; female incubates 4–6 white eggs for 32–37 days; both adults tend the young.

Feeding: surface gleans and occasionally grazes submerged and emergent vegetation, grain and pasture grasses; especially when young, also eats small fish and eggs and invertebrates.

Voice: loud, resonant, buglelike *koh-hoh*, usually by male in flight; gentle, nasal honking; high-pitched calls of the immature deepen over first winter.

Similar Species: *Tundra Swan* (p. 69): smaller; more commonly in large flocks; often shows yellow at base of bill; softer, more nasal calls; rounder head. *Snow Goose* (p. 64) and *Ross's Goose* (p. 65): smaller; shorter neck; stubbier, pink bill and legs; black in wing tips.

Best Sites: Malheur NWR and surrounding area. *In migration* and *winter:* Sauvie I.; Forest Grove; Lower Klamath NWR; Summer L. *Winter:* lower Columbia R. lakes; Polk Co. farmlands.

TUNDRA SWAN

Cygnus columbianus

The long neck and powerful bill of the Tundra Swan are adaptations to a life in shallow wetlands. It can graze and glean on land like a goose, skim the water's surface or tip up like a dabbling duck. With its exceptional underwater reach and strong bill, it can grasp and root out bottom-growing tubers and shoots—foods unavailable to geese and ducks. Such specialization allows large flocks of waterfowl to gather together in huge numbers without overly depleting the same food resources. • Tundra Swans depend largely on federally managed wetland refuges, but some smaller flocks winter at widely scattered sites in the interior valleys and along the coast. • Swans have long been celebrated in poetry and dance for their grace, and the first sight of swans flying in formation overhead is something that few people forget.

ID: rounded head; long neck, held mostly straight; heavy, black, slightly concave bill; black facial skin; most have yellow "teardrop" in front of eye; big, black feet. *In flight:* neck held horizontally; flies in family groups.
Size: *L* 4–4¾ ft; *W* 5½–6¾ ft.
Status: common to locally abundant migrant; uncommon to locally common in winter; fall migration usually begins in early November; most winter residents and spring migrants leave by early April.
Habitat: permanent or seasonal wetlands in undisturbed open country; large, shallow lakes, riparian marshes and shallow estuarine tidal areas with nearby grassland or cropland; prefers clear line of sight in all directions.

Nesting: does not nest in Oregon.
Feeding: tips up, dabbles and surface-gleans for aquatic vegetation, mollusks and invertebrates; grazes for tubers, roots, grasses and waste grain.
Voice: muffled, hollow honking or hooting *whoo-hoo-wu-whoo* call in flight and by nervous flocks on land or in water; large flocks make gooselike barking sounds.
Similar Species: *Trumpeter Swan* (p. 68): larger; heavier bill; no yellow "teardrop"; loud, buglelike calls; immature retains grayer plumage into fall; longer neck in flight. *Snow Goose* (p. 64) and *Ross's Goose* (p. 65): smaller; shorter neck; stubbier, pink bill and legs; black in wing tips; faster wingbeats.
Best Sites: lower Columbia R. *In migration:* large lakes in Klamath, Harney and Lake Counties; Sauvie I. *Winter:* along the coast; Willamette Valley; Klamath Basin.

WOOD DUCK

Aix sponsa

The image of the gaudy male Wood Duck has adorned innumerable calendar leaves, postcards and bird-book jackets as well as wooded ponds. The drake's plumage throughout much of the year suggests that he bathed in the palette left over after all the other North American birds had been painted. The female is much less dramatic than the male, but she is lovely in her own right, clothed in delicate mouse gray, her large, liquid eyes given added expression by elongated white patches. • In the wild, Wood Ducks usually flush and fly off almost immediately after coming into view, but at park ponds they often accommodate close-range admiration. • Wood Ducks are sometimes found well away from water when foraging for acorns, and they perch in trees and low overhanging riparian tangles more often than any other duck.

ID: *Male:* glossy, green-and-purple head with white-bordered, slicked-back crest; white "chin," throat and neck lines; reddish-pink-and-white bill; red eyes; white-spotted chestnut breast; golden brown sides, bordered by white and black; dark back and hindquarters of brown, purple and blue; dark tail; dull green speculum. *Female:* white "teardrop" around brown eye; brownish gray upperparts; mottled brown breast streaked with white; white belly.

Size: *L* 17–21 in; *W* 28–31 in.

Status: common summer breeder and migrant west of the Cascades; uncommon east of the Cascades; uncommon winter resident.

Habitat: freshwater ponds, marshes, lakes and rivers, usually bordered by dense stands of trees.

Nesting: in a natural hollow, tree cavity or nest box, up to 30 ft above the ground and usually near water; nest is lined with down; female incubates 9–14 creamy white to tan eggs for 27–30 days.

Feeding: gleans the water's surface and tips up for aquatic vegetation; feeds in woodlands; eats fruits and nuts and waste grains.

Voice: male utters an ascending *ter-wee-wee*; female gives a squeaky *woo-e-e-k*.

Similar Species: *Hooded Merganser* (p. 93): slim, dark bill; pointed tail; black-and-white speculum; male has black, crested head with white patch and black-and-white breast; female is brown, with shaggy crest.

Best Sites: *Summer:* valleys and coastal lowlands west of the Cascades; Klamath Basin; rivers in Malheur, Hood River and northern Wasco Counties. *Winter:* coastal Coos Co. and Curry Co.; Klamath Basin; Bend area; Portland's Westmoreland Park and Crystal Springs L.

GADWALL

Anas strepera

Being called an "odd duck" implies an unusual appearance and habits. The image of a blandly plumaged Gadwall doesn't leap to mind, yet this often-overlooked species displays nuances of habitat selection, temperament and behavior distinct from the other dabblers with which it is often found. • Gadwalls favor undisturbed ponds and sloughs with muddy bottoms, abundant aquatic plants and adjacent cover of marsh vegetation or overhanging willows or other trees. In such seclusion, they glean from the surface, dabble in shallows and repeatedly dive to reach submerged food items. Methodical feeders, they move slowly around a feeding site. • A combination of blackish bill, black-and-white speculum and black hindquarters confirms the male. A female is generally close at hand, because Gadwalls start forming pair bonds for the next breeding season as early as July, remaining together in the interim.

ID: steeply angled forehead; rounded head; black-bordered small, white speculum patch; yellowish orange legs. *Breeding male:* mostly subtly barred and streaked gray; dark bill; black hindquarters. *Female* and *eclipse male:* mostly mottled brown; less white in speculum; orangy yellow bill with dark ridge.
Size: *L* 18–22 in; *W* 29–33 in.
Status: locally common summer resident and breeder east of the Cascades; breeds sparingly in western Oregon; locally common migrant and winter resident throughout Oregon.
Habitat: *Breeding:* marshes; moves with ducklings to open water with emergent vegetation. *In migration* and *winter:* ponds, lakes and coastal and brackish waters.

Nesting: well concealed in tall, emergent vegetation, often on an island and can be far from water; grassy, down-lined hollow; female incubates 7–12 dull creamy white to grayish green eggs for 24–27 days; female leads brood to more open habitat to feed on aquatic invertebrates.
Feeding: dabbles, tips up and dives for aquatic and estuarine plants and invertebrates; also eats waste grain, tadpoles and small fish; often steals food from American Coots.
Voice: male has a simple, single quack; often whistles harshly; female utters a high *kaak kaaak kak-kak-kak* series with changing volume.
Similar Species: *Female Mallard* (p. 74): blue or purplish speculum bordered on both sides with white; white sides to tail; darker eye line.
Best Sites: Harney, Lake and Klamath Counties, including Malheur NWR.

71

EURASIAN WIGEON

Anas penelope

Large flocks of migrating or overwintering American Wigeons scattered throughout Oregon, chiefly at principal waterfowl concentration sites along the Pacific Flyway, typically contain one to several Eurasian Wigeons. Following an avian rule that echoes the saying, "when in Rome, do as the Romans do," Eurasian Wigeons consort almost exclusively with American Wigeons. • As with most ducks, wigeon males in their breeding plumage (mid-fall until late spring) are more easily distinguished and the females are often overlooked. Eurasian females are patterned much like their female American cousins and differ only in having warmer buff flanks, less contrast between the neck and breast and, usually, more reddish heads. Scanning throngs of American Wigeons for Eurasian Wigeons offers observers of all abilities valuable practice in picking out the odd bird from among the host of the mundane—one of the keys to discovering rarities.

ID: bluish gray bill with black tip; dark legs and feet; pointed tail; white belly; green-and-black speculum. *Male:* rich orangy brown head; creamy yellow forehead stripe; chestnut breast; lightly barred gray sides and back; black-and-white hindquarters; white belly and forewing. *Female:* brown head and breast, usually with rufous tints; rufous tan sides.

Size: *L* 17–21 in; *W* 30–33 in.

Status: locally uncommon migrant and winter visitor.

Habitat: shallow lakes with abundant submergent vegetation; open expanses of sprouting grass close to water; intertidal eelgrass beds.

Nesting: does not nest in Oregon.

Feeding: dabbles or tips up for stems, leaves and seeds of submergent vegetation; grazes lawns and pastures; occasionally dives, especially in eelgrass beds.

Voice: male utters a high-pitched, 2-toned *thweeeeeeer* whistle; female's quack is rougher than an American Wigeon's.

Similar Species: *American Wigeon* (p. 73): white "wing pits"; breeding male has clear white forehead and crown, broad, iridescent green facial patch and rusty back and sides; female has grayish head and neck contrasting with browner breast.

Best Sites: near Portland; in the lower Columbia R. lowlands; along the coast.

AMERICAN WIGEON

Anas americana

Expanses of short, lush grass in open country attract flocks of American Wigeons from fall until spring. These ducks like to graze on young shoots while walking steadily along in dense, formless flocks, each individual no more than a few feet from its nearest neighbor. Golf courses provide much the same opportunity for grazing. American Wigeons also occur in the managed wetlands and croplands of wildlife refuges and sanctuaries, massing by day in reed-fringed impoundments and flying off at dusk to glean waste grains and sprouting grasses from outlying agricultural lands. A few flocks settle in for winter in estuarine shallows with eelgrass beds, which they share with Brant and other waterfowl. • Amid the wetland orchestra of buzzes, quacks and ticks, the male American Wigeon's piping, three-syllable whistle is in striking contrast.

ID: large white wing patch; cinnamon breast and flanks; white belly; green-and-black speculum; bluish gray bill with black tip. *Breeding male:* whitish forehead and crown; broad, iridescent green patch behind eye; cinnamon breast and sides; conspicuous white shoulder patch. *Female:* grayish head; brown breast and sides. *Eclipse male:* like female, but with more white on upperwing and warmer brown on underparts.
Size: *L* 18–23 in; *W* 30–33 in.
Status: common migrant and winter resident; uncommon summer breeder east of the Cascades.
Habitat: *Breeding:* small water bodies. *In migration* and *winter:* shallow lakes and slow-moving rivers with submergent vegetation; open expanses of short grass,

protected fresh water, brackish marshes and intertidal eelgrass beds.
Nesting: always on dry ground, often far from water; well-concealed nest of grass and leaves is lined with down; female incubates 7–11 creamy white eggs for 23–25 days.
Feeding: dabbles and tips up for stems, leaves and seeds of submergent vegetation, insects, small mollusks and crustaceans; grazes short grasses.
Voice: male frequently repeats a nasal, whistled *whee wick weew;* female gives a soft, seldom-heard quack, mostly uttered when with the young.
Similar Species: *Eurasian Wigeon* (p. 72): breeding male has rich orangy brown head, creamy yellow forehead and crown; gray back and sides; female has little contrast between rufous or grayish neck and breast.
Best Sites: intertidal eelgrass beds; city parks and golf courses.

73

MALLARD
Anas platyrhynchos

The Mallard is among the most abundant, distinctive and familiar of all water-fowl. In many parts of Europe, its common name translates as "wild duck," and it was likely the ancestor of many wild and domesticated species. • Highly successful, Mallards do well anywhere from tiny ponds to extensive wetlands. Often the last ducks to be pushed out of wetlands under human pressure or deterioration of habitat, they are the first to recolonize if conditions improve. • Mallard drakes will mate with females of closely related species, including domestic ducks, especially Muscovy Ducks (*Cairina moschata*)—the offspring are the ducks usually accepting handouts at park ponds. • Males molt after breeding, losing much of their extravagant plumage. This eclipse plumage camouflages them during the flightless period. Molting into new breeding plumage usually occurs by early August.

ID: orange feet. *Breeding male:* iridescent, green head; bright yellow bill; unmarked chestnut breast; white neck ring; upcurled, black central tail feathers; pale gray underparts. *Female:* finely patterned brown overall; long, thin, dark eye line; dark-mottled dull orange bill; white outer tail feathers. *Eclipse male:* like female, but with dull yellow bill and richer brown breast. *In flight:* white-bordered dark blue speculum (purple or green on hybrids).

Size: *L* 20–28 in; *W* 31–35 in.

Status: common year-round resident and breeder.

Habitat: freshwater and brackish habitats of nearly every description; favors grain-fields, stubble, flooded fields and sprouting pastures, but will visit city parks and even garden ponds; molting, flightless adult moves to tall emergent vegetation near open water.

Nesting: in tall vegetation or under a bush, usually near water; nest of grass and other material is lined with down; female incubates 7–10 white to olive buff eggs for 26–30 days.

Feeding: tips up, gleans and dabbles in shallows for seeds of aquatic plants; takes some mollusks and other invertebrates, larval amphibians, fish eggs and crop wastes; city ducks readily take handouts at ponds and beneath feeders.

Voice: very vocal; male quacks deeply but quietly; female quacks loudly.

Similar Species: *Northern Shoveler* (p. 77): long, wide-tipped bill; green speculum with narrow white borders; breeding male has white breast with chestnut flanks and dark back; female is paler, with fainter eye line.

Best Sites: anywhere near water.

BLUE-WINGED TEAL

Anas discors

Less common along the Pacific Coast than most other dabbling ducks and not very tolerant of cold, Blue-winged Teals arrive late at their breeding sites and leave before the cold weather sets in. Most birds appear between late April and early June. Individuals, pairs and small groups frequent marshes, reed-bordered ponds, mudflats and seasonal wetlands in both spring and fall. Modest numbers of Blue-winged Teals appear during the summer months, most merely passing through, but with some remaining to breed. A few birds occasionally linger through winter in favored areas. • The male defends his nesting territory and may remain with the female and brood through the early part of summer, increasing nesting success. • It is difficult to consistently identify females and males in eclipse plumage.

ID: broad-based, bluish black bill; brown eyes; yellow legs and feet. *Breeding male:* bluish gray head; blackish forehead and crown; white crescent in front of eye; black-spotted brown breast and sides. *Female:* mottled brownish gray overall; dark eye line; whitish "chin" spot. *Nonbreeding male:* like female, but with gray "chin" and faint white crescent that extends up through eye line. *In flight:* conspicuous sky blue forewing patch; green speculum; agile flight.
Size: *L* 14–16 in; *W* 21–23 in.
Status: uncommon migrant from mid-April to early June and from early August to late October; rare breeding summer resident; very rare in winter west of the Cascades.

Habitat: freshwater wetlands, lakes, ponds and marshes; migrants may visit estuarine-edge habitats, such as mudflats, secluded tidal channels and salt marsh pools; rarely on coastal bays.
Nesting: in grass along a shoreline or in a wet meadow, usually near water; grass nest includes considerable amounts of down; female incubates 8–11 creamy eggs for 23–24 days.
Feeding: gleans the water's surface for sedge and grass seeds, pondweeds, duckweeds and aquatic invertebrates.
Voice: male makes a soft *keck-keck-keck* and whistles; female quacks softly.
Similar Species: *Female Cinnamon Teal* (p. 76): broader end on longer bill; face is more uniform.
Best Sites: Harney, Lake and Klamath Counties; nests in Willamette Valley, Rogue Valley and along the coast in Tillamook, Coos and Clatsop Counties.

75

CINNAMON TEAL

Anas cyanoptera

Every spring, Cinnamon Teals push northward from southern wintering grounds to dot the reed-fringed ponds and marshes of Oregon. They nest on both sides of the Cascades and are most common in south-central and south-eastern Oregon. • The intensely reddish brown breeding plumage of the male, accented by his ruby red eyes, is worth an admiring gaze at any time of day, and, during the low, slanting light of early morning or near sunset, he can be a real showstopper. • Females often have the company of their mates throughout the nesting cycle, which contributes greatly to nesting success.

ID: broad-ended bill. *Breeding male:* intensely cinnamon red head, neck and underparts; red eyes. *Female:* mottled warm brown overall; plain face; brown eyes. *Nonbreeding male:* like female, but with rufous tint and red eyes. *In flight:* conspicuous sky blue forewing patch.

Size: *L* 15–17 in; *W* 20–22 in.

Status: common migrant and summer breeder; rare in winter west of the Cascades.

Habitat: freshwater ponds, marshes, sloughs, stock ponds, ditches and flooded swales with floating or submergent aquatic vegetation; prefers sites close to marshes; less apt to feed in large flocks far out in stubble fields or pastures.

Nesting: nest is hidden in sedges, grass or rushes, possibly in aquatic bulrushes or cattails; female incubates 7–16 off-white to pale buff eggs for 21–25 days.

Feeding: gleans the water's surface for grass and sedge seeds, pondweeds, duckweeds and aquatic invertebrates; often feeds with head partially submerged and bill held just below the surface.

Voice: usually silent; male utters a whispered *peep* and a rough *karr-karr-karr*; female gives a soft, rattling *rrrrr* and a somewhat weak *gack-gack-ga-ga*.

Similar Species: *Blue-winged Teal* (p. 75): narrower tip on shorter bill; nonbreeding male has white crescent in front of dark eye and more contrasting grayish brown plumage; female has sharper facial pattern and lighter blue on forewing. *Breeding male Ruddy Duck* (p. 96): mostly rufous; large, blue bill; white "cheeks"; rufous-and-gray upperwings; tail often angled upward.

Best Sites: Malheur NWR; other managed sites in Harney, Lake and Klamath Counties.

NORTHERN SHOVELER

Anas clypeata

You can't fail to be impressed by the Northern Shoveler's remarkable bill. Its broad, spatulate shape and the hairlike ridges that line it allow this duck to sift small water plants and invertebrates from the surface of still waters, where it is by far the most common duck. Shovelers eat much smaller organisms than do most waterfowl, and their digestive systems are elongated to prolong the digestion of these hard-bodied invertebrates.

• When nesting duties are over, drake Shovelers move to molting areas and, like other dabbling ducks, acquire an eclipse plumage that resembles that of the female. Partial development of the chestnut belly and bottle green head then results in a distinctive, subtly attractive "supplementary" stage that lasts until late winter.

ID: large, wide-ended bill; yellowish legs and feet; white outer tail feathers. *Breeding male:* green head; white breast; chestnut sides. *Female:* mottled brown overall; large, orange-tinged bill. *Eclipse male:* like female, but less mottled, with brighter blue forewing, grayer head and darker bill. *In flight:* green speculum with 1 white bar.

Size: *L* 18–20 in; *W* 27–30 in.

Status: locally common breeding resident east of the Cascades, rare breeder in the west; common migrant and generally common winter resident throughout Oregon.

Habitat: *Breeding:* margins of open, shallow wetlands with submergent vegetation, including ponds, marshes and sloughs. *In migration* and *winter:* sites rich in aquatic plants and invertebrates, such as sewage and farm ponds, lagoons and mudflats

with algal growth; regularly visits upper reaches of estuaries.

Nesting: usually on dry land within 150 ft of water, in a shallow scrape; female builds a nest of dry grass and down and incubates 10–12 pale blue eggs for 25 days.

Feeding: dabbles in water and gleans on land and in mud; strains most plants and animal matter, especially aquatic crustaceans and insect larvae, through the bill from just below the water's surface or in mud; sometimes gleans seeds and other plant material in croplands and stubble fields.

Voice: occasionally gives a raspy chuckle or quack, most often heard during spring courtship.

Similar Species: *Mallard* (p. 74): smaller bill; blue speculum with 2 white bars; breeding male has chestnut breast, white flanks, upcurled black tail and yellow bill; female has richer brown on underparts and stronger eye line.

Best Sites: shallow waters; sewage settling ponds.

NORTHERN PINTAIL

Anas acuta

Several million waterfowl, many from just a handful of migratory species, visit the marshes, lakes and grainfields of the Pacific Flyway each year. Most Northern Pintails seen in Oregon are en route between California and Canada or Alaska. Spring migration begins in late February, peaking in early spring. A few southbound migrants regularly show up along the coast by late June, but the main flocks don't crowd the roosting sites at reservoirs and marshes until well into fall. The species is common in winter, especially in the Willamette Valley. • Northern Pintails are particularly attracted to winter grainfields. Lands managed to provide staging and feeding habitat have relieved the pressure on croplands and proven to be of critical importance to Northern Pintails and many other ducks.

ID: long neck; grayish blue bill; long, pointed tail; dark wings. *Breeding male:* white neck and breast; dark nape; brown head; very long, tapering central tail feathers; speculum is dark green and brown. *Female:* mottled brown overall; slightly pointed tail; white-bordered brown speculum. *Nonbreeding male:* like female, but with grayer body and whiter foreneck. *In flight:* white line divides dark brown wing linings and gray flight feathers.
Size: *Male: L* 25–28 in. *Female: L* 20–22 in. *Both: W* 30–34 in.
Status: common summer breeder in south-central and southeastern Oregon; common migrant throughout; uncommon winter resident east of the Cascades; common winter resident and rare summer lingerer west of the Cascades.

Habitat: *Breeding:* open wetlands, especially those with islands. *In migration:* shallow wetlands, larger lakes and reservoirs close to foraging fields and estuarine habitats. *Winter:* wide variety of shallow freshwater and intertidal habitats.
Nesting: on the ground near water, in brushy cover; female makes a small scrape lined with grass and down, incubates 6–8 pale greenish or buff eggs for 22–24 days and tends young for up to 42 days.
Feeding: tips up and dabbles for seeds; also eats aquatic invertebrates, especially crustaceans and snails, and larval salamanders; grazes on waste grain during migration.
Voice: male whistles softly; female gives a rough quack.
Similar Species: *Female Gadwall* (p. 71): chunkier; grayer head; orange-and-dusky bill; shorter tail.
Best Sites: Harney, Lake and Klamath Counties support the most breeding birds. *In migration:* shallow freshwater habitats; larger estuaries.

GREEN-WINGED TEAL

Anas crecca

The name "teal" is applied to 16 of the world's smaller waterfowl, of which the Green-winged Teal is the best known. This widespread bird exemplifies the diminutive build, speedy flight and small habitat requirements of teals. This dabbling duck favors the frontier between the cover of marsh vegetation and the expanses of open country, so it is quite likely to flush up from waterlogged ditches, overgrown irrigation canals, park ponds and any marshes offering some semi-open water with a muddy border. • Green-wings will happily forage on mudflats and at the edge of salt marshes, sifting through semifluid mud like overgrown sandpipers. On the wing, their small size, dark plumage and habit of making tight turns in wheeling flocks further suggest shorebirds in flight.

ID: *Breeding male:* chestnut head; gray bill; glossy green swipe extends back from eye; vertical white shoulder slash; black-spotted creamy or buff breast; barred grayish back. *Female:* mottled brown overall; pale belly; dark eye line. *Nonbreeding male:* like female, but grayer upperparts and darker head. *In flight:* green speculum bordered with white or pale buff bars; flies in compact, agile flocks.

Size: *L* 12–16 in; *W* 20–23 in.

Status: common migrant and uncommon to common winter resident in most of Oregon; locally uncommon breeder east of the Cascades; locally uncommon in summer in the west, with nesting reported from several locations.

Habitat: *Breeding:* marshes. *In migration:* well-vegetated, shallow, muddy inland wetlands and coastal marshes and estuaries. *Winter:* wetlands, flooded farmlands, slough and backwater edges, coastal salt water and brackish marshes and estuaries.

Nesting: on the ground; well concealed beneath a tussock or bush in tall vegetation; shallow bowl of grass and leaves is lined with down; female incubates 6–11 creamy white eggs for 20–23 days and tends young until fledging at 25–30 days.

Feeding: dabbles in shallow water; walks about probing wet mud for sedge seeds, pondweeds, aquatic invertebrates and larval amphibians; forages in grain fields in winter.

Voice: male whistles crisply; distinctive gurgling and wheezing notes in a unique courtship display; female quacks softly.

Similar Species: *Blue-winged Teal* (p. 75) and *Cinnamon Teal* (p. 76): somewhat larger; males are distinctively patterned; females are lighter colored, with larger bills and blue forewing patches.

Best Sites: almost anywhere there is water.

CANVASBACK

Aythya valisineria

The uniquely sloping head profile—the long bill meets the forecrown with no apparent break in angle—allows Canvasbacks of either gender to be distinguished from far away. • The Canvasback resembles other *Aythya* ducks—a sizeable genus of diving ducks of deep marshes, larger freshwater bodies and estuaries—by being "dark at both ends and pale in the middle." Legs set far back on their bodies make these ducks clumsy on their rare land excursions but help them be elegant, powerful divers and underwater swimmers. Most members of the genus require a brief running start in order to become airborne, and they fly with rapid, flickering wingbeats, offering repeated glimpses of their characteristic wing patterns. • Canvasbacks breed chiefly in interior U.S. and Canadian marshes, but they also nest in Oregon.

ID: hefty body; long bill; evenly sloped forecrown. *Male:* deep chestnut red head; whitish back and underparts; black breast and hindquarters; red eyes. *Female:* warm brown head, neck and breast; pale grayish body; dark eyes.

Size: *L* 19–22 in; *W* 27–29 in.

Status: common breeding resident in south-central and southeastern Oregon; common migrant and locally common winter resident east of the Cascades; uncommon migrant and winter resident in inland western valleys; common coastal migrant and winter resident.

Habitat: *Breeding:* extensive marshes with open water pools. *In migration* and *winter:* large lakes, reservoirs, lagoons and estuaries.

Nesting: concealed in a marsh; platform built on emergent vegetation over water

has a deep inner cup lined with down; female incubates 7–9 olive gray eggs for 24–29 days and tends young until shortly before fledging at 60–70 days.

Feeding: dives to or near the bottom in water up to 30 ft deep in search of the roots, tubers, basal stems and seeds of aquatic and estuarine plants; prefers wild celery and eelgrass; takes some invertebrates.

Voice: generally quiet; male occasionally coos, squeaks and growls during courtship; female utters a purring quack and also growls.

Similar Species: *Male Redhead* (p. 81): darker gray back and sides; shorter, black-tipped, bluish bill; more squared-off forehead profile; yellow eyes.

Best Sites: breeds mainly in the large marshes of Harney, Lake and Klamath Counties, especially at Malheur NWR. *Winter:* as above, plus coastal estuaries and large inland lakes.

REDHEAD

Aythya americana

Redheads select very different breeding and nonbreeding habitats. During the breeding season, pairs scatter across the marshes, lake edges and wetlands of central and western North America. They choose clean water with plenty of skirting emergent vegetation, lush bottom growth and enough depth to accommodate their foraging dives. In southern Oregon, these needs are met in the large marshes of Harney, Lake and Klamath Counties. During the rest of the year, flocks migrate through Oregon or overwinter at widely scattered open-water sites. Like Canvasbacks, Redheads are quite traditional in their choice of wintering locations, often reappearing in about the same numbers year after year on large, shallow reservoirs and in the upper reaches of estuaries; they visit smaller lakes, reservoirs and estuaries in only token numbers.

ID: stocky body; black-tipped bluish gray bill. *Male:* red head; black breast; finely barred gray back and sides; yellow eyes. *Female:* dusky brown overall with some gray; pale facial areas; dark eyes. *In flight:* dark gray forewing and lighter hindwing.
Size: *L* 18–22 in; *W* 26–29 in.
Status: locally common summer breeding resident and common migrant east of the Cascades; rare to uncommon winter resident throughout Oregon.
Habitat: freshwater marshes; lakes and reservoirs with bottom plants. *Winter:* estuarine shallows, tidal channels and eelgrass beds.
Nesting: well concealed at the base of emergent vegetation, suspended over water; deep basket of reeds and grass is lined with fine, white down; female incubates 9–13 creamy white eggs for 24–28

days and tends young for 21–35 days; female sometimes lays eggs in the nests of her own and other species.
Feeding: dives for aquatic vegetation, especially pondweeds and duckweeds; occasionally eats aquatic invertebrates.
Voice: generally quiet; courting male utters nasal notes; female gives soft, low grunts and harsher quacks plus an occasional rolling growl.
Similar Species: *Canvasback* (p. 80): elongated bill-and-crown profile; more uniform upperwing color and whiter underparts on female; male has white or lighter back, darker head and red eyes; less measured flight. *Female scaups* (pp. 83-84): brown parts are darker; broader, paler bill with white patch immediately behind it; yellow eyes; broad, white hindwing stripe in flight.
Best Sites: *Summer:* Harney, Lake and Klamath Counties, especially at Malheur NWR; Umatilla NWR. *In migration:* Malheur NWR; Upper Klamath NWR; Summer L. *Winter:* Yaquina Bay.

RING-NECKED DUCK

Aythya collaris

Visits to secluded ponds during the colder months will soon reveal Ring-necked Ducks. These scauplike waterfowl typically assemble in small flocks on wooded reservoirs, along shallow, vegetated coves of lakes and in the still water of shaded river eddies. At times, however, they venture into the open in flooded fields, sewage ponds and on exposed impoundments at waterfowl refuges. In summer, a few pairs remain to breed at scattered, forested lakes in the Cascades and eastward. • The dark brown neck ring of the male, for which the species was named, is rarely visible—a more fitting name would be "Ring-billed Duck". • When alarmed, these ducks stretch their necks and raise their fluffy crowns.

ID: elevated hindcrown; black and white bands on bluish gray bill; white belly. *Breeding male:* purple-glossed head; yellow eyes; black breast and back; light gray sides. *Female:* light brown head with variable pale patches; brown eyes; white eye ring; dark back; lighter brown breast and flanks. *Nonbreeding male:* smudgy brown flanks and shoulder slash.

Size: *L* 14–18 in; *W* 23–25 in.

Status: locally uncommon summer and breeding resident in the Cascades and eastward; common migrant and uncommon winter resident east of the Cascades; common migrant and winter resident and rare in summer in the west.

Habitat: *Breeding:* shallow, permanent freshwater wetlands. *In migration:* small water bodies; prefers slow-moving wooded or vegetated fresh water.

Nesting: in a depression, over water on a vegetated hummock or raised shoreline with a platform of bent-over vegetation; female adds vegetation and down as eggs are laid; female incubates 8–10 olive tan eggs for 25–29 days; young can dive after 5 days and are fed by the female for several weeks.

Feeding: dives underwater for vegetation, including seeds, tubers and pondweed leaves; also eats aquatic invertebrates.

Voice: seldom heard; male hisses; female utters a growling *churr.*

Similar Species: *Scaups* (pp. 83-84): prominent white hindwing stripe in flight; males have almost entirely bluish gray bills and lighter backs, with whiter flanks in breeding plumage; females have darker brown heads and necks and yellow eyes.

Best Sites: *Summer:* Timothy L.; Detroit L.; Foster Reservoir; L. Selmac; Klamath Forest NWR ponds; Upper Klamath NWR; Phillips Reservoir. *In migration and winter:* small water bodies, generally Henry Hagg Lake.

GREATER SCAUP

Aythya marila

Distinguishing Greater Scaups from Lesser Scaups offers a chronic challenge. In Oregon, Greater Scaups favor larger, deeper and more exposed saltwater habitats including estuaries, coastal bays, lagoons and reservoirs in the coastal lowlands. They do not nest in Oregon, although a few may stay over summer. In contrast, Lessers have a more widespread interior distribution, prefer fresh water and do breed in Oregon. Greaters often disperse among large, mixed-species flocks and are more inclined to mix with dabbling ducks. The observer must also rely on subtle field marks to distinguish the species for sure, because there is too much habitat crossover to be certain. • Greater Scaups appear to be more leisurely feeders than other *Aythya* ducks and often look to be resting.

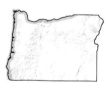

ID: heavyset; large, rounded head; heavy-based, bluish bill with small black tip; yellow eyes.
Breeding male: dark head, often with green iridescence; dark breast; pale gray back; white sides; dark hindquarters.
Female: dark to rufous brown overall; bold white area encircles base of bill.
Nonbreeding male: brown-smudged flanks and back. *In flight:* prominent white wing stripe extends onto primaries.
Size: *L* 16–20 in; *W* 26–29 in.
Status: common coastal migrant and winter resident and rare summer lingerer; rare to uncommon migrant and winter resident inland, except locally common along the Columbia R.

Habitat: protected waters of estuaries, harbors, lagoons, large lakes, reservoirs and tidal rivers; often seen migrating along the outer coast and occasionally in rafts with scoters beyond the surf line.
Nesting: does not nest in Oregon.
Feeding: dives for mollusks, especially mussels, other aquatic and marine invertebrates and some vegetation.
Voice: generally quiet in migration; deep *scaup* alarm call; male may issue a 3-note whistle and a soft *wah-hooo*; female sometimes gives a subtle growl.
Similar Species: *Lesser Scaup* (p. 84): slightly smaller; smaller bill; peaked head; shorter, white wing stripe; male shows less contrast between back and sides and has purplish gloss to head; female rarely shows extensive area of white behind bill and on face; prefers inland habitats.
Best Sites: coastal saltwater habitats; Columbia R.

LESSER SCAUP

Aythya affinis

Greater Scaups and Lesser Scaups are very similar at first glance, and, compared to other waterfowl, have what can politely be called a low glamour quotient, eliciting few artistic outpourings. Being widespread and quite abundant, Lesser Scaups are more familiar to most beginner birders. Lessers tend to occur on freshwater lakes, in open marshes and along slow-flowing rivers much more commonly than Greaters, but Lessers are also common in freshwater coastal habitats. Both species mingle together in unpredictable ratios, and the head iridescence and shape are not reliable identification features. Male Lessers often flash green gloss instead of purple in certain light, and, in the moment prior to submerging in a feeding dive, they can compress their plumage to squeeze out air, lowering the fluffy crown so that the head angle looks remarkably like that of Greaters.

ID: black-tipped grayish blue bill; angled head with peak behind eye; yellow eyes. *Breeding male:* head often has purple gloss; black breast and hindquarters; grayish, barred back; gray-tipped white side feathers. *Female:* dark brown, sometimes rufous, overall, with lighter sides; variable white area encircling base of bill. *Nonbreeding male:* brown-smudged flanks and back. *In flight:* white wing stripe confined to secondaries.
Size: *L* 15–18 in; *W* 23–25 in.
Status: uncommon to locally common summer breeder east of the Cascades and rare nonbreeder elsewhere; common migrant and locally common winter resident throughout Oregon.
Habitat: *Breeding:* large, shallow freshwater lakes and seasonal or semipermanent wetlands with emergent vegetation.

In migration and *winter:* shallow, fresh and estuarine waters; prefers large wetlands and lakes.
Nesting: in tall, concealing vegetation; close to water, occasionally on an island; nest hollow is built of grass and lined with down; female incubates 8–10 olive buff eggs for 22–25 days; fledges at 47–71 days.
Feeding: dives for aquatic and estuarine invertebrates, especially amphipods, but also submergent vegetation, mainly sedges.
Voice: deep *scaup* alarm call; courting male utters soft *whee-oooh*; female gives rough, purring *kwah*.
Similar Species: *Greater Scaup* (p. 83): more rounded head without central peak; larger bill with more black at tip; wing stripe extends onto primaries; prefers marine habitats.
Best Sites: breeds in Klamath Basin and elsewhere in south-central and southeastern Oregon; park ponds in towns, such as Westmoreland Park in Portland.

HARLEQUIN DUCK
Histrionicus histrionicus

Ocean waters surging around rocky headlands or among sea stacks and clusters of intertidal boulders attract Harlequin Ducks. These small ducks are at home in the turbulent roar-and-tumble of the roughest whitewater, diving among the crashing waves with bravado. • Most birds seen here hatch beside swift mountain streams and rivers to the north of Oregon. Modest numbers of Harlequins appear in fall, remain through winter and then return north in spring. • Harlequins prefer rocky shorelines that support a healthy intertidal invertebrate fauna and plenty of kelp and other algae. • The uniformly brown females are difficult to see among the foam and dark rocks, and even the colorful males can be surprisingly well camouflaged. • "Harlequin" refers to a multicolored traditional Italian court character who used "histrionics" (tricks).

ID: rounded profile; short, pale bill; high forehead; raises and lowers tail while swimming. *Breeding male:* grayish blue body; chestnut sides; narrow chestnut stripe on lower crown; white-spotted and striped head, neck and flanks; longish tail. *Female:* dark brown with pale belly; 3 white areas on side of head. *Nonbreeding male:* like female, but with chestnut-tinted flanks, darker head and white-marked lower back.
Size: *L* 15–18 in; *W* 25–27 in.
Status: common coastal migrant and winter resident and rare in summer; rare summer resident and regular breeder in the northern and central Cascades; federal species of concern and state-listed as sensitive.
Habitat: *Breeding:* by shallow, fast-flowing mountain streams; stages along banks or

near gravel bars of larger rivers. *In migration* and *winter:* rocky inshore coastal waters and surf lines near kelp beds; roosts and preens on rocks.
Nesting: in a tree cavity or stump, under bushes or among rocks near a rushing watercourse; shallow nest is lined with conifer needles, moss, leaf litter, grass and down; female incubates 4–6 creamy to pale buff eggs for 27–29 days.
Feeding: dabbles; gleans from rocks; makes short, shallow dives to the bottom; eats invertebrates and small fish.
Voice: generally silent; courting pair may give high-pitched whistles.
Similar Species: *Female Surf Scoter* (p. 86): larger; heavier; larger, darker bill; different head pattern; pale eyes.
Best Sites: *Summer:* Santiam R.; other western mountain streams. *In migration* and *winter:* Garibaldi and Barview Jetty (Tillamook Bay); Yaquina South Jetty; Cape Arago SP; Cape Blanco SP.

SURF SCOTER
Melanitta perspicillata

The looks and habits of Surf Scoters are easily learned. Much of the year, these sturdy, heavily built ducks are at home within the zone of steepening swells and breaking surf along the open ocean coast. Huge rafts of Surf Scoters assemble at frequent intervals off beaches and headlands and around harbor entrances. • Surf Scoters are very common here in winter months, but it is the spectacle of their migration that has served most to stamp them in the minds of Oregon birders. Throughout most of spring and fall, immense numbers pass steadily just offshore. Flock after flock may race past a given point over the course of several hours, and a thorough scan of the ocean will reveal that the slowly wavering lines extend to the horizon and often well above it.

ID: large, broad-based bill; squarish head. *Male:* black overall; white patches on forehead and back of neck; clownish bill is black, white, yellow and reddish; pale yellow eyes. *Female:* deep sooty brown overall; large, grayish black bill; 2 large, whitish patches on side of head; pale brown eyes. *In flight:* flies in long lines, usually close to water, but can be higher in migration.
Size: *L* 17–21 in; *W* 29–31 in.
Status: common migrant and winter resident, uncommon nonbreeding summer lingerer along the coast; rare migrant and winter resident inland.
Habitat: varied oceanic and estuarine situations, mostly within 1 mi of shore; some birds visit coastal and inland freshwater bodies.
Nesting: does not nest in Oregon.

Feeding: feeds singly or in large, well-coordinated flocks; dives in shallow to moderately deep water (up to 30 ft) for mussels and clams, herring eggs, crustaceans and other attached and free-swimming marine invertebrates and some plant material; swallows small pebbles and gravel to aid digestion.
Voice: generally quiet; infrequently utters low, harsh croaks; male occasionally whistles or gargles; female utters a guttural *krraak krraak*.
Similar Species: *White-winged Scoter* (p. 87): white area on hindwing; male's head shows white around eye only and slimmer, more ridged, less colorful bill with bulbous base; female has less pronounced forehead and crown angle. *Black Scoter* (p. 88): more smoothly rounded head; shorter bill; male has bright yellow knob on bill and completely black head; female has pale "cheeks" and dark crown.
Best Sites: on ocean near the shore.

WHITE-WINGED SCOTER

Melanitta fusca

White-winged Scoters are the largest of the three North American scoter species. As mixed flocks take off, White-wings take a moment longer to become airborne, stumbling across the water on their pinkish feet and thrashing across the surface with deep wingbeats. When diving for food, their bulk, combined with a habit of projecting part of the wing's leading edge forward before submerging, causes their splash to rise 3 feet—a telltale identifying characteristic.
• White-wings are typically somewhat warier than Surf Scoters, often seeming not to tolerate the close proximity of human activity. When they aren't agitated, White-winged Scoters are elegant and efficient divers and powerful fliers. • During their extended spring and fall migrations, pairs, small lines and bunched strings of White-winged Scoters can be seen from nearly any ocean viewpoint. Locally abundant in open harbors and over sandy bottoms offshore, White-wings are often outnumbered by Surf Scoters.

ID: conspicuous white area on hindwing; bulbous bill with much basal feathering; distinctive head profile. *Male:* black overall; pale eye within upward-curved, white crescent; orange to yellowish tip to bill. *Female:* dark, brownish gray plumage; 2 large, indistinct pale patches on side of head.
Size: *L* 19–24 in; *W* 32–35 in.
Status: common coastal migrant and winter resident and uncommon nonbreeding summer lingerer; rare migrant inland.
Habitat: varied nearshore oceanic and estuarine habitats, often just beyond the

surf line; some birds may visit large inland lakes during migration.
Nesting: does not nest in Oregon.
Feeding: dives in water up to 90 ft deep for bivalve mollusks and some crustaceans, taking larger prey than other scoters; like other scoters, swallows small stones to aid in digestion.
Voice: courting pair produces coarse quacking; otherwise usually silent; male's wings whistle in flight (like other scoters).
Similar Species: *Surf Scoter* (p. 86): all-dark wings; male has white forehead and nape and more colorful bill; female has more distinct white facial patches. *Black Scoter* (p. 88): male has completely black head and bright yellow knob on bill; female has light "cheeks" and darkish crown.
Best Sites: *In migration:* most coastal sites.

BLACK SCOTER
Melanitta nigra

Black Scoters are greatly outnumbered by other scoters in Oregon. Just an individual or a pair of Blacks will likely be found among scoters rafting in estuaries, and they are the least likely scoters to be found inland. Blacks are more likely to be seen in outer-coastal waters, especially in surge zones around headlands, sea stacks, reefs, jetties and breakwaters. Here they form loose associations with other scoters, Pelagic Cormorants, alcids, grebes and, in particular, Harlequin Ducks. • Black Scoters are rarely seen in any numbers in migration. Thousands of Surf Scoters and hundreds of White-winged Scoters may wing by before a pair of Black Scoters eventually appears. • Although adult Black males are distinctive, immature or eclipse-plumaged male Surf Scoters are routinely mistaken for them. Female Blacks are unlike the two other species but can easily be overlooked.

ID: distinctive, high-domed head. *Male:* plumage completely black; bold, yellowish orange knob at base of bill. *Female:* dark, blackish brown overall, except for paler, dingy whitish face, throat and upper foreneck; grayish black bill. *In flight:* rather rounded body and wings.

Size: *L* 19 in; *W* 27–28 in.

Status: uncommon coastal migrant and winter resident and very rare nonbreeding summer lingerer.

Habitat: outer coast, most often in the surf zone near rocky shores and islands, edges of kelp beds or around jetties; sometimes gathers in small flocks to the lee of headlands; can visit lower reaches of estuaries and even coastal freshwater lagoons; prefers rocky headlands and waters with gravelly bottoms.

Nesting: does not nest in Oregon.

Feeding: dives for mollusks and other invertebrates, small fish and some plant material; known to eat herring eggs in spring; often swallows gravel to aid in digestion.

Voice: rarely heard in Oregon; courting male utters an unusual *cour-loo* and a long, drawn-out *whe—oo-hoo* or rattling *tuka-tuka-tuka-tuk*; female growls.

Similar Species: *White-winged Scoter* (p. 87): larger; longer, larger-based bill; white on hindwing; female has darker face; male has white area around eye and less orangy yellow on bill; immature male has more angled head, with yellow only at bill tip. *Surf Scoter* (p. 86): larger, heavier bill; male shows white at least on nape; female has 2 whitish areas on side of head.

Best Sites: Ecola SP and Cannon Beach; Yaquina South Jetty; Coos Bay river mouth; Cape Arago; Cape Blanco.

LONG-TAILED DUCK

Clangula hyemalis

These odd-looking ducks, previously known as "Oldsquaws," mostly summer on the arctic tundra and appear only sparingly in Oregon. Numbers vary considerably from year to year, with the great majority being either immatures or females, but nonbreeding males are more likely in summer. While in Oregon from late October to mid-April, Long-tails prefer nearshore ocean shallows over shoals or in the lee of headlands or jetties. One or two, and rarely a small flock, establish winter quarters near harbor entrances, around piers and waterfronts, and on lagoons, seemingly at intervals of many miles along the length of the coast. A few turn up inland, often on sewage lagoons and ponds. • The Long-tailed Duck remains distinctive throughout its complex series of plumages.

breeding

nonbreeding

ID: white underparts; rounded or oval brown eyes, reddish on male.
Nonbreeding male: long, trailing tail feathers; black bill with broad pink ring; white head; grayish "cheek"; blackish brown neck patch; white lower neck and upper breast; blackish lower breast; brownish back with white patches. *Nonbreeding female:* bluish gray bill; white face; dark brown top of head, lower neck patches, back and breast.
Size: *Male: L* 17–21 in (including tail). *Female: L* 16–17 in. *Both: W* 26–28 in.
Status: rare to uncommon migrant and winter resident along the coast; very rare inland in winter.

Habitat: inshore coastal waters, including bays, harbors, lagoons and estuaries; can appear some miles out to sea; rarely seen on inland freshwater lakes and ponds.
Nesting: does not nest in Oregon.
Feeding: dives up to 180 ft deep (usually less than 35 ft) to catch mollusks, crustaceans and some small fish.
Voice: heard only occasionally in Oregon; quiet in early winter; very vocal from February onward; male utters musical, throaty yodels; female softly grunts and quacks.
Similar Species: *Male Northern Pintail* (p. 78): much longer neck and bill; brown head; wings mostly pale gray; most common on fresh water.
Best Sites: mouth of Yaquina Bay; possible at headlands and bays.

BUFFLEHEAD

Bucephala albeola

The energetic Bufflehead is among the first diving ducks to be positively identified by beginning birders. Simply and boldly patterned, it resembles few other species. The black-and-white male's most characteristic feature is the broad white patch on the rear of his head. The female is somber but appealing, her sooty head ornamented with a white "cheek" spot. • A small goldeneye, the Bufflehead is classified in the same genus, and it employs the same feeding techniques and nesting strategies—all three *Bucephala* species nest in tree cavities or nest boxes. • Although the female attends her brood and defends her feeding territory for 35–40 days, ducklings often switch broods.

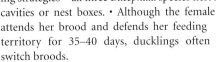

ID: bluish gray or blackish bill; dark eyes; pinkish feet with brownish webs; white belly. *Breeding male:* white wedge on back and sides of head; black forecrown, lower face, neck and back; dark portion of head flashes iridescent purple and green. *Female:* brownish gray head and upperparts with lighter breast and flanks; small, elongated white patch behind and below eye. *Nonbreeding male:* like female, with larger white areas on head and wing.

Size: *L* 13–15 in; *W* 20–21 in.

Status: common migrant and winter resident throughout Oregon from late September to early May; locally uncommon breeding summer resident in the central and southern Cascades; state-listed as sensitive.

Habitat: *Breeding:* small ponds and lakes with wooded margins. *In migration* and *winter:* prefers larger lakes and estuaries,

but also uses smaller water bodies, including urban ponds.

Nesting: in an aspen or poplar woodpecker cavity (sometimes in a natural cavity or nest box); can be unlined or down-filled; female incubates 6–11 creamy or pale olive buff eggs for 28–33 days; egg dumping is quite common.

Feeding: eats small fish, crustaceans and mollusks; in summer, dives for aquatic or estuarine invertebrates, such as large insects and larvae and amphipods.

Voice: seldom heard in Oregon; male growls and squeaks sharply; female quacks harshly.

Similar Species: *Hooded Merganser* (p. 93): larger; yellow eyes; slim bill; breeding male has black-bordered white crest and buff to rufous flanks; female has brownish crest and no white on face. *Harlequin Duck* (p. 85): prefers turbulent water; female has 3 small white areas on head and browner plumage.

Best Sites: *Summer:* high-elevation mountain lakes in Linn, Deschutes, Klamath and Douglas Counties. *Winter:* widespread.

COMMON GOLDENEYE

Bucephala clangula

The boldly patterned plumage and peaked head of the male Common Goldeneye lend themselves to an elaborate series of courtship displays, beginning on the wintering grounds and continuing during the northward migration of late winter. Some birds may linger well into May, and, although Common Goldeneyes typically nest beside boreal lakes, bog pools and beaver ponds, a few have summered in northeastern Oregon and may even have nested. • One of the last diving ducks to leave mountain lakes before freeze-up, Common Goldeneyes often remain until only narrow channels or pools remain. Fall migrants return to Oregon from mid-October to early December, whistling wings signaling their arrival. Single birds and small flocks usually winter at some distance from one another, but they are quite happy to join other ducks, loons, grebes, cormorants and gulls.

ID: white inner wing patches, continuing onto shoulder; yellow eyes; steeply angled head. *Male:* glossy, dark green head (may appear purplish); round, white "cheek" patch from base of dark bill; black back with white wing markings; white underparts; black tail. *Female:* dark brown head; dark bill tipped with dull yellow; narrow white collar; grayish brown body; white belly.
Size: *L* 16–20 in; *W* 25–26 in.
Status: uncommon to common migrant and winter resident; very rare nonbreeding summer visitor to northeastern Oregon and along the coast.
Habitat: shallow coastal bays, estuaries and harbors, larger inland lakes and rivers (in winter, especially those kept open by warm wastewater). *In migration:* also temporary wetlands and ponds.
Nesting: not known to nest in Oregon.
Feeding: dives for a variety of aquatic or estuarine food items, such as crustaceans, mollusks, amphibians, small fish and plant material; consumes several prey items underwater in prolonged dives.
Voice: usually silent in migration; late-winter courting male utters a nasal *peent* and a hoarse *kraaagh*; female croaks harshly.
Similar Species: *Barrow's Goldeneye* (p. 92): male has longer, often purple-glossed head with white crescent behind bill and smaller white marks on back; female has more yellow on bill.
Best Sites: *In migration* and *winter:* wooded wetland habitats; shallow coastal locations; lakes and rivers.

BARROW'S GOLDENEYE
Bucephala islandica

Often near the top of a birder's "wish list," this duck is certainly worthy of the honor: both the male and female are neatly attired and have a subtle charm. • Barrow's Goldeneyes breed largely in western North America, but the range is quite extensive, with small numbers staying on to nest on subalpine lakeshores in the Cascades. These ducks are loyal to favored wintering locations, where the same number of individuals occur year after year. Very few birds migrate along the Oregon coast, but they are quite regularly seen in bays and estuaries in Washington and British Columbia, Canada. Although Barrow's Goldeneyes join Common Goldeneyes in winter and often indulge in aggressive courtship displays in a mixed flock, hybrids are extremely rare.

ID: bright yellow eyes and feet; stubby bill; long, angled head. *Male:* black head, often with dark purple gloss (may appear greenish); distinctive white crescent between eye and black bill; white-spotted black back; black extension downward from shoulder. *Female:* dark brown head; yellowish orange bill; white collar; grayish brown body.

Size: *L* 17–20 in; *W* 27–29 in.

Status: rare to uncommon migrant and winter resident east of the Cascades and on reservoirs on the western slope of the Cascades; rare winter resident west of the Cascades and along the coast; local summer breeder in the Cascades; state-listed as sensitive.

Habitat: *Breeding:* clear, still waters and fast-flowing streams and rivers with standing trees or piles of boulders. *In migration*

and *winter:* lakes, reservoirs, estuaries, lagoons and rivers.

Nesting: in an old woodpecker hole in a decaying tree or stump or in a rock pile; female revisits former or prospected site; down is added as eggs are laid; female incubates 8–11 whitish or bluish green eggs for 28–30 days; female sometimes dumps eggs in other nests.

Feeding: dives to 15 ft deep for aquatic invertebrates and larvae and some plant material.

Voice: generally silent; spring male gives a cawing call; female croaks hoarsely.

Similar Species: *Common Goldeneye* (p. 91): less elongated head; male has glossy green head with round white face spot and whiter scapular marking with more lines than spots; female has yellowish-tipped dark bill.

Best Sites: *Summer:* Lost L. (Santiam Pass area); northern lakes along the Cascades Highway. *Winter:* Haystack, Ochoco and Prineville Reservoirs; Hatfield L.; Upper Klamath L.; Pete's Pond (Enterprise); Wallowa L.

HOODED MERGANSER

Lophodytes cucullatus

Second only to the Wood Duck and tied with the Harlequin drake for sheer brilliance of plumage, the male Hooded Merganser is always a treat to see. The adult male's colorful plumage would be spectacularly obvious in the sunlight, but it blends well with the dappled and irregular rays of sunlight cast upon the water through overarching vegetation. Given a choice between sunny and shady shorelines or banks, Hooded Mergansers opt for the shady side. • These merganser shun large open bodies of water, instead favoring secluded, sheltered or overgrown smaller water bodies, but they will use a variety of habitats, from coastal estuaries to mid-elevations in the Cascades. • Hooded Mergansers are most commonly seen in small flocks, but larger flocks sometimes occur, especially when migrants start reappearing in October.

ID: slim body; thin, dark bill; crested head; yellow to brownish eyes; yellowish legs and feet.
Breeding male: black head and back; bold white crest outlined in black; white breast with 2 black shoulder slashes; finely barred, warm buff to deep rufous sides. *Female:* dusky brown body; reddish brown crest; yellow lower mandible. *Nonbreeding male:* much like female, but duller. *In flight:* white speculum with dark bar; flickering flight.
Size: *L* 16–19 in; *W* 23–24 in.
Status: uncommon migrant and winter resident; locally uncommon summer breeder west of the Cascades.
Habitat: *Breeding:* shallow wetlands, small lakes, forested creeks and rivers. *In migration* and *winter:* forested freshwater wetlands; tidal brackish and saltwater creeks.

Nesting: in an old woodpecker hole in a tree in or near water, sometimes in a broken stump, large limb or nest box; little lining except for down; female incubates 5–13 almost spherical white eggs for 35–40 days; female sometimes dumps eggs in other nests.
Feeding: dives for small fish, aquatic insects and larvae, snails, amphibians and crustaceans, often in murky water.
Voice: low grunts and croaks; courting male utters a froglike *crrrrooo;* generally quiet female gives an occasional harsh *gak* or a croaking *croo-croo-crook.*
Similar Species: *Bufflehead* (p. 90): smaller; chunkier; breeding male is much whiter and has white patch across back of head; female has small white patch on side of head.
Best Sites: Henry Hagg L.; Foster Reservoir. *In migration* and *winter:* Coffenbury L.; Cascade Gateway Park; Fern Ridge Reservoir.

COMMON MERGANSER

Mergus merganser

Rafts of big, black-and-white ducks massed on fish-bearing lakes and reservoirs in winter often prove to be Common Mergansers. In spring, winter flocks break up and Common Mergansers disperse throughout much of forested Oregon to nest. Pairs are soon swimming or resting every few miles along foothill rivers, within coastal creek entrances and high into drainage headwaters. • After breeding, single-sex flocks are the norm until courtship resumes in late winter. Females assume full responsibility for raising the sometimes unruly young. As family groups move downriver, they gather in larger groups at river bars, pools and smaller estuaries toward late summer. • These heavy-bodied, low-slung diving ducks require a running start for takeoff and prefer to dive to escape danger.

ID: elongated body; long, slender, hook-tipped, red bill; dark eyes; red legs. *Breeding male:* glossy, dark green, uncrested head; mostly white body; black back; black stripes on shoulders and flanks. *Female:* gray body; rusty brown head; small, shaggy crest; clean white "chin" and throat. *Nonbreeding male:* like female, with larger white areas and whiter flanks.

Size: *L* 22–27 in; *W* 32–34 in.

Status: common breeding summer resident, migrant and winter resident.

Habitat: prefers fresh or brackish water. *Breeding:* fast, deep streams and rivers; clear, tree-ringed foothill and mountain lakes with drainage channels to lead ducklings downstream. *In migration* and *winter:* clear rivers, lakes and estuaries.

Nesting: in a natural tree cavity or a large woodpecker hole; occasionally on the ground, under a bush or log, among boulders, in an underground hole or in a large nest box; usually near water; female incubates 8–11 creamy eggs, often nest-stained, for 30–32 days.

Feeding: singly or in a flock cooperating to drive fish; swims with its head and bill extended; dives underwater (up to 30 ft deep) for small fish, shrimp, frogs, salamanders, freshwater mussels and even small mammals and birds.

Voice: usually silent; male utters a harsh *uig-a;* female gives a harsh *karr karr,* usually in flight or when tending the brood.

Similar Species: *Red-breasted Merganser* (p. 95): smaller; red eyes; shaggier crest; slimmer bill; prefers salt water; breeding male has dark-spotted chestnut breast, white-spotted black shoulder patch and grayish sides; female has brownish "chin."

Best Sites: *Summer:* clear, fast-flowing streams; large freshwater lakes. *In migration* and *winter:* large rivers and lakes.

RED-BREASTED MERGANSER

Mergus serrator

It requires a bit of effort to discover the habits and habitats of Red-breasted Mergansers. Rarely seen away from open water and flat shorelines, they are relatively widespread and common waterfowl that few people know well. To the north of Oregon, they nest in boreal forests and above the treeline, but in migration and winter they prefer shallows, boat channels and protected ocean along the outer coast. Very few will venture inland, generally to large, open reservoirs, during migration periods, typically in late fall and early winter. • Red-breast flocks rarely join other waterfowl or Common Mergansers, even when they are found together, but individual birds are often seen in the company of grebes and loons, perhaps because of the presence of shared prey.

ID: thin, serrated, red or dull orangy yellow bill; red or pale orange legs; shaggy, wild-looking crest; red eyes; white belly. *Breeding male:* glossy, green head; black-spotted light rusty breast; broad, white collar; black-and-white wing coverts. *Female:* reddish brown head; gray sides and lower breast. *Nonbreeding male:* much like female.

Size: *L* 19–26 in; *W* 28–30 in.

Status: common migrant and winter resident and rare nonbreeding summer lingerer along the coast; very rare migrant and winter resident inland.

Habitat: inshore coastal waters, including saltwater bays, harbors, lagoons and estuaries with limited tidal action; rarely freshwater lakes and large rivers.

Nesting: does not nest in Oregon.

Feeding: often "snorkels" at the surface, sometimes in loose flocks; makes shallow dives for small fish, aquatic insects, fish eggs, crustaceans, worms and amphibians; rarely uses wings for underwater propulsion.

Voice: generally quiet; courting or feeding male utters a catlike *yeow;* female gives a harsh *kho-kha,* especially when tending her brood.

Similar Species: *Common Merganser* (p. 94): larger; elongated look; dark eyes; breeding male has smoother crest and white breast and flanks, extending into wing; female has distinct white "chin" and lower throat.

Best Sites: along the coast, inside the surf zone, in estuaries and shallows.

RUDDY DUCK

Oxyura jamaicensis

Ask a kid with a box of crayons to draw a duck, and the result may well resemble a Ruddy Duck. With his big head, outsized bill, pointed tail and bold coloration, a male Ruddy Duck in his spring finery looks like a cartoon come alive. The male's intent is serious, however, as he advertises for prospective mates with a vigorous bill-pumping display accompanied by staccato grunting notes and a stream of surface bubbles. • The nondescript yet appealing female's main claim to fame is the extraordinarily large eggs she lays. • These ducks can sink slowly underwater to escape detection—easier than flying, which requires a laborious running take-off and extremely rapid wingbeats.

breeding

breeding

ID: dark tail of stiff, pointed feathers, usually uptilted; pale belly; dark eyes. *Breeding male:* bold white (rarely black) "cheeks"; chestnut red neck, body and back; blue bill; black crown and hindneck. *Female:* brown overall, darker on crown and back; brown stripe across whitish "cheek." *Nonbreeding male:* gray bill; grayish brown replaces chestnut; gray crown and hindneck. *In flight:* head looks heavy; uniformly dark upperwings.
Size: *L* 15–16 in; *W* 18–19 in.
Status: common migrant and winter resident; locally common summer breeder east of the Cascades; rare, locally regular breeder in the west.
Habitat: *Breeding:* around openings in deep marshes or on marsh-skirted ponds and lakes. *In migration:* ponds, lakes, sewage ponds and reservoirs. *Winter:* large flocks assemble on protected freshwater lakes or tidal waters.

Nesting: in cattails, bulrushes or other emergent vegetation; occasionally on a muskrat lodge or a log or in the abandoned nest of another duck or coot; basketlike, sometimes domed nest is always suspended over water; female incubates 6–10 whitish eggs for 23–26 days; female often dumps eggs in other nests.
Feeding: dives to the bottom in shallow water for seeds, leafy parts of aquatic or estuarine plants and some aquatic invertebrates.
Voice: courting male delivers *chuck-chuck-chuck-chur-r-r-r* display "song" with panache, punctuated with air bubbles on the water; female is generally silent.
Similar Species: *Breeding male Cinnamon Teal* (p. 76): more slender; reddish head; red eyes; smaller, more slender, dark bill.
Best Sites: *Spring* and *summer:* Harney Basin and smaller basins in Lake Co. and Klamath Co.; a few pairs breed in the Willamette Valley; nonbreeders in the Willamette Valley and along the north coast.

OSPREY

Pandion haliaetus

The highly successful Osprey is thriving on all continents. The only species in its genus, the Osprey is so superbly adapted for catching fish that it has been able to succeed in many different niches. Its primarily white undersides disappear against the sky as it flies high above lakes, rivers and bays in search of fish just below the surface, and its dark "mask" reduces the blinding glare of sunshine skipping off the water. Two other important features also aid in catching fish. Two toes facing forward and two toes facing backward, and a heavily scaled sole, help the Osprey clamp tightly onto slippery fish. Also, frequent preening makes Osprey feathers more water resistant than those of other raptors.

ID: dark brown upperparts; white underparts; yellow eyes; bluish gray legs and feet; dark eye line; light crown; long wings extend beyond tail at rest; white throat; fine "necklace," darkest on female. *In flight:* long, narrow, distinctively kinked wings; dark "wrist" patch; white underparts; narrowly banded tail.

Size: *L* 22–25 in; *W* 4½–6 ft.

Status: uncommon to locally common summer breeder and common migrant; very rare in winter.

Habitat: lakes, reservoirs and rivers; open seacoast. *In migration:* urban lakes and ponds.

Nesting: on an exposed treetop, pole or tower; builds a nest of sticks and twigs, possibly on a platform or base of sticks;

male helps female incubate 2–3 pale, usually pinkish eggs with brown or olive markings for 32–43 days; young fledge in 48–59 days.

Feeding: hovers, then dives feet first from up to 100 ft in the air for small fish, usually under 2 lb in weight, sometimes plunging below the surface; also eats rodents, birds, other small vertebrates and crustaceans.

Voice: pair is very vocal around the nest site; piercing, whistled *chewk-chewk-chewk* and far-carrying *kip-kip-kip*.

Similar Species: *Red-tailed Hawk* (p. 106): smaller; dark head; shorter, broader wings are held flat when soaring; reddish tail; darker wing linings; underparts are pale rufous to dark brown.

Best Sites: lower Columbia R.; lakes in the Cascades and Blue Mts.; many coastal lakes; Tahkenitch L.; Oxbow CP; Whitehorse CP; L. Selmac; Ochoco Reservoir; Crane Prairie Reservoir; Upper Klamath L.; Phillips Reservoir; Clackamas R. near Portland.

WHITE-TAILED KITE
Elanus leucurus

Formerly known as "Black-shouldered Kite," the White-tailed Kite is the North American representative of a widespread family. Flying with grace and buoyancy uncommon among raptors, it has the look and general color pattern of a tern. • The White-tailed Kite hunts from dawn until deep evening twilight. When it spots a vole scurrying through the grass, it parachutes down on the rodent with wings held high. • White-tailed Kites nest in trees and tall bushes in semi-open areas, with the bulky nest placed near the treetop away from the main trunk and larger limbs, perhaps as protection against arboreal predators. • After being persecuted almost to extinction in the early 1900s, the White-tailed Kite was first sighted in Oregon in the 1920s, becoming regular since the 1960s. Population fluctuations, apparently in tune with prey populations, are normal.

ID: long, white tail with gray central feathers; pointed wings; dark shoulders; light gray back (female is darkest); white underparts; red eyes; dark eye patch; small bill; yellow cere and feet. *In flight:* small, black "wrist" patch; buoyant flapping; hovers with body at steep angle; flies with wings in a shallow "V."

Size: *L* 15–17 in; *W* 3¼ ft.

Status: locally uncommon fall migrant and winter resident from late August to April along the coast and in interior valleys of western Oregon; rare summer breeder in western Oregon; rare in winter in the Klamath Basin.

Habitat: tree-dotted lowland or hillside fields; ungrazed or fallow grasslands; croplands; marshes; loose groups sometimes form in open fields.

Nesting: high in a tree, often an oak; pair builds a bulky stick platform, lined with grass and other soft vegetation; female incubates 4 brown-blotched, creamy white eggs for 26–32 days.

Feeding: hovers over open country and dives after prey feet first; eats rodents, especially voles, but also small birds, snakes, frogs, lizards and large insects.

Voice: largely silent; short, repeated *keep keep keep* call; also utters a raspy *keerak* and a more guttural *grrrkkk.*

Similar Species: *Male Northern Harrier* (p. 100): wings dark only at tips and trailing edge, otherwise all gray on top and white beneath; banded tail; hovers infrequently. *Hawks* (pp. 100–08): shorter, broader, rounded wings. *Falcons* (pp. 110–13): more pointed wings; longer, narrower tails.

Best Sites: Nehalem Meadows; lower Coquille Valley Bay; Bandon Dunes; Fern Ridge Reservoir; Tillamook Bay marshlands.

BALD EAGLE
Haliaeetus leucocephalus

Symbolic in both aboriginal myth and modern American culture, the Bald Eagle is listed as threatened, but habitat protection, restoration of salmon stocks and less harassment at nesting and feeding sites have helped return it to a position of preeminence in Oregon. • Benjamin Franklin, a respected naturalist of his day, opposed selecting the Bald Eagle as our national bird because of its "dishonorable" habits of scavenging carrion and stealing fish from the smaller Osprey. Although most of an adult's food does consist of spawned-out salmon and other carrion, it is capable of catching its own prey. • A female returning to her nest site will put her mate through a series of aerial maneuvers to confirm his suitability for the coming season, and not all males pass the test.

immature

ID: white head and tail; dark brown body; large yellow bill and cere. *1st year:* brown overall; white patches; dark eyes. *2nd year:* whiter back and underparts; light belly; dark head; blackish terminal band on white tail. *3rd year:* some white on head; dark eye stripe; paler eyes; yellow cere. *4th year:* largely white head and tail; mainly dark underparts; some white on back and underwings. **Size:** *L* 30–43 in; *W* 5½–8 ft.
Status: common year-round breeding resident throughout the Klamath Basin; locally uncommon breeder on the coast, along the Columbia R. and in the southern Cascades; rare breeder elsewhere; locally common on the coast and at lower elevations inland in winter; federal- and state-listed as threatened.
Habitat: *Breeding:* lakeshores, river corridors, estuaries and seacoasts. *In migration*

and *winter:* coastal and inland waterways; occasionally farmlands.
Nesting: in a tree bordering a lake or wide river, occasionally on a cliff ledge or nest platform; huge stick nest; pair incubates 2, rarely 3, white eggs for 34–36 days.
Feeding: opportunistic; fish are caught by swoops to the water's surface or are pirated from Osprey; some birds eat waterfowl; scavenges fish and carcasses.
Voice: weak squeaks and chirps; sometimes *kek-kek-kek-kek;* immature's calls are somewhat shriller; argumentative squawks and shrieks in group foraging.
Similar Species: adult is unmistakable. *Golden Eagle* (p. 109): similar to immature Bald Eagle, but with fully feathered legs and broad, dark terminal tail band.
Best Sites: *Summer:* around Upper Klamath L.; along the coast and the Columbia R.; around lakes in the Cascades south of Crook Co. *Winter:* Bear Valley NWR (Klamath Basin); Sauvie I.; Columbia R.; southern Willamette Valley.

NORTHERN HARRIER

Circus cyaneus

The Northern Harrier is the only North American representative of its world-wide genus. It may be the easiest raptor to identify on the wing, because no other hawk routinely flies so close to the ground. As it cruises low across fields, meadows and marshes in search of prey, it uses both its excellent vision and its hearing, which is enhanced by its owl-like parabolic facial disc. • Males are less numerous than females. In areas with a plentiful food supply, a male can have as many as five mates, supplying all five ground nests with food. • The genus name *Circus* is a reference to this bird's somewhat erratic flight pattern. The high maneuverability of this species inspired the British Royal Air Force's name for its Harrier aircraft.

ID: facial disc; small bill and talons; banded tail. *Male:* gray upperparts; white under-parts; black wing tips and trailing edge; white under-wings. *Female:* brown overall; brown-streaked buffy underparts; barred underwings. *In flight:* long, somewhat pointed wings; long, narrow tail; white rump patch; unmistakable when coursing with wings held in a clear "V."

Size: *L* 16–24 in; *W* 3¾–4 ft.

Status: locally common east of the Cascades; locally common in interior valleys west of the Cascades and along the coast in winter; breeds commonly east of the Cascades and locally along the northern coast and in the Willamette Valley.

Habitat: open country, including fields, marshes and alpine meadows.

Nesting: on the ground, often on a mound started by the male and completed by the female; usually in shrubs, cattails or tall vegetation; nest of grass, sticks and cat-tails; female incubates 4–6 pale bluish eggs for 30–32 days; male provides food.

Feeding: glides low to the ground; eats mostly small prey, including birds and mammals, especially mice and voles, reptiles, amphibians and grasshoppers.

Voice: vocal during courtship, near the nest site and when repelling other harriers; rather peevish, high-pitched, repeated *kek* or *ke* alarm notes; female attracts attention with a piercing, descending *eeyah eeyah* scream.

Similar Species: *Red-tailed* (p. 106), *Red-shouldered* (p. 104) and *Swainson's* (p. 105) *hawks:* chunkier; brownish rump; shorter, wider tail. *Rough-legged Hawk* (p. 108) and *Ferruginous Hawk* (p. 107): larger; broader wings; distinctively patterned, fanlike tail; different underwing pattern.

Best Sites: open country and wetlands.

SHARP-SHINNED HAWK

Accipiter striatus

When delivering food to his nestlings, a male Sharp-shinned Hawk is understandably cautious around his mate—she is typically one-third larger than he is. The small prey supplied by the male is suitable for small nestlings, but the female does much of the hunting when they get larger. Preying on different-sized mammals and birds helps increase the total food available to the species. • Accipiters have short, rounded wings, long, rudderlike tails and a flap-and-glide flight, allowing these woodland hawks to negotiate a maze of tree trunks and foliage at high speed. • Sharp-shins can be secretive in summer, until the nest is approached. They are more visible in migration and at urban sites in winter. Rural bird feeders attract small and medium-sized songbirds, which in turn attract Sharp-shins, especially immatures, that might otherwise not over-winter here.

ID: yellow legs; bluish gray crown, back and upper-wings; fine rufous bars on underparts; red eyes; buffy rufous underwing coverts; pale flight feathers spotted and barred with dark brown. *Immature:* thicker, brown markings on underparts; brown upperparts; yellow eyes. *In flight:* small head; short, rounded wings; long, heavily barred, squared-off tail.

Size: *Male: L* 10–12 in; *W* 20–24 in. *Female: L* 12–14 in; *W* 24–28 in.

Status: uncommon year-round resident; good numbers of migrants move southward from mid-August to late October and northward from mid-March to late April.

Habitat: dense to semi-open forests; riparian edges; small woodlots. *In migration:* alpine areas; foothills.

Nesting: in a tree, often in an abandoned crow nest; stick or twig nest, normally about 2 ft across; female incubates 4–5 pale bluish white eggs for up to 35 days; male feeds the female during incubation and leaves food at the nest after hatching.

Feeding: operates mainly from a perch; pursues small birds in rapid, high-speed chases, taking more birds than other accipiters; occasionally takes small mammals, amphibians and insects.

Voice: generally silent; intense, repeated *kik-kik-kik-kik* effectively warns intruders during the breeding season; migrating fall juvenile utters a clear *tewp*.

Similar Species: *Cooper's Hawk* (p. 102): larger, although male can be same size as female Sharp-shinned; heavy-headed; rounded tail with more noticeable white terminal band.

Best Sites: most habitats from the coast to timberline.

COOPER'S HAWK

Accipiter cooperii

With blinding speed, the Cooper's Hawk bursts from an overhead perch to ambush and pursue songbirds, grabbing them in midair with its sharp talons. • Even where it is common, the Cooper's Hawk is generally secretive and inconspicuous in breeding season. • Since DDT was banned in the U.S. and Canada, these forest hawks have slowly recolonized many of their former breeding sites, but many of them still suffer from the use of insecticides on their South and Central American wintering ranges. • Misinformed farmers and poultry producers sometimes shoot Cooper's Hawks, calling them "Chicken-Hawks." Although they do take some domestic poultry and wild grouse, they usually target smaller birds and small mammals.

immature

ID: yellow cere and feet; bluish gray crown, back and upperwings; fine, horizontal, reddish barring on underparts; red eyes. *Immature:* brown upperparts; narrow, blackish streaks on underparts; yellow eyes. *In flight:* longish wings; long, round-ended, banded, white-tipped tail; white undertail coverts.

Size: *Male: L* 15–17 in; *W* 27–32 in. *Female: L* 17–19 in; *W* 32–37 in.

Status: uncommon summer breeding resident; common migrant from mid-August to October and in March and April; uncommon to common at lower elevations in winter.

Habitat: *Breeding:* broken woodlands, including woodlots, and brushland, especially in riparian areas, canyons and floodplains. *In migration* and *winter:* soars on thermals in open areas and along ridge-lines; often visits urban areas and winters near feeders.

Nesting: in a tree fork, often in the outer branches of a Douglas-fir, sometimes in a remodeled crow's nest; stick-and-twig nest is lined with bark flakes; female incubates 4–5 bluish eggs for 34–36 days and broods young for 14 days; male brings food until the female starts to hunt; pair feeds nestlings until fledging at around 50 days.

Feeding: often hunts from a perch; pursues prey in rapid flight through the forest or at its edges; takes prey to a "plucking-post" or eats on the ground; male hunts birds up to robin size and mammals up to chipmunk size; female pursues grouse, occasionally small ducks, squirrels and hares.

Voice: largely silent, except around nest; fast, barking, woodpecker-like *cac-cac-cac-cac* alarm.

Similar Species: *Sharp-shinned Hawk* (p. 101): smaller; smaller head; square-ended tail; darker nape; thicker, redder streaks on immature's underparts.

Best Sites: most habitats.

NORTHERN GOSHAWK

Accipiter gentilis

The Northern Goshawk, the largest of the accipiters, has a legendary disposition. This hawk will attack a perceived threat of any size, including people too near its nest. It chases and catches prey in a high-speed aerial sprint and will even crash through brush to chase its quarry on foot. The Northern Goshawk kills by repeatedly stabbing its victim's internal organs with its long talons. • Attila the Hun, impressed by this hawk's strength and tenacity, had one adorning his helmet. • The scientific species name derives from this hawk's use as the preferred "falcon" of the gentry, with the similar-sized Gyrfalcon (*Falco rusticolus*) and smaller Peregrine Falcon reserved for kings and emperors.

ID: dark "cap" and "cheek" patch; white "eyebrow"; long, unevenly banded tail; well-feathered legs; yellow cere and feet; bluish gray crown, back and upperwings; finely barred gray underparts; 2-toned gray upperwings; fluffy, white undertail. *Juvenile:* brown-streaked white underparts; dark-banded tail; yellow eyes. *In flight:* more robust and uniform in color than other accipiters; short, broad wings; brown-and-white-barred wings on juvenile; purposeful flight.
Size: *Male: L* 21–23 in; *W* 3¼–3½ ft. *Female: L* 23–25 in; *W* 3½–4 ft.
Status: uncommon year-round resident in mountains of central and northeastern Oregon; rare to uncommon migrant and winter resident elsewhere; federal species of concern and state-listed as sensitive.
Habitat: *Breeding:* mature montane coniferous forests; nonbreeding birds summer in riparian and open woodlands, canyons and forest edges; adversely affected by clear-cutting. *In migration* and *winter:* above mountain ridges and open country; any forest.
Nesting: in deep woods; in a fork, usually high in a deciduous tree; may be reused for several years; bulky nest is made of sticks and twigs; female incubates 2–4 dirty white eggs for 28–32 days.
Feeding: perches briefly or flies at a low level across open areas; flies through cover to snatch ground-dwelling birds, especially grouse, and rabbits and ground squirrels; sometimes continues pursuit on the ground.
Voice: silent, except around nest site; aggressive, loud *kyk-kyk-kyk;* other loud, accipiter-type calls.
Similar Species: *Cooper's Hawk* (p. 102): smaller; narrower tail; fine, reddish breast bars; immature is whiter below, with narrower underpart streaking.
Best Sites: *Summer:* Santiam Pass; Cascade Lakes; Crater Lake NP; Spring Creek; Eagle Cap Wilderness; Thief Valley Reservoir; Anthony L.

RED-SHOULDERED HAWK

Buteo lineatus

Following nearly a century of absence from Oregon, Red-shouldered Hawks began reappearing in Oregon in 1971, in Curry County. Since then, pairs and individuals have also been noted in Coos County and, recently, in the Rogue Valley. Most sightings are between August and March in wetter woodlands, with birds at various locations through winter. The species is increasingly found in the Willamette Valley and along the northern coast. • Red-shouldered Hawks nest in forest-edge and woodland habitats, but they forage a great deal from exposed perches well removed from cover. • The *B.l. elegans* subspecies of the Pacific Coast is more richly colored on the head, back and underparts and has broader white tail bands than eastern or southeastern birds.

ID: dark-streaked orangy brown head; small, dark-tipped yellowish bill; yellow feet; finely barred, reddish orange underparts; multi-banded tail; boldly dark-and-light checkered upperparts; reddish orange shoulder patch. *Juvenile:* more brown, less orange; coarser underpart barring. *In flight:* wings may be slightly raised or lowered.
Size: *L* 17–19 in; *W* 3¼ ft.
Status: uncommon year-round resident and scarce nester in the coastal lowlands of Curry Co. and Coos Co.; rare in northern coastal lowlands, interior western valleys and south-central and southeastern Oregon.
Habitat: varied, semi-open woodlands and forest-edge situations; prefers wooded river bottoms, especially with nearby open meadows and marshes; some birds move to oak woodlands in spring.

Nesting: within the canopy of live trees, well above the ground; nest is often reused; pair assembles a stick platform with a lining of bark and vegetation; male supplies food as the female incubates 2–4 blue-tinted white eggs marked with brown and light purple; pair raises the young.
Feeding: swoops down from an elevated perch to capture birds, small mammals, reptiles, frogs, crayfish and insects on the ground or in water.
Voice: distinctive, deliberate *kee-aaaah* with downslurred, drawn-out end, almost always repeated; *kip* alarm call.
Similar Species: *Red-tailed Hawk* (p. 106): slightly larger; heavier head; dark bar on underwing's leading edge; upperwings nearly consistently dark; dark belly band in most plumages; underparts reddish buff to dark brown. *Cooper's Hawk* (p. 102): very similar in flight from below, but whiter.
Best Sites: coastal Oregon south of Cape Arago; lower Coquille Valley; Fern Ridge Reservoir; occasionally Umpqua, Rogue and Willamette Valleys.

SWAINSON'S HAWK

Buteo swainsoni

The Red-tailed Hawk may dominate the skies over much of Oregon, but the Swainson's Hawk takes center stage in eastern Oregon's open country, especially where ground squirrels are abundant. • Swainson's Hawk numbers have diminished with the loss of native grasslands and with pesticide use on its wintering grounds. • Traveling in large flocks (sometimes numbering in the thousands in other regions), all of North America's Swainson's Hawks migrate to South American wintering areas as far as Patagonia—a feat among raptors exceeded only by the arctic-breeding *tundrius* Peregrine Falcon race. • This bird's name honors William Swainson, who illustrated a bird collected by the 1827 Franklin Expedition's John Richardson. Incorrectly identified as the European Common Buzzard, it was correctly named by Charles Lucien Bonaparte 10 years later.

light morph

dark morph

ID: white or pale face; dark eyes; gray bill; yellow cere; yellow feet; reddish or dark "bib"; underparts white or reddish to dark brown. *Juvenile:* mottled dark and white. *In flight:* dark-barred flight feathers; dark wing tips; broad, finely barred, white-tipped tail with dark subterminal band; white to reddish brown wing linings.
Size: *Male: L* 19–20 in; *W* 4¼ ft. *Female: L* 20–22 in; *W* 4¼ ft.
Status: locally common breeding resident from April to September east of the Cascades; rare migrant in interior western valleys and along the coast; state-listed as sensitive.
Habitat: open grasslands and pastures, low-crop fields and small woodlands; sometimes with other hawks over mountain ridges.

Nesting: in a well-spaced tree in an open area or riparian edge, sometimes in a bush, abandoned building or haystack; male chooses the site; female adds sticks and debris plus a lining of leaves, grass, stalks and bark; female incubates 1–4 plain whitish eggs for 34–35 days.
Feeding: swoops to the ground for voles, mice and ground squirrels; also eats snakes, small birds and large insects.
Voice: not very vocal; shrill, somewhat plaintive, screaming *kreeee* and repeated *pi-tik*.
Similar Species: *Red-tailed Hawk* (p. 106): wings are flatter when soaring; bulkier; larger bill; reddish tail; silvery underwing flight feathers; reddish to dark wing linings; broader tail on immature. *Red-shouldered Hawk* (p. 104): reddish shoulders, underwing linings and underparts; pale, well-barred flight feathers; strongly banded tail.
Best Sites: *Summer:* L. Abert; Warner Valley; La Grande Airport; Crow Creek; Thief Valley Reservoir; near Malheur NWR.

RED-TAILED HAWK
Buteo jamaicensis

One of North America's best-known, most widely distributed hawks, the Red-tailed Hawk is often seen perched on a branch or pole overlooking open fields, or even soaring over downtown Portland. • Size, coloration and tail markings distinguish up to 16 subspecies of Redtail. Most races exhibit dark, intermediate and light morphs. Western Red-tails usually have deep cinnamon to brick red tails, except for the less colorful immatures and the rare Harlan's Hawk. • Most Red-tails are year-round residents, but others migrate through from late August to late October. • The distinctive, shrill "scream" uttered during courtship flights or when defending the nest is often used in movies to lend wildness to outdoor scenes but is sometimes misattributed to another species, such as the Bald Eagle.

light morph

light morph

ID: dark upperparts with indistinct pale markings; yellow cere and feet; brown eyes. *Light morph:* pale rufous breast; streaky belly band; dark head. *Harlan's:* dark overall; black-and-white-streaked breast; pale grayish, occasionally banded tail. *Juvenile:* yellow eyes; whitish outer wing; clearly banded tail. *In flight:* fan-shaped rufous tail; variable dark wing lining with darker leading edge and whitish underwing flight feathers; dark wing tips and trailing edges.
Size: *Male: L* 18–23 in; *W* 3¾–4¾ ft. *Female: L* 20–25 in; *W* 4–4¾ ft.
Status: common summer breeding resident, migrant and winter resident.
Habitat: almost anywhere with open areas and high perches.
Nesting: in the crown of a woodlot tree, usually deciduous, or on a cliff; usually next to open fields or shrub lands; bulky platform nest, augmented yearly with sticks and twigs and lined with bark, green sprigs, husks, stalks and catkins; both adults incubate 2–3 whitish, brown-blotched eggs for 28–35 days; young fledge at 42–46 days.
Feeding: sit-and-wait predator on an elevated perch; also dives after prey while soaring or pursues prey on the ground; eats small mammals, mid-sized birds, amphibians and reptiles, with occasional insects and fresh carrion.
Voice: distinctive, exuberant, down-slurred, single *keee-(eee)-rrrr;* shrill *chwirk* and low, nasal *gannk;* at the nest, adults yelp and juveniles whistle.
Similar Species: tail not red on other medium or large hawks; immature and dark-morph adults are often distinguishable only if close. *Swainson's Hawk* (p. 105): dark "bib," white face and light underwing linings on pale and intermediate morphs.
Best Sites: rising thermals above open or semi-open habitat; migrates over mountain ridges.

FERRUGINOUS HAWK

Buteo regalis

Coursing the contours of rolling, grassy hills, circling high above the landscape, or sitting alertly in a barren field, the majestic Ferruginous Hawk spends much of its time perched low in a tree or on a fence post watching for prey. The largest of the buteos, this grassland hawk also hunts from the air, swooping from great heights and striking with great force. • Formerly shot and poisoned as pests, Ferruginous Hawks eat mostly rabbits, ground squirrels and gophers, so they can actually be of service to farmers and ranchers. Unfortunately, conversion of grasslands to agricultural areas and rodent control campaigns have reduced and localized Ferruginous Hawks. On the Great Plains, they used to nest in areas with wandering bison, which provided bones and wool as nest material, until the herds were eliminated.

dark morph

light morph

ID: heavy head; feathered legs; pale brown eyes; yellow cere and feet. *Light morph:* brown-mottled rusty upperparts; white underparts; rusty flanks and "leggings"; pale head; pale tail washed with cinnamon above. *Dark morph:* gray-mottled dark reddish brown upperparts, underparts and wing linings. *Juvenile:* coloration is dark brown instead of rusty; yellow eyes. *In flight:* long wings; dark-lined white underwings; pale upperwing patch.
Size: *L* 22–27 in; *W* 4½–4¾ ft.
Status: locally common summer breeding resident east of the Cascades; rare in winter; vagrant in the rest of Oregon; federal species of concern; state-listed as sensitive.
Habitat: arid grasslands. *In migration:* foothills and mountain ridges.

Nesting: in a solitary tree, on a cliff or on the ground, possibly on a pole, farm building or haystack; wide, massive platform of sticks, twigs, sagebrush stems and debris, lined with finer, drier material; male helps female incubate 2–4 creamy white, heavily spotted and blotched eggs for 32–33 days.
Feeding: hunts from a soaring flight, low perch or the ground; preys on ground squirrels, rabbits, mice and pocket gophers and also snakes and small birds.
Voice: generally silent; loud, squealing alarm call, usually a down-slurred *kaaarr*.
Similar Species: *Red-tailed Hawk* (p. 106): smaller; darker underparts; adult's tail is cinnamon to red, immature's tail is darker and more banded. *Swainson's Hawk* (p. 105): smaller; darker flight feathers contrast with pale wing linings, or wings are all dark below; banded tail.
Best Sites: Fort Rock SP; L. Abert; Pilot Rock; Virtue Flats (Pleasant Valley); Diamond area; Crow Creek; near Riley.

ROUGH-LEGGED HAWK

Buteo lagopus

Each fall, subarctic-nesting Rough-legged Hawks drift south in search of warmer southern meadows and sagebrush habitat. The abundance of Rough-legs in Oregon varies with the weather to the north and the success of the breeding season. When small mammals are common in the north, a pair of Rough-legs can fledge up to seven young, but in lean years one chick is the norm. Most birds return north by early April, but some birds linger until late May. • Easily identified at great distances when foraging, the Rough-legged is one of the few large hawks that routinely hovers over prey. • Oddly, light-morph females generally appear much darker than light-morph males and the reverse is true in dark-morph birds. • The name *lagopus*, meaning "hare's foot," refers to this bird's distinctive feathered feet, an adaptation to its subarctic lifestyle.

light morph

dark morph

ID: feathered down to toes; yellow cere and toes; brown eyes. *Light morph:* wide, dark belly band; white-streaked dark brown head and breast; dark upperparts mottled with buff and white. *Dark morph:* generally dark; white-and-dark underwings and undertail. *Juvenile:* paler eyes. *In flight:* indistinctly barred white underwing flight feathers; dark patch at "wrist"; white tail with broad, dark terminal band tipped with white; shallow, effortless wingbeats; soars and glides with wings held in a slight "V"; regularly hovers when hunting.
Size: *L* 19–24 in; *W* 4–4¾ ft.
Status: uncommon to common from October to April.

Habitat: open grasslands, sagebrush flats, coastal plains, fields and meadows.
Nesting: does not nest in Oregon.
Feeding: hunts from a perch, from a hovering flight or on the ground; eats mostly small rodents, especially mice and voles; occasionally captures smaller birds, amphibians, reptiles and large insects.
Voice: rarely vocal; catlike *kee-eer* alarm call.
Similar Species: *Other* Buteos (pp. 104–07): rarely hover; "wrist" patch much smaller; tail is a single color or multi-banded. *Northern Harrier* (p. 100): smaller and slimmer; long, narrow tail; facial disc; white rump; slow, low-level cruising. *Golden Eagle* (p. 109): much larger; broader wings; dark, unpatterned underwings; immature's broader white tail has dark terminal band extending to tip.
Best Sites: open country.

GOLDEN EAGLE

Aquila chrysaetos

Throughout the world, the Golden Eagle with wings spread is a corporate and national symbol of strength and power. Few people ever forget their first encounter with a Golden Eagle—the wingspan of adults exceeds seven feet. • The high mountains and rolling foothills of eastern Oregon provide a spectrum of varied habitats for this impressive hunter. In summer, observers might chance upon a breeding pair of Golden Eagles hunting together or displaying breathtaking aerial acrobatics. In spring and fall, migrating eagles that breed farther north can be seen soaring over mountain ridges, often no more than specks in the sky.

juvenile

ID: all-brown; gold-tinted neck and head; yellow feet and cere; gray bill; pale-edged wing feathers; buffy undertail; banded tail with broad, dark terminal band. *Juvenile:* white on wings and tail. *In flight:* relatively long tail; measured, effortless wingbeats; soars with wings held in a slight "V."
Size: *L* 30–40 in; *W* 6½–7½ ft.
Status: uncommon to common breeding resident east of the Cascades; very uncommon summer breeder high in the Cascades; rare breeder in the southwest and in the foothills next to the southern Willamette Valley; locally rare west of the Cascades in winter.
Habitat: open or broken woodlands and open country, from lower foothills to high alpine in summer, dropping to lower elevations afterward.

Nesting: on a cliff ledge or in a tall tree; nest platform to 10 ft across is built of sticks, branches and roots; pair incubates 2–3 creamy buff, brown-marked eggs for 43–45 days; young fledge at 66–75 days.
Feeding: swoops on prey from a fast, soaring flight; opportunistic feeder on small mammals and birds; also lizards, snakes and some larger mammals (usually stillbirths or carrion).
Voice: generally quiet; utters yelps, lower *chiup* calls and a short bark.
Similar Species: *Immature Bald Eagle* (p. 99): bare legs; larger head; heavier bill; more diffuse white patches in wings; wings held flat in flight. *Turkey Vulture* (p. 62): naked head looks small in flight; dark wing linings; silvery flight feathers; rocks and teeters in flight with wings in a sharp "V."
Best Sites: Prineville Reservoir; John Day Fossil Beds; Fort Rock SP; Abert Rim; Hart Mt.; OK Gulch; Imnaha area; Thief Valley Reservoir; Virtue Flats (Pleasant Valley); Malheur NWR.

109

AMERICAN KESTREL

Falco sparverius

The American Kestrel is North America's smallest falcon, but it is not merely a miniature version of its relatives. The kestrel is more buoyant in flight, and it is not inclined toward the all-out, full-speed-ahead aerial attacks that have made other falcons such admired predators. The kestrel often "wind-hovers" to scan the ground, flapping rapidly to maintain a stationary position while facing upwind. It also perches on telephone wires above roadsides and along open fields, peering intently downward into the grass below for any sign of small rodents or birds, but large insects form the majority of its summer diet. • The species name, *sparverius*, is Latin for "pertaining to sparrows," even though sparrows are only an occasional prey item. Old field guides referred to this bird as "Sparrow Hawk."

ID: 2 distinctive dark facial stripes and nape patch; rufous back and wings with dark brown barring; gray forehead and crown; white "chin"; small bill; yellow cere and feet; long tail. *Male:* rufous upper crown patch; dark-spotted bluish gray wings and pale buff underparts; white-tipped rufous tail with broad, blackish terminal band. *Female:* less contrasting head pattern and browner back; heavily rufous-streaked pale underparts; dark-banded rufous tail. *In flight:* long, thin, pointed wings; rufous back and tail; much lighter flight than other falcons.
Size: *L* 7½–8 in; *W* 20–24 in.
Status: uncommon to common permanent breeding resident in western Oregon; common summer breeder, migrant and winter resident east of the Cascades.

Habitat: open fields, oak woodlands, forest edges, grasslands, sagebrush flats, roadsides and farmland with hunting perches; post-breeding birds may move into mountain alpine areas.
Nesting: in a natural cavity or an abandoned woodpecker hole, old magpie or crow nest, or in a nest box; pair incubates 4–6 brown-spotted, white to buff eggs for 28–31 days; pair feeds young until fledging at 30–31 days and sometimes beyond.
Feeding: swoops from a perch or hovers; eats mostly insects, including grasshoppers, crickets, dragonflies and beetles, small rodents, birds, reptiles and amphibians.
Voice: loud, often repeated, shrill piping notes.
Similar Species: *Merlin* (p. 111): slightly larger; stockier; gray or brown back and wings; plainer face; dark or dark-banded tail.
Best Sites: *Winter:* Klamath Basin; Willamette Valley.

MERLIN

Falco columbarius

Only slightly larger than an American Kestrel, the Merlin considers itself the equal of any falcon, emulating the Peregrine Falcon in high-speed flight and in snatching other birds in midair. Its sleek body design, long, narrow tail and pointed wings increase aerodynamic efficiency in high-speed pursuits. The elements of speed and surprise work best in open country close to forest edges, where the Merlin is most at home. • The scientific name *columbarius*, Latin for dove or pigeon, and the former name "Pigeon Hawk" refer to the bird's appearance in flight, not its preferred prey. • The Black Merlin, *F.c. suckleyi*, is most often seen along the coast and inland in the west. The less dark Taiga Merlin, *F.c. columbarius*, is seen mostly east of the Cascades. The paler Prairie Merlin, *F.c. richardsonii*, may occur in eastern Oregon.

ID: long, narrow, dark or heavily banded tail; heavily brown-streaked white or buffy underparts; indistinct facial markings; dark eyes; yellow eye ring; yellow feet. *Male:* plain bluish gray back and crown. *Female:* plain brown back and crown. *In flight:* very rapid, shallow, swiftlike wingbeats; dark or banded tail; pointed wings with straight trailing edge; light-speckled, generally dark underwings.
Size: *L* 10–12 in; *W* 23–26 in.
Status: uncommon migrant and winter visitor in coastal lowland areas and western Oregon and rare to uncommon elsewhere; first fall migrants appear in late August or early September; spring migrants usually leave by late April, but some may linger until mid-May.
Habitat: semi-open to open country, including estuaries, seacoast, open woodlands,

windbreaks, forest glades and hedgerows; often winters in towns and cities.
Nesting: not known to nest in Oregon; has nested east of the Cascades and possibly elsewhere in the distant past.
Feeding: stoops or pursues smaller birds, particularly flocking songbirds and shorebirds, and larger flying insects, especially dragonflies; also eats other insects, small mammals and reptiles, usually pouncing from a perch.
Voice: rapid, high-pitched *ki-ki-ki-kee*, sometimes imitated by jays.
Similar Species: *American Kestrel* (p. 110): slightly smaller; more colorful; 2 bold facial stripes; rufous tail; often hovers; perches on roadside wires. *Prairie Falcon* (p. 113): much larger; sandy brown upperparts; whiter underparts; dark "wing pits."
Best Sites: *In migration:* open country. *Winter:* near coastal beaches and estuaries; farmland and in towns.

PEREGRINE FALCON

Falco peregrinus

The well-known Peregrine Falcon is believed to be the world's fastest bird. Named for its propensity for wandering, it is found on every continent except Antarctica. • Although migrants and wintering birds commonly hunt waterfowl and shorebirds, hence the former name of "Duck Hawk," summering Peregrines typically concentrate on birds of the forest canopy or, in city habitats, species such as the Rock Dove. • The Peregrine's legendary speed and hunting skills were no defense against the insidious effects of pesticides during the mid-1900s. In the space of 30 years, Peregrines almost disappeared from Oregon and elsewhere, prompting a public outcry that resulted in a 1972 ban on DDT. Intensive conservation and reintroduction efforts have brought about a strong and heartening recovery across much of the Peregrine's North American range.

ID: bluish gray back, wings and tail; broad, dark "mustache" joins "cap" to form distinctive "helmet"; light underparts with fine, dark barring and spotting. *In flight:* broad-based pointed wings; dark-banded tail; strong, steady wingbeats.

Size: *Male: L* 15–17 in; *W* 3–3½ ft. *Female: L* 17–19 in; *W* 3½–3¾ ft.

Status: very rare breeder along the coast and inland; uncommon migrant and winter resident along the coast; rare to uncommon migrant and winter resident elsewhere; reintroduced at various locations; *anatum* and *tundrius* ssp. state-listed as endangered.

Habitat: lakeshores, seacoast, estuaries and coastal marshlands; mountainous areas with cliffs and open country; even urban areas.

Nesting: wild birds use cliff ledges or rocky ridges; many introduced birds use artificial platforms and flat, protected sites on ledges and bridges; nest sites are traditionally reused with no material added; male helps the female incubate 3–4 yellowish white eggs spotted with cinnamon brown for 32–36 days; pair feeds young in the nest for 49–56 days until fledging.

Feeding: stoops at high speed from a soaring flight, striking birds in midair with clenched feet; also chases down birds on the wing.

Voice: generally silent; loud, harsh, persistent *kak-kak-kak-kak* near the nest.

Similar Species: *Prairie Falcon* (p. 113): sandy brown above; dark "wing pit" on whiter underwing; smaller "mustache" separate from crown patch; brown-spotted underparts.

Best Sites: *Summer:* Cape Meares SP; Portland's Fremont Bridge. *Winter:* northern Willamette Valley; Clatsop Spit; Nehalem Meadows; Bayocean Spit; greater Portland area.

PRAIRIE FALCON

Falco mexicanus

Rocketing overhead more like supercharged fighter jets than stealth bombers, Prairie Falcons nonetheless seem to appear out of nowhere. A Prairie Falcon can outfly the closely related Peregrine in level flight and can rival it in downward swoops. During spring and summer, Prairie Falcons often concentrate their efforts over ground squirrel colonies, swooping over expanses of windswept grass to pick off naïve youngsters. As summer fades to fall, large flocks of migrating songbirds capture their attention. • Inexperienced and over-eager birds risk serious injury or death when pushing the limits in early hunting forays. Young falcons swooping at close to 200 miles per hour can easily misjudge their flight speed or their ability to pull out of a dive. • Prairie Falcons commonly soar for long periods on updrafts or along ridgelines.

ID: sandy brown upperparts; pale face; narrow, dark brown "mustache"; white underparts with brown spots heaviest on flanks; brown eyes; yellow eye ring; yellow cere and feet; barred tail. *In flight:* black "wing pit" line unique among falcons.
Size: *Male: L* 14–15 in; *W* 3–3¼ ft. *Female: L* 17–18 in; *W* 3½ ft.
Status: locally common permanent breeding resident east of the Cascades; rare fall and winter visitor to the west.
Habitat: arid grasslands. *Breeding:* deserts; cliffs and rocky promontories. *In migration* and *winter:* croplands and pastures; hardly ever along the coast.
Nesting: on a cliff ledge, in a crevice or on a rocky promontory, rarely in an abandoned crow or hawk nest or on an artificial

structure; nest is usually unlined; female, with some help from the male, incubates 3–5 pale, dark-speckled, spotted and clouded eggs for 29–33 days; young fledge at 35–42 days.
Feeding: high-speed strike-and-kill follows diving swoop, low flight or chase on the wing, sometimes from a perch; eats ground squirrels, pocket gophers, small birds and other small vertebrates, supplemented by lizards and large insects.
Voice: generally silent; yelping *kik-kik-kik-kik* alarm, more intense and screamlike than the Peregrine's.
Similar Species: *Peregrine Falcon* (p. 112): somewhat bulkier; broader, pointier wings; uniform underwing coloration; distinctive dark "helmet." *Female Merlin* (p. 111): much smaller; darker underwings; back and upperwings are usually darker; narrower, dark or heavily banded tail.
Best Sites: *Summer:* Steens Mt.; Hart Mt.; Snake River Canyon.

CHUKAR

Alectoris chukar

First introduced east of the Cascades in the 1950s, this Old World species was well established by 1968. Further releases have helped it become widespread and fairly common in southeastern and northeastern Oregon. Rarely seen in open grasslands or heavy forest, the Chukar prefers steep, rocky areas with brush and grass; it does not compete for habitat with native grouse and quail species. • The Chukar has impressive reproductive capabilities—a female can lay more than 20 eggs in a single clutch, and she will sometimes provide another, usually smaller, clutch for the male to incubate separately. • In fall and winter, Chukars feed in family groups, using the distinctive call for which the bird was named to reassemble. The same call may help disperse breeding pairs into separate territories in summer.

ID: generally gray; brownish back and crown; black "mask" and "necklace" border creamy white throat and "cheeks"; black-and-chestnut vertical bars on pale buff sides; gray tail; rufous undertail coverts; brown eyes; reddish pink bill, eye ring, legs and feet. *In flight:* gray rump, plain brownish wings; red-sided gray tail; whirring wingbeats.
Size: *L* 13 in; *W* 20 in.
Status: introduced east of the Cascades; widespread and common year-round in suitable habitat; privately released birds are sometimes seen west of the Cascades.
Habitat: steep, rocky hillsides; arid foothills; canyons; dry sagebrush; drier mid-elevation valleys.
Nesting: on the ground on rocky, brush-covered slopes; nest is a shallow scrape lined with grass and feathers; female (and sometimes male) incubates 10–20 heavily chestnut-spotted, pale yellow to buff eggs

for 23–24 days; family stays together throughout winter.
Feeding: gleans the ground for weed and grass seeds; plucks green leaves from grasses and other plants; also takes berries and some insects, especially grasshoppers; occasionally feeds on carcasses, perhaps to eat maggots.
Voice: short clucking introduction precedes a distinctive *chuc-kar chuc-kar chuc-kar;* flushed bird utters a soft, clucking *whitoo whitoo.*
Similar Species: *Gray Partridge* (p. 115): chestnut brown bars on gray sides; pale bill and legs; buff to rufous face with gray patch. *Northern Bobwhite:* much smaller; more chestnut and brown; strong facial stripes; pale legs. *Other quails* (pp. 122–23): smaller; more uniform bluish gray on breast, back and tail; distinctive belly and flank stripes; black bill; grayish legs; crest on male.
Best Sites: Deschutes R.; Abert Rim; Hart Mt.; Eagle Cap Wilderness Area; Diamond Craters.

114

GRAY PARTRIDGE

Perdix perdix

Quite secretive most of the year, Gray Partridges are rarely seen in the open, except when they venture onto quiet country roads, particularly during early morning. • Social outside the incubation period, Gray Partridges sometimes form coveys. If flushed, the birds burst suddenly from cover and fly off in all directions, flapping furiously and then gliding to a nearby safe haven to reunite. During cold weather, they huddle together in a circle, with each bird facing outward, always ready to burst into flight. • Like other seed-eating birds, the Gray Partridge regularly swallows small amounts of gravel to help crush hard seeds. This gravel accumulates in the bird's gizzard, a muscular pouch of the digestive system. • Preserving hedgerows and limiting pesticide use benefit the Gray Partridge, which has declined in intensive agricultural areas.

♂

ID: short, gray tail with rufous outer tail feathers; chestnut-barred flanks; gray underparts; mottled brown back; brown eyes; pale grayish blue bill, legs and feet. *Male:* orangy brown face and throat; dark brown horseshoe-shaped patch on belly. *Female:* buffy face. *In flight:* whirring flight close to the ground.
Size: *L* 12–13 in; *W* 19 in.
Status: introduced permanent breeding resident; fairly evenly distributed east of the Cascades but most common in the northeast.
Habitat: grassy or weedy fields and crop-lands with hedgerows or brushy edge cover; prefers grainfields; also established in some desert areas and grasslands; moves to crop stubble and wooded cover in winter.
Nesting: in a hay field, pasture, weedy fenceline or brushy margin; scratched-out ground depression is rimmed and lined with grass; female incubates 10–20 buff, brown or olive eggs for 21–26 days; pair feeds the young; family stays together until early spring.
Feeding: at dusk and dawn in summer, throughout the day in winter; gleans the ground for seeds and stems, waste grains and seeds; picks apart seedheads; also eats insects and larvae; sometimes tunnels in the snow to find waste grain.
Voice: male's *kshee-rik* dawn and dusk call sounds like a rusty hinge; squeaks and clucks; flushed covey utters a barrage of cackling *keep* notes.
Similar Species: *Chukar* (p. 114): generally gray and brown; black-bordered creamy throat and "cheeks"; white belly and boldly dark-barred flanks; red eye ring, bill, legs and feet; pale chestnut undertail coverts.
Best Sites: Ladd Marsh WMA; Grand Ronde Valley; Upper Wallowa Valley; Crow Creek.

RING-NECKED PHEASANT

Phasianus colchicus

The spectacular Asian Ring-necked Pheasant was introduced to North America in the mid-1800s mainly for hunting purposes. Unlike most other introductions, Ring-necks became established and thrived almost everywhere they were introduced. A combination of harsh winter conditions, hunting pressure and diminished habitat associated with more intensive farming practices has since reduced numbers to a point where annual replenishment by hatchery-raised young is required to maintain populations in much of their Oregon range. • The distinctive, loud *krahh-krawk* of male pheasants is often heard echoing near farmyards, brushy suburban parks and national wildlife refuges, but the birds are less frequently observed. The drab females are more circumspect but may be seen shuffling away to safety in farm fields and brushy cover. • Like other game birds, pheasants have poorly developed flight muscles and rarely fly far.

ID: unfeathered gray legs; very long tail. *Male:* glossy, green-and-purple head; red face and wattle; bronze neck and underparts; white-spotted brownish back; long, neatly barred bronze tail; yellowish pink bill; pale yellow eyes. *Female:* dull buff overall; brown-mottled back and sides; dark eyes; dark gray bill. *In flight:* short, rounded wings; long tail feathers well spaced at ends.

Size: *Male: L* 30–36 in; *W* 28–33 in. *Female: L* 20–26 in; *W* 19–25 in.

Status: common introduced year-round resident.

Habitat: agricultural lands, brushy and weedy fields, stubble fields, croplands and shrubby, overgrown hillsides at lower elevations.

Nesting: on the ground, among grass or sparse vegetation, or next to a log or other ground cover; nest is in a slight depression, barely lined with leaves or grass; female incubates 10–12 brownish olive eggs for 23–25 days; occasionally dumps eggs in other game bird or duck nests.

Feeding: gleans the ground and lower vegetation for weed seeds and invertebrates; winter diet of buds, seeds and waste grain.

Voice: male utters a loud, raspy *kraah-krawk*, followed by a muffled whirring of wings; flushed or startled bird gives a hoarse *ka-ka-ka, ka-ka*; female usually clucks.

Similar Species: male is unmistakable. *Greater Sage-Grouse* (p. 118): grayer brown overall; short, feathered legs; dark belly. *Ruffed Grouse* (p. 117): smaller; fan-shaped tail; feathered legs.

Best Sites: grain-growing areas of north-central Oregon; agricultural areas of Malheur Co.; larger urban parks and suburban areas.

RUFFED GROUSE

Bonasa umbellus

The sounds of a displaying male Ruffed Grouse are felt more than heard. Strutting on a fallen log with his tail fanned and neck ruffled, the male beats the air with accelerating wing strokes and then falls back from the sheer force of his solo. This "drumming" occurs mainly in the spring courtship season but in fall as well. By erecting the black ruffs on the sides of his neck during this nonvocal display, the male impresses females by appearing larger. • As winter approaches, Ruffed Grouse toe feathers gain an elongated bristle, providing a temporary snowshoe. • This grouse is more likely to be seen close to town than other grouse. • *Bonasa* is thought to compare the male's drumming sound to the bellow of a bull aurochs (an extinct species of European wild cattle); *umbellus* refers to the umbrella-like black ruff.

ID: rufous brown overall; small, ragged crest; black shoulder patches expand into ruff (larger on male) in display or threat; thick, dark, vertical barring on sides; brown-barred rufous tail tipped with broad, dark band (incomplete on female) and narrow, pale band. *In flight:* rounded wings; fan-shaped tail; stiff, shallow wingbeats; usually flies close to the ground.
Size: *L* 15–19 in; *W* 22 in.
Status: common year-round resident.
Habitat: forests of all types, from near sea level to over 5000 ft; prefers deciduous 2nd-growth or mixed forests with birch or aspen; often occurs close to urban areas.
Nesting: on the ground, typically at the base of a tree, stump or boulder, possibly in deadfall or a brush pile; female makes a bowl-like depression lined with dry vegetation and incubates 9–14 cinnamon buff eggs for 23–24 days.
Feeding: gleans on the ground and in bushes and trees for buds, leaves, flowers, catkins, fruit, acorns and small invertebrates; occasionally perches high in deciduous trees in winter and early spring to eat buds.
Voice: female utters nasal squeals, soft clucks and hisses and also squirrel-like chirps and a loud *peta peta peta peta* flushing call; male gives a quiet *queet* flushing call.
Similar Species: *Female Spruce Grouse* (p. 119): finely dark-barred underparts; no crest or ruff; shorter, darker tail. *Female Blue Grouse* (p. 120): duskier; barred tail; spotted flanks.
Best Sites: many forested areas.

117

GREATER SAGE-GROUSE

Centrocercus urophasianus

In March and April, groups of large, spectacular Greater Sage-Grouse assemble at their courtship "leks" at dawn to perform a traditional springtime dance. Males enter the arena, inflate their pectoral sacs, spread their pointed tail feathers and really strut their stuff to intimidate their rivals and attract prospective mates. The most fit and experienced males take center stage, and the others are banished to the edges. The best performer will mate with up to 75 percent of the nearby females. • Sage-grouse do not run well, preferring to hide or fly, so close encounters of the finest kind are usually possible only while the birds are gathered in leks. • Flocks flush with a startling burst of wingbeats.

breeding

ID: light-mottled grayish brown upperparts; black belly; brown eyes; yellow eye comb; stubby, dark bill; feathered yellowish legs and feet; long, pointed, barred tail. *Male:* black "bib" and neck stripes; white underparts; inflatable yellow pectoral sacs; spiked tail. *Female:* smaller; less dark than male; white "chin". *In flight:* heavy-looking body; long tail feathers are widely separated at tips; black belly; brown underwings with white linings.

Size: *Male: L* 27–34 in; *W* 38 in. *Female: L* 18–24 in; *W* 33 in.

Status: uncommon and declining year-round resident east of the Cascades; *phaios* ssp. is a federal species of concern and is state-listed as sensitive.

Habitat: sagebrush; ventures into nearby woodlands and farmlands to feed; display leks are often located in or on fields, airstrips, gravel roads or pits, ridges, grassy swales or dry beds of lakes or streams.

Nesting: on the ground, in shaded cover; shallow bowl is filled with leaves and twigs and lined with feathers; female incubates 7–9 brown-marked, pale olive or greenish eggs for 25–29 days and tends young for up to 12 weeks.

Feeding: gleans mostly sagebrush leaves and buds; pursues insects; juveniles are fed insects for the first 20 days.

Voice: generally silent; male at lek site makes a unique, hollow *oop-la-boop* with air released from quivering air sacs; both genders give guttural clucking and cackling notes.

Similar Species: *Female Ring-necked Pheasant* (p. 116): smaller; mostly dark-marked dull buff body; naked legs. *Female Blue Grouse* (p. 120): browner; white-spotted, dark-mottled underparts; rounded tail end, open or closed.

Best Sites: Hart Mt.; Virtue Flats (Pleasant Valley); Malheur NWR; Steens Mt.; Alvord Basin.

SPRUCE GROUSE
Falcipennis canadensis

Spruce Grouse spend much of their secretive lives hidden in dark, dense conifer stands as they search for food. They trust their camouflaged plumage even in open areas, often allowing people to approach within a few feet before flushing. Overall, more Spruce Grouse probably escape detection than are seen. • The Spruce Grouse is most conspicuous in late April and early May, when the female issues her cackling notes from trees and the male struts across open areas. The male's courtship call is largely beyond human hearing, but we can see him transform from a dark and somber bird to a red-browed, puff-necked, fan-tailed dandy in display. Unlike the Taiga subspecies male of the northeastern U.S., the Franklin's male found in Oregon ends his short, whirring courtship flight with two loud wing claps.

ID: mottled, gray-and-brown upperparts; grayish bill; straw-colored feet. *Male:* prominent red eye comb; black throat and neck; indistinct white collar line; heavily white-marked dark breast and underparts; dark tail; white-tipped upper tail coverts. *Female:* browner upperparts than male's; mottled, dark-barred white or rufous-washed underparts. *In flight:* heavyset body; shortish wings and tail; short flights to tree branches.

Size: *L* 14–16 in; *W* 22 in.

Status: uncommon local year-round resident in the Wallowa Mountains; state-listed as sensitive.

Habitat: young successional conifer stands; avoids single-species plantations; high-elevation stunted growth.

Nesting: on the ground, often below a conifer, in a natural or enhanced depression; nest is lined with needles, leaves and some feathers; female incubates 4–5 tawny olive eggs for 22–24 days; young leave the nest when dry and can flutter to lower tree branches at 6–8 days.

Feeding: usually forages at mid-level on pine and spruce needles; also eats berries and leaves off trailing junipers and shrubs, as well as forbs, small arthropods and snails.

Voice: female makes a loud, wavering cackle from a tree perch at dawn and dusk; male utters extremely low, barely audible hoots, accompanied by whirring flight and 2 wing claps; both genders also utter guttural notes and clucks.

Similar Species: *Blue Grouse* (p. 120): larger; more bluish gray; male has orange comb, pale-tipped tail and yellow air sacs, with less white in plumage.

Best Sites: *Summer* to *mid-fall:* Moss Springs; Wallowa Lake SP; Bonny Lakes.

BLUE GROUSE
Dendragapus obscurus

In high coniferous forests, the male Blue Grouse sometimes begins his low, owl-like hooting while patches of snow remain. One of the earliest signs of spring, this mating call is intended to attract multiple females. So deep that the human ear can detect only a fraction of the sounds produced, the resonant notes make the ear vibrate at close range, producing a humming sensation in the head. • Some birds fatten up on berries along timberline ridges before overwintering at more sheltered lower elevations. • *Dendragapus*, Greek for "tree-loving," accurately reflects this bird's attachment to forest cover and its roosting in conifers, but it spends much of its time on the ground. • Like other forest-dwelling grouse, the Blue Grouse is often easily approached, earning it the name "Fool Hen."

ID: longish, broad tail; dark bill and eyes; feathered legs. *Male:* bluish gray crown and nape; brownish back, rump and upper tail coverts; black tail with light terminal band; orange eye comb; displays with inflated yellow or red throat patches surrounded by white and blackish feathers. *Female:* grayish brown overall, lightly white-speckled neck and back; banded brown rump and tail with paler terminal band.

Size: *Male:* L 18–22 in; W 25–27 in. *Female:* L 17–19 in; W 23–25 in.

Status: uncommon year-round resident.

Habitat: coniferous forests, from coastal rainforests to high mountain subalpine associations; occasionally wanders to open country, especially in summer; prefers denser forests in winter.

Nesting: female selects a site with some overhead cover; nest is a shallow scrape sparsely lined with dead vegetation and some feathers; female incubates 6–7 buffy eggs for 25–28 days; young leave the nest the morning after hatching and can flutter to cover after 9 days.

Feeding: flies into foliage and perches; eats mainly leaves, flowers and conifer needles in spring, berries and invertebrates in summer and conifer needles, buds, twigs and seeds in winter.

Voice: male produces a series of 5–8 extremely deep hoots in his neck sacs; male also utters soft and harsh calls; female gives a loud whinny and quavering cackles.

Similar Species: *Spruce Grouse* (p. 119): male has black throat and upper breast, prominent red comb and large, white spots on underparts and tail; female is more heavily barred on underparts.

Best Sites: forests in the Coast Ranges, on the western slopes of the Cascades, and in the Blue Mts. and Wallowa Mts.

WILD TURKEY
Meleagris gallopavo

The wary Wild Turkey has acute senses and a highly developed social system. Feeding largely in the open and highly visible to predators, it forms flocks of up to 60 birds, with some individuals always on alert. Turkeys sometimes cooperatively flush grasshoppers. • Like other game birds, turkeys consume grit to assist in grinding down hard-shelled materials in the gizzard. Objects requiring more than 400 pounds of pressure per square inch to crush have been found flattened within a day when fed to a turkey. • The turkey is the only widely domesticated animal native to North America. Perhaps with that in mind, the Wild Turkey was Benjamin Franklin's choice for America's national emblem, but it lost to the Bald Eagle by one congressional vote.

♂

ID: dark, glossy, iridescent plumage of green, copper and brown; naked, bluish head; barred copper tail tipped with white; long, unfeathered pinkish legs. *Male:* red wattles; conspicuous central breast tuft. *Female:* smaller; less iridescent body.
Size: *Male: L* 4–4¼ ft; *W* 5¼ ft. *Female: L* 3 ft; *W* 4¼ ft.
Status: uncommon introduced year-round resident.
Habitat: chiefly openings and forest edges in the oak-conifer zone of valley edges, rolling foothills and lower mountain slopes; prefers oak, hackberry and cottonwood; needs adequate surface water.
Nesting: in open woods or forest glade; female scratches a slight depression at the base of a tree, close to shrubs or under a brush pile, lines it with grass and leaves, and incubates 5–17 reddish-spotted pale buff eggs for 27–31 days.
Feeding: omnivorous diet includes sedge and grass seeds, fruits, bulbs, leaves, nuts, berries, roots, invertebrates and even small amphibians and reptiles.
Voice: wide array of sounds; male gobbles loudly; female clucks and whines; birds leaving the roosting area cackle.
Similar Species: none.
Best Sites: White River WMA; Blue Mts. of Union Co. and Wallowa Co.; southern Morrow Co.; near Medford.

121

MOUNTAIN QUAIL

Oreortyx pictus

As spring arrives, the foothill and mountain slopes throughout much of Oregon resound with the resonant, querulous calls of male Mountain Quails. In other seasons, Mountain Quails are less readily detected. Family groups vanish from roadsides, quickly concealing themselves among dense brush and sheltering thickets. Flushed coveys scatter and then reunite. • The Mountain Quail is known for its ability to exploit a wide variety of plant food and to travel long distances to take advantage of seasonally abundant food in various high-elevation habitats. Newly hatched quails quickly follow their parents as they travel many miles a day by foot, often moving to lower elevations where there is more cover. • The largest of the North American quails, the Mountain Quail is also the one with the least sexual dimorphism.

gray morph

ID: brownish gray back, wings, rump and tail; bluish gray neck and head; white-bordered brown "cheeks" and throat; 2 straight, black head plumes (may intertwine); strongly white-barred rufous sides; unbarred rufous belly; reddish buff undertail coverts; short tail. *In flight:* grayish underwings.
Size: *L* 11–12 in; *W* 16 in.
Status: common year-round resident in mountainous and hilly areas; generally absent from urban and agricultural areas used by California Quail or close to the ocean; state-listed as sensitive.
Habitat: shrubby growth after a fire or clear-cutting; woodlands; streamside habitats; birds may move downslope to the coast in winter.
Nesting: on the ground, usually in dense cover; shallow nest scrape in loose, dry soil is lined with dry pine needles and grass; pair incubates 6–14 cream or buff eggs for 24–25 days.
Feeding: digs and scratches among leaf litter; sometimes gleans in trees or shrubs; eats seeds, berries, bulbs, green leaves, flowers, acorns, fungi and grit; female eats bone fragments and forages for ants and other insects with young.
Voice: male's distinctive courtship call is a loud, clear, 2-noted, whistling *quee-yark;* similar, less raucous alarm call; other calls by both genders include a whistling *wit-wit-wit* and *tu-tu-tu-tu* assembly call.
Similar Species: *California Quail* (p. 123): grayer plumage; "scaly" neck and belly; horizontally streaked flanks; darker face and teardrop-shaped plume on male; plainer face and short, upright plume on female.
Best Sites: Saddle Mountain SP; Larch Mt.; Scoggins Valley; William L. Findley NWR; Foster Reservoir; Lake Selmac CP; Roxy Ann Butte (near Medford).

CALIFORNIA QUAIL

Callipepla californica

Although the male's spring courtship call sounds remarkably like the name of mid-America's famous windy city, Chicago, the California Quail rarely strays from its western homeland. Native to southwestern Oregon, the California Quail has, since the 1880s, been successfully introduced to other regions, but it is largely absent from the northern coast, heavily forested areas and higher elevations. • Spending most of their time scuttling about in tight, cohesive coveys of up to 200 birds, these quails run the risk of attracting feral cats and other predators. Even though they stay largely within the protective confines of their brushland habitat, noisy scratching for food and soft vocalizations to keep the covey together usually give them away. A flushed covey will erupt from cover, scatter and later reassemble.

ID: gray breast, back and tail; very "scaly" neck and belly; horizontally white-streaked brown sides. *Male:* dark crown; white-bordered black "cheeks" and throat; prominent white "eyebrow"; forward-drooping black plume. *Female:* grayish brown face and throat; small, upright black plume. *In flight:* gray underwings.

Size: *L* 10–11 in; *W* 14 in.

Status: common breeding permanent native resident in Jackson, Josephine and Curry Counties; introduced elsewhere with general success but absent along the coast from Coos Co. north and rare at high elevations.

Habitat: chaparral; brush, even in suburban parks; oak and riparian woodlands.

Nesting: usually on the ground, well concealed under cover of a shrub, log, brush pile or debris; sometimes in an abandoned nest of another species; shallow depression lined with leaves and grass can be quite substantial; female, with some help from the male, incubates up to 21 brown-blotched, off-white eggs for 22–23 days.

Feeding: gleans and scratches on the ground; eats seeds, fresh leaves, plant shoots, berries, acorns, bulbs, flowers and catkins, plus occasional plant galls, insects and waste grain; sometimes takes birdseed.

Voice: male gives a loud, low-pitched *chi-ca-go* call for courtship from April to May and at other times of year; other calls are softer and usually 2 notes, except for the spitting alarm call.

Similar Species: *Mountain Quail* (p. 122): 2 (or 1) long, straight head plumes; strongly white-barred rufous sides and unbarred rufous belly.

Best Sites: often in suburbs, urban areas and farmlands.

123

YELLOW RAIL

Coturnicops noveboracensis

The Yellow Rail might be Oregon's most challenging breeding bird to meet. It is most active at night, when most naturalists are dreaming of birds behind closed eyelids. Under a blanket of darkness, the Yellow Rail steals quietly through tall sedges, grass and cattails, picking food from the ground and searching for snails and earthworms. By day, this shy bird hides behind a cover of dense marsh vegetation. Only in spring does the Yellow Rail reveal its presence by issuing its distinctive, repetitive "ticking" calls. • Rails are masters at slipping through tightly packed stands of marsh vegetation with their laterally compressed bodies, and the name "rail" might reflect their looking "as thin as a rail." Their large feet, which help them rest atop thin mats of floating plant material, add to their strange appearance.

ID: short, pale bill; black (finely barred with white) and tawny stripes on upperparts; broad, dark eye line; whitish throat and belly; yellowish tan throat and breast; pinkish legs. *Juvenile:* dark streaks and white speckles across head, neck, breast and flanks. *In flight:* short, rounded, straight, grayish wings with black-and-tawny shoulders, prominent white secondary patch and white underwing leading edge; trailing legs.
Size: *L* 6½–7½ in; *W* 11 in.
Status: very local summer resident; state-listed as sensitive.
Habitat: sedge marshes; wet grassy meadows.

Nesting: on the ground or low over water, hidden by overhanging plants; shallow cup nest is made of grass or sedges; female incubates 8–10 eggs for up to 18 days.
Feeding: picks food from the ground and aquatic vegetation; eats mostly snails, aquatic insects, spiders and possibly earthworms; occasionally eats seeds.
Voice: metallic *tik, tik, tik-tik-tik*.
Similar Species: *Sora* (p. 126): white-streaked, black-mottled brown back; gray underwing, white at leading edge only; gray face; black "mask"; black throat and bright yellow bill on breeding bird; distinctly different call. *Virginia Rail* (p. 125): long, orange bill; brown-mottled rusty back; broad-tipped, forward-swept wings; gray underwing, white at leading edge only; face is mostly gray.
Best Sites: Klamath Basin.

VIRGINIA RAIL

Rallus limicola

A time-honored way to meet a Virginia Rail is to sit alongside a wetland marsh, clap your hands three or four times and wait patiently. With luck, this slim bird may reveal itself for an instant, but more often a metallic return call is all that betrays a Virginia Rail's presence. • With its short, stubby wings, the Virginia Rail prefers to escape the attention of an intruder or predator by scurrying off into dense vegetation, particularly so in late summer, when molted wing and tail feathers leave it temporarily flightless. Escape is made easier by the laterally compressed body, modified feather tips resistant to wear and tear, and flexible vertebrae. • The ability of rails to disappear so quickly and their habit of feeding by twilight ensure that their numbers are almost always underestimated.

ID: rusty orange throat and breast; black-and-white, vertically barred flanks; gray face; red eyes; long, downcurved, orange bill; pinkish orange legs and feet; long toes; brown-mottled rusty back; short tail with white undertail coverts. *In flight:* broad-tipped, forward-swept wings; gray underwings, white at leading edge only; rusty shoulders on brownish upperwings; dangling feet.

Size: *L* 9–11 in; *W* 13 in.

Status: common breeding summer resident; very rare to common in winter.

Habitat: *Breeding:* freshwater wetlands, especially cattail, bulrush and tule marshes; flooded riparian woodlands; sometimes coastal saltwater marshes. *In migration* and *winter:* wetland areas with suitable overhead cover, particularly coastal freshwater marshes in winter.

Nesting: usually suspended just over the water in emergent marsh vegetation; concealed loose basket nest of coarse grass, cattail stems or sedges; pair incubates 7–12 brown-dotted, pale buff eggs for 18–20 days; pair feeds and tends the young, which fledge at 25 days.

Feeding: probes soft substrates for soft-bellied invertebrates, such as earthworms, beetles, snails, spiders, insect larvae and nymphs; often snatches prey from vegetation; sometimes eats seeds or small fish.

Voice: easily imitated, repeated, metallic *kid-dik* given day or night; also gives an accelerating series of wheezy grunts that eventually trail off; female ends a series of sharp notes with a rough trill.

Similar Species: *Sora* (p. 126): short, yellow bill; black "mask"; greenish yellow legs; straight wings. *Yellow Rail* (p. 124): smaller; stubby, yellow bill; striped, black-and-tawny upperparts; yellowish tan breast; straight wings.

Best Sites: widespread. *Winter:* unfrozen wetlands.

SORA
Porzana carolina

Sounding halfway between a crazed laugh and a horse's whinny, the call of a male Sora hidden deep within a marsh puzzles the uninitiated. Easier to imitate is the plaintive, two-note whistle that the Sora gives day and night, but most often in the clear, still twilight hours. This call is often the only definite sign of a Sora's presence, because this bird is especially elusive even in places where it is common. • Even without webbing between its toes, the Sora swims well as it moves from one patch of wet vegetation to another, and its wings are strong enough to enable many North American birds to migrate to South America. • The Sora habitually flicks its short, stubby tail, perhaps to confuse prey. • *Porzana*, meaning "crake," indicates this bird's resemblance to Europe's Corn Crake (*Crex crex*).

breeding

ID: gray face, neck and breast; black "mask" in front of eye, extending onto "chin" and throat in breeding plumage; yellow bill; reddish brown eyes; brown crown and nape; white-streaked, black-mottled brown back and tail; greenish yellow legs and feet; whitish undertail coverts. *In flight:* longish, straight wings; gray underwings; chestnut shoulders, back and tail.
Size: *L* 8–10 in; *W* 14 in.
Status: locally common breeding summer resident; very rare in winter west of the Cascades.
Habitat: *Breeding:* freshwater marshes with standing water and abundant emergent vegetation; grassy or marshy borders of streams, lakes and ponds; more likely than the Virginia Rail to be found at higher elevations.

In migration and *winter:* freshwater wetlands; saltwater and brackish coastal marshes.
Nesting: under concealing vegetation, usually over water, but possibly in a wet meadow; well-built basket nest of grass and aquatic vegetation; pair incubates 10–12 brown-spotted buff eggs for 16–19 days; pair feeds and tends the young until just beyond fledging at 20–25 days.
Feeding: gleans and probes vegetation for seeds, plants, aquatic insects and mollusks; also picks food from the ground or the water's surface.
Voice: distinctive, loud, uneven whinny; also a high, clear, 2-note, whistling *koo-ee* and a sharp alarm call.
Similar Species: *Virginia Rail* (p. 125): rusty underparts; long, orange, downcurved bill; pinkish legs. *Yellow Rail* (p. 124): striped, black-and-tawny upperparts; yellowish tan breast; some white secondaries; pinkish legs.
Best Sites: freshwater wetlands, including flooded fields and ditches.

AMERICAN COOT

Fulica americana

The expression "crazy as a coot" may at first seem very inappropriate for such well-adapted, successful waterbirds, but watch American Coots in spring and summer and you will understand where the expression came from. During the breeding season, coots are among the most spirited and aggressive waterbirds in the world, quick to take offence and always finding something to squabble about. They can often be seen running across the surface of the water on their lobed feet or swimming head down with white frontal "shields" flashing to intimidate rivals and other, larger waterfowl. Yet, in winter they are highly sociable and often form large rafts, swimming and diving together as if they didn't have a care in the world.

ID: dark gray overall; black head; sturdy, white bill with broken dark ring; white forehead "shield" with reddish spot; red eyes; sturdy, greenish yellow legs; long, individually lobed toes; white undertail coverts. *Juvenile:* dark brown upperparts; pale grayish brown underparts. *In flight:* trailing legs; secondaries are white-tipped at trailing edge.
Size: *L* 13–16 in; *W* 24 in.
Status: uncommon to common breeding summer resident, migrant and winter resident.
Habitat: freshwater marshes, ponds and wetlands with open water and emergent vegetation; city parks and golf courses. *Winter:* coastal saltwater marshes, lagoons and estuaries.

Nesting: in emergent marsh vegetation; pair builds a bulky, floating nest of cattails and grass; pair incubates 8–12 brown-spotted, pale buffy eggs for 21–25 days; pair feeds young until fledging at 49–56 days.
Feeding: gleans the water's surface for algae, aquatic vegetation and invertebrates; grazes short grasses; dives for submerged water plants, tadpoles and fish.
Voice: usually very vocal; single notes often accelerated into a long, loud *priki priki priki...* series with emphasis on "*ki.*"
Similar Species: *Common Moorhen:* less stocky; unlobed long toes; yellow-tipped red bill; red forehead "shield"; brown back; whitish flank streak; prominent white undertail coverts. *Male scoters* (pp. 86–88): larger; colorful bills; smaller, webbed, pinkish feet.
Best Sites: *Summer:* marshes and lakes east of the Cascades; Fern Ridge Reservoir. *In migration:* Klamath Co.; Harney Co. *Winter:* coastal ponds and estuaries.

SANDHILL CRANE

Grus canadensis

Deep, resonant, rattling yet melodious croaks betray the approach of a flock of migrating Sandhill Cranes. At some locations, flock after flock may sail effortlessly overhead. The expansive, V-shaped lines suggest geese, but the long necks, trailing legs and distinctive bugling calls quickly establish them as cranes. • Lesser Sandhills (*G.c. canadensis*) migrate through the state between wintering areas in California and breeding grounds in Alaska. The larger Greater Sandhills (*G.c. tabida*) summer and breed in eastern and south-central Oregon, reaching their meadow and marsh territories in late February and March and leaving by mid-November. • Cranes mate for life, reinforcing their pair bond each spring with an elaborate, exuberant courtship dance in which partners leap high into the air with their wings half spread and then bow like courtiers.

ID: long neck; long, dark legs; pale gray plumage, often stained rusty by iron oxides in the water; long, straight bill; red above pale "cheek" patch; bright yellow eyes; scapular feathers form large "bustle." *In flight:* straight neck; trailing legs; black-tipped silvery flight feathers; slow, steady wingbeats; flocks fly in a line or "V" formation.
Size: *Greater Sandhill: L* 3¾–4¼ ft; *W* 6¼–7 ft. *Lesser Sandhill: L* 3¼–3¾ ft; *W* 5¾–6¼ ft.
Status: *Greater Sandhill:* locally common migrant and breeding summer resident. *Lesser Sandhill:* common migrant; occasional winter resident; state-listed as sensitive.
Habitat: *Breeding:* isolated, open, wet grassy meadows and shallow marshlands; grasslands, mudflats and freshwater lakeshores. *In migration* and *winter:* agricultural fields.

Nesting: on a large mound of aquatic vegetation over water or along a shoreline; platform of vegetation is lined with smaller surrounding material selected by the female; pair incubates 1–3, usually 2, olive-splotched eggs for 29–32 days.
Feeding: probes and gleans the ground and shallow water for insects, soft-bodied invertebrates, especially worms, berries, waste grain, shoots and tubers.
Voice: unmistakable, loud, resonant, rattling, croaking *gu-rrroo gu-rrroo gurrroo*, sometimes extended into a long, exuberant chorus, especially with several birds calling.
Similar Species: *Great Blue Heron* (p. 55): white head with black crown stripe; mainly yellow bill; chestnut thighs; black head plumes and pale neck plumes in breeding plumage; flies with neck folded; all-gray underwings.
Best Sites: *Greater Sandhill Crane:* Harney, Lake, Klamath, Grant, Baker, Union and Deschutes Counties; Malheur NWR. *Lesser Sandhill Crane:* Sauvie I.

BLACK-BELLIED PLOVER
Pluvialis squatarola

Most often seen in its nonbreeding plumage, the Black-bellied Plover breeds across the High Arctic. Some of the most northerly breeding birds winter in the tropics whereas others winter as far north as coastal British Columbia, Canada. • Black-bellies benefit from their sociable nature and ability to adopt a variety of feeding strategies. Dense flocks roost together in migration and at wintering grounds but spread out to forage on the receding tide on mudflats. At high tide, they forsake the shore for freshwater and field habitats. Their large eyes allow them to readily feed at night. • Wary and quick to give alarm and take flight, the Black-bellied Plover serves as a sentinel for mixed flocks of shorebirds. • *Pluvialis* refers to rain, but the connection to this genus of birds is not known.

breeding

nonbreeding

ID: black bill; relatively long, blackish legs. *Breeding:* black face, breast and belly (less bold on female); light gray crown; white shoulders; white-spangled black back; white undertail coverts. *Nonbreeding:* grayish brown upperparts; brown-smudged pale underparts; traces of black on belly until September. *In flight:* diagnostic black "wing pits."
Size: *L* 11–13 in; *W* 29 in.
Status: common migrant and locally common winter resident along the coast; locally uncommon migrant and winter resident in inland valleys west of the Cascades.
Habitat: coastal sand- and mudflats, especially at high tide; fields flooded by heavy

rain; roosts on salt marshes, dunes and pastures and above beaches.
Nesting: does not nest in Oregon.
Feeding: run-and-snatch technique to pick prey from the surface; sometimes probes in mud or moist soil; winter diet of mollusks, crustaceans and marine worms, also insects and some plant material.
Voice: rich, plaintive 3-syllable *pee-oo-ee* whistle; flocks may utter mellow 2-note whistles.
Similar Species: *Pacific Golden-Plover* (p. 131) and *American Golden-Plover* (p. 130): gold-flecked upperparts; more black on crown and rump in breeding plumage; buffier head and breast in non-breeding plumage; grayish underwings.
Best Sites: Fern Ridge Reservoir; Nehalem Bay; Tillamook Bay; Coos Bay; Coquille R. estuary.

AMERICAN GOLDEN-PLOVER
Pluvialis dominica

The American Golden-Plover breeds in the Canadian and Alaskan Arctic and migrates along both the Atlantic and Pacific Coasts, as well as along the Mississippi Flyway. It once numbered among the most common shorebirds in the world, but hunting greatly reduced its numbers—reports indicate over 9000 birds being shot in a single day in the 1800s! Since hunting of this species mostly stopped in the early 1900s, populations have recovered considerably. • The breeding plumage, occasionally seen in spring and late-summer migrants, is a fine example of both disruptive and cryptic coloration. Although the bird is boldly marked, the pattern breaks up the bird's outline in the rock, lichen and snow cover of its arctic summer home. • Any golden-plovers seen inland in Oregon are likely to be American Golden-Plovers.

nonbreeding

nonbreeding

ID: straight, black bill; long, blackish legs; gold-, white- and brown-flecked upperparts; dark "cap"; dark-barred rump and tail; folded wings extend beyond tail. *Breeding:* black face and underparts, including undertail coverts; white "S" stripe extends from forehead to shoulders only; female may have white splotching on flanks and undertail coverts. *Nonbreeding:* finely brown-streaked pale gray neck; brown-spotted pale underparts; pale "eyebrow"; fewer, less distinct gold flecks on upperparts. *In flight:* narrow, pointed wings; indistinct pale upperwing stripe.
Size: *L* 11–14 in; *W* 24–26 in.
Status: rare to uncommon fall migrant; very rare spring migrant.
Habitat: pastures, farmlands, golf courses, airports, mudflats and shorelines, especially along the edges of reservoirs, marshes and sewage lagoons; also estuaries and beaches.
Nesting: does not nest in Oregon.
Feeding: run-and-stop foraging technique, snatching insects, mollusks and crustaceans from the ground; also eats spiders, earthworms, berries and seeds.
Voice: soft, melodious *quee, quee-dle* whistle in flight; soft *chu-leek* on the ground; loud *keleep* or *killik-killik* alarm call.
Similar Species: *Pacific Golden-Plover* (p. 131): longer bill and legs; brighter yellow upperpart markings; male has white-barred black flanks and undertail, and female's are pure white in breeding plumage; nonbreeding adult and juvenile are much more golden on back, with yellow-washed face. *Black-bellied Plover* (p. 129): upperparts are black, white and gray in breeding plumage; plainer gray-and-white upperparts in nonbreeding plumage; white undertail coverts; black "wing pits"; stronger upperwing stripe; dark-barred white tail.
Best Sites: Sauvie I.; Fern Ridge Reservoir; Hatfield L. (near Bend); Lower Klamath NWR; Cold Springs NWR.

PACIFIC GOLDEN-PLOVER

Pluvialis fulva

Until recently, both the Pacific Golden-Plover and the American Golden-Plover were known collectively as "Lesser Golden-Plover." Separate species ranking was accorded to each species because there is no evidence of hybridization in the few locations where both breed together in Alaska. • Although both species pass through Oregon each fall, and in smaller numbers in spring, only the Pacific Golden-Plover has been positively identified in winter. The Pacific is the commoner species along the coast but is rarely seen in inland locations. • The theory that the oceanic migratory cycle of what we now know as the Pacific Golden-Plover led sea-faring Polynesians to Hawaii resulted in the bird being portrayed on the 1984 U.S. postage stamp commemorating the 25th anniversary of Hawaii's statehood.

nonbreeding

ID: straight, blackish bill; long, bluish black legs; gold-, white- and brown-flecked upperparts; dark "cap"; dark-barred rump and tail. *Breeding:* black face and underparts; white "S" stripe extends from forehead to shoulders only; black-and-white splotched flanks and undertail coverts; female has more white on "cheeks," flanks and undertail coverts. *Nonbreeding:* finely brown-streaked buffy neck and breast; brown-spotted pale buffy gray underparts; conspicuous dark ear spot. *In flight:* fairly long, pointed wings; indistinct pale upperwing stripe.
Size: *L* 10–11 in; *W* 24 in.
Status: uncommon fall migrant and rare spring migrant along the coast; rare inland and in winter.
Habitat: estuaries; drier tidal mudflats; upper intertidal zone of sandy beaches; coastal salt marshes; inland on fields and large areas of short grass.
Nesting: does not nest in Oregon.
Feeding: pecks and probes for insects and spiders, small mollusks and crustaceans; also eats some berries and may scavenge at carcasses.
Voice: loud, whistled *chu-wee* call; also utters a short *peee* or a longer *deed-leek* alarm call.
Similar Species: *American Golden-Plover* (p. 130): shorter bill and legs; black flanks and undertail coverts on breeding male; folded wings extend well beyond tail. *Black-bellied Plover* (p. 129): upperparts are black, white and gray in breeding plumage; plainer gray-and-white upperparts in nonbreeding plumage; white undertail coverts; black "wing pits"; stronger upperwing stripe; dark-barred white tail.
Best Sites: ponds at Columbia River South Jetty; Bayocean Spit; Siletz Bay; Yaquina Bay; Bandon Marsh.

SNOWY PLOVER

Charadrius alexandrinus

An inconspicuous and often overlooked year-round patron of undisturbed coastal beaches, the Snowy Plover also nests among the barren shorelines of interior alkaline lakes in southern Oregon. • Human development and activity threaten this unassuming little plover, which blends almost unseen into its surrounding environment, moving like a silent ghost over isolated coastal dunes, open sandy beaches and blazing white alkali pans. Attempts by birders to find Snowy Plovers and their well-camouflaged nests and young usually result in disruption of the parents' activities and can lead to the crushing of eggs or death of the young. Snowies should only be sought out in the nonbreeding season, when human disturbances are less harmful.

breeding

ID: light brown upperparts; white underparts; thin, black bill; gray legs; dark eyes; white eye ring, forehead and "collar"; wings shorter than tail. *Breeding:* black patches on forehead, ear and shoulder (dark gray on female). *Nonbreeding:* brown ear and shoulder patches. *In flight:* broad, white upperwing stripe; whitish underwings; gray-tipped, white-edged upper tail.
Size: *L* 6–7 in; *W* 16–17 in.
Status: locally uncommon breeding year-round resident and rare migrant along the coast; locally common breeding summer resident in Harney Co., Lake Co. and, less regularly, in Klamath Co.; *nivosus* ssp. is federal- and state-listed as threatened.
Habitat: sandy beaches, dunes, sandspits, drier areas of tidal estuaries and sand flats and shorelines of alkaline lakes.

Nesting: on bare ground, often near cover of grass or driftwood; shallow scrape is lined with pebbles, shells, grass and other debris; pair incubates 3 dark-spotted pale buff eggs for 26–32 days; young leave the nest within hours of hatching.
Feeding: run-and-stop foraging is supplemented by probing in sand; eats mainly tiny invertebrates; scavenges some items from beached marine mammal carcasses.
Voice: both genders make soft *purrt* calls and utter low, tinkling *ti* alarm notes; male's flight call is a soft, whistled *tur-wheet*.
Similar Species: *Semipalmated Plover* (p. 133): slightly larger; much darker above and on head; full dark breast band; heavier, dark-tipped orange bill; yellowish orange legs; longer wings with less black on underwing edges.
Best Sites: Coos Bay North Spit; Ten Mile Creek Spit; beaches south of Bandon and near Floras; Harney L.; Alvord Basin; Summer L.; L. Abert.

SEMIPALMATED PLOVER

Charadrius semipalmatus

The Semipalmated Plover's varied food choices and habitats have enabled it to expand its range while other plovers have declined in numbers. • During their seasonal long-distance flights, flocks of Semipalmated Plovers routinely touch down on Oregon's shorelines for a brief stopover—or sometimes an extended winter stay. Their feeding methods distinguish them amidst flocks of sandpipers: they dart here and there in short runs interspersed with deliberate pauses or stabbing probes. • One pair successfully raised young in three consecutive years at Malheur National Wildlife Refuge, and another pair has nested at nearby Harney Lake—the world's southernmost breeding record for the species. • The scientific name *semipalmatus* reflects the partial webbing between the toes.

nonbreeding

ID: sandy brown above and white below; dark crown, facial patch and full breast band; stubby, black-tipped orange bill; white forehead spot; dark eyes; yellow eye ring; yellowish orange legs; folded wings extend just beyond tail. *Breeding:* black forecrown extends to black "mask"; complete black breast band, narrowing at neck and throat (less dark on female). *In flight:* longish, pointed wings; broad white upperwing stripe; mainly dark tail.
Size: *L* 7 in; *W* 18–19 in.
Status: common migrant and rare winter resident along the coast; uncommon migrant inland; scarce, irregular nester.
Habitat: drier areas of coastal mudflats and estuaries and upper intertidal beach areas; shorelines of interior lakes, rivers

and marshes; sometimes uses city ponds and sewage lagoons.
Nesting: nests on sand or gravel, usually near extensive salt or brackish marshes; in a depression sparsely lined with vegetation; pair incubates 4 creamy buff eggs, cryptically marked at the larger end, for 23–25 days.
Feeding: run-and-snatch technique; occasional probing; eats bottom-dwelling invertebrates in both salt and fresh water, including crustaceans, worms and mollusks.
Voice: crisp, high-pitched, rising *tu-wee* whistle.
Similar Species: *Snowy Plover* (p. 132): narrow, incomplete breast band; paler upperparts; less distinct facial markings; gray legs; shorter, black bill. *Killdeer* (p. 134): much larger and heavier; longer, heavier, dark bill; 2 black breast bands; red eye ring; pale pink-tinged legs; long tail; rusty rump; more relaxed flight.
Best Sites: coastal sites, including Tillamook Bay and Coos Bay.

133

KILLDEER
Charadrius vociferus

The Killdeer is among North America's most widely distributed shorebirds and certainly the best known. No other shorebird has its combination of double black breast bands and rusty tail, and its boisterous call accurately reflects its name. • Unusual for its far-flung family, the Killdeer often uses habitats many miles from water, including urban ones. Active at any hour, it might be heard calling overhead at night, lured by lights in parking lots and ball fields. • Like many other plovers and some other shorebirds and ducks, the Killdeer has a method of luring intruders away from its nest or young. Feigning injury, one of the pair will drag a wing along the ground and fan its conspicuous tail while its mate utters loud cries—hence *vociferus*, which means "very loud voiced."

ID: pale legs; black bill; white breast with 2 black bands; brown head; white forehead and "eyebrow"; dark eyes; red eye ring; brown back and wings; rusty rump and tail with dark tip; tail projects beyond tips of folded wings. *In flight:* white underwing with dark trailing edge; black outer upperwing with white stripe; unhurried, bouncy, somewhat erratic flight.

Size: *L* 9–11 in; *W* 23–24 in.

Status: common summer resident and migrant; uncommon to locally abundant in winter west of the Cascades; rare to uncommon in winter east of the Cascades.

Habitat: any wet or dry open environment, from gravel to grass, including urban wasteland, anywhere from sea level to mountains; most numerous at lower elevations.

Nesting: on any open ground, such as a shoreline, beach, field or the edge of a gravel road; in a shallow depression, usually unlined but sometimes lined with pebbles, grass or debris; pair incubates 4 dark-blotched pale eggs for 24–28 days; may hatch a 2nd brood.

Feeding: typical plover technique of run-stop-snatch, mainly for insects, but also eats some seeds.

Voice: loud, distinctive *kill-dee kill-dee kill-deer* and variations, including *deer-deer;* high, rapid trilling when nervous or before flight.

Similar Species: *Mountain Plover:* light grayish brown upperparts; white underparts and on throat and face; black at forecrown and ahead of eye in breeding plumage; grayish brown breast; brown center on tail. *Semipalmated Plover* (p. 133): much smaller; single breast band; shorter, 2-toned bill; yellowish orange legs; brown center on tail.

Best Sites: southern Willamette Valley.

BLACK OYSTERCATCHER

Haematopus bachmani

Above the background roar of surf and the cries of gulls, piercing flight calls announce the most conspicuous member of the rocky intertidal community. Whereas other birds will desert the shoreline to roost, feed or nest, the Black Oystercatcher rarely leaves its chosen gravel or rocky shorelines—they provide both feeding and nesting territory for breeding pairs, which tend to return to the same site each year. • The long, narrow, blood red bill is well adapted for prying open the tightly sealed shells of mollusks and other shellfish that constitute this bird's main food supply. • The genus name *Haematopus*, Greek for "blood red eye," refers to Old World species. The species name honors Reverend John Bachman, a close friend of John James Audubon in the 19th century, who first described the bird.

ID: black head, neck and breast and brownish black elsewhere; long, straight, blood red bill; bright yellow eyes; orangy red eye ring; sturdy, pale pink legs; female is slightly heavier, with longer bill. *In flight:* short tail; broad wings; underwing feathers are slightly paler on juvenile.

Size: *L* 16–18 in; *W* 31–32 in.

Status: common year-round coastal resident.

Habitat: rocky shorelines and islands; sea stacks; breakwaters, jetties and reefs; bathes at freshwater outfalls.

Nesting: on bare ground or rocks well above the high-water mark; nest is sometimes lined with pebbles and shells; pair incubates 1–3 dark-marked buff eggs for 26–28 days; pair tends the young until fledging at 38–40 days and then moves them to remote feeding sites for winter.

Feeding: forages at low tide on mussel beds, prying open shells; pries limpets, barnacles and other shellfish from rocks and cavities; also eats sea urchins, marine worms, crabs and other invertebrates; rarely eats oysters.

Voice: loud, piercing *wheep* or *wik* repetitions are usually given in flight; longer series of notes, accelerating into a frantic, uneven trill, is given in spring or in territorial disputes.

Similar Species: none.

Best Sites: Ecola SP; Tillamook Bay (entrance); Boiler Bay SP; Yaquina Bay (entrance); Seal Rock SP; Shore Acres SP; Cape Blanco SP.

BLACK-NECKED STILT

Himantopus mexicanus

A bird of contrasts, the Black-necked Stilt is black above and white below, and it wades with dignity on its long, pink legs along the margin of a smelly sewage lagoon or a stark, white, alkaline lakeshore. • All semblance of dignity disappears if an intruder approaches a nest and agitated adults scream at the would-be predator. Soon afterward, the adult Black-necked Stilts return to taking turns sheltering their eggs from the warmth of the hot sun. Some individuals may even be observed wetting their belly feathers to cool off their offspring during their next stint of incubation duty. • Border disputes commonly erupt between two neighboring pairs. Unlike American Avocets, their colonial-nesting colleagues, Black-necked Stilts are fiercely territorial.

ID: very long, orangy pink legs; long, needlelike black bill; black on back, nape and crown extends around eyes on otherwise white face; red eyes; short, white "eyebrow"; white flanks and underparts. *Male:* black parts are glossy. *Female:* black parts are brownish. *In flight:* white triangle from back onto tail; extremely pointed dark wings with white "wing pits"; legs extend far beyond tail.
Size: *L* 14–15 in; *W* 29 in.
Status: locally common breeding summer resident east of the Cascades; rare in western Oregon; recent very local breeder in the Willamette Valley.
Habitat: *Breeding:* edges of salt ponds, sewage lagoons and shallow, inland wetlands. *In migration:* may visit shallow lagoons with muddy shores.

Nesting: in a shallow depression made in short, emergent stubble over water, or on a dike, island or mound with sparse vegetation; pair incubates 3–4 heavily dark-marked drab brown or gray eggs for 24–29 days; pair tends the young until independent at about 21 days.
Feeding: picks prey, mostly aquatic invertebrates, from the water's surface or from the bottom.
Voice: loud, shrill *yip yap yip yap* at the nest site; also utters *kik-a-rik* or *kek kek kek kek* flight calls.
Similar Species: *American Avocet* (p. 137): bulkier; shorter, bluish legs; upturned black bill; peach-colored head and neck on breeding bird but otherwise light gray; broad wings with striking black-and-white upperwing pattern.
Best Sites: Lower Klamath NWR; Summer Lake WMA; L. Abert; Burns–Hines area; Malheur NWR.

AMERICAN AVOCET

Recurvirostra americana

The American Avocet, unlike avocets native to other parts of the world, takes on a characteristic peach glow on its head, neck and upper breast in early spring, making it one of North America's most elegant birds. • Avocets can be identified at any season, even at a distance, by their habit of whisking their long, upward-curved bills back and forth through shallow water when feeding. The tip of the bill is so sensitive that it will recoil at the slightest touch. Female avocets are slightly smaller than the males and have shorter, more curved bills, enabling them to locate different aquatic prey than their mates. • Avocets don't always conduct their business in a quiet, controlled manner—the sometimes-noisy parents are noted for their complicated array of both deceptive and aggressive anti-predator behaviors.

nonbreeding

breeding

ID: long, slim, upturned, black bill; long, light bluish gray legs; black wings with broad white patches; white underparts; dark eyes. *Breeding:* peach-colored head, neck and upper breast. *Nonbreeding:* light gray replaces peach. *In flight:* white back with black-and-white patterned upperwings; white underwings with large, dark tips; long legs extend beyond tail.

Size: *L* 17–18 in; *W* 30–31 in.

Status: locally abundant breeding summer resident in Klamath, Lake, Harney and Malheur Counties and locally uncommon elsewhere east of the Cascades in summer; rare in western Oregon in summer.

Habitat: shallow alkaline ponds and depressions; mudflats; marshes with short vegetation; sewage lagoons.

Nesting: semi-colonial; along a dried mud-flat or exposed shoreline, in an open area or on a mound or island; in a shallow depression, usually with sparse vegetation; pair incubates 3–4 dark-marked dusky eggs for 22–29 days.

Feeding: scythes bill through shallow water (male goes deeper) to pick up small fish and crustaceans, aquatic insects and sometimes seeds; sometimes wades or swims into deeper water and pecks, plunges, lunges or tips up.

Voice: noisy aerial pursuits near the nest; melodic *kleet* repetitions are usually loud and shrill.

Similar Species: *Black-necked Stilt* (p. 136): slimmer; straight bill; mostly white body with black pattern on head, black nape and largely black back and wings; orangy pink legs.

Best Sites: Lower Klamath NWR; Summer Lake WMA; L. Abert; Burns–Hines area; Malheur NWR.

137

GREATER YELLOWLEGS

Tringa melanoleuca

The Greater Yellowlegs is the most widespread North American shorebird of a group once collectively termed "tattlers" or "tell-tales"—around the world, these species serve as sentinels among mixed flocks of shorebirds. At the first sign of danger, a Greater Yellowlegs begins calling, bobbing its head and moving slowly away from any perceived threat, eventually retreating into deeper water or taking flight, still uttering its three- or four-note warning. This loud, whistled alarm helps distinguish the Greater Yellowlegs from the smaller Lesser Yellowlegs, one of the first challenges to face a novice birdwatcher in Oregon. • The heavy black streaking and barring on northward-migrating birds in breeding plumage seen here in March and April explains the species name *melanoleuca*, which is Greek for "black-and-white."

nonbreeding

ID: long, yellow legs; long, slender, slightly upcurved, dark bill; white eye ring. *Breeding:* white-spangled brownish black back and wings; finely dark-streaked white head, neck and upper breast; dark-barred white lower breast and flanks. *Nonbreeding:* white-speckled brownish gray upperparts and lighter-streaked neck; white belly and flanks. *In flight:* dark grayish upperwings and paler underwings; dark-streaked white tail.

Size: *L* 13–15 in; *W* 27–28 in.

Status: common migrant; rare winter resident in western Oregon; very rare east of the Cascades in winter; has irregularly bred in Wallowa Co.

Habitat: *Breeding:* bogs, alluvial wetlands, sedge meadows and beaver ponds. *In migration:* almost any wetland habitat, including river shorelines and flooded fields.

Nesting: on the ground, usually on a ridge near an open bog or muskeg; concealed depression is sparsely lined with leaves and moss; female incubates 4 brown-marked buff eggs for 23–25 days; pair loosely tends young until fledging at 18–20 days.

Feeding: wades in water and snatches prey from the surface or just below or probes into soft mud; eats mostly aquatic invertebrates, but also takes small fish and frogs plus some seeds and berries.

Voice: quick, whistled *tew-tew-tew* series (sometimes 4 notes); soft, single notes possible when feeding.

Similar Species: *Lesser Yellowlegs* (p. 139): smaller; shorter bill; legs extend farther beyond tail in flight; softer, typically 1–2 note calls. *Willet* (p. 141): stockier; stouter bill; grayish legs; flashy black-and-white wing markings in flight; different calls.

Best Sites: *Summer:* Downie L. *Winter:* near Coos Bay.

LESSER YELLOWLEGS

Tringa flavipes

A daintier, gentler version of its larger cousin, the Lesser Yellowlegs neverthe-less appears considerably larger than the small sandpipers with which it readily mixes. It is shorter-billed, longer-legged and less stocky than any accompanying dowitchers. • All but a few of the Lesser Yellowlegs seen in Oregon are merely passing through on their way to nest sites in boreal woodlands and tundra in northern Canada and Alaska or to wintering grounds along Gulf and South American shorelines. Northbound spring migrants appear in early April and con-tinue to pass through until about mid-May, with the first southbound adults return-ing in late June. Juveniles begin to appear in mid-August, and most birds leave Oregon by early October. Stragglers appear until late November, and, rarely, a few immatures may overwinter.

nonbreeding

ID: long, yellow legs; slender, dark bill slightly longer than head; white eye ring and "eye-brow"; folded wings extend well beyond tail. *Breeding:* white-spangled brownish black back and wing coverts; fine, dense, dark streaking on white head, neck and upper breast; lim-ited dark barring on white lower breast and flanks. *Nonbreeding:* white-speckled brownish gray upperparts; fine pale brownish gray streaking on white head, neck and breast; white belly and flanks. *In flight:* grayish upperwings and paler under-wings; dark-streaked white tail.
Size: *L* 10–11 in; *W* 23–24 in.
Status: uncommon spring migrant, common fall migrant and very rare winter resident.

Habitat: equally likely in freshwater and saltwater habitats; lake, pond and marsh edges, flooded fields and wet meadows, mudflats and coastal estuaries.
Nesting: does not nest in Oregon.
Feeding: makes quick probes into shallow water and mud and scythes bill back and forth for aquatic invertebrates, small fish and tadpoles; snatches airborne insects and picks prey off vegetation.
Voice: typically gives a high-pitched pair of *tew* or *tip* notes; rising, trilled *kleet* alarm call.
Similar Species: *Greater Yellowlegs* (p. 138): larger; much longer, slightly upturned bill; more dark barring on flanks in breeding plumage; more ringing alarm call with more notes; legs extend less beyond tail in flight.
Best Sites: *Winter:* along the coast; interior valleys west of the Cascades.

139

SOLITARY SANDPIPER

Tringa solitaria

The somewhat reclusive Solitary Sandpiper is rarely seen in flocks, but single birds may forage close together. This sandpiper's nesting strategy remained a mystery until someone discovered shorebird eggs in an abandoned songbird nest in a tree. Even though the closely related yellowlegs regularly perch in trees, the Solitary Sandpiper is the only North American shorebird to take the next logical step. • Shorebirds lay relatively large eggs that are incubated long enough for the young to grow body feathers before they hatch—such highly developed hatchlings, known as precocial young, must learn quickly to fend for themselves. (The altricial young of songbirds hatch naked; they stay in the nest for concealment and protection until they can fly.) Once hatchling Solitary Sandpipers are lured down to the ground by the waiting parents, they act like typical shorebird young.

breeding

breeding

ID: white-spotted dark back and wings; white eye ring; dusky bill; greenish yellow legs; white underparts. *Breeding:* darker upperparts; fine dark streaking on head and neck extends onto upper breast. *Nonbreeding* and *juvenile:* grayish brown upperparts; brown-streaked head and neck. *In flight:* center of tail and rump are dark; dark-barred outer tail; unique, butterfly-like flight close to the water's surface.

Size: *L* 8–9 in; *W* 21–22 in.

Status: rare to uncommon spring and fall migrant; a few pairs may have bred in the central Cascades, but no nests have been found.

Habitat: *Breeding:* higher-elevation lakes and ponds. *In migration:* small wet or muddy areas.

Nesting: in a tree, usually in an abandoned robin, thrush or other songbird nest; female incubates 4 purple-blotched pale green eggs for 23–24 days as male stands guard; hatchlings clamber or jump down to the ground; pair tends the young.

Feeding: gleans at the water's surface, probes in water and soft mud and stirs up food with its feet; eats aquatic and terrestrial invertebrates.

Voice: high, thin *peet-wheet* and clipped *plik*.

Similar Species: *Spotted Sandpiper* (p. 143): dark eye line and white "eyebrow"; dark spotting on under- and upperparts (most conspicuous on breast), orange legs and dark-tipped orange bill in breeding plumage; unmarked brown upperparts, white underparts, throat and breast (brown-smudged at edges) and yellowish legs in nonbreeding plumage.

Best Sites: *Summer:* Gold Lake Bog in Lane Co. *In migration:* small freshwater wetland habitats throughout Oregon.

WILLET

Catoptrophorus semipalmatus

Just as "you can't judge a book by its cover," you certainly can't judge a bird solely by its initial appearance. If you spot a Willet walking slowly along a wetland shore, there is little to indicate its spirited nature. This stocky shorebird cuts a rather staid, dull, gray figure on the ground, but the instant it begins to take flight it becomes a whirling dervish of flashing black-and-white wings and loud, rhythmic *pill-will-willet!* calls. The bold wing flashes may serve as a warning signal to other shorebirds or may intimidate predators during a parent's dive-bombing defense of its young. • The common name imitates the Willet's calls, and the genus name *Catoptrophorus* is Latin for "mirror-bearing," an obvious reference to the genus's flashy white wing patches.

breeding

breeding

ID: dark-tipped bluish gray bill; bluish gray legs; light belly; white tail with dark terminal barring.
Breeding: buff neck and breast with dark streaks; wavy-barred flanks; dark blotches and bars on gray back and wings.
Nonbreeding: lightly mottled, dull gray upperparts; white throat, belly and under-tail; gray breast. *In flight:* distinctive black-and-white wing pattern.
Size: *L* 14–16 in; *W* 25–26 in.
Status: common breeding summer resident in southeastern and south-central Oregon; very rare to rare spring and early fall migrant throughout Oregon but most prevalent along the coast; rare winter resident along the coast.
Habitat: *Breeding:* wet meadows; edges of freshwater marshes and lakes. *In migration:* wet fields; shores of marshes, ponds, lakes,

estuaries and lagoons; tidal flats, beaches, rocky coastal reefs and breakwaters.
Nesting: semi-colonial; shallow depression in tall grass is lined with finer grass; pair incubates 4 brown-blotched, dull gray or olive eggs for 22–29 days; pair tends young for up to 21 days.
Feeding: walks in shallow water, probes muddy areas and gleans the ground for insects, worms, crustaceans, mollusks and fish; occasionally eats shoots and seeds.
Voice: loud, rolling *will-will willet, will-will-willet;* monotonous repeated *wik* alarm call reminiscent of Wilson's Snipe or Northern Flicker.
Similar Species: *Nonbreeding Hudsonian Godwit:* grayer overall with darker crown; longer, slightly upcurved, dark-tipped orangy bill; longer, black legs; black tail; narrower white stripe on more pointed wing with unique black covert.
Best Sites: *Summer:* Malheur, Harney, Lake and Klamath Counties; Stinking L. (Malheur NWR).

141

WANDERING TATTLER

Heteroscelus incanus

Named for its migratory prowess, the Wandering Tattler remains unknown to most Oregon residents. Its breeding sites were unknown until the first nest was discovered on a gravel bar alongside a Yukon stream in 1912; others were later found in northeastern Siberia, Alaska and northwestern British Columbia. • Many birds head out to sea and winter on distant shores, but a small number hug the Pacific coastline and linger on rocky headlands, jetties and tide pools before continuing on as far south as Peru and as far west as eastern New Guinea and Australia. • The Wandering Tattler tends to stand and walk in a horizontal posture, bobbing its tail and occasionally its head. The stout legs and bill are likely adaptations to its favored summer nest sites in fast-flowing streams and winter feeding habitats along wave-washed rocks.

breeding

nonbreeding

ID: shortish, stout yellowish legs; stout, dark bill; dark eye line; unmarked gray upperparts. *Breeding:* dense, blackish barring on head and underparts. *Nonbreeding* and *juvenile:* underparts gray except for white belly and undertail coverts. *In flight:* 2-toned gray wings; gray tail; low, flicking flight.
Size: *L* 10–11 in; *W* 25–26 in.
Status: common migrant and very rare in winter along the coast; very rare elsewhere.
Habitat: rocky coastlines, gravel beaches, jetties and breakwaters; rarely on lower portions of sandy beaches among freshly washed-up seaweed or on tidal mudflats.
Nesting: does not nest in Oregon.
Feeding: creeps deliberately among intertidal rocks and seaweed, picking off crustaceans, mollusks, marine worms and other invertebrates.
Voice: generally silent; short 1-pitch series of rapid-fire whistles *lididididi* or a crisp *klee-ik* in alarm.
Similar Species: *Willet* (p. 141): larger; paler and browner; longer, bluish gray legs; rarely seen among rocks. *Surfbird* (p. 149): chunkier; browner; stubby, dark-tipped yellow bill; white wings and tail in flight. *Black Turnstone* (p. 148): black head, breast and upperparts; short, dark bill; complex white pattern on back, wings and tail in flight. *Nonbreeding Rock Sandpiper* (p. 157): slightly smaller; slightly downcurved bill; dark breast; dark-flecked belly and sides; white upperwing stripe in flight.
Best Sites: Columbia River South Jetty; Barview Jetty (Tillamook Bay); Seal Rock SP; Shore Acres SP; Harris Beach SP (Brookings); rocky shore near Bandon's south jetty.

SPOTTED SANDPIPER

Actitis macularia

Apart from the ubiquitous Killdeer, the Spotted Sandpiper is perhaps North America's best-known and most easily identified shorebird. Its characteristic "teeter-totter" behavior, stiff-winged flight and large, dark breast spots all serve to make it instantly recognizable in summer. • The Spotted Sandpiper is among a tiny minority of birds that have reversed the typical gender roles. As with phalaropes, the females arrive on the breeding grounds first, stake out territories and then go about attracting mates. A large female may mate with up to four males, each of which has the job of incubating her eggs and caring for the young (but some females are loyal to one mate and help raise their chicks). The male's relatively high level of prolactin—a pituitary hormone known for its promotion of parental care—helps ensure his follow-through.

breeding

nonbreeding

ID: tail bobs distinctively and extends well beyond folded wings; dark eye line; white "eyebrow." *Breeding:* white underparts are heavily dark-spotted, especially in female; yellowish orange legs; dark-tipped orange bill; white undertail coverts. *Nonbreeding:* brown back; white throat, neck, belly and breast (brown-smudged at edges). *In flight:* short white streak on dark trailing edge of upperwing; gray-patterned white underwing with dark trailing edge; distinctive, flickering flight with short glides close to water.
Size: *L* 7–8 in; *W* 14–15 in.
Status: locally common breeding summer resident and migrant; rare winter resident, mostly along the coast, but also along the Columbia R. and in western inland valleys.
Habitat: beaches and gravel bars along freshwater streams, lakes, ponds and estuaries; wet meadow margins.

Nesting: among logs or under bushes, usually well above the water's edge; shallow depression is lined with grass; male, occasionally with some help, incubates 4 brown-blotched buff eggs for 20–24 days and tends the young.
Feeding: picks and gleans along shorelines for invertebrates; occasionally snatches flying insects from the air.
Voice: sharp, crisp *eat-wheat, eat-wheat, wheat-wheat-wheat-wheat.*
Similar Species: *Solitary Sandpiper* (p. 140): white-speckled back and wings; streaked upper breast and white underparts year-round; greenish yellow legs; dark-barred white outer tail. *Lesser Yellowlegs* (p. 139): larger; longer, bright yellow legs; slimmer, all-dark bill; more upright; white-speckled back, streaked breast and white belly year-round; white upper tail; deeper wingbeats.
Best Sites: wetland habitats throughout Oregon. *Winter:* coastal estuaries.

WHIMBREL

Numenius phaeopus

Whimbrels nest across the northern latitudes of North America, Europe and Asia. They spend their winters on the shores of six continents, with some migrants undertaking nonstop ocean flights of up to 2500 miles. • Unlike its smaller relative, the probably-extinct Eskimo Curlew (*N. borealis*), the Whimbrel withstood the ravages of 19th-century market hunters largely because of its more wary nature. • Heard long before they come into sight, Whimbrels fly in V-formations and keep in touch with almost continuous whistles—one of the truly wild sounds of fall and spring. Flocks spread out to feed and often forage on the drier parts of mudflats, which most other shorebirds avoid. • The genus name for curlews comes from the Greek words *neos* and *mene*, meaning "new moon"—a clear reference to the crescent-shaped bills.

ID: long, down-curved, dark bill (lower mandible has pinkish base from late fall through winter); stocky, bluish legs; dark-striped head with lighter central strip; dark eyes; partial white eye ring; pale-dappled grayish brown back and upperwings; pale, buff-washed underparts; brown-streaked head, neck and breast; brown-barred flanks; brown-barred tail. *Siberian race:* rare; white lower back patch; whiter underparts; grayish barring on underwings. *In flight:* brown-barred buff wing linings; gray flight feathers.
Size: *L* 17–18 in; *W* 31–32 in.
Status: common migrant, uncommon summer lingerer and rare winter resident along the coast; very rare inland, mostly in spring.

Habitat: various coastal habitats, including beaches, mudflats, estuaries, rocky shores, saltwater marshes, reefs and breakwaters; also uses pastures, flooded fields, freshwater marshes and coastal lake and river margins.
Nesting: does not nest in Oregon.
Feeding: picks from the ground or probes just under the surface in mud or vegetation; eats mainly marine invertebrates, especially small crabs, marine worms and mollusks.
Voice: incoming flocks utter a distinctive, easily imitated, rippling *bibibibibibibi*.
Similar Species: *Long-billed Curlew* (p. 145): larger; much longer, pink-based bill; distinctly buffy underparts; warm cinnamon wing linings and upper flight feathers; unstriped crown. *Willet* (p. 141): smaller; much grayer; shorter, straight bill; gray crown; distinctive black-and-white wing pattern in flight.
Best Sites: Tillamook Bay; Siletz Bay; Yaquina Bay; Coos Bay.

LONG-BILLED CURLEW

Numenius americanus

North America's largest sandpiper, the Long-billed Curlew comes equipped with a downcurved bill that may be more than 7 inches long on some females. The bill is used as a dexterous tool to pick grasshoppers and beetles from dense prairie grasslands or extract deeply buried aquatic invertebrates from soft mud. • Male curlews engage in spectacular displays over their nesting territory, uttering loud, ringing calls while fluttering high and then gliding down in an undulating flight. • Long-billed Curlews breed on grasslands often with scattered lakes and marshes, habitat found largely in southeastern and south-central Oregon. The future of the Long-billed Curlew is largely tied to the adoption of conservative range and grassland management strategies designed to provide enough grassland habitat for nesting.

ID: very long, downcurved bill with pink base; buff-brown underparts; mottled brown upperparts; streaked neck and breast; streaked crown; partial dark eye stripe; pale eye ring; long, bluish legs. *In flight:* cinnamon wing linings; barred rufous brown upperwing flight feathers; toes extend just beyond tail.
Size: *L* 20–26 in; *W* 34–35 in.
Status: locally common breeding summer resident and migrant east of the Cascades; rare migrant and both summer and winter lingerer, mostly along the coast; federal species of concern and state-listed as sensitive.
Habitat: *Breeding:* grasslands often interspersed with freshwater lakes and marshes. *In migration:* tidal mudflats, estuaries and saltwater marshes; grasslands and pastures.
Nesting: on the ground in the open, often near a rock, bush or other small landmark;

slight depression is sparsely lined with grass and other debris; pair incubates 4 brown-spotted olive or buff eggs for 27–30 days; young fledge in 32–45 days.
Feeding: probes tall grass for insects, especially grasshoppers and beetles; probes shorelines and coastal mudflats for invertebrates; may take eggs, nestlings and berries.
Voice: most common call is a loud, whistling *cur-lee cur-lee cur-lee;* also gives shorter whistles; male's display song is low whistle series with slurred crescendo.
Similar Species: *Whimbrel* (p. 144): smaller; shorter bill; dark and pale crown stripes; unmarked pale belly; plain, brown wings. *Marbled Godwit* (p. 146): smaller; plain orange upperwing flight feathers; shorter bill slightly upturned toward tip; dark legs.
Best Sites: *Summer:* Lower Klamath NWR; Summer Lake WMA; Warner Valley; Logan Valley; Burns–Hines area; Malheur NWR. *In migration:* Yaquina Bay; Pony Slough (Coos Bay).

MARBLED GODWIT

Limosa fedoa

The Marbled Godwit is generally a scarce migrant in Oregon, though it is common on Willapa Bay, Washington and just to the south on the California coast. Some Oregon migrants go up the coast to Alaska to nest, while others migrate across southeastern Oregon to nest in Montana or the Canadian prairie provinces. • The Marbled Godwit's large size, warm brown color and long, pink-based, slightly upturned bill makes it easy to recognize. Unlike the other godwit species that occur in North America, the Marbled Godwit has a summer dress that is not much different from what it wears the rest of the year.

breeding

breeding

ID: long neck; long, dark legs; long, slightly upturned, dark-tipped pinkish bill; buff brown overall; dark-and-light-patterned back; pale tan underparts; dark eyes; fairly noticeable dark crown and eye stripes. *Breeding:* fine dark barring on underparts; brown streaks on neck. *In flight:* unbarred cinnamon underwing; unmarked orangy buff secondaries; darker leading edge on upperwing.
Size: *L* 16–20 in; *W* 29–30 in.
Status: uncommon migrant and rare winter resident along the coast; rare migrant inland.
Habitat: coastal estuaries, salt marshes, lagoons, sandy beaches, wet fields and lake margins.

Nesting: does not nest in Oregon.
Feeding: walks slowly and probes deeply in soft substrates for polychaete worms, small bivalve mollusks, crabs and earthworms.
Voice: unique resonant, anxious, gull-like *ka-rek* cries.
Similar Species: *Long-billed Curlew* (p. 145): larger; longer, downcurved bill; bluish gray legs; barred rufous brown upperwing flight feathers. *Hudsonian Godwit* and *Bar-tailed Godwit:* breeding females are similar to nonbreeding and juvenile Marbled Godwits but with underwings mostly gray or black. *Dowitchers* (pp. 159–60): much smaller; stockier; long, straight, dark bills; greenish legs; white back patch; grayish underwing with light trailing edge.
Best Sites: Coquille R. estuary; Siletz Bay; Coos Bay; Yaquina Bay.

RUDDY TURNSTONE

Arenaria interpres

Although most people get barely a glimpse into the life of a Ruddy Turnstone, something about this bird screams "individualist." Perhaps it's the harlequin spring markings that are gone when the flocks return in early fall, or maybe it's the foraging behavior that sees it dashing past static sandpipers to poke into every nook and cranny, or it could be the flashy wing and tail markings as it flies. • The Ruddy Turnstone has among the most widely separated summer and winter ranges of any bird species, breeding in the arctic tundra of North America and Eurasia and wintering in tropical and temperate habitats well into the southern hemisphere. • As their name suggests, turnstones find food by flipping over pebbles, shells, driftwood and other objects to find invertebrates, exploiting a niche unused by other shorebirds.

breeding

nonbreeding

ID: white belly; U-shaped "bib" curves up to shoulders; short, tapered, black bill. *Breeding:* orangy red legs; ruddy upperparts; black bands on upper and lower back; black-and-white face; dark-streaked crown; black "collar." *Nonbreeding:* yellowish orange legs; ruddy areas are replaced with brown and mottled with buff and white; dusky brown head and breast markings. *In flight:* unmistakable pattern of red (or brown), black and white bands on upperwings, back and tail; white underwings with dark trailing edges.
Size: *L* 9–10 in; *W* 21 in.
Status: common migrant and rare winter resident along the coast; very rare migrant inland.
Habitat: sand or cobble beaches with pebbles, shells and abundant wrack and wave-tossed debris; estuarine mudflats, tide pools and breakwaters.
Nesting: does not nest in Oregon.
Feeding: forages by gleaning from the ground or probing in mud and sand or under dislodged objects; takes mostly invertebrates, but will eat carrion, moss, fish eggs and discarded human food.
Voice: clear, rattling, staccato *cut-a-cut* alarm call and lower, repeated contact notes.
Similar Species: *Black Turnstone* (p. 148): black upperparts; whitish edges accent back and wing feathers; more hectic, higher-pitched calls; similar upperwing pattern is all black and white. *Surfbird* (p. 149): bulkier; yellow legs; stout, dark-tipped, yellowish orange bill; streaky, grayish head, black-spotted flanks and paler pinkish brown back in breeding plumage; nonbreeding plumage is mostly plain gray.
Best Sites: rocky shorelines; Columbia River South Jetty; Yaquina Bay; Seal Rock SP; Bandon Marsh.

BLACK TURNSTONE

Arenaria melanocephala

The aptly named Black Turnstone does much of its foraging by probing and flipping over small, loose objects to expose concealed food items. This visual feeder moves slowly over rocks to dislodge prey, including barnacles, which it hammers or pries open to extract the soft parts. • Black Turnstones prefer rocky habitats, which they share with Black Oystercatchers, Surfbirds and Rock Sandpipers, but they also occur in small numbers on sand beaches and mudflats, often with Ruddy Turnstones. Unlike Ruddy Turnstones, Black Turnstones have a fairly constant plumage year-round. • Flock size is usually small, and individuals always show a certain amount of aggression toward each other and to other species. • The Greek-derived species name *melanocephala* means "black head."

nonbreeding

ID: black upperparts with whitish feather edges; black head and breast; white belly; brownish or blackish orange legs; short, tapered black bill. *Breeding:* white "eyebrow" and "teardrop" in front of eye. *In flight:* distinctive black-and-white pattern on wings, back and tail.

Size: *L* 9 in; *W* 21 in.

Status: common migrant and winter resident along the coast; vagrant inland.

Habitat: rocky shorelines, breakwaters, jetties and reefs; may also visit beaches with seaweed wracks as well as mudflats, gravel bars and temporary ponds.

Nesting: does not nest in Oregon.

Feeding: forages on rocks or other substrates; pries open shells or hammers them apart; flips over pebbles and other items to find food; eats mostly crustaceans and mollusks such as barnacles and limpets.

Voice: shrill, high-pitched *skirrr* call turns into chatter as flock erupts into flight.

Similar Species: *Ruddy Turnstone* (p. 147): legs clearly orange; ruddy back and wing bars and distinctive black markings on head and breast in breeding plumage; light-mottled brownish upperparts and head in nonbreeding plumage; lower-pitched calls. *Surfbird* (p. 149): larger; mostly gray upperparts; dark-tipped yellow bill; yellowish legs; back and wing coverts all gray or with pinkish brown; black- or gray-spotted flanks. *Wandering Tattler* (p. 142): slimmer; all-gray upperparts, wings and tail; white belly; dark-barred underparts in breeding plumage; longer bill; teeters and bobs as it feeds.

Best Sites: Columbia River South Jetty; Barview Jetty (Tillamook Bay); Boiler Bay SP; Newport South Jetty; Seal Rock SP; Shore Acres SP; Coquille Point.

SURFBIRD

Aphriza virgata

Wreathed in the mist from another breaking Pacific roller, a Surfbird treks slowly but surely through a mix of tide pools and seaweed-covered rocks until a larger wave forces it to take off. At this point, what appeared to have been three or four birds suddenly transforms into a much larger flock of two dozen or more birds hidden in the backdrop of dark and glistening seaweed and mussels encrusting the boulders. In its tight foraging flocks, the Surfbird occasionally appears by the hundreds at favored feeding sites. • The Surfbird has the longest wintering range of any North American shorebird breeder—more than 10,000 miles from Kodiak Island, Alaska, to Chile's southernmost peninsula, and yet it never strays far above the tide line during this period. When not feeding, it frequents rocky shores or jetties, staying close to the waterline.

nonbreeding

ID: sturdy, yellow-based bill with dark tip; mainly dull gray overall; white belly; yellow legs; dark eyes. *Breeding:* black-marked pinkish brown wing coverts; blackish spots and chevrons on flanks and lower breast; more fine, white streaking on head. *Nonbreeding* and *juvenile:* gray-spotted flanks. *In flight:* white stripe on gray upper wing; black-tipped white tail; white underwings with gray edges.
Size: *L* 9–10 in; *W* 26 in.
Status: common coastal migrant and winter resident.
Habitat: wave-washed rocky shorelines, including ledges, reefs and pinnacles; rarely on sand beaches or intertidal mudflats.
Nesting: does not nest in Oregon.

Feeding: pries young mussels, barnacles and limpets from rocks to eat whole, later regurgitating shells; picks invertebrates, such as snails, from intertidal rocks.
Voice: generally silent; soft, single, high-pitched notes and a *yif-yif-yif* flight call; feeding flocks may utter turnstonelike nasal chatter.
Similar Species: *Black Turnstone* (p. 148) and *Ruddy Turnstone* (p. 147): slightly smaller; plumage more striking; pointier, darker bills; orange or dark orange legs; white-striped back in flight; much noisier. *Nonbreeding Rock Sandpiper* (p. 157): longer, thinner, darker, slightly downcurved bill; dusky greenish legs; white tail with gray center on top.
Best Sites: Columbia River South Jetty; Barview Jetty (Tillamook Bay); Boiler Bay SP; Newport South Jetty; Seal Rock SP; Shore Acres SP; Coquille Point; Bandon's south jetty area.

RED KNOT

Calidris canutus

S urely the Cinderella of shorebirds, the Red Knot, though lost in a mass of brown and gray sandpipers in fall, is an absolute knockout during its brief spring appearance. Among its usual tidal-flat neighbors, only the dowitchers undergo a similar transformation. Whereas the Red Knot's dull nonbreeding plumage blends into the uniform grays and browns of mudflats and sandy beaches, its bright summer wardrobe matches rusty-tinged arctic grasses, sedges, shrubs and wildflowers. • Red Knots feeding together in tightly packed knots at a few favored spots along Oregon's coast in spring may have started as far south as the shores of South America. • The scientific species name refers to King Canute, who commanded the tide to halt, something a flock of Red Knots may seem to be doing on its shoreline food patrol.

breeding

nonbreeding

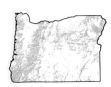

ID: blackish yellow legs; straight, headlength dark bill; dark eyes. *Breeding:* largely rufous orange head, neck and underparts; grayish upperparts flecked with dark brown and chestnut; dark barring on white undertail coverts. *Nonbreeding:* pale brownish gray upperparts; white underparts with buffy wash; faint brown streaks on breast; some brownish gray barring on flanks; dark eye line.

Size: *L* 10–11 in; *W* 23 in.

Status: uncommon to common spring migrant, locally uncommon fall migrant and very rare winter resident along the coast; very rare migrant inland.

Habitat: almost entirely coastal; prefers tidal and estuary margins; also in saltwater marshes with tidal channels and sandy beaches.

Nesting: does not nest in Oregon.

Feeding: probes in sand and mud; occasionally pecks at washed-up seaweed; eats invertebrates and various plant materials; may join Ruddy Turnstones to pick at beach carcasses.

Voice: usually silent; utters occasionally repeated low *knut* reminiscent of its name.

Similar Species: *Nonbreeding Surfbird* (p. 149): yellow legs; stubby, dark-tipped yellow bill; gray-spotted flanks; dark-tipped white tail; more contrast on underwings. *Nonbreeding Wandering Tattler* (p. 142): yellow legs; more uniformly gray upperparts, head, breast, wings and tail.

Best Sites: Tillamook Bay (especially in mid-May); Coquille R. estuary; Coos Bay.

SANDERLING

Calidris alba

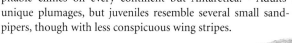

Anyone who has spent time on a sandy beach from very late summer to late spring knows Sanderlings. Flocks scamper about like wheeled mechanical toys as they zigzag up and down the beach following every wave. Resembling fledgling surfers having fun, they are after tiny crustaceans of the fluid–sand zone. If a wave catches a flock unprepared, it will rise in unison. Sanderlings also peck and probe with other sandpipers on sand- and mudflats. After feeding, the birds slowly reassemble in densely packed roosting flocks, seemingly asleep but ready to escape at any disturbance. Sometimes flocks whirl about like gusts of giant snowflakes. • The Sanderling breeds across the Arctic and overwinters on beaches in more hospitable climes on every continent but Antarctica. • Adults have unique plumages, but juveniles resemble several small sandpipers, though with less conspicuous wing stripes.

nonbreeding

nonbreeding

ID: black bill and legs; white underparts. *Breeding:* rusty orange head and breast with dark spots and streaks (much grayer female has hints of rufous); rufous-marked grayish brown upperparts; dark centered, pale-edged feathers on and near back. *Nonbreeding:* pale gray upperparts; small black shoulder patch. *In flight:* gray upperwing with darker edges and conspicuous white stripe; gray-edged white underwing.
Size: *L* 7–8 in; *W* 16–17 in.
Status: abundant migrant, often throughout most of summer (except possibly late June to mid-July), and common winter resident along coast; rare to uncommon migrant inland; rare winter resident in the Willamette Valley.
Habitat: sand beaches, but also estuaries, rocky shores, wet grassy fields and shorelines of large reservoirs.

Nesting: does not nest in Oregon.
Feeding: runs and pecks along the line of advancing and retreating waves; eats various coastal invertebrates, especially sand crabs, marine worms, amphipods, insects and small mollusks.
Voice: easily distinguished sharp *kip* flight call.
Similar Species: *Western Sandpiper* (p. 152): smaller; breeding bird has black-tipped scapular feathers and dark-spotted breast and flanks, with rufous restricted to crown, ear patch and sides of back; lightly streaked upper breast area on nonbreeding bird. *Semipalmated Sandpiper:* smaller; darker "cap" and mark in front of eye; lightly brown-marked breast; "scaly" upperparts; little rufous in breeding plumage.
Best Sites: Columbia R. mouth; Sunset Beach, Clatsop Co.; Tillamook Bay; Yaquina Bay; Florence; Coos Bay.

WESTERN SANDPIPER

Calidris mauri

The Western Sandpiper is the largest of a group of small *Calidris* sandpipers known as "peeps" in North America and "stints" elsewhere in the English-speaking world. Members of this group can be notoriously difficult to identify because of the changeable nature of their plumage and the similarity of the species. If subtleties of size, plumage and calls are not of particular interest, then enjoy these sprites for their sheer exuberance and grace of movement—just about everyone appreciates the aerial maneuvers of a Western Sandpiper flock wheeling over estuarine tidal flats in July and August. • Western Sandpipers breed only in Alaska and extreme northeastern Siberia but fan out across the continent in migration, wintering as far south as the coasts of South America.

nonbreeding

breeding

ID: long, black, slightly down-curved bill (longer in female); white belly and undertail coverts. *Breeding:* rusty crown, ear and scapular patches; heavily dark-spotted and chevroned upper breast and flanks and less so on upper belly. *Nonbreeding:* pale gray upperparts; faint streaks on sides of breast; pale gray head with indistinct white "eyebrow" and lower face. *In flight:* tail has dark center; gray upperwing with white stripe; dark-edged white underwing; large, tightly packed flocks.

Size: *L* 6–7 in; *W* 14 in.

Status: locally abundant migrant from mid-April to October; rare to uncommon in winter along the coast.

Habitat: tidal estuaries, saltwater marshes and sandy beaches; freshwater shorelines, flooded fields and pools.

Nesting: does not nest in Oregon.

Feeding: gleans and probes in soft mud, moist sand, washed-up seaweed and shallow water (occasionally submerges its head); eats mainly small aquatic invertebrates.

Voice: squeaky, high-pitched *cheep* or *chireep* flight call, more liquid than that of other peeps; twittering chatter from flocks.

Similar Species: *Semipalmated Sandpiper:* breeding bird is plainer brown, with few rufous tints and less spotting on flanks; nonbreeding bird has slightly darker mottling. *Dunlin* (p. 158): larger; longer bill; breeding bird has black area on lower belly and more rufous on back; nonbreeding bird is darker and browner; juvenile has darker back markings and more breast streaking.

Best Sites: Columbia R. mouth; Bayocean Spit; Siletz Bay; Siuslaw R. estuary; Bandon Marsh; Coos Bay; Lake Co.; Harney Co.

LEAST SANDPIPER

Calidris minutilla

As indicated by its species name, this shorebird is the smallest of the small, yet its tiny size doesn't preclude impressive migratory feats. As with most peeps and other small sandpipers, some females migrate from the Arctic to South America and back again each year. • Least Sandpipers optimize their breeding efforts during the brief arctic summer, and in fall the parents start their journey south earlier than their brood, leaving the juveniles on their own to fatten up, learn to fly and prepare for the long journey south. Many birds stop off at coastal salt marshes and tidal estuaries, often using the more vegetated areas to replenish their food supplies and to get some protection from aerial predators.

nonbreeding

ID: sharp, black bill; distinctive yellowish or greenish legs; clearly defined white belly, white flanks and undertail coverts. *Breeding:* mottled warm brown upperparts, head and breast; dark-centered back and wing feathers. *Nonbreeding:* dark-marked dull grayish brown upperparts, head and breast. *Juvenile:* brighter than adult; extensive dark-centered rufous feathering on back and wings. *In flight:* short, dark wing, often bent, with white lining and thin upperwing stripe; short flight when flushed.
Size: *L* 6 in; *W* 13 in.
Status: common migrant from mid-March to mid-October; uncommon along the coast, rare to uncommon inland west of the Cascades and very rare elsewhere in winter.
Habitat: tidal estuaries, saltwater marshes, lagoons and kelp-wracked sandy beaches

along the coast; flooded fields and fresh-water shorelines inland.
Nesting: does not nest in Oregon.
Feeding: picks and probes in mud, sand and low marsh vegetation for mosquitoes, beach fleas, amphipods, snails, marine worms, other aquatic invertebrates, flies and occasional seeds; does not wade much.
Voice: usual call is a high-pitched *kreee;* spring male often utters a high, fast trill during his advertising flight of alternating glides and rapid flutters, with each phrase rising to a crescendo as he descends.
Similar Species: dark legs on other small sandpipers. *Semipalmated Sandpiper:* little rufous on plain grayish brown breeding bird; dull, uniformly gray upperparts on nonbreeding bird; no rufous and less distinctly streaked breast on juvenile. *Western Sandpiper* (p. 152): slightly larger; longer bill; rufous crown, "cheeks" and scapulars on breeding bird; less defined breast streaking on grayish brown nonbreeding bird.
Best Sites: widely distributed in suitable habitat inland and along the coast.

153

BAIRD'S SANDPIPER

Calidris bairdii

Baird's Sandpipers are the largest of the small sandpipers commonly referred to as "peeps." As with other arctic-nesting shorebirds, when the chicks can fend for themselves, the parents abandon them and then embark on the long, arduous return trip to wintering areas in western and southern South America. A few weeks later, the juveniles are ready to make their first migration flights, some following the adults' interior routes but others spreading out across Canada to reach both the Atlantic and Pacific coasts. The juveniles join up with other species of sandpipers from early August to late September; they can be picked out in roosting flocks by their taller stature. • This modestly plumaged but elegant shorebird was named for Spencer Fullerton Baird, an early Smithsonian Institute official who organized several natural history expeditions across North America in the mid- to late 1800s.

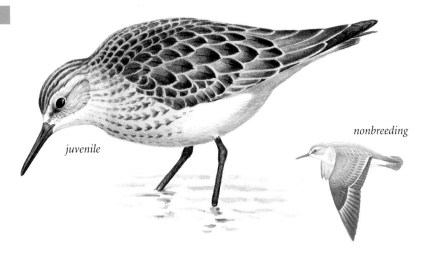

juvenile

nonbreeding

ID: straight, black bill; black legs; long wings project well beyond tail when folded; white underparts; pale grayish brown breast band. *Breeding:* silvery scapulars with large dark spots. *Nonbreeding:* indistinctly "scaly" grayish brown back. *Juvenile:* "scaly" back; light brown upper breast.
Size: *L* 7 in; *W* 17 in.
Status: uncommon fall migrant (mostly juveniles) and rare spring migrant.
Habitat: upper ocean beach tide lines, dry estuarine flats, damp freshwater alkaline flats and margins of sewage ponds; grassy fields and dunes; even above timberline during fall migration.
Nesting: does not nest in Oregon.
Feeding: alone, with other small sandpipers or with plovers; walks slowly and picks insects and other invertebrates from the water's surface; rarely probes; not inclined to wade.
Voice: usually silent; soft, reedy *creeeep, creeep* is often extended into a trill in flight.
Similar Species: *Pectoral Sandpiper* (p. 155): dull, yellow legs; streaky pectoral band is darker and more clearly defined; male is noticeably larger; undertail coverts are more obvious in flight.
Best Sites: Clatsop Spit; Bayocean Spit; Siletz Bay; Siuslaw R. estuary; Sauvie I.; Forest Grove; Baskett Slough NWR; Cabell Marsh; Fern Ridge Reservoir.

PECTORAL SANDPIPER

Calidris melanotos

Widespread world travelers, Pectoral Sandpipers have been observed in every state and province in North America during their epic migrations from arctic Siberia, Alaska and Canada to the pampas of South America—and even to Australia and New Zealand in small numbers. Siberian individuals may undertake a return trip of 20,000 miles—comparable to that of the Arctic Tern. In spring, most migrants take an inland route to the Arctic. Once there, the males court by filling their pectoral sacs with air and producing a remarkable, rapid, foghornlike hooting, but in migration they hide in long grass and give no indication of their unique abilities. • Adults first appear in Oregon in mid-July and leave by early September, but juveniles are most abundant from late August to the end of October, with a few birds lingering until late November.

adult

juvenile

ID: dark breast streaking with distinct boundary; yellow-tinged legs; dark-tipped, dusky yellowish bill; dark-centered tail with white sides; white underparts. *Breeding:* pale buff edges to upper feathers; darker breast streaking and back markings. *Juvenile:* brighter, more rufous upperparts; 2 distinctive white back and scapular stripes.
Size: *Male: L* 8–9 in; *W* 17–18 in. *Female: L* 6–7 in; *W* 16–17 in.
Status: locally common fall migrant; rare spring migrant.
Habitat: especially coastal salt marshes; also grassy margins of saltwater and brackish pools and lagoons, wet or grassy fields, ponds and drained lake beds.
Nesting: does not nest in Oregon.
Feeding: pecks and probes the ground and grass for small invertebrates, including flies, beetles, amphipods, spiders and insect larvae; also takes some seeds and algae.
Voice: gives a sharp, short, low and distinctive *krrick krrick* when flushed; a feeding male occasionally utters a low, throaty note series or louder, more persistent threat call.
Similar Species: *Sharp-tailed Sandpiper* (p. 156): pale buff breast with less and coarser streaking; usually some rufous on crown of nonbreeding adult; juvenile has brighter reddish "cap" and upperparts, strong white "eyebrow" and buffier, mostly unstreaked breast. *Buff-breasted Sandpiper* (p. 363): warm buff underparts; small, rounded head; unmarked "cheeks" and throat; large eyes; "scaly," brown-and-buff back; short, pointed black bill.
Best Sites: Tillamook Bay; Nehalem Meadows; Bayocean Spit; Drift Creek (Siletz Bay); Siuslaw R. estuary; Sauvie I.; Forest Grove (Fern Hill Wetlands); Hatfield L. (Bend); Malheur NWR.

SHARP-TAILED SANDPIPER

Calidris acuminata

Sharply attired Sharp-tailed Sandpipers are rather surprising regular visitors to Pacific Northwest coastlines. Most of the Siberian population heads out over the Pacific to wintering grounds as far south as Australia, but a few adults and many more juveniles cross to the Alaskan coast and then go southward to regular stop-offs in British Columbia, Washington and Oregon before heading off to who-knows-where. Some birds linger past October, often with late-leaving Pectoral Sandpipers, but none are known to have wintered, and very few Sharp-tails are seen in spring. Sharp-tailed Sandpipers like the same kind of habitats as Pectoral Sandpipers but are much more likely to be seen along the coast. • When not associating with dowitchers or Dunlins, individual Sharp-tails are the rule, so be sure to check any lone medium-sized grassland sandpipers you see.

juvenile

ID: short, black-tipped, dull olive or yellowish bill; conspicuous white eye ring; greenish yellow legs. *Nonbreeding:* pale buff breast with scattered spots and streaks. *Juvenile:* conspicuous reddish "cap"; largely unstreaked, bright buff breast; strong white "eyebrow."
Size: *L* 8 in; *W* 18 in.
Status: rare but regular fall migrant to the coast and the Willamette Valley from early September to mid-November; very rare east of the Cascades in fall.
Habitat: estuaries; salt marshes; bare margins of small ponds and large lakes; wet grasslands; plowed fields.
Nesting: does not nest in Oregon.

Feeding: pecks and probes the ground and grass for small invertebrates, including flies, beetles, amphipods, spiders and insect larvae; also takes some seeds and algae.
Voice: calls are like the Pectoral Sandpiper's, but sweeter, with rapid, trilling notes in mixed flocks.
Similar Species: *Pectoral Sandpiper* (p. 155): browner on back and wings; less prominent wing stripe; more extensive breast streaking; juvenile usually looks duller and has browner "cap." *Buff-breasted Sandpiper* (p. 363): buff underparts and breast with some spots; "scaly" back; brighter yellow legs; no wing stripe; darker tail edges.
Best Sites: tidal ponds at Clatsop Spit; Nehalem Meadows; Bayocean Spit; Yaquina Bay; Sauvie I.; Forest Grove; Fern Ridge Reservoir; Danebo Pond; Bandon Marsh NWR.

ROCK SANDPIPER

Calidris ptilocnemis

This well-camouflaged bird is the smallest and rarest of the several "rock-pipers" seen along the Oregon coast. With the shape and size of a Dunlin and the overall plumage of a Surfbird, the Rock Sandpiper might easily be overlooked as it feeds with larger, showier Black Turnstones and Surfbirds on wave-washed jetties, rock ledges and rocky shorelines. In Oregon it is almost always seen in the cryptic purplish gray nonbreeding plumage rather than the more colorful breeding or juvenile plumages. • Often seen in small numbers, Rock Sandpipers normally reach the Oregon coast in early November and leave by the end of April, although a few adults have returned by late August and a few lingerers have stayed until mid-May. The most reliable site is Seal Rock State Park.

nonbreeding

ID: folded wings shorter than tail; blackish bill with dull olive base; short, dusky greenish legs; bold, gray spots on sides and undertail coverts. *Nonbreeding:* mottled gray back, wings and breast; uniformly gray head and neck; pale mark between base of bill and eye. *Juvenile:* back feathers narrowly edged in rufous; indistinct, pale mantle stripe.
Size: *L* 9 in; *W* 17 in.
Status: rare to uncommon winter resident along the coast, most common in the north.
Habitat: rocky shorelines, jetties, breakwaters, sea stacks and tide pools; very rarely on estuarine sites.

Nesting: does not nest in Oregon.
Feeding: picks small marine invertebrates off rocks and seaweed; may also eat plant material.
Voice: generally silent; scratchy, low *keesh* flight call may change to a rougher *cherk;* flocks utter a sharper *kwitit-kwit.*
Similar Species: *Dunlin* (p. 158): slightly longer, more downcurved bill; brownish gray upperparts and plainer underparts in nonbreeding plumage; juvenile has more, darker streaking on breast and black-marked belly. *Surfbird* (p. 149): much heavier; stubbier bill; black-tipped white tail; yellow legs; paler gray upperparts in nonbreeding plumage.
Best Sites: Seal Rock SP; Columbia River South Jetty; Ecola SP; Barview Jetty (Tillamook Bay); Boiler Bay SP; Yaquina Bay South Jetty; Siuslaw R. jetties.

DUNLIN

Calidris alpina

Named for its brownish color and small size, the Dunlin (originally "Dunling") only fully lives up to its name in winter, when grayish brown blankets of this small sandpiper are scattered along chilly shorelines. As spring approaches, the dingy nonbreeding plumage gradually takes on the dazzling russet back and bold, black belly of spring. But, all too soon, the flocks leave for more northerly destinations. Before they do, we marvel at the dynamic, swirling clouds of individuals flying wing tip to wing tip, all changing course simultaneously. Unlike other small sandpipers, the Dunlin prefers to fly with its own kind and can often be seen in more discrete flocks at tide-line roosts. • The Dunlin is among the swiftest of the shorebird migrants. Its speed helps it escape from raptors such as Merlins and Peregrine Falcons.

breeding

ID: long, slightly downcurved black bill; black legs. *Breeding:* black belly; russet crown, back and scapulars; gray, lightly streaked head and neck; white undertail coverts. *Nonbreeding:* brownish gray upperparts; pale underparts. *In flight:* prominent white stripe on dark upperwing; dark center to tail; long wings; usually in highly coordinated flocks.

Size: *L* 7–9 in; *W* 17 in.

Status: common migrant and winter resident along the coast and in the Willamette Valley; uncommon migrant and winter resident in the Rogue Valley and the Umpqua Valley; locally common migrant east of the Cascades.

Habitat: tidal and saltwater marshes, estuaries and lagoon shorelines; open, sandy ocean beaches; flooded fields and muddy edges of freshwater wetlands; occasionally seen beside city ponds and sewage lagoons.

Nesting: does not nest in Oregon.

Feeding: jabs, picks and probes, often with the bill open and usually at the tide line; varied diet of mostly bivalve mollusks, amphipods and arthropods, plus other invertebrates, small fish and some plant material.

Voice: grating *cheezp* or *treezp* flight call; male's display song is a descending, creaky, high-pitched trill.

Similar Species: *Rock Sandpiper* (p. 157): slightly shorter bill; gray upperparts and heavily gray-marked underparts in nonbreeding plumage; juvenile has whitish belly; prefers rocky areas. *Curlew Sandpiper:* slightly longer bill and legs; all-white rump; breeding adult is deep rufous over most of body; nonbreeding adult has lighter gray upperparts and white "eyebrow."

Best Sites: *Winter:* along the coast; Willamette Valley; a spectacular flock roosts at Ankeny NWR.

SHORT-BILLED DOWITCHER

Limnodromus griseus

Subtle plumage differences, feeding habits and calls usually distinguish Short-billed Dowitchers from Long-billed Dowitchers. • Having short legs, dowitchers feed in mud or in shallow pools, where their extra-long bills with flexible tips can reach hidden invertebrates unavailable to longer-legged but shorter-billed shorebirds. While foraging along shorelines, these birds "stitch" up and down into the mud with a rhythm like a sewing machine. • Short-billed Dowitchers are saltwater mudflat specialists, whereas Long-billed Dowitchers prefer freshwater pools and marshes, but there is enough of an overlap to cause confusion. Bill length is unreliable—the bills of female Short-bills are often as long as, if not longer than, the bills of male Long-bills—and not all birds call. A more reliable identification feature, in good light and at least for juveniles, is a combination of tertial and tail feather patterns.

breeding

ID: long, sturdy bill; greenish yellow legs; dark line from bill to eye; conspicuous white "eyebrow"; spotted, rarely barred, undertail coverts; white belly. *Breeding:* largely orange head and spotted neck; lighter orange on barred and spotted breast and heavily barred sides; dark centers and pale buff edges to scapulars. *Nonbreeding:* pale grayish overall; gray-speckled breast; heavily dark-barred flanks. *Juvenile:* indistinctly streaked orangy buff breast. *In flight:* equal dark-and-white tail barring; triangular white lower back area.
Size: *L* 11–12 in; *W* 19 in.
Status: common coastal migrant; rare to uncommon spring migrant and uncommon to fairly common fall migrant through

western interior valleys; rare migrant east of the Cascades.
Habitat: estuaries and salt marshes along the coast; lakeshores, shallow marshes, sewage lagoons, ponds and flooded fields inland.
Nesting: does not nest in Oregon.
Feeding: wades in shallow water or soft mud, picking off surface and swimming invertebrates; probes for buried prey with the full length of the bill; occasionally eats seeds, aquatic plants and grasses.
Voice: generally silent; flight call is a mellow, repeated *tututu, toodulu* or *toodu.*
Similar Species: *Long-billed Dowitcher* (p. 160): heavier dark barring on tail; redder orange continues onto flanks and belly of breeding bird; more uniform brownish gray head and upperparts in nonbreeding plumage.
Best Sites: Columbia River South Jetty tidal ponds; Tillamook Bay; Siletz Bay; Yaquina Bay; Coos Bay; Bandon Marsh NWR.

LONG-BILLED DOWITCHER

Limnodromus scolopaceus

Long-billed Dowitchers favor freshwater habitats, even along the coast, preferring lakeshores, flooded pastures, grass-dotted marshes and the mouths of brackish tidal channels, where their slightly longer legs give them an advantage over Short-billed Dowitchers. • Nesting only along the edge of the Beaufort Sea in extreme northern Alaska and western Canada, Long-bills spread out over the continent and make a more leisurely fall migration than their cousins, with juveniles appearing as late as November at coastal and southern wintering sites. Long-bills are also later to leave their wintering areas, not getting on the move until mid-April to early May. Their breeding plumage makes them one of Oregon's most-anticipated returning shorebirds.

breeding

nonbreeding

ID: long, sturdy bill; greenish yellow legs; conspicuous, pale "eyebrow"; dark-barred undertail coverts. *Breeding:* rufous head and underparts; dark-streaked neck; some white streaking on dark-barred breast and sides. *Nonbreeding:* drab brownish gray overall; heavily barred pale flanks. *Juvenile:* buffy gray breast. *In flight:* thickly dark-barred white tail; triangular, white lower back area; dark-barred wing linings.
Size: *L* 11–12 in; *W* 19 in.
Status: common migrant; uncommon in winter along the coast and in western interior valleys; rare in winter east of the Cascades.

Habitat: along lakeshores, shallow marshes and fresh water; even along the coast.
Nesting: does not nest in Oregon.
Feeding: probes in shallow water and moist mud with a rapid up-and-down bill motion, often with the head underwater; eats mostly larval flies, worms and other soft-bodied invertebrates, but will take mollusks, crustaceans and seeds of aquatic plants.
Voice: usual call is a single *peek*, sometimes quickening into *kik-kik-kik-kik;* feeding flocks chatter steadily.
Similar Species: *Short-billed Dowitcher* (p. 159): breeding plumage is less rufous, with white belly; browner upperparts and more obvious streaking and barring on underparts in nonbreeding plumage.
Best Sites: Sauvie I.; Finley NWR; Baskett Slough NWR; Ankeny NWR; Fern Ridge Reservoir; Summer Lake WMA; Malheur NWR.

WILSON'S SNIPE

Gallinago delicata

The eerie, hollow, ascending winnowing of the male Wilson's Snipe (formerly Common Snipe, *G. gallinago*) is one of spring's most memorable wetland sounds. Specialized outspread outer tail feathers vibrate like saxophone reeds as the courting bird performs aerial maneuvers. • Both genders are well camouflaged and normally secretive. With large eyes set far back on the head, Wilson's Snipes can detect predators approaching from almost any direction. They explode from cover of grass or sedges and escape in a characteristic zigzag flight, usually uttering a rasping call. • "Snipe" comes from *snite*, an old version of "snout," in reference to the long bill and the bird's habit of feeling for prey deep in soft ground. *Gallinago* comes from a Latin word meaning "hen"—a reference that is lost in obscurity.

ID: long, straight, grayish bill; relatively short, pale yellowish or bluish legs; heavy brown and white stripes on head and back; large, dark eyes; dark-barred breast and sides; white belly; rusty tail. *In flight:* short wings; dark underwings with barred linings; rapid wingbeats; often rises high in the air and then drops rapidly back into cover.

Size: *L* 10–12 in; *W* 18 in.

Status: common in and east of the Cascades and locally uncommon west of the Cascades in summer; generally uncommon east of the Cascades and common to uncommon at lower elevations west of the Cascades in winter; common migrant.

Habitat: grassy edges of freshwater marshes, ponds, lakes, rivers and streams, beaver meadows, flooded grasslands; sometimes stages in salt marshes and at brackish stream outlets in migration.

Nesting: usually in dry grass, often under vegetation; female lines a small depression with grass, moss and leaves and incubates 4 brown-marked, olive buff to brown eggs for 18–20 days; pair splits the brood, feeding them for about 20 days, sometimes up to 60 days.

Feeding: probes deliberately into soft substrates for soft-bodied invertebrates, mostly larvae and earthworms, but also eats small amphibians and some seeds.

Voice: nasal *scaip* alarm call; often sings *wheat wheatawheat* from an elevated perch; male uses tail feathers to produce an accelerating *woo-woo-woo-woo-woo-woo* courtship song in flight.

Similar Species: *Dowitchers* (pp. 159–60): triangular, white back area; more orangy breeding plumage and otherwise grayer; usually seen in flocks in the open; rapid up-and-down feeding method.

Best Sites: almost any grassy wetland.

161

WILSON'S PHALAROPE
Phalaropus tricolor

Among the most colorful and graceful of all North American shorebirds, phalaropes also have unusual breeding strategies. The flashy females pursue the less colorful males, sometimes mating with several, laying eggs in each of their nests and then leaving the males with all the duties of a single parent. This polyandrous strategy maximizes use of the breeding territory. For the most part, however, female Wilson's Phalaropes are monogamous and defend the nesting territory. Soon after the young hatch, the females head for several lakes in Harney County and Lakes County, as well as California's Mono Lake, to fatten up and partially molt. The males and juveniles join them later. As many as 100,000 phalaropes may gather at one such location before they all leave for Bolivia or Argentina.

breeding

nonbreeding

ID: long, dark, needlelike bill; dark eyes; white "eyebrow," "cheeks," belly, sides and under-tail coverts; lobed toes. *Breeding female:* gray "cap"; black eye stripe and neck sides; cinnamon foreneck and upper breast; gray back with 2 broad chestnut stripes; black legs; brownish upperwings. *Breeding male:* grayish brown upperparts and "cap"; chestnut and light brown neck; white throat. *Nonbreeding:* light gray upperparts; yellow legs.

Size: *L* 8–9 in; *W* 17 in.

Status: common breeding summer resident and migrant east of the Cascades; generally rare in summer and in migration in western Oregon.

Habitat: *Breeding:* boggy ponds, marshes and wet meadows, including marshy mountain lakes. *In migration:* alkaline lakes; sewage ponds; freshwater shorelines; flooded fields.

Nesting: near water; usually well concealed; a depression is lined with grass and other vegetation; male incubates 3–4 brown-blotched buff eggs for 22–25 days and tends the young.

Feeding: whirls in tight circles in water to stir up aquatic invertebrates and picks prey from surface or just below; makes short jabs for invertebrates on land.

Voice: deep, grunting, *work work* or *wu wu wu*, usually in flight on breeding grounds.

Similar Species: *Red-necked Phalarope* (p. 163): shorter bill; dark "cap"; white upperwing stripe; red (female) or buff (male) neck sides and gray breast in breeding plumage. *Red Phalarope* (p. 164): shorter, thicker bill; rufous (female) or cinnamon (male) neck, breast and underparts, yellow bill, dark "cap" and white eye patch in breeding plumage.

Best Sites: Lower Klamath NWR; Summer Lake WMA; L. Abert; Pelican L. and Crump L. (Warner Valley); Burns-Hines area; Malheur NWR.

RED-NECKED PHALAROPE

Phalaropus lobatus

This tiny mite of a shorebird is, for most of the year, the world's smallest seabird. Seeming all but lost among the troughs, the dainty Red-necked Phalarope rides out all the open ocean has to offer. • Other sea-feeding birds search far and wide for concentrations of food and then plunge, dive or swim to reach their food. Phalaropes use their individually lobed toes to swim and dab in tight circles, stirring up tiny invertebrates that live in the upper layer of seawater. As prey items funnel toward the water's surface, phalaropes pick and choose with their needlelike bills. • Most of these arctic breeders migrate along the coast or well out to sea, but small flocks of Red-necks may suddenly appear along freshwater shores.

breeding

nonbreeding

ID: long, thin, dark bill; white "chin" and belly; dark legs; lobed toes. *Breeding female:* dark gray head; chestnut on neck and upper breast; white "chin"; tiny white "eyebrow"; gray breast; buff-striped gray back. *Breeding male:* dark gray upperparts with buff stripe; cinnamon neck stripe; black "cap" and eye line; whitish "eyebrow." *Nonbreeding:* gray-streaked upperparts; white underparts and face; black eye patch. *Juvenile:* buff-striped dark back; dark "cap"; black eye patch; smudgy breast.

Size: *L* 7–8 in; *W* 15 in.

Status: common migrant from mid-April to mid-May and from August through September, mostly offshore; occasionally seen on or near shore, especially during storms.

Habitat: open ocean, from just beyond the surf line to well offshore; harbors, estuar-ies, lagoons and saltwater marshes with tidal channels; alkaline lakes; sewage ponds; open freshwater marshes.

Nesting: does not nest in Oregon.

Feeding: whirls in tight circles in shallow or deep water, picking small invertebrates from the surface or just below; totters jerk-ily on land, lunging for invertebrates with short jabs.

Voice: often noisy with a soft *krit krit krit* in migration.

Similar Species: *Red Phalarope* (p. 164): chunkier; heavier bill; rufous or cinnamon neck and underparts in breeding plumage; paler, plainer upperparts in nonbreeding plumage. *Wilson's Phalarope* (p. 162): longer, thinner bill; breeding female has black on neck and cinnamon foreneck; male and nonbreeding female have pale gray upperparts and mostly white face; plainer wings.

Best Sites: Clatsop Spit; Nehalem sewage ponds; Bay City sewage ponds (Tillamook Bay); Yaquina Bay; Siuslaw R. estuary; Umpqua R. estuary; Coos Bay.

RED PHALAROPE

Phalaropus fulicarius

Getting a good view of a Red Phalarope, the most pelagic of shorebirds, usually requires a boat trip well offshore—or going out in a storm on land. The effort is worth it, especially in spring, when the birds are in their striking breeding plumage. Heavy weather in November and December may drive hundreds of Red Phalaropes close to or onto land. At such times, beaches, coastal ponds, wet meadows and even parking lots may harbor exhausted phalaropes. • Red Phalaropes have been seen snatching parasites off the backs of surfacing whales, acting much like the tickbirds of the African plains. • John James Audubon, fooled by female phalaropes assuming typical male roles on their arctic breeding grounds, mislabeled the genders on his phalarope illustrations.

nonbreeding

ID: grayish legs; lobed toes. *Breeding female:* striking, reddish orange neck and underparts; white eye patch; black crown, forehead and "chin"; buff-striped brown back; black-tipped, bright yellow bill. *Breeding male:* like female, but paler. *Nonbreeding:* white head, neck and underparts; plain, light gray upperparts; black nape and eye patch; black bill has pale base.

Size: *L* 8–9 in; *W* 17 in.

Status: common offshore migrant in late spring and from late July to late December; probable rare winter offshore resident; irregular migrant close to shore and in coastal locations; rare spring and fall vagrant inland.

Habitat: open ocean waters far from shore, preferring upwellings and current edges; occasionally seen close to shore off headlands and jetties, and inshore in bays, lagoons and estuaries; hardly ever found inland, except when blown in by storms.

Nesting: does not nest in Oregon.

Feeding: gleans the ocean's surface, largely for euphausiids, usually while swimming in tight circles; eats small invertebrates on land.

Voice: calls include a shrill, high-pitched *wit* or *creep* and a low *clink clink*.

Similar Species: *Red-necked Phalarope* (p. 163): daintier; white underparts (all plumages); slimmer bill; breeding bird has gray upper breast and different facial pattern; nonbreeding bird has darker, streakier upperparts. *Wilson's Phalarope* (p. 162): longer, thinner, dark bill; white underparts; breeding female has black eye line and black-and-cinnamon neck; breeding male has grayer upperparts and light brown neck; nonbreeding bird has yellow legs and gray eye line; plainer wings.

Best Sites: birds driven inshore by storms prefer sewage ponds, reservoirs and lakes.

POMARINE JAEGER
Stercorarius pomarinus

Powerful, swift pirates of the open ocean, jaegers chase down hapless terns and small gulls to steal their hard-earned food. On their arctic nesting grounds, jaegers defend their eggs and young by attacking any intruders with stooping dives or hectic pursuits. • During much of the year, lone birds and loose groups of jaegers may be encountered at sea. Most jaegers occur far from land where ocean currents and upwellings bring food to the surface, but some can be seen from land and a few individuals may even make it to a harbor entrance or inland lake. • The "Pom" appears heavier than other jaegers. Its wings have broader bases, and its flight is more labored with slower wingbeats. • With their heavy build and prominent primary patch, juveniles can be mistaken for South Polar Skuas.

dark morph breeding

light morph breeding

ID: dark-tipped, pale yellowish bill; twisted, spoonshaped tail feathers. *Light morph:* dark "cap" and front of face; creamy yellow upper neck; dark brown upperparts; possible brownish black breast band; white underparts, often with dark brown or barred flanks and undertail. *Dark morph:* all-dark plumage. *Juvenile:* light-tipped, dark upperpart feathers; brown head and underparts; dark-barred white rump. *In flight:* prominent, white primary underwing flash with corresponding white shafts visible on upperwing.
Size: *L* 18–23 in; *W* 4¼ ft.
Status: common migrant offshore from mid-July to mid-November and rare in mid-spring; occasional visitor inshore, particularly after storms, but very rare inland;

rarely seen from shore, except from October to mid-November.
Habitat: usually open ocean, often far from land; regularly seen around fishing vessels.
Nesting: does not nest in Oregon.
Feeding: snatches food from the ocean's surface; harasses other birds, including larger shearwaters and gulls, into dropping or ejecting their food; chases and eats small birds.
Voice: generally silent; may give a sharp *which-yew*, a squealing *weak-weak* or a squeaky, whistled note during migration.
Similar Species: *Parasitic Jaeger* (p. 166): more slender; smaller head; long, pointed tail feathers; all-dark bill; often no breast band.
Best Sites: Columbia R. mouth beach; Barview Jetty CP; Cape Meares SP; Yaquina Bay South Jetty; Coos Bay North Spit; Boiler Bay SP.

PARASITIC JAEGER

Stercorarius parasiticus

Alert, speedy and able to turn on a dime, Parasitic Jaegers intimidate small gulls and terns into dropping or coughing up their latest meal. Any concentrations of feeding seabirds often attract vigilant jaegers. In the Arctic, pairs of nesting jaegers will cooperate to drive off predators. Jaegers will also follow people and bird-hunting mammals in hopes of getting any eggs and young left behind by fleeing nesters of other bird species. • Parasitic Jaegers occur in three color phases (morphs). About one in five juveniles is either a light or dark morph, with the rest being intermediate. • Of the three jaegers species found along the Oregon coast, the Parasitic is the most widely and regularly seen from shore. It is also a rare visitor to inland lakes.

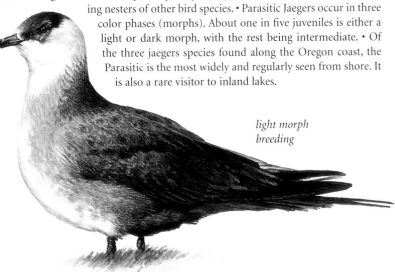

light morph breeding

ID: long, pointed, dark wings; pointed central tail feathers; dark "cap," eye patch, upperparts, bill and legs. *Light morph:* white face and neck tinged with pale yellow; may have smudgy breast band; white underparts; dull brown bars or streaks on flanks and undertail coverts. *Dark morph:* all-dark plumage. *Juvenile:* lighter-tipped dark upperpart feathers; dark-streaked lighter brown head and underparts. *In flight:* white primary underwing flash with corresponding white shafts visible on upperwing.
Size: *L* 16–21 in; *W* 3¾ ft.
Status: common migrant offshore from late August to mid-October and uncommon migrant from March to late May; rare winter and summer visitor; regularly observed inshore but rarely inland.
Habitat: mainly on the open ocean from the outer surf zone to the edge of the

continental shelf; some birds, especially immatures, enter estuaries and harbors or visit inland lakes.
Nesting: does not nest in Oregon.
Feeding: eats small schooling fish (usually stolen from Bonaparte's Gulls, Black-legged Kittiwakes and migrant terns); scavenges food from the ocean's surface.
Voice: generally silent; may make shrill calls in migrating groups of the same or other jaegers.
Similar Species: *Pomarine Jaeger* (p. 165): bulkier; dark-tipped pale bill; larger, darker breast band; larger dark "cap"; blunt, twisted, elongated central tail feathers. *Long-tailed Jaeger* (p. 364): slimmer; pale underparts; whitish lower head and neck; little or no breast band; particularly long, pointed central tail feathers and crisp black "cap" on breeding bird; all-brown underwings.
Best Sites: Columbia R. mouth beach; Barview Jetty CP; Bayocean Spit; Cape Meares SP; Yaquina Bay South Jetty; Coos Bay North Spit.

FRANKLIN'S GULL

Larus pipixcan

The Franklin's Gull, more than any other gull, is no "seagull." Affectionately known on the Great Plains and the Prairies as "Prairie Dove" because of its dovelike profile, it follows tractors to find stirred-up food in much the same way its cousins follow fishing boats. • The first Oregon record of the Franklin's Gull was at Malheur National Wildlife Refuge in 1943, where the first pair nested in 1948. Now, over 1000 pairs can nest there in a season. • First appearing in late April and early May, birds can be seen throughout the Harney Basin and neighboring Alvord Basin and Catlow Valley. More and more small summer flocks are appearing in other parts of eastern Oregon, especially in Klamath County and Lake County, but birds in interior western Oregon and along the coast are mainly fall migrants.

breeding

ID: gray mantle; dark reddish legs; prominent white spots on black primary tips. *Breeding:* black "hood"; partial broad, white eye ring; red bill; possible pinkish tinge on breast. *Nonbreeding:* partial "hood"; white forehead and "chin"; dark legs. *Juvenile:* light brown upperparts and hindneck. *In flight:* gray upperwing with white trailing edge; white underwing; small dark area at wing tip; white tail (partially dark tip on 1st-winter bird).
Size: *L* 14–15 in; *W* 3 ft.
Status: common summer resident and local breeder in the Harney Basin; locally uncommon from spring to fall elsewhere east of the Cascades; rare migrant in western Oregon; state-listed as sensitive.
Habitat: *Breeding:* freshwater marshes; grassy fields; sloughs; marshy lakes.

In migration: marshlands; meadows; farm fields; lakes; river mouths.
Nesting: colonial; usually in water, anchored to a large, floating platform of dead reeds and lined with fine grass and plant down; pair incubates 3 lightly marked buff eggs for 24–25 days.
Feeding: opportunistic; follows agricultural machinery to seize flushed insects and worms; catches flying insects in midair.
Voice: gives shrill, "mewing" *weeeh-ah* and hollow *kowee-ee* calls; longer calls are more varied than those of other inland gulls.
Similar Species: *Bonaparte's Gull* (p. 168): slimmer; thinner, black bill; paler back; primaries have conspicuous white wedge and narrow, black trailing edge above and below; dark ear spot in nonbreeding plumage; pink or red legs.
Best Sites: Harney Basin, especially at Malheur NWR; Burns–Hines area.

BONAPARTE'S GULL

Larus philadelphia

Bonaparte's Gulls are occasionally seen inland in Oregon in spring, but most of the population chooses a coastal migration route to boreal and subarctic breeding areas. The abundance of Bonaparte's Gulls becomes evident from late April to early May, when small flocks and long lines appear along the coast. Some flocks migrate as far as 40 miles out to sea, but birds hugging the coast often rest and feed at estuaries, sewage ponds and flooded fields and on water close to shore. A similar influx is seen from late September to the end of November, when these gulls are common on both estuaries and inland lakes. • This elegant gull was named after the French emperor's nephew, zoologist Charles Lucien Bonaparte. The first specimen was collected in Philadelphia.

nonbreeding

breeding

ID: thin, black bill; pale gray upperparts; white underparts; short tail. *Breeding:* black "hood"; white eye-arcs; orangy red legs. *Nonbreeding:* white head; neat, round, dark ear patch; pink legs. *1st winter:* elongated ear patch; paler legs; dark upperwing trim. *In flight:* primaries have conspicuous white wedge and narrow, black trailing edge above and below; white tail; 1st-winter bird has dark terminal tail band and thin, dark "M" on upperwings.
Size: *L* 12–14 in; *W* 32–33 in.
Status: common migrant and uncommon summer and winter lingerer along the coast; locally common migrant and rare in summer and winter inland.

Habitat: protected coastal waters; beaches; sewage ponds; rivers; large lakes; reservoirs; open ocean.
Nesting: does not nest in Oregon.
Feeding: dabbles and tips up for aquatic and marine invertebrates, especially small fish, shrimps and other crustaceans, worms and tadpoles; gleans the ground for land invertebrates; catches flying insects in midair.
Voice: utters a scratchy, soft *ear ear;* large flocks can be very noisy when feeding.
Similar Species: *Franklin's Gull* (p. 167): larger; dark legs; darker back; prominent white spots on black primary tips; slightly heavier bill is red in breeding plumage; half "hood" in nonbreeding plumage.
Best Sites: along the coast; Fern Ridge Reservoir; Upper Klamath L.

HEERMANN'S GULL

Larus heermanni

Any novice coastal birder struggling to identify confusingly colored gulls can be grateful to the Heermann's Gull for providing a sequence of completely distinctive plumages. Something else sets this dusky gull apart: whereas most gulls migrate north to breed and return south for winter, the Heermann's Gull travels south to sun-baked Isla Raza in the Sea of Cortez to raise its chicks and then heads north for the balance of summer and much of fall. In Oregon, observations peak from mid-July to early November, and this gull is rarely seen here after late November. • The Heermann's Gull often steals food from Brown Pelicans, especially juveniles, or any other waterbirds it can bully into giving up their catch. The feathers of jaegers, which also steal food from other birds, are not very water-resistant, but the Heermann's Gull has no such excuse for its kleptoparasitism. How and why it developed this strategy is not known.

nonbreeding

breeding

ID: dark back and wings; light ashy gray underparts and neck; dark red eyes; black-tipped red bill; black legs; white-tipped black tail. *Breeding:* white head. *Nonbreeding:* brownish gray mottling or streaking on head. *1st winter:* dark brown overall, darkest on head, wing tips and tail; dark-tipped pale bill. *In flight:* wings and tail usually all dark except for white trailing edges (narrower on 2nd-winter bird).

Size: *L* 16–19 in; *W* 4¼ ft.

Status: common nonbreeding late summer and fall resident along the coast; extremely rare away from the coast.

Habitat: coastal ocean waters, usually close to shore, including bays, beaches, offshore islands, lagoons and coastal creek outfalls.

Nesting: does not nest in Oregon.

Feeding: dips to the water's surface to snatch items while in flight; often pirates food from other birds, especially pelicans; eats mainly small fish but also invertebrates, eggs, carrion and human waste.

Voice: common call is a nasal *kawak;* also gives a series of whining *ye* notes and low-pitched honking; noisy and argumentative when feeding.

Similar Species: *Dark morphs* of *Pomarine Jaeger* (p. 165) and *Parasitic Jaeger* (p. 166): resemble immature Heerman's but have white primary flashes and narrower tail, often with projecting central feathers; Parasitic has much smaller bill.

Best Sites: Columbia R. mouth; Miami Cove (Tillamook Bay); Boiler Bay SP; Yaquina Bay; Seal Rock SP; Salmon Harbor (Umpqua R.); Sport Haven CP (Brookings).

MEW GULL

Larus canus

T he first few Mew Gulls appear around river mouths and along coastal shore-lines by early August, and a major invasion occurs from mid-October to early December. Most birds head north again between mid-March and the end of May. • The Mew Gull is a common nester from British Columbia northward only, so few purely white-headed adults are seen in Oregon. • Winter storms bring Mew Gulls from their usual open coast estuary habitats into flooded fields and pastures, where they forage for earthworms and other invertebrates driven to the surface. Some birds, starting to adopt the fast-food approach favored by Ring-billed Gulls, scavenge food scraps instead. • The scientific name *canus* means "dog," but the "mewing" calls made by this small, dainty gull sound catlike.

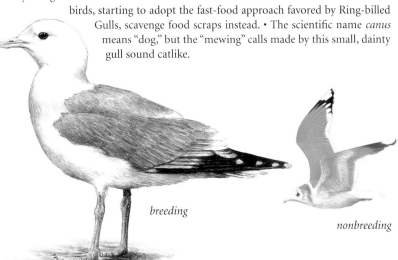

breeding

nonbreeding

ID: medium gray back and wings; wings extend well beyond the tail at rest; walks rapidly.
Nonbreeding: small, thin, yellow bill with indistinct dark spot; greenish yellow legs; variable dusky streaking or smudging on head, neck and upper breast. *1st winter:* dark-tipped dull pink bill; smudgy brown underparts; barred tail coverts. *In flight:* broad, white tail; mostly pale underwing and gray upperwing with wide white trailing edges and white-spotted black tip (visible at rest); 1st-winter bird is mostly grayish brown, with dusky wedge and trailing edge on upperwing.
Size: *L* 16 in; *W* 3½ ft.
Status: locally abundant winter resident along the coast and in the northwest; rare to uncommon elsewhere in western Oregon and in the Klamath Basin.

Habitat: tidal waters, ranging from upper estuaries out to the open coast; concentrates in and around fields, harbors and ocean beaches.
Nesting: does not nest in Oregon.
Feeding: opportunistic; captures fish and crustaceans and other invertebrates by plunging to the water's surface, plucking from wave-washed seaweed or picking from the ground; does not normally visit garbage dumps or accept handouts.
Voice: among the quietest of small gulls; gives high, squeaky, nasal notes, a "mew-ing" call and a high-pitched, coughing *queeoh*.
Similar Species: *Ring-billed Gull* (p. 171): paler gray above; paler eyes; heavier, black-ringed yellow bill or black-tipped pink bill (immature); nonbreeding bird has less brown on head; more black and less white at wing tips; dark tail band and sharper wing coloration in 1st winter.
Best Sites: Tillamook Bay; coastal estuaries and nearby fields.

RING-BILLED GULL

Larus delawarensis

At home amid concrete buildings and paved roads, Ring-billed Gulls are in some places a routine sight at shopping mall parking lots, ball fields and garbage dumps. Some Ring-bills have taken to the urban lifestyle, with its opportunity for food everywhere, and have learned the fine art of pursuing lunch handouts at city parks, followed by dinner outside a choice fast-food outlet. To be fair, Ring-bills also help out farmers by following agricultural machinery to feast on many crop pests, and they are unobtrusive in most places. • Long-established and temporary nesting colonies in southeastern and south-central Oregon are shared with California Gulls, and there are fair-sized colonies along the Columbia River.

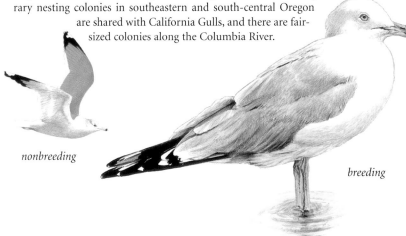

nonbreeding

breeding

ID: pale gray upperparts; white neck and underparts; yellow eyes; yellow bill with prominent black ring; yellow legs. *Breeding:* all-white head. *Nonbreeding:* faintly brown-streaked lower crown and nape. *1st winter:* gray-and-brown back and wings; dark-barred neck and flanks; black-tipped pink bill; pink legs. *In flight:* mostly pale underwing; white trailing wing edge; white spot on black wing tip (visible at rest); white tail (with blackish band on 1st-winter bird).
Size: *L* 18–20 in; *W* 4 ft.
Status: locally common breeding summer resident and common nonbreeder east of the Cascades; uncommon nonbreeding summer resident and common migrant and winter resident west of the Cascades; common in winter in the Klamath Basin and along the Columbia R.
Habitat: *Breeding:* sandbars; beaches in freshwater wetlands. *In migration and*

winter: various open environments close to water, including urban ones.
Nesting: colonial; on the ground, in driftwood or on bare rock next to or under low plants; nest of twigs, sticks, grass and leaves is lined with lichens and mosses; pair incubates 2–4 brown-splotched grayish eggs for 25–28 days and feeds young until fledging at 35–40 days.
Feeding: opportunistic; gleans, stabs and flycatches for fish, flying insects, earthworms, termites and rodents; scavenges for carrion, human leftovers and waste grain.
Voice: high-pitched *kakaka-akakaka;* low, laughlike *yook-yook-yook.*
Similar Species: *Mew Gull* (p. 170): smaller; dark eyes; smaller, faintly ringed or unringed bill; darker mantle; larger white spots on wing tips; breeding bird has streakier head and neck; less contrasting immature plumages.
Best Sites: *Summer:* Lake, Klamath and Harney Counties; Miller Rocks (near Deschutes R. mouth); Three Mile Canyon I. (near Boardman). *Winter:* Willamette Valley; Columbia R.; Klamath Basin.

171

CALIFORNIA GULL

Larus californicus

Seeing a "seagull" so far from the ocean may puzzle summer observers in eastern Oregon, but the California Gull makes use of fluctuating inland water bodies, even in arid environments, by breeding only when the water level is right. Wherever there are islands for nesting, this opportunistic gull can find food on the lakes—or, more often, in surrounding terrain. • In winter, California Gulls can be found throughout Oregon. During the March smelt run, thousands of birds gather along the Columbia River. • Despite the California Gull's name and coastal abundance, this interior prairie-and-basin nester first became well known to the general public when it was celebrated for consuming hordes of crop-threatening grasshoppers in Utah in 1848 and 1855.

breeding

nonbreeding

ID: dark gray mantle; dark eyes; heavy, yellow bill with black band; red spot on lower mandible; pale greenish yellow legs. *Breeding:* white head. *Nonbreeding:* brown-streaked hindcrown and nape. *2nd winter:* grayish blue legs; black tail band; dark-ringed gray bill. *1st winter:* black-tipped pink bill; pinkish gray legs; dark-streaked head, neck and breast; blotched brown back; barred tail coverts; dark brown tail. *In flight:* white tail and underwing; mostly gray upperwing; white spot on dark wing tip; 1st-winter bird is brown overall.
Size: *L* 18–20 in; *W* 4–4½ ft.
Status: uncommon to locally abundant breeder and locally uncommon in winter east of the Cascades; uncommon nonbreeding summer visitor and locally common winter visitor west of the Cascades; widespread migrant, often abundant along the coast.

Habitat: lakes; marshes; estuaries; croplands; cities; garbage dumps; open ocean, especially in fall and winter.
Nesting: colonial; usually on an island, often next to shrubs; a depression is lined with bones, feathers and other materials; pair incubates 2–3 dark-marked buff, olive or greenish eggs for 24–27 days and feeds young until fledging at 48 days.
Feeding: takes a large variety of insects, brine shrimp, worms, fish, birds and small mammals, as well as garbage.
Voice: the usual calls are loud, ringing *kyow-kyow* barks and mellower, laughlike notes, mostly at the nesting colony.
Similar Species: *Ring-billed Gull* (p. 171): smaller; shorter bill without red spot; yellow eyes; yellower legs. *Herring Gull* (p. 173): larger; yellowish eyes; pinkish legs.
Best Sites: *Summer:* Lake, Klamath and Harney Counties. *In migration:* along the coast; Columbia R. *Winter:* Columbia R.; Willamette Valley; Klamath Basin.

HERRING GULL

Larus argentatus

Aggressive and opportunistic by nature, the Herring Gull still finds itself outcompeted by Western Gulls and Glaucous-winged Gulls at many coastal feeding sites. It is, therefore, generally more common well up in the larger estuaries and at landfills beyond the normal foraging range of its larger competitors. • The proliferation of subspecies designations around the world, recent division into several species and continuing hybridization make it difficult to confidently identify a Herring Gull. These gulls hybridize freely with other large, white-headed gulls, including the Glaucous-winged Gull. Because these species readily crossbreed, some ornithologists consider them a "super-species"—an intermediate grouping of several species within the same genus.

breeding

nonbreeding

ID: heavy, yellow bill with red spot; pale yellow eyes; pinkish legs; light gray back and wings.
Breeding: all-white head and neck. *Nonbreeding:* heavy brown streaking on head, neck and upper breast. *3rd winter:* dark-tipped yellow bill; residual brownish areas. *2nd winter* and *1st winter:* pale brown plumage, usually mottled; dark tail; blackish bill, often with pink base; barred undertail coverts. *In flight:* white tail and underwing; mostly gray upperwing; white spot on dark wing tip; 1st- and 2nd-winter birds are mostly brown, with lighter primary upperwing patch.
Size: *L* 23–26 in; *W* 4¾ ft.
Status: uncommon to fairly common migrant and winter resident along the coast, offshore and in the Willamette

Valley and rare elsewhere; rare along the coast in summer.
Habitat: ubiquitous; generally any habitat near water; concentrates at landfills, river mouths and on agricultural land; migrates along beaches and the surf line.
Nesting: does not nest in Oregon.
Feeding: scavenges dead fish, carrion and human waste; catches crabs, snails, insects and other invertebrates on or under the water's surface; is a major predator of colonial seabird eggs and young.
Voice: utters a loud, buglelike *kleew-kleew;* alarm call is a loud *kak-kak-kak.*
Similar Species: *California Gull* (p. 172): smaller; darker mantle; dark eyes; yellowish or grayish (immature) legs; black band and red spot on bill. *Thayer's Gull* (p. 174): pale underwing tips; shorter, slimmer bill; eyes mostly dark; legs mostly redder.
Best Sites: Columbia R. (March and early April); Portland area; Sauvie I.; Willamette Valley near Eugene.

THAYER'S GULL

Larus thayeri

Just when you thought you had your gulls all sorted out, along comes a Thayer's Gull and everything goes out the window. The Thayer's Gull was long considered to be a subspecies of the Herring Gull until it was elevated to full species status by the American Ornithologists' Union in 1973. A majority of gull researchers now argue that its closest ally is the Iceland Gull (*L. glaucoides*), which shares the same nest sites in the eastern Canadian Arctic but winters along the Atlantic Coast. • Thayer's Gulls arrive on the Oregon coast in late September, with most wintering birds choosing the areas around Portland, Salem and Eugene. Smelt runs on the Columbia River in late February and March attract good numbers of Thayer's Gulls, but few birds remain past April.

nonbreeding

breeding

ID: yellow bill with red spot; dark eyes; pinkish legs; light gray back and wings; black wing tips with prominent white spots. *Breeding:* white head; brighter bill. *Nonbreeding:* heavy brown streaking on head, neck and upper breast. *1st winter* and *2nd winter:* pale brown plumage; blackish brown tail; blackish bill with pink base; barred undertail coverts. *3rd winter:* dark-ringed yellow bill; all-black wing tips. *In flight:* white underwings; gray upperwings with white trailing edges; black markings at wing tips; plain, brownish 1st- and 2nd-winter birds have darker tail and wing tips.

Size: *L* 22–25 in; *W* 4½ ft.

Status: fairly common migrant and uncommon winter resident along the coast; fairly common winter resident along the lower Columbia R. and in the Willamette Valley; rare elsewhere.

Habitat: disperses widely from night roosts and concentrates in harbors, river mouths, plowed fields and pastures.

Nesting: does not nest in Oregon.

Feeding: omnivorous and opportunistic but not predatory; gleans and picks food items from the land and the water's surface; eats anything edible from berries to garbage.

Voice: generally silent in winter; notes are usually short and flat.

Similar Species: *Herring Gull* (p. 173): more black on wing tips; longer, heavier bill; pale yellow eyes; immature is more heavily streaked and patterned. *Glaucous-winged Gull* (p. 176): heavier head and bill; dark eyes; gray-and-white wing tips; immature is paler.

Best Sites: Sauvie I.; Portland area; parts of Willamette Valley, notably Salem and Eugene; Columbia R. (late February and March).

WESTERN GULL
Larus occidentalis

Big, bold and married to salt water, the dark-backed Western Gull is the casual observer's Pacific Coast "seagull." This large, heavyset gull is conspicuous whether sitting atop a piling, splashing in a stream outfall or sailing on a stiff breeze above coastal bluffs. • Many large, pink-footed gulls inhabit Oregon's coast, but the Western Gull is the only one that stays and nests on the outer coast, rather than in estuaries. • The Western Gull has a smaller population than most other North American gulls, with breeding pairs concentrating at fewer than 200 colony sites in total. It is also of possible conservation concern because of the effects of pesticides on reproduction, threats from oil spills and extensive hybridization with other species.

breeding

nonbreeding

ID: dark gray back and wings; white head and underparts; yellow to dark eyes; stout, yellow bill with red spot; pink legs. *3rd winter:* black-ringed yellow bill; black wing tips. *2nd winter:* brownish wings; streaked head; dark-tipped pinkish bill. *1st winter:* patterned medium brown overall; barred tail coverts; mainly dark bill. *In flight:* white tail; white underwing with long gray triangle; dark wing tips; 1st- and 2nd-winter birds have pale brownish underwings and dark tail.

Size: *L* 24–26 in; *W* 4¾ ft.

Status: locally common year-round coastal resident; rare to uncommon winter visitor along the lower Columbia R. and in the Willamette Valley.

Habitat: *Breeding:* offshore rocks. *In migration* and *winter:* offshore rocks; intertidal and shallow inshore zones; open ocean upwellings; coastal fields; coastal towns.

Nesting: colonial; on or near rock with vegetation cover; scrape nest is filled with vegetation; pair incubates 2–3 heavily marked pale eggs for 30–32 days.

Feeding: eats various open-ocean and intertidal invertebrates and fish; follows feeding marine mammals to scavenge fish; is a major predator (eggs to adults) at seabird colonies; also eats human refuse.

Voice: *keow* note is the most common call.

Similar Species: *Herring Gull* (p. 173): paler upperparts; paler eyes; nonbreeding bird has brown-streaked head and neck; whiter underwings; immature is often indistinguishable. *Thayer's Gull* (p. 174): paler upperparts; whiter underwings; eyes normally dark; immature much paler.

Best Sites: along the coast. *Summer:* Haystack Rock, Clatsop Co.; Three Arch Rocks and Haystack Rock, Tillamook Co.; Table Rock, Coos Co.; Island Rock, Hunter's I. and Goat I., Curry Co.

GLAUCOUS-WINGED GULL

Larus glaucescens

L ook for large, heavyset Glaucous-winged Gulls among winter gatherings of Western Gulls along the open coast and in estuaries. The paler-backed Glaucous-winged adults have noticeably whitish wings and rather indistinct white primary "mirrors" in their gray wing tips. Scattered immature birds remain through spring and early summer, their drab, brownish first-winter plumage wearing and fading visibly before most of them leave for summer. • In northern Oregon and Washington, the Glaucous-winged Gull routinely hybridizes with the Western Gull, resulting in a confusing range of intergrades. • Over the last few decades, the Glaucous-winged Gull has begun to move up estuaries and river systems well beyond the influence of the tides and therefore cannot be fully considered a "seagull."

breeding

nonbreeding

ID: heavy, yellow bill with red spot; eyes are usually darkish; pinkish legs; pale gray upperparts. *Breeding:* white head, neck and upper breast. *Nonbreeding:* dingy head, neck and upper breast. *3rd winter:* dark-tipped pinkish bill. *2nd winter:* grayish brown overall; gray mantle; white tail coverts and throat; mainly dark bill. *1st winter:* buffy white or pale brown overall with paler flight feathers; dark bill. *In flight:* gray spots on trailing edge near wing tip.

Size: *L* 24–27 in; *W* 4¾ ft.

Status: breeds locally along the northern coast; from fall to spring, abundant along the coast and the Columbia R., common in the Willamette Valley, uncommon in southwestern interior valleys and rare to uncommon in central Oregon.

Habitat: saltwater and brackish bays, estuaries, harbors and the open ocean; also city dumps and parks, wet fields and offshore islands.

Nesting: colonial but territorial; on bare rock or in low ground cover on island ledges; nest consists of loosely stacked grass, weeds, moss, roots, string, bones and seaweed; pair incubates 2–4 heavily marked greenish eggs for 27–28 days.

Feeding: forages while walking, wading, swimming or plunging; omnivorous diet includes fish, mollusks, crustaceans, nestling birds, plant material, garbage and carrion.

Voice: usual calls are a squealing *kjau,* a high-pitched, repeated *kea* and a "mewing" *ma-ah;* flight call is a single, throaty *kwoh;* attack call is *eeja-ah.*

Similar Species: *Herring Gull* (p. 173): pale yellow eyes; black-and-white wing tips; darker, more patterned immature. *Western Gull* (p. 175): darker upperparts; eyes usually yellow; whiter head and neck on nonbreeding bird; darker, more patterned immature.

Best Sites: Sand I. (Columbia R. mouth); along the Columbia R. east of the Cascades; along the coast; many locations in Portland, including the South Park Blocks.

176

SABINE'S GULL

Xema sabini

The easy, buoyant flight and highly contrasting plumage of the Sabine's Gull make it instantly recognizable and unforgettable. Commercial fishermen and residents of the Arctic have the best regular opportunities to appreciate this dainty and stunning bird, which wanders far out to sea, often beyond the limits of the continental shelf. Avid birders occasionally see single Sabine's Gulls or small flocks from shoreline viewpoints in Oregon, mostly in May and September and usually with the aid of a spotting scope, but most birds pass by offshore, far from view. Considering the pelagic nature of the species, the arrival of a few immature Sabine's Gulls inland each fall is somewhat surprising but highly anticipated. Beware, though, of misidentifying immature Black-legged Kittiwakes.

breeding

nonbreeding

ID: red-ringed dark eyes; yellow-tipped black bill; medium gray upperparts; dark legs. *Breeding:* dark gray "hood." *Nonbreeding:* partial "hood." *Juvenile:* brownish partial "hood," neck and back; barred back and wings; pale legs. *In flight:* mostly pale underwing; upperwing has gray triangle, white triangle and extensive black strip; notched white tail (black-tipped on juvenile).
Size: *L* 13–14 in; *W* 3 ft.
Status: uncommon to fairly common migrant offshore; rarely observed from land; rare inland visitor, usually in fall.
Habitat: highly pelagic; most birds remain well out of sight of land throughout their stay in Oregon waters.
Nesting: does not nest in Oregon.

Feeding: dips or swoops to the water's surface; gleans small fish and pelagic crustaceans while swimming; if forced to shore by storms, picks marine worms, crustaceans and insects from the water's surface or scavenges dead or dying fish.
Voice: generally silent; high-pitched calls at sea resemble those of the Arctic Tern.
Similar Species: *Juvenile Black-legged Kittiwake* (p. 178): black-marked gray mantle and black "collar"; dark "M" on upperwings in flight. *Bonaparte's Gull* (p. 168): paler mantle; pink or orangy (breeding) legs; head of nonbreeding bird is white except crown and ear spot; rounded tail and dark underwings in flight. *Franklin's Gull* (p. 167): red bill; reddish legs; darker mantle; partial white eye ring; mostly gray upperwing.
Best Sites: open ocean; Clatsop Spit; Cape Meares SP; Boiler Bay SP; Siuslaw R. mouth; Cape Blanco SP.

BLACK-LEGGED KITTIWAKE

Rissa tridactyla

Apart from the usually open-ocean Sabine's Gull, the Black-legged Kittiwake is the only true "seagull" (pelagic gull) regularly found in Oregon. This small, highly marine gull breeds on coastal cliffs at higher latitudes and spends the balance of the year on the open ocean, though some immature birds may spend the entire summer at sea farther south. Most sightings in Oregon are from pelagic boat trips or coastal headlands in fall, winter and spring. Late fall and winter storms that persist for several days may tire these small gulls and push them into nearshore waters and even onto exposed ocean beaches or into more sheltered harbors and estuaries. At such times, the unique combination of short, black legs and yellow bill readily identify Black-legged Kittiwakes as "birds of a different feather."

breeding

nonbreeding

1st winter

ID: black legs; dark eyes; white head and underparts; medium gray upperparts; yellow bill.

Nonbreeding: smudgy, grayish ear patch. *1st winter:* black bill; black ear patch and "collar"; gray mantle; dark wing markings. *In flight:* notched tail; small, crisply defined black wing tips; white underwings; juvenile has heavy, black "M" on upperwings and black-tipped tail.
Size: *L* 16–18 in; *W* 3 ft.
Status: fairly common migrant offshore from September to November and from early April to early June; uncommon winter resident offshore; irregular and uncommon migrant, summer lingerer and winter resident along the coast.
Habitat: mainly the open ocean, preferring areas along the edge of the continental

shelf and upwellings; young birds occasionally associate with other gulls in coastal locations, especially the mouth of the Columbia R.
Nesting: does not nest in Oregon.
Feeding: plunges, dips and surface-feeds for marine invertebrates, fish and offal; can dive to 20 ft below the surface.
Voice: generally silent in Oregon.
Similar Species: *Nonbreeding Sabine's Gull* (p. 177): much smaller; partial dark "hood"; yellow-tipped black bill; more black on upper wing tip and less below; gray wing coverts; wider tail. *Nonbreeding Bonaparte's Gull* (p. 168): much smaller; rounded tail; small, black bill; black-tipped white primaries.
Best Sites: Columbia R. mouth, especially during the May–June smelt run; Barview Jetty CP; Bayocean Spit; Cape Meares SP; Yaquina Head lighthouse; Yaquina Bay; Siuslaw R. estuary; Cape Arago SP.

CASPIAN TERN

Sterna caspia

A giant among its fellow terns, the Caspian Tern makes its presence known to the most casual observer by its robustness, size, eye-catching whiteness and commanding voice. Its heavy bill, deliberate flight and broad wings seem to span the conceptual gap between gulls and terns, but unlike even the smaller gulls, this tern is strictly a fish-eater. • The breeding colony at the mouth of the Columbia River, with over 9000 pairs, is the world's largest for this species. Historically, the Caspian Tern was a regular breeding resident on the large lakes of southern Oregon, but the only current large inland colony, which is shared with Forster's Terns, is on the Columbia River at Three Mile Island.

breeding

ID: daggerlike, blood red bill; white or pale gray underparts; black legs; folded wings extend beyond short tail. *Breeding:* peaked black "cap." *Nonbreeding:* white-streaked dark "cap." *Juvenile:* dull orange bill; white-streaked dark "cap"; "scaly" back. *In flight:* short, notched tail; wings mostly pale gray above and white below, darker areas near tips.

Size: *L* 19–23 in; *W* 4¼–4½ ft.

Status: locally common summer breeder along the Columbia R. and in south-central and southeastern Oregon; common migrant on the coast, locally common east of the Cascades, and uncommon but increasing inland in western Oregon.

Habitat: *Breeding:* sandy islands at the mouth of the Columbia R.; islands and spits on fresh water; reservoirs and larger rivers; less often in mixed colonies on flat, rocky islands. *In migration:* large bodies of water; estuaries; coastal beaches.

Nesting: colonial, with other species; in sand or gravel; scrape nest with mollusk- and crayfish-shell rim is lined with clam shells, rocks, twigs or vegetation; pair incubates 1–3 lightly spotted buff eggs for 25–28 days; family remains together until spring.

Feeding: hovers over water and plunges headfirst after small fish; also eats tadpoles and aquatic invertebrates.

Voice: gives a low, harsh *ca-arr;* parents utter a loud *kraa-uh* that juveniles answer with a high-pitched whistle.

Similar Species: *Forster's* (p. 182), *Arctic* (p. 181) and *Common* (p. 180) *terns:* much smaller; long tail streamers; red to orangy legs and bill (thinner, with dark tip, except on Arctic) on breeding birds; black bill on nonbreeding birds.

Best Sites: Columbia R. mouth area. *Summer:* Upper Klamath L.; Summer L.; L. Abert; Crump L.; Malheur NWR. *In migration:* Bayocean Spit; Yaquina Bay; Coos Bay North Spit.

COMMON TERN
Sterna hirundo

Terns are effortless fliers, and most people concede the title of "world's best long-distance traveler" to the Arctic Tern. Recently, however, a Common Tern banded in Great Britain was recovered in Australia—a record distance for any bird. • Preferring to hug the coastline in migration, the Common Tern regularly visits beaches and estuaries. It is especially common in the larger estuaries in fall migration, when it may also appear on interior lakes, reservoirs and larger rivers. • Difficulty in the identification of the three smaller *Sterna* terns seen in Oregon makes many out-of-habitat and out-of-season sighting claims suspect. In general, any tern seen in eastern Oregon is most likely to be a Forster's Tern, those in coastal habitats are probably Common Terns, and any flocks seen well out at sea are very likely Arctic Terns.

breeding

ID: light gray upperparts; white underparts; white rump and undertail coverts; tail streamers (longest on breeding bird) normally do not reach tips of folded wings. *Breeding:* black "cap"; thin, orangy red bill, usually with small, black tip; short, orangy red legs; grayish belly and breast. *Nonbreeding:* black bill and legs; partial black "cap" and poorly defined white forehead; dark shoulder bar. *Juvenile:* white-barred brownish or gray upperparts; bill and legs initially orangy or pinkish. *In flight:* strongly forked white tail with gray outer edges; gray upperwings; dark primary tips on nonbreeding bird; juvenile has shorter outer tail streamers.
Size: *L* 12–15 in; *W* 29–30 in.
Status: common migrant along the coast from late April to early June (especially early to mid-May) and from late July and October, with some birds occasionally lingering past October; very rare spring migrant and uncommon fall migrant inland.
Habitat: open ocean offshore, coast, bays, harbors and lagoons; rarely on interior freshwater lakes, reservoirs and rivers.
Nesting: does not nest in Oregon.
Feeding: hovers over water and plunges headfirst, mostly for small fish, but also crustaceans and insects.
Voice: high-pitched, drawn-out *keee-are* given mostly at the colony but also during foraging.
Similar Species: *Forster's Tern* (p. 182): slightly bulkier; thicker bill (orange on breeding bird) and longer legs; underparts always white; black eye-to-ear patch is diagnostic on nonbreeding bird and juvenile; broader wings; more white on upperwings; longer, all-white outer tail feathers.
Best Sites: Columbia R. mouth; Bayocean Spit; Yaquina Bay; Siuslaw R. estuary; Coos Bay North Spit.

ARCTIC TERN

Sterna paradisaea

This elegant tern rates among the most accomplished of avian migrants, with some arctic-nesting birds flying to and from the Antarctic each year. Most Arctic Terns take the oceanic route, and any small "white" tern seen far out on the open ocean is likely an Arctic Tern. • These terns take short rests at sea, using any piece of driftwood or other floating platform that comes along. They are often harassed by Parasitic Jaegers, which follow them southward from the Arctic. • Arctic Terns are rarely seen from land in Oregon, but if they are blown inshore by spring or fall storms, hundreds can appear along the coast, often in association with Red Phalaropes. No interior spring sightings of Arctic Terns have been confirmed in Oregon, but some birds have appeared inland in June and July.

breeding

ID: light gray upperparts; white "cheeks"; white rump and undertail coverts; long tail streamers reach beyond wing tips at rest. *Breeding:* black "cap"; small, red bill; very short, red legs; gray underparts. *Nonbreeding:* clearly defined white forehead; black bill and legs; partial black "cap"; indistinct dark shoulder bar. *Juvenile:* white bars on upperparts; dusky legs; short, notched tail. *In flight:* long, forked, darker-edged white tail; pale gray upperwings with little darkening at tips.
Size: *L* 14–17 in; *W* 31 in.
Status: common pelagic migrant from April to June (especially May) and from mid-July to mid-November (especially late August to September); rare coastal migrant; vagrant inland.
Habitat: open ocean in migration; occasionally visits estuaries, beaches and jetties if driven inshore by storms.

Nesting: does not nest in Oregon.
Feeding: hovers over water and swoops or plunges for small fish and crustaceans.
Voice: common call is a harsh, high-pitched, down-slurred *kee kahr;* most calls are harsh and buzzy; attack call is a dry, nasal *raaaaz;* also utters single short *kip* notes.
Similar Species: *Common Tern* (p. 180): longer legs; larger bill, usually black-tipped on breeding bird; shorter tail streamers compared to folded wings; nonbreeding bird and immature have darker primaries and more pronounced shoulder bar; juvenile often has some brown on upperparts. *Forster's Tern* (p. 182): longer legs; thicker bill, orange and black-tipped on breeding bird; nonbreeding bird and juvenile have diagnostic, black eye-to-ear patch.
Best Sites: open ocean; Columbia R. mouth; Barview Jetty CP; Yaquina Bay; Siuslaw R. estuary.

FORSTER'S TERN

Sterna forsteri

The Forster's Tern is Oregon's only strictly North American tern. It was once considered the same species as the very similar Common Tern. German naturalist Johann Reinhold Forster was the first person to recommend, based on tern specimens sent to him from the Hudson Bay region of Canada, that the Forster's Tern deserved full species status. • Forster's Tern is widespread in interior Oregon and fairly common as a colonial nesting bird on the large, shallow lakes and marshes of Klamath, Lake and Harney Counties and southwestern Deschutes County. There is one colony on the Columbia River at Three Mile Island, with other small colonies here and there east of the Cascades. Forster's Tern rarely reaches the coast.

nonbreeding

breeding

ID: light gray upperparts; white underparts, rump and undertail coverts; tail normally longer than folded wings. *Breeding:* black "cap"; black-tipped orange bill; short, orangy red legs. *Nonbreeding:* black bill; black eye-to-ear patch; white crown; dull orange legs. *Juvenile:* plain gray upperparts, initially tan-barred. *In flight:* long, forked, mostly white tail (shorter, darker streamers on juvenile); primaries white above on breeding bird and otherwise darkish.

Size: *L* 13–16 in; *W* 30–31 in.

Status: locally common breeding summer resident and migrant east of the Cascades; rare migrant and nonbreeding summer resident west of the Cascades; spring migration peaks in mid-spring; fall migration generally ends by late September.

Habitat: *Breeding:* large freshwater lakes and marshes; large rivers with islands; alka-line lakes. *In migration:* wetlands; coastal estuaries; open beaches.

Nesting: mainly colonial, often with other species; on the ground in mud or sand, or on a muskrat house, old grebe nest or floating vegetation platform; nest is lined with shells and grass; pair incubates 2–5, usually 3, brown-marked buff eggs for 23–24 days.

Feeding: hovers above the water and plunges headfirst after small fish, frogs and aquatic invertebrates; also catches airborne insects and eats carrion.

Voice: gives a short, nasal *keer keer* flight call; utters a grating *tzaap* at predators and intruders.

Similar Species: *Common Tern* (p. 180): more slender; redder bill and gray underparts in breeding plumage; partial "cap," dark shoulder bar and black legs in nonbreeding plumage; grayer upperwings; gray outer (not inner) tail feathers; more coastal.

Best Sites: *Summer:* Davis L. (Cascades Lakes); Klamath Forest NWR; Upper Klamath L.; Lower Klamath NWR; Summer Lake WMA; L. Abert; Malheur NWR.

BLACK TERN

Chlidonias niger

Even without brilliant colors, Black Terns are strikingly beautiful birds. Depending on what they are doing, their flight can be reminiscent of nighthawks, flycatchers, swallows or butterflies. Their zest and grace is unparalleled as they fly erratically but buoyantly across their nesting marsh. • Unmistakable in their breeding plumage, nesting Black Terns arrive at their Oregon colonies in late April and May, with most leaving by late September. Highly social, terns often breed in colonies and forage in flocks. • Black Tern populations have dropped in the past few decades partly as a result of wetland breeding habitat loss, but they often benefit from the restoration of upland habitat surrounding managed wetlands.

breeding

nonbreeding

ID: gray back, tail and wings; white undertail coverts; slender, black bill. *Breeding:* black head, breast and belly; reddish black legs. *Nonbreeding:* white forehead, neck and underparts; black hindcrown, nape, eye spot and ear spot; partial dark gray "collar." *Juvenile:* orange legs; plumage like nonbreeding adult, but browner and with pale barring on back and wings. *In flight:* plain, dark-gray wings; white undertail; mildly notched tail; irregular, wandering flight.

Size: *L* 9–10 in; *W* 24 in.

Status: locally common breeding summer resident and widespread uncommon migrant east of the Cascades; very rare west of the Cascades; state-listed as sensitive.

Habitat: shallow freshwater marshes, ponds and lakes. *In migration:* flooded fields; rarely on coastal estuaries.

Nesting: loosely colonial; in still water with emergent vegetation; on a muskrat house, abandoned grebe nest or platform of loose, dead vegetation; nest is usually flimsy and unlined; pair incubates 2–4 dark-blotched, buff or olive eggs for 19–21 days.

Feeding: flies across water and vegetation, hovering, dipping and landing for brief moments; snatches insects from the air or from tall grass; takes fish and aquatic insects from the water's surface; also eats small amphibians, earthworms, spiders, small crustaceans and leeches.

Voice: gives a shrill, metallic *kik-kik-kik-kik-kik* greeting call; *kreea* is the alarm call.

Similar Species: *Nonbreeding Forster's Tern* (p. 182) and *Common Tern* (p. 180): larger; much lighter coloration; different head patterns; much longer tail streamers.

Best Sites: wetlands throughout southeastern and south-central Oregon.

COMMON MURRE

Uria aalge

The alcids (auk family) occupy the same niche in the northern hemisphere that penguins do in the south. ("Penguin" comes from *Pinguinus pinguinus*, the now-extinct large, flightless Great Auk of the northern Atlantic.) • The slender, upright-standing Common Murre has typical alcid attributes: small wings, webbed feet and sleek, water-proof plumage for pursuing fish underwater, and it nests in huge, tightly packed colonies on offshore islands. • Some birds go northward from August to October, with some of them returning to nest. Nesting murres arrive at their colonies beginning in late March, possibly following a winter visit. • Although shaped to roll around in circles and stay on the nesting ledge, many murre eggs are dislodged in panic departures caused by predators or by boats approaching too closely.

breeding

ID: long, straight, pointed, black bill; dark legs and feet; white underparts; gray-streaked flanks. *Breeding:* dark brown head and upperparts with sharp demarcation on upper breast. *Nonbreeding:* blackish brown upperparts; white lower face, "chin" and neck; thin, dark line curving down from eye. *In flight:* body tilted upward; rapid, whirring wingbeats.
Size: *L* 17–18 in; *W* 26 in.
Status: abundant at coastal colonies and in nearshore waters in summer; common inshore and uncommon offshore in winter.
Habitat: *Breeding:* offshore islands, islets and sea stacks, rarely headland cliff ledges. *Foraging:* on the open ocean from just beyond the surf line to far offshore; father-and-chick pairs regularly visit the lower reaches of estuaries from July to August.

Nesting: highly colonial; lays eggs on bare, flat rock of cliff ledges or islands close to water; pair incubates 1 heavily marked pale egg for 30–35 days; young bird leaves the nest at 21 days and joins the father in the water below.
Feeding: dives for fish, squid, crustaceans, mollusks and marine worms; most birds in the water below colonies are nonbreeding immatures and unpaired adults.
Voice: utters a low, harsh *murrr;* dependent juvenile gives a high-pitched, quavering, repeated *feed-me-now* whistle.
Similar Species: *Murrelets* (pp. 186–87): much smaller; stubby bills; stocky bodies; very fast wingbeats; more erratic flight. *Nonbreeding Rhinoceros Auklet* (p. 189): slightly smaller; stockier; grayish brown overall except for white belly and under-tail; stubbier, yellowish bill.
Best Sites: Three Arch Rocks, Tillamook Co.; Ecola SP; Cape Meares SP; Yaquina Head; Cape Arago SP; Cape Blanco SP; Goat I., Curry Co.

PIGEON GUILLEMOT

Cepphus columba

Pigeon Guillemots are among the most widespread and commonly seen alcids along the Pacific Coast, and they are the most likely to remain inshore. • The distinctively patterned black breeding plumage, with its large white wing patches, vermilion gape and startling red feet, is designed for breeding displays and for visual stimulation of the chicks in the dark nest site. The Pigeon Guillemot's much different gray-and-white winter look, which is reminiscent of the Rock Dove, as well as its similarity in size and body form, inspired its common and scientific names. It is still called "Sea Pigeon" in Alaska. • During summer, these black-and-white seabirds forage close to their small colony sites.

breeding

ID: *Breeding:* black overall, except for white wing patch; dark bill and eyes; bright red legs and feet. *Nonbreeding:* whitish head, neck and underparts; dark eye patch; mottled gray-and-white back and crown. *In flight:* stubby wings; white wing patch split by brownish black line; gray underwings; conspicuous trailing red feet.

Size: *L* 13–14 in; *W* 23 in.

Status: fairly common in spring and summer and rare in winter along the coast; rare offshore in winter.

Habitat: shallow water with offshore islands; rocky or cliff-edged seashores. *Breeding:* estuaries with piers and other shoreline structures.

Nesting: loosely colonial or solitary; on the ground or a rock, inside a crevice, cranny or cavity in a cliff, in boulder rubble or on an artificial structure; nest scrape is lined with loose stones and shells; pair incubates 1–2 pale cream eggs with gray-and-brown blotches for 29–32 days; young leave the nest on fledging at 33–37 days.

Feeding: prefers 30–95 ft deep inshore water; dives to seabed for small fish, mollusks, crustaceans, worms and other marine invertebrates; probes underwater rocky recesses and vegetation for freshwater and marine invertebrates; also eats herring eggs.

Voice: distinctive series of wheezy, stuttering, whistled trills and screams, especially near the nest site.

Similar Species: *Breeding Common Murre* (p. 184): larger; longer bill; dark brown upperparts; white underparts; all-dark upperwing; highly colonial on ledges and stack tops. *Murrelets* (pp. 186–87): smaller; browner or black above, white below; small bills; dark feet; all-dark upperwing; usually in pairs.

Best Sites: coastal headlands and lookout points; Yaquina Bay; Charleston; Bandon.

MARBLED MURRELET

Brachyramphus marmoratus

Although Marbled Murrelets were first described as early as 1789, their nests were not found until 1961 in Asia and 1974 in North America. Most Marbled Murrelets nest individually high atop old-growth rainforest trees. They visit their nests at night to avoid diurnal raptors and fly high, fast and directly to thwart nocturnal owls of the lower canopy. • Adults and young may stay together well past summer. Pair bonds are very strong, and pairs can be found well out to sea, even in winter. When one bird takes off from the water, it will call until it hears a reply from its partner. These stocky birds are sometimes seen in small flocks, especially when feeding close to nest sites.

nonbreeding

breeding

ID: appears flat-headed. *Breeding:* mottled dark brown throughout; paler on throat and undertail coverts. *Nonbreeding:* black "helmet," narrow nape line, back and wings; white "collar," underparts and shoulder stripe. *In flight:* all-dark wings.
Size: *L* 9–10 in; *W* 16 in.
Status: local breeding resident from April to July; uncommon from spring to fall and rare in winter in nearshore waters; *marmoratus* ssp. is federal- and state-listed as threatened.
Habitat: *Breeding:* old-growth rainforests. *In migration* and *winter:* open ocean, usually close to shore; some birds may retain nest sites and territories over winter.
Nesting: usually in a tree crown, but often on a lower horizontal limb of a tall rainforest tree; nests in a depression in moss or

lichens; pair incubates 1 dark-spotted pale green egg for 28–30 days; both parents feed the chick until it jumps to the ground at 27–40 days.
Feeding: dives for food, usually within 3 mi of the shore and in depths of less than 200 ft; eats mainly small schooling fish, adding small crustaceans in winter.
Voice: common location call in the water or in flight is a shrieking *keer;* various whistles and groans are given at the nest.
Similar Species: *Cassin's Auklet* (p. 188): heavier bill; rounder head; sooty gray overall with lighter belly; whitish crescent above yellowish eye; light stripe on underwing. *Nonbreeding Rhinoceros Auklet* (p. 189): larger; heavier, yellow bill; grayish brown overall except for white belly and undertail; feeds farther offshore.
Best Sites: Barview Jetty CP (Tillamook Bay); Cape Meares SP; Boiler Bay SP; Yaquina Head; Yaquina Bay South Jetty; Umpqua Lighthouse SP; Cape Arago SP.

ANCIENT MURRELET
Synthliboramphus antiquus

During the breeding season, this proficient mariner's feathery white "eyebrows" and gray mantle give it a distinguished, aged look. Unfortunately, few birders will ever see the Ancient Murrelet in breeding plumage along the Oregon coast, because this small, relatively slender alcid is mainly an offshore migrant and winter resident, but a few birds do occasionally summer here. • The Ancient Murrelet's feet and wings are not as suited to diving as those of other small alcids. • At its island nesting colonies in Alaska and northern British Columbia, this murrelet typically raises two nestlings (most alcids raise one). Nestlings leave the nest burrow only one to three days after hatching and are reared entirely at sea. • The long and awkward genus name simply means "small bill."

breeding

ID: black "hood"; dark gray back; white-mottled gray flanks; white lower neck and belly; short, pale yellow bill; dark eyes; pale blue legs and feet. *Breeding:* black throat; wispy white streaks on crown and nape. *Nonbreeding* and *juvenile:* white throat; upper head all or mostly black. *In flight:* all dark above; white underparts and wing linings.
Size: *L* 9–10 in; *W* 17 in.
Status: fairly common offshore migrant, uncommon in winter and rare in summer.
Habitat: from inshore tidal upwellings to the edge of the continental shelf; often

seen from headlands, jetties and beaches; rarely occurs in harbors and protected bays.
Nesting: does not nest in Oregon.
Feeding: swims and dives to 50 or 60 ft for krill, other crustaceans and very small fish.
Voice: generally silent; gives a clipped whistle at sea; nesting birds utter a variety of wheezy and whistled notes.
Similar Species: *Xantus's Murrelet:* daintier; black above and white below; dark bill; broken white eye ring; white below eye and bill; blackish flanks. *Cassin's Auklet* (p. 188): sooty gray overall with white belly and undertail coverts; dusky bill with light area on lower mandible base; gray underwing with light stripe.
Best Sites: headlands and jetties from November to March; Barview Jetty CP; Cape Meares SP; Boiler Bay SP; Yaquina Head.

CASSIN'S AUKLET

Ptychoramphus aleuticus

The small size and the ground-nesting habits of the Cassin's Auklet make it extremely vulnerable to predators—including foxes, cats and rats—introduced near its island nesting colonies. Southern populations try to compensate for such losses by raising a second chick later in the breeding season. • Natural oils secreted by an alcid's uropygial gland help to waterproof its feathers against cold water, but waterproofed feathers are useless against petrochemical spills. Matted, oil-contaminated feathers lose their insulative properties, and, in preening, the birds ingest much of the heavy oil, which then coats the digestive system, resulting in a slow and painful death by starvation and exposure.

ID: bold white crescent above pale yellow eye; sooty gray upperparts; paler gray underparts; white belly and undertail coverts; stubby, dark bill with light area at base of lower mandible. *In flight:* rounded wings; gray underwing with short, lighter stripe near body; flies close to water.
Size: *L* 8–9 in; *W* 15 in.
Status: common in nearshore waters in fall but otherwise rare; uncommon to common offshore; rare breeding summer resident on coastal islands.
Habitat: *Breeding:* offshore islands and sea stacks, steep cliffs and slopes. *Foraging:* ocean waters, especially over upwellings along the continental shelf and deeper water near nest sites.

Nesting: colonial; pair digs an underground burrow or uses a natural rock crevice for the normally unlined nest; pair incubates 1 creamy white egg for 37–42 days; pair feeds the chick until fledging at 42 days; it leaves the nest at 50 days and swims out to sea.
Feeding: swims underwater to a depth of 120 ft for small crustaceans, squid and small fish.
Voice: usually silent away from the nest site; foraging pair may utter short, sharp *krik* location notes.
Similar Species: *Nonbreeding Rhinoceros Auklet* (p. 189): much larger; heavier, yellow bill; dark all around eye; unmarked dark underwings. *Breeding Marbled Murrelet* (p. 186): heavily mottled brown plumage; slimmer, usually uptilted bill; unmarked dark underwings.
Best Sites: pelagic boat trips; occasionally seen from shore anywhere along the coast.

RHINOCEROS AUKLET
Cerorhinca monocerata

The Rhinoceros Auklet is named for its striking "horn," which is present only during the March-to-June breeding season. • During winter storms, "Rhinos" ride out mountainous waves, seemingly unaffected by the chilling wind and ocean spray. These stocky, medium-sized alcids may be common along the coast in winter, but the better weather conditions of spring and summer allow more dependable viewing near their scattered breeding sites. • Feeding birds can remain submerged for up to two minutes. Unlike other alcids, Rhinoceros Auklets sometimes cooperate in flocks to herd sand lance and herring schools by blowing bubbles from the sides of their mouths, much like feeding humpback whales do. • Other auklets use their throat pouches to carry food to their nests, but the Rhinoceros Auklet uses its bill, as do its close relatives, the puffins.

breeding

ID: drab grayish brown overall; white belly and undertail coverts; pale, yellowish or bluish legs and feet. *Breeding:* fleshy, ivory-colored, vertical "horn" at base of orangy yellow bill; yellow eyes; 2 whitish plumes at side of head. *Nonbreeding:* dull yellow bill. *In flight:* all-dark wings.
Size: *L* 14–16 in; *W* 22 in.
Status: locally uncommon summer breeder; uncommon offshore from late August to early November and locally uncommon in March and April; rare inshore in winter.
Habitat: *Breeding:* small islands, sea stacks and cliffs with enough soil for burrowing. *Foraging:* inshore coastal waters and offshore on the open ocean over the continental shelf; prefers deeper water.
Nesting: colonial; in a burrow, up to 20 ft long, in deep soil, usually into a grassy slope at least 30 ft above sea level; nest is a cup of moss and twigs; pair incubates 1 lightly spotted off-white egg for 42–49 days; night-fed young fledges in 45–52 days.
Feeding: dives to 120 ft deep to catch small schooling fish and crustaceans; switches to pelagic fish and squid in winter.
Voice: usually silent; utters a rasping squeak at sea; gives growling and braying calls at the nest site.
Similar Species: *Cassin's Auklet* (p. 188): much smaller; white crescent above eye; darker bill; light underwing stripe. *Breeding Common Murre* (p. 184): bulkier; dark brown above and white below; long, dark, pointed bill; white wing linings. *Immature Tufted Puffin* (p. 190): wider bill; dark undertail coverts.
Best Sites: Goat I. and Hunters I., Curry Co.; Sea Lion Caves, Lane Co.; Yaquina Head, Otter Crest and Cape Foulweather, Lincoln Co.; Cape Meares and Cape Lookout, Tillamook Co.

189

TUFTED PUFFIN
Fratercula cirrhata

Puffins, the clowns of the alcid world, are among the most photographed and painted of birds. Their colorful bills and chunky bodies set them apart from most other coastal inhabitants. • The Tufted Puffin, with its massive, brightly colored bill, may look awkward in the air and clumsy on land, but its stubby wings propel it with surprising speed and agility when it swims in pursuit of prey or to avoid aerial predators. • During the breeding season, Tufted Puffins can be seen at the entrances to their burrows and on the water near colonies, but they forage well out to sea. In August, adults abandon their chicks and move offshore. The chicks remain in the burrow for a week and then, still flightless, leap into the water and paddle out to sea, where they remain until they attain breeding maturity at age four or five.

breeding

ID: massive, laterally flattened bill; large head; yellow eyes; soot-black plumage; pinkish orange legs and feet. *Breeding:* bill is reddish orange and yellow; white face; long, downcurved, yellow tuft behind eye; red eye ring. *Nonbreeding:* dull orange bill with dark base; sooty face; short, golden gray tuft behind eye.
Size: *L* 15–16 in; *W* 25 in.
Status: locally common breeding summer resident at island and headland colonies; generally uncommon offshore in summer; winters well offshore and very rarely close to land.
Habitat: *Breeding:* offshore islands with enough soil to construct burrows; nearshore waters, especially with upwellings. *Winter:* open ocean offshore.

Nesting: colonial; burrow, usually 1–3 ft long (may be up to 20 ft), leads to a nest chamber, which may be lined with grass and feathers; pair incubates 1 dark-spotted white egg for 41 days; the young fledges in 35–40 days.
Feeding: dives to great depths, often for up to 2 minutes, to capture small schooling fish; also eats crustaceans, mollusks, sea urchins and rarely, marine algae.
Voice: generally silent; softly growls and grunts at the nesting colony.
Similar Species: *Nonbreeding Horned Puffin:* white breast; gray face. *Rhinoceros Auklet* (p. 189): smaller bill; white undertail coverts. *Male Surf Scoter* (p. 86): larger; white patches on forehead and nape; bill is orange, white and black.
Best Sites: Three Arch Rocks, Tillamook Co.; Haystack Rock, Clatsop Co. (colony viewable from the beach at Cannon Beach); Haystack Rock, Tillamook Co.; Island Rock and Goat I., Curry Co. (visible from Harris Beach SP).

ROCK DOVE

Columba livia

Our Rock Doves are the feral version of Eurasian birds that were first domesticated around 4500 BC. Introduced to North America in the 1600s, they have settled wherever cities, towns, farms or grain elevators exist. Some birds have reverted to nesting on tall cliffs—their original nesting habitat. • Rock Doves have been used as food, as message couriers (both Caesar and Napoleon used them) and as scientific subjects. Much of our understanding of bird migration, endocrinology, sensory perception, flight, behavior and other biological functions derives from experiments involving Rock Doves. • The Rock Dove's great variation in coloration is a result of extensive inbreeding over time.

ID: highly variable build and color; most birds have a white rump, orangy pink feet and dark-tipped tail; birds closest to wild ancestors are gray overall with bluish gray head, iridescent, green-and-purple neck and upper breast and 2 dark wing bars; other birds may be mostly white, tan, or blackish brown. *In flight:* broad, fan-shaped tail; powerful, deep, irregular wingbeats; holds wings in deep "V" while gliding and in display flight; often in large flocks; wings often make clapping sound on takeoff.
Size: *L* 12–14 in; *W* 28 in.
Status: common year-round resident.
Habitat: urban and suburban areas, railroad yards, grain terminals, farms and ranches; wilder birds use cliffs and canyon walls; absent only from dense forests and arctic-alpine habitats.

Nesting: on ledges of barns, cliffs, bridges, buildings and towers; flimsy nest of sticks, grass and assorted vegetation is adorned with debris in urban sites; pair incubates 2 eggs for about 18 days; parents feed the young with regurgitated food and crop "milk"; young are independent at fledging; pair may raise up to 5 broods a year.
Feeding: gleans the ground for waste grain, seeds, fruits and human scraps; occasionally eats insects.
Voice: female occasionally clucks; male and female utter a slow series of low hoots; male's song is a soft, cooing *coorrr-coorrr-coorrr.*
Similar Species: *Band-tailed Pigeon* (p. 192): slightly larger; gray rump; dark band at base of paler tail; yellow bill and feet; white half-"collar"; unbarred wings. *Mourning Dove* (p. 193): much slimmer; grayish fawn overall plumage, less gray on head, breast and belly; dark wing spots; long, diamond-shaped tail; shorter wings.
Best Sites: at ship docks and railroad yards where grain is available.

BAND-TAILED PIGEON

Columba fasciata

Clinging clumsily to twigs that may barely support their weight, Band-tailed Pigeons reach into adjacent foliage to pick nuts and fruit. Their presence overhead is often revealed by the occasional noisy slapping of their broad wings as they shift position in the canopy. These large, heavy pigeons forage anywhere from sea-level forests to the upper limits of the oak woodlands, especially in canyons where the oak is mixed with madrones, and in mixed woodlands, such as fir and maple. They are also found in residential areas with large evergreens. • This bird's common and scientific names both refer to the broad gray band on its tail—*fascia* means "a band" in Latin.

ID: gray overall; purple-tinged head and breast; dark eyes; black-tipped yellow bill; yellow legs and feet; white "collar" on iridescent green nape. *In flight:* much like Rock Dove, but has longer, mostly pale tail with darker base band and more direct flight, often in small flocks.
Size: *L* 13–15 in; *W* 26 in.
Status: fairly common breeding summer resident and migrant in dense coniferous and mixed forests from the coast to the western slope of the Cascades; locally uncommon in winter in the interior valleys of western Oregon; very rare along the coast in winter; very rare east of the Cascades from March to October.
Habitat: *Breeding:* mainly coniferous rainforests, especially riparian or moist bottomland ones. *In migration* and *winter:* agricultural lands, interior valleys and forested habitats throughout western Oregon.

Nesting: in a tree; twig nest is lined with conifer needles, moss or breast feathers; female incubates at night, male by day, 1 (rarely 2) all-white egg for 16–22 days; young is fed regurgitated food and crop "milk" and fledges at 22–29 days; pair raises 2–3 broods per year.
Feeding: seeds; grain; fruit; tree and shrub flower buds; attracted to salt licks.
Voice: call notes include a nasal *waaaaa;* male's song is a repetition of 2 owl-like *hwoo* notes.
Similar Species: *Rock Dove* (p. 191): variable build and color; usually has white rump and dark wing bars; no half-"collar." *Mourning Dove* (p. 193): much smaller; grayish fawn overall, less gray on head, breast and belly; dark wing spots; long, diamond-shaped tail.
Best Sites: coastal rainforests; mixed woodlands along the coast, in the Willamette Valley and on the western slope of the Cascades; oak-conifer woodlands in the southwest.

MOURNING DOVE

Zenaida macroura

The soothing, rhythmic *coo* of the Mourning Dove is a common sound in Oregon's woodlands, farmlands and suburban parks and gardens, as it is throughout much of North America. Ranked second to the Red-winged Blackbird in the number of breeding bird survey routes that it is found in, and ranked eleventh in relative abundance, the Mourning Dove is one of the most common and widespread land birds of North America. • All members of this family feed their young with "milk"—a nutritious liquid produced by glands in the bird's crop. • Mourning Doves are swift, direct fliers, and their wings make a distinctive, whistling sound as the birds accelerate. • The Mourning Dove's name reflects its sad-sounding song. The genus name *Zenaida* honors Zénaïde, Princess of Naples and wife of zoologist Charles Lucien Bonaparte in the early 1800s.

ID: sleek profile; grayish fawn overall; pinkish tinges on neck and upper breast, especially on male; several blackish spots on upperparts; slender, gray bill; pinkish red feet. *In flight:* fast and direct flight on short, rounded wings; gray underwings; very long, tapering, black-and-white-trimmed tail.
Size: *L* 11–13 in; *W* 18 in.
Status: rare to common breeding summer resident; common migrant in March and April and from August to early October; rare to fairly common winter resident; very scarce in north coastal counties.
Habitat: *Breeding:* open woodlands and forest edges next to grasslands and parks, rarely uses extensive woods or forests. *In migration* and *winter:* widespread in agricultural areas, waste areas, gravelly areas and suburbs.

Nesting: usually in a tree, but occasionally on the ground; flimsy twig platform is sometimes built on top of a songbird nest; pair incubates 2 white eggs for 14 days and feeds the young by regurgitation and crop "milk"; the young fledge at 15 days and are independent 1 week later.
Feeding: picks seeds and waste grains from the ground; readily takes to city and suburban feeders, often arriving in small flocks.
Voice: mournful, soft, slow *oh-woe-woe-woe* is often misidentified as an owl hooting.
Similar Species: *Rock Dove* (p. 191): stockier; typically with iridescent neck, white rump, dark wing bars and broad, fan-shaped tail. *Band-tailed Pigeon* (p. 192): much larger; partial white "collar"; iridescent, green nape; yellow bill and feet; broad, fan-shaped tail.
Best Sites: *Summer:* widespread. *Winter:* agricultural areas east of the Cascades; interior western valleys.

193

BARN OWL

Tyto alba

The haunting look and eerie screams of this night hunter have inspired many superstitions, yet people who know the Barn Owl appreciate its subtle beauty and the benefits it brings to farmers by eating so many rodents. • Nest boxes have stabilized populations in some areas, but intensive agriculture and the loss of hedgerows and barns have threatened others. Almost any open area serves as a foraging site, and Barn Owls are surprisingly tolerant of human activities as long as their nest sites are not threatened. Some birds have been known to roost even in large garages with people working below. • If food is plentiful, Barn Owls often raise a second, and even a third, brood in the same nest. • Barn Owls have rather slow wingbeats, but they are capable of speeds of 50 mph.

ID: gray-patterned tawny upperparts with lighter markings; white underparts; dark brown or blackish eyes; heartlike reddish border around white face; ivory colored bill; pinkish white cere; light gray feet and legs. *In flight:* mostly whitish below with some gray underwing barring; feet extend beyond tail.

Size: *Male: L* 13–14 in; *W* 34 in. *Female: L* 14–15 in; *W* 35 in.

Status: common year-round resident west of the Cascades; locally uncommon year-round resident east of the Cascades.

Habitat: almost any open habitat, including grasslands, deserts, marshes and farm fields.

Nesting: cavity in a tree, cliff, cave, riverbank, building, haystack or nest box;

female incubates 5–7 nest-stained dull white eggs for 29–34 days; male delivers food while female broods and tends the young.

Feeding: usually hunts in full darkness; mostly flies close to the ground in quartering flights for small mammals; also eats some amphibians, reptiles, fish, invertebrates and roosting birds.

Voice: calls include harsh, raspy screeches and hisses; also makes metallic clicking sounds; often heard flying high over cities and residential areas late at night.

Similar Species: *Snowy Owl* (p. 198): larger; stockier; mostly white, often with dark barring and spots; yellow eyes; winter only. *Short-eared Owl* (p. 205): dark area accentuates yellow eye; vertical brown streaks on breast and belly; black "wrist" patches in flight; hunts by twilight.

Best Sites: agricultural lands at lower elevations in western and north-central Oregon; along the Columbia R. in Sherman, Morrow and Umatilla Counties.

FLAMMULATED OWL

Otus flammeolus

As the campfire settles into glowing embers, an odd, low-pitched sound comes from beyond the clearing edge. A Flammulated Owl has just shaken off its daytime lethargy and is preparing to begin its nocturnal hunt for large insects and anything else it can track down and overpower. • Once the summer supply of insects has dwindled and the season's youngsters have been safely fledged, the Flammulated Owl bids farewell to its mountain forests for another year and heads off for the warmth of Mexico or Guatemala. • Increased attention by birders and raptor researchers has revealed that this small, dark-eyed, nocturnal insectivore, once considered rare, is actually widespread and numerous in many areas.

gray morph

ID: variable gray or rufous overall; dark-streaked whitish breast; dark-centered white spots on shoulders and wing coverts; white "eyebrows" indent top of rusty or gray facial disc; grayish bill; dark eyes; often shows small "ear" tufts. *In flight:* wings are generally white-barred brown and gray.
Size: *L* 6–7 in; *W* 15 in.
Status: fairly common breeding summer resident east of the Cascades; rare breeding summer resident in southwestern Oregon; birds return in late spring and leave in September and October; state-listed as sensitive.
Habitat: forests of ponderosa pine alone or mixed with Douglas-fir, grand fir and western larch. *Breeding:* often near clearings or in riparian areas with aspens and a brushy understory of saplings, oak or other hardwoods.

Nesting: uses a natural cavity or an old hole of a sapsucker or other woodpecker, occasionally taking over an active nest of another species; female incubates 2–3 cream-tinted white eggs for 21–24 days; the young fledge at 25 days.
Feeding: strictly nocturnal; catches prey in flight, on the ground and from the foliage of both the canopy and understory; eats mostly arthropods, especially moths, beetles, crickets and grasshoppers.
Voice: utters low-frequency notes like those of a distant larger owl; very difficult to locate.
Similar Species: *Western Screech-Owl* (p. 196): larger; generally brown or gray with similar markings; large, yellow eyes; face usually has less pronounced white markings and less rusty coloration. *Northern Saw-whet Owl* (p. 207) and *Northern Pygmy-Owl* (p. 199): heavier; no prominent "ear" tufts; yellow eyes.
Best Sites: Starr Campground (Blue Mts.); Ochoco Ranger Station; Spring Creek; Elkhorn Mts.; Bear Valley, Grant Co.; Logan Valley; Idlewild Campground (Burns).

195

WESTERN SCREECH-OWL

Otus kennicottii

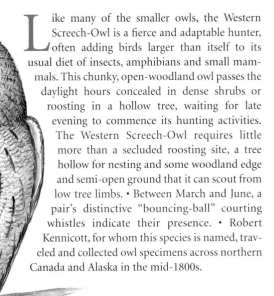

Like many of the smaller owls, the Western Screech-Owl is a fierce and adaptable hunter, often adding birds larger than itself to its usual diet of insects, amphibians and small mammals. This chunky, open-woodland owl passes the daylight hours concealed in dense shrubs or roosting in a hollow tree, waiting for late evening to commence its hunting activities. The Western Screech-Owl requires little more than a secluded roosting site, a tree hollow for nesting and some woodland edge and semi-open ground that it can scout from low tree limbs. • Between March and June, a pair's distinctive "bouncing-ball" courting whistles indicate their presence. • Robert Kennicott, for whom this species is named, traveled and collected owl specimens across northern Canada and Alaska in the mid-1800s.

ID: usually streaky brown overall along the humid coastal plain and gray overall elsewhere; narrow, dark, vertical breast stripes; partially dark-bordered facial disc; often shows small "ear" tufts; gray bill; yellow eyes. *In flight:* pale-lined, barred, grayish or brownish wings; dark "wrist" patch; white spots on upperwing.

Size: *Male:* L 8–9 in; W 18–20 in. *Female:* L 10–11 in; W 22–24 in.

Status: common year-round resident in interior western valleys, along the coast and at lower elevations in the mountains; uncommon year-round resident at lower elevations east of the Cascades.

Habitat: mid-elevation forests of all types, including coniferous forests with juniper stands, chaparral and oak woodlands, riparian woodlands, towns, orchards, farms, ranches and desert oases.

Nesting: in an abandoned woodpecker cavity, stump, nest box, or magpie nest; adds no nest material; female, fed by the male, incubates 2–5 white eggs for about 26 days; both adults feed the young through summer.

Feeding: nocturnal; swoops from a perch to capture invertebrates, mice, voles, amphibians and occasionally songbirds, often taking prey larger than itself.

Voice: courtship song is a distinctive series of soft, accelerating, even-pitched whistles and clear notes, with a rhythm like that of a bouncing ball coming to a stop; also gives a short trill followed by a longer trill; pairs often harmonize.

Similar Species: *Flammulated Owl* (p. 195): smaller; at least some rusty coloration on face and upperparts; dark eyes; whitish "eyebrows"; coarser breast markings; prefers conifers at higher elevations.

Best Sites: riparian areas; suburbs and city parks in western interior valleys; towns, orchards and desert oases east of the Cascades.

GREAT HORNED OWL

Bubo virginianus

The Great Horned Owl, the most widely distributed avian predator in the Western Hemisphere, is arguably the most formidable. Unchallenged in any habitat from desert to dense forest, the large, power-fully built, aggressive Great Horned Owl normally lives a long life in almost any habitat except arctic-alpine areas. • The Great Horned Owl tends to hunt in low light, when its prey is more active. Its strong talons, which take 30 pounds of force to open, can sever the spinal column of prey that outweigh it, and its acute hearing and sight allow it to hunt for a wide variety of nocturnal mammals, amphibians and other birds, including roosting waterfowl and hawks. With its poorly developed sense of smell, this owl happily hunts skunks, but even its molted feathers often retain the odor!

ID: heavily mot-tled, gray-, brown-and-black upper-parts; dark horizontal bar-ring on white or buffy underparts; prominent "ear" tufts; large, yellow eyes; interrupted brownish facial disc with partial dark border. *Juvenile:* paler; no ear tufts; whitish fore-head. *In flight:* broad, barred wings; paler below; slow, measured wingbeats; short glides; will fly over open water.
Size: *Male: L* 18–22 in; *W* 3¼–3¾ ft. *Female: L* 21–25 in; *W* 3¾–4¼ ft.
Status: common year-round resident.
Habitat: almost any open habitat below timberline; agricultural areas; suburban woodlots and parks.
Nesting: typically uses a tree-platform nest of another species, sometimes uses a tree cavity, cliff, deserted building or artificial platform or nests on the ground; nest may be lined with bark shreds, leaves, downy breast feathers or fur; female, fed by the male, incubates 2–4 dull white eggs for 30–37 days.
Feeding: opportunistic; mainly nocturnal, from a perch, but may hunt on the ground or from flight; eats large invertebrates and birds as large as geese, as well as rodents, amphibians and reptiles.
Voice: breeding male gives 4–6 deep hoots: *hoo-hoo-hoooo hoo-hoo* or *eat-my-food, I'll-eat you;* female in a pair duet gives the higher-pitched hoots.
Similar Species: *Long-eared Owl* (p. 204): much smaller; very slim appearance; more startled-looking stare; largely vertical breast markings; narrower head and "ear" tufts; dark "wrist" patch in flight. *Barred Owl* (p. 202): smaller; more rounded body; paler; tuftless, rounded head; more conspicuous facial disc; coarse vertical belly streaks.
Best Sites: any wooded site.

SNOWY OWL
Nyctea scandiaca

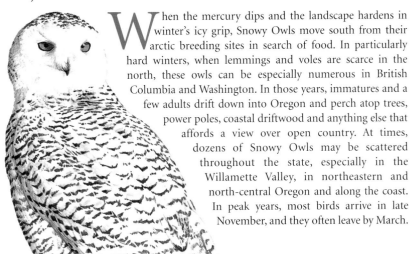

When the mercury dips and the landscape hardens in winter's icy grip, Snowy Owls move south from their arctic breeding sites in search of food. In particularly hard winters, when lemmings and voles are scarce in the north, these owls can be especially numerous in British Columbia and Washington. In those years, immatures and a few adults drift down into Oregon and perch atop trees, power poles, coastal driftwood and anything else that affords a view over open country. At times, dozens of Snowy Owls may be scattered throughout the state, especially in the Willamette Valley, in northeastern and north-central Oregon and along the coast. In peak years, most birds arrive in late November, and they often leave by March.

ID: yellow eyes; black bill and talons; white feet. *Male:* becomes almost entirely white with age; very little dark flecking. *Female:* white with dark barring on breast and upperparts. *Immature:* heavier brownish gray barring. *In flight:* underwings mostly or all white; upperwings often have dark barring.
Size: *Male: L* 22–23 in; *W* 4¾ ft. *Female: L* 24–25 in; *W* 5¼–5½ ft.
Status: irregular, rare, but sometimes widespread winter resident.
Habitat: open-country habitats, including farmlands, grasslands, marshes, wet meadows, salt marshes and sand dunes.
Nesting: does not nest in Oregon.
Feeding: opportunistic; usually uses a sit-and-wait technique; eats mostly rodents,

but is capable of catching large waterfowl and mammals as large as hares.
Voice: generally silent on wintering grounds, but will utter low grunting sounds when flushed, as well as quite musical, soft warbles and soft barking sounds; may scream at territorial rivals.
Similar Species: *Barn Owl* (p. 194): much smaller; slimmer; red-bordered heartlike white facial disc; dark eyes; gray-and-tawny upperparts; finely spotted white underparts. *Short-eared Owl* (p. 205): much smaller; mottled, tawny brown upperparts; bold brown streaks on breast; pronounced facial disc with dark areas around eyes; short, centrally placed "ear" tufts; hunts by twilight. *Great Gray Owl* (p. 203): all-gray plumage; prominent facial disc; mainly nocturnal.
Best Sites: Clatsop Spit jetty; Bayocean Spit; Sauvie I.; Fern Ridge Reservoir; farmlands outside Boardman; Cold Springs NWR; Grande Ronde Valley; Crow Creek area.

NORTHERN PYGMY-OWL

Glaucidium gnoma

Ounce for ounce, the Northern Pygmy-Owl may be the fiercest predator in North America. Oregon's smallest owl, it regularly catches prey that outweighs it. Prey may even be dragged some distance before the owl can finally subdue and dispatch its hard-won meal. • The Northern Pygmy-Owl is a daytime predator. With a poorly developed facial disc, it must depend more on vision than hearing to locate prey. • These owls are most likely to be seen outside of the breeding season, when individuals move into towns and farms to hunt birds and small mammals. They often end up at bird feeders, where they can wreak havoc on wintering flocks. • The dark black "eyes" on the back of this owl's head trick predators into believing that the Northern Pygmy-Owl is watching them.

red morph

ID: brown uperparts; white-spotted crown, neck and back; boldly dark-streaked pale underparts; large, rounded head with 2 black "eyes" on back; indistinct facial disc; fierce, yellow eyes; light-colored bill; inconspicuous "ear" tufts; long, narrow, barred tail. *In flight:* rounded, white-and-dark-barred wings with brownish linings; usually short, woodpecker-like flights.
Size: *L* 7 in; *W* 15 in.
Status: uncommon to common year-round resident; state-listed as sensitive.
Habitat: coniferous and mixed forests, including high-elevation conifers.
Nesting: tree cavity, sometimes lined with cedar strips or feathers; female incubates 3–7 glossy white eggs for about 28 days; young fledge at about 23 days and disperse from the nesting area.
Feeding: mostly by day and early evening; eats beetles, butterflies, grasshoppers,

moths, birds up to woodpecker-sized, mammals as large as red squirrels, amphibians and reptiles.
Voice: often calls throughout the day for much of summer; main song is an easily imitated series of monotonous, low-pitched *toot* notes, sometimes preceded by a faster, quieter trill.
Similar Species: no other owl has false eyes. *Northern Saw-whet Owl* (p. 207) and *Boreal Owl* (p. 206): slightly larger and chunkier; shorter, weakly or unbarred tail; white-spotted dark brown upperparts; blurrier streaking on underparts; prominent facial disc. *Western Screech-Owl* (p. 196): larger; often shows conspicuous "ear" tufts; prominent facial disc; gray bill; unspotted head; unbarred tail.
Best Sites: *Summer:* Indian Ford Campground and Cold Spring Campground (Sisters); Cascades Lakes. *Winter:* Grande Ronde Valley; Hurricane Creek (Enterprise); Wallowa Lake SP; Imnaha area; Powder River Valley; Idlewild Campground (Burns).

BURROWING OWL

Athene cunicularia

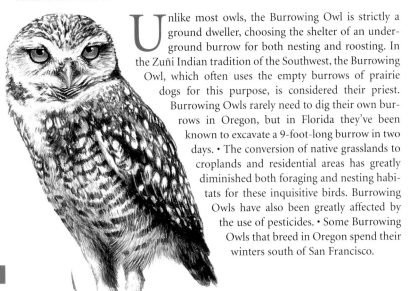

Unlike most owls, the Burrowing Owl is strictly a ground dweller, choosing the shelter of an underground burrow for both nesting and roosting. In the Zuñi Indian tradition of the Southwest, the Burrowing Owl, which often uses the empty burrows of prairie dogs for this purpose, is considered their priest. Burrowing Owls rarely need to dig their own burrows in Oregon, but in Florida they've been known to excavate a 9-foot-long burrow in two days. • The conversion of native grasslands to croplands and residential areas has greatly diminished both foraging and nesting habitats for these inquisitive birds. Burrowing Owls have also been greatly affected by the use of pesticides. • Some Burrowing Owls that breed in Oregon spend their winters south of San Francisco.

ID: generally slightly rufous brown with white spots; horizontal belly barring and fine streaking on rounded head; yellow eyes; yellowish bill; white "eyebrows" and throat; long, pale, feathered legs; upright stance. *Male:* plumage is often sun-bleached lighter. *In flight:* feet extend beyond tail; short, pale-lined, white-barred wings, also spotted above.

Size: *L* 8–9 in; *W* 21–24 in.

Status: uncommon and declining breeding summer resident east of the Cascades; rare winter visitor west of the Cascades; *hypugea* ssp. is a federal species of concern and state-listed as sensitive.

Habitat: *Breeding:* dry, open grasslands and deserts; also agricultural lands, especially in winter.

Nesting: open terrain; in a 6–9 ft long burrow dug by a ground squirrel, prairie dog or other mammal, or in a nest box; female incubates 6–11 white eggs for 28–30 days; male guards the burrow and supplies food.

Feeding: opportunistic; active hunter mainly at dawn and dusk but often by day; eats mostly arthropods, small mammals and birds, but also takes some reptiles and amphibians.

Voice: utters a variety of clucks and rasping notes, screams or makes a snakelike rattle when threatened; male's song is a loud, monotonous, dovelike *coo-cooo*.

Similar Species: *Short-eared Owl* (p. 205): larger; vertical breast streaking; short legs; prominent facial disc; small "ear" tufts; long wings with dark "wrist" patches; bouncy, quartering flight. *Western Screech-Owl* (p. 196): stockier; stronger facial disc; "ear" tufts are often prominent; vertical breast streaking; short legs; perches in trees.

Best Sites: Summer Lake WMA; Lakeview; Warner Valley; Hart Mt.; Umatilla NWR; Grande Ronde Valley; Virtue Flats (Pleasant Valley); Burns–Hines area; Malheur NWR; Succor Creek SP.

SPOTTED OWL

Strix occidentalis

In the last decades of the 20th century, the Spotted Owl unwittingly became notorious as the focal point of discussions about timberland management across its range in the Pacific Northwest. The northern *caurina* subspecies needs large areas of old-growth rainforest to nest and forage—a pair may have a home range as large as 16 square miles. Unfortunately for the Spotted Owl, old-growth rainforest is favored for cutting by the forest industry. Another pressure on the Spotted Owl is the range expansion of its slightly larger relative, the Barred Owl, into Spotted Owl habitat. • The Spotted Owl hunts at night, usually by sitting on a perch and waiting until it detects prey, mostly arboreal or terrestrial rodents.

ID: large, rounded head; white-tipped brown feathers give chest a spotted look; large, dark eyes; whitish throat; pale yellowish bill. *In flight:* nearly rectangular, barred, brown wings, paler below and white-spotted above.

Size: *Male L* 17–18 in; *W* 3¼ ft. *Female: L* 18–19 in; *W* 3½–3¾ ft.

Status: fairly common year-round resident in old-growth coniferous forests and rare in younger stands in western Oregon and on the eastern slopes of the Cascades; *caurina* ssp. federal- and state-listed as threatened.

Habitat: old-growth rainforests, fir and mixed forests of ponderosa pine, white fir and Douglas-fir to 6000 ft; forages in unlogged areas and tends to avoid crossing bushy areas and clear-cuts.

Nesting: in a stump or tree cavity or, rarely, on a tree platform; female incubates 2–3 white or pearly gray eggs for 28–32 days; young leave the nest at 35 days and stay with the parents throughout summer.

Feeding: strictly nocturnal; sits-and-waits to pounce on small mammals, especially ground squirrels, woodrats, voles and snowshoe hares; also eats insects, amphibians and birds, occasionally including other forest owls.

Voice: much like the Barred Owl's *hoo-hoo, hooooo* notes, but generally higher pitched and without pace changes; female makes loud barking and nasal cries.

Similar Species: *Barred Owl* (p. 202): slightly larger; often paler; horizontal breast bars; thick, vertical belly streaks; more likely in moist bottomlands. *Western Screech-Owl* (p. 196): much smaller; gray (or brown) overall; vertically streaked underparts; yellow eyes; "ear" tufts are often prominent.

Best Sites: near Larch Mt.; Timothy L.; Detroit Reservoir; Foster Reservoir; Waldo L.; Umpqua R. east of Glide.

201

BARRED OWL

Strix varia

Anyone who hears the excited *who-cooks-for-you, who-cooks-for-you-all* courtship call of this forest owl is tempted to mimic it. Imitating the call will certainly bring any Barred Owl within range, but it may also provoke an attack from this easily stressed and highly territorial bird. • Barred Owls are usually most active between midnight and 4 AM, when the forest floor rustles with the movements of mice, voles and shrews. These birds' eyesight in darkness is 100 times as keen as that of humans, but they can also locate prey using sound alone. • First discovered in Oregon in 1974, following southward range expansion along the mountains, this owl may now be found almost anywhere in Oregon with sufficient forest habitat.

ID: white-spotted brown upperparts; brown-barred white breast and heavily streaked white underparts; large, round head; dark eyes; yellowish bill. *In flight:* nearly rectangular, barred, brown wings, paler below and white-spotted above.

Size: *Male: L* 17–19 in; *W* 3¼–3¾ ft. *Female: L* 22–24 in; *W* 3¾–4¼ ft.

Status: rare to fairly common year-round resident.

Habitat: most forest types, including mixed, Douglas-fir and ponderosa pine, mature and old-growth forests; prefers riparian and lower elevation woodlands.

Nesting: cavity in a hardwood tree, especially a dead one, but sometimes uses a nest box or platform nest of another species; nest is lined with lichens or fresh conifer twigs; female incubates 2–4 pure white eggs for 28–33 days; pair feeds the young.

Feeding: from a perch, or less often, from low, fairly direct flight, catches a wide range of invertebrates, reptiles, amphibians, smaller mammals and other birds.

Voice: gives the most characteristic call of all owls; loud, hooting, rhythmic, laughlike *Who cooks for you? Who cooks for you all?* is heard year-round, but mostly in spring.

Similar Species: *Spotted Owl* (p. 201): slightly smaller; white-spotted brown breast and underparts; paler bill; limited to old-growth forests. *Great Gray Owl* (p. 203): larger; generally grayer; large, concentrically barred facial disc; small, deep-set, yellow eyes; black-centered partial white "collar" on throat; diffusely patterned breast.

Best Sites: Tollgate; Spring Creek; Grande Ronde Valley; Eagle Cap Wilderness Area; Upper Wallowa Valley; Elkhorn Mts.; eastern Douglas Co. and Lane Co., especially along the Umpqua R. east of Glide; grounds of Portland Audubon Society.

GREAT GRAY OWL

Strix nebulosa

This largely silent hunter is the only *Strix* owl to breed on both sides of the Atlantic. Although it is North America's largest owl, the Great Gray Owl owes its bulk largely to a mass of fluffy insulation, and the Snowy Owl and Great Horned Owl outweigh it by about 15 percent. • Often active by day, the Great Gray prefers areas near bogs, forest edges, montane meadows and other open areas offering an unobstructed view. Its small eyes are less important for hunting than its incredibly acute hearing, made possible by the large facial disc. • The Great Gray's habitat preferences restrict where it can breed, but Great Horned Owls or woodland hawks rarely disrupt its foraging and nesting activities.

ID: white-marbled grayish brown plumage; large, rounded head; prominent, concentrically barred facial disc; small, deep-set, yellow eyes; yellow bill; black-centered, white partial "collar" on throat. *In flight:* large, nearly rectangular, mostly barred, brown wings, paler below; long, faintly banded tail.
Size: *Male: L* 25–28 in; *W* 4½–4¾ ft. *Female: L* 29–33 in; *W* 4¾–5 ft.
Status: rare to uncommon year-round resident in the central and southern Cascades, mostly on the eastern slope, and in the northeastern mountains; state-listed as sensitive.
Habitat: open pine forests or mixed conifers with nearby large meadows or open bogs for foraging; lower elevations in winter.
Nesting: in a broken-topped snag, but may use an old raptor nest or an artificial platform; female incubates 3–5 dull white eggs for 28–31 days; male feeds the young for up to 3 months after fledging at 26–29 days.
Feeding: at dawn and dusk, from a perch or sometimes in flight; eats mostly small rodents, but can catch medium or large birds.
Voice: gives a hard-to-hear, very low, evenly spaced *hoo* note series and low, soft, doubled hoots.
Similar Species: *Barred Owl* (p. 202): smaller; less pronounced facial disc; dark eyes; horizontally barred breast; vertically streaked underparts; prefers moist, low-elevation woodlands. *Great Horned Owl* (p. 197): conspicuous "ear" tufts; interrupted facial disc; large, bright yellow eyes; dark bill; dense horizontal underpart streaking; mottled dark upperparts.
Best Sites: Howard Prairie Reservoir; Hyatt Reservoir; Ochoco Mts.; Cascades Lakes; Fort Klamath; Spring Creek; Wallowa Mts.; Logan Valley; Sun River Resort.

LONG-EARED OWL

Asio otus

A master of disguise and illusion, the Long-eared Owl hides from intruders by assuming a thin, vertical form to blend into its wooded background. If that tactic fails, this medium-sized owl will expand its air sacs, puff up its feathers, spread its wings to double its size and hiss defiantly in an exaggerated threat display. • Most owl species are fiercely territorial, but nonbreeding Long-eared Owls will often form communal roosts—typically fewer than two dozen birds but sometimes up to a hundred. • The "ear" tufts seen on many owls are purely ornamental feathers. The real ears are hidden under the facial disc feathers, and their asymmetrical size, shape and placement enhance the owl's judgment of distance and direction.

ID: slim body; white-blotched grayish brown upperparts; long "ear" tufts; dark, roughly crisscross pattern on underparts; pale rusty brown facial disc; large, yellow eyes; white "eyebrows" and "mustache." *In flight:* pale buff underwing; mostly gray upperwing with orangy patch near tip; dark-barred tips and trailing edges; prominent black "wrist" patch.

Size: *Male: L* 13–14 in; *W* 3–3¼ ft. *Female: L* 15–16 in; *W* 3¾–4 ft.

Status: locally uncommon year-round resident east of the Cascades; rare breeding summer resident in the Willamette Valley; rare in western interior valleys in winter.

Habitat: *Breeding:* near open country in juniper forests, riparian woodlands and other coniferous and mixed forests. *In migration* and *winter:* open habitats.

Nesting: in an abandoned stick nest of another species, or sometimes in a tree or cliff cavity or even on the ground; female incubates 5–7 slightly glossy white eggs for 26–28 days; young start leaving the nest at 21 days and fledge at 30–35 days.

Feeding: actively searches for small rodents and birds; perches or flies along forest edges to flush prey.

Voice: gives a low, soft, ghostly *quoo-quoo* breeding call; utters a *weck-weck-weck* alarm call; also issues various shrieks, hisses, whistles, barks, hoots and dovelike coos.

Similar Species: *Short-eared Owl* (p. 205): buffier and less grayish overall; light underpart streaking denser at breast; tiny "ear" tufts usually hidden. *Great Horned Owl* (p. 197): larger; much bulkier; wider-set "ear" tufts; darker around eyes; horizontally streaked underparts; plainer wings.

Best Sites: *Summer:* widespread but difficult to locate. *Winter:* streamside thickets and dense juniper stands east of the Cascades.

SHORT-EARED OWL

Asio flammeus

This open-country owl is the most likely owl to be seen hunting and is one of the easiest owls to identify. The Short-eared Owl flies so characteristically that after a first encounter even a distant view of one in flight is sufficient for a positive identification. Its long wings beat slowly, almost butterfly-like, as it courses low over wet meadows, often by day. • As with other owls that have fluctuating food resources, Short-eared Owl populations show considerable local variation in both numbers and reproductive success, and birds may be very nomadic in times of shortage. • In fall and winter, as many as several dozen birds will parcel out a feeding territory and communally roost on or near the ground.

ID: tawny golden dappling on brown upperparts; paler face and underparts; vertical brown striping, heaviest on upper breast and thinning on belly; tiny, often hidden, close-set "ear" tufts; yellow eyes in black sockets; white "eyebrows" and "mustache." *In flight:* dark "wrist" patch and wing tip on buffy underwing; buff-and-brown barring above.
Size: *L* 13–17 in; *W* 3–4 ft.
Status: common breeder east of the Cascades and scarce in the west; widespread in open habitats in winter, in highly variable numbers.
Habitat: *Breeding:* wet meadows, marshes, grasslands, fields. *In migration* and *winter:* mountain meadows, deserts, coastal salt marshes, interior valleys; roosts communally in trees and brush.
Nesting: semicolonial in prime habitats; nests on the ground on matted-down vegetation; female incubates 4–10 nest-stained creamy white eggs for 26–32 days; young fledge at 28–36 days.
Feeding: hunts by day or night, especially at twilight; eats small mammals and some small birds.
Voice: generally quiet; breeding male produces a soft *toot-toot-toot;* utters a loud *keee-ow* in winter.
Similar Species: *Long-eared Owl* (p. 204): grayer, more mottled plumage; crisscrossing underpart markings; prominent "ear" tufts; pale rusty brown face; less likely to perch in the open. *Burrowing Owl* (p. 200): smaller; mostly white-spotted, slightly rufous brown, with horizontal belly barring; yellowish bill; stubbier wings; long, feathered legs; ground dweller.
Best Sites: *Summer:* large meadows and marshes of Klamath, Lake and Harney Counties; cultivated areas, grasslands and marshes elsewhere east of the Cascades. *Winter:* interior western valleys; Klamath Basin.

BOREAL OWL

Aegolius funereus

The Boreal Owl (known elsewhere as Tengmalm's Owl) lives primarily in the boreal forests of Canada and Alaska, as well as boreal forests in Europe and Asia from Siberia to Scandinavia. The Boreal Owl is also scattered across the northern coterminous states, but Oregon had only two old records for it until eight individuals were found at several sites in northeastern Oregon in 1987–88. Since then, this owl has been recorded in the central Cascades in Deschutes County and Lane County and at various locations in the Wallowa and Blue Mountains, always above 5000 feet. This day-roosting owl may well be widespread and even fairly common in forests above that level—deep snow restricts observation from February to April, when it is most vocal, and it usually doesn't wander in winter like other owls.

ID: white-spotted dark brown upperparts; heavy, vertical, brown streaks on white underparts; white-speckled forehead; large, pale facial disc with partial dark border; fluffy, white "eyebrows" and "mustache"; dark-ringed yellow eyes; dusky ivory bill. *In flight:* short, weakly barred tail; coarsely brown-barred whitish underwings.

Size: *Male: L* 9–10 in; *W* 22–24 in. *Female: L* 11–12 in; *W* 26–29 in.

Status: locally fairly common year-round resident at higher elevations in the Cascades, Blue Mts. and Wallowa Mts.; state-listed as sensitive.

Habitat: subalpine pine, fir and spruce forests and transition forests just below.

Nesting: in a cavity excavated by a woodpecker or in a nest box; female incubates 2–5 dull white eggs for 26–32 days and broods the nestlings until fledging at 28–36 days; pair feeds the young outside the nest for another 3–6 weeks.

Feeding: mainly nocturnal hunter, from a low perch, for small mammals; also eats small birds and insects.

Voice: gives a loud, hoarse *hooo-aaak* and a grating, hissing threat call; male's main spring song is a low, trilled toot series with increasing loudness.

Similar Species: *Northern Saw-whet Owl* (p. 207): slightly smaller; dark bill; white-streaked head and nape; tawnier belly markings; paler underwings. *Western Screech-Owl* (p. 196): gray bill; fiercer look; often shows "ear" tufts; streaky gray or brown upperparts; thinner dark vertical streaks on grayish or brownish belly.

Best Sites: Tollgate; Moss Springs Guard Station area (Wallowa Mts.); Bonny Lakes; Eagle Cap Wilderness Area; Elkhorn Mts.; Anthony L.; high elevations in the central Cascades.

NORTHERN SAW-WHET OWL

Aegolius acadicus

Northern Saw-whet Owls are opportunistic hunters that take whatever they can, whenever they can. When temperatures drop below freezing, these small owls catch and store extra food in tree caches, where it quickly freezes. When pickings are slim, a hungry owl can thaw out its frozen cache by "incubating" it as it would a clutch of eggs. • By day, Northern Saw-whets roost quietly in the cover of dense lower branches and brush to avoid attracting mobbing forest songbirds. • "Saw-whet" reflects the perceived likeness of the bird's call to the filing of a large saw, and *acadicus* refers to Acadia in Atlantic Canada, where the first specimen was collected. • With its dark upperparts and buff belly, the juvenile Northern Saw-whet Owl shows more color difference from the adult than any other North American owl.

ID: white-spotted brown upperparts; rufous brown vertical streaks on white underparts; finely buff- and brown-streaked facial disc, forehead and nape; dark-ringed yellow eyes; thick white "eyebrows"; dark bill. *Juvenile:* buff-marked brown upperparts; rich buff, unstreaked underparts; white forehead patch. *In flight:* short tail; coarsely brown-barred pale buff underwings.

Size: *Male:* L 7–8 in; W 16–17 in. *Female:* L 8–9 in; W 17–18 in.

Status: common year-round resident west of the Cascades; common breeding summer resident and uncommon in winter east of the Cascades; anywhere in migration.

Habitat: *Breeding:* moist woodlands, especially with conifers. *Winter:* dense riparian growth and deciduous trees around farms and urban areas; conifer forests.

Nesting: in a cavity made by a woodpecker or in a nest box, usually lined with wood chips or other debris; female incubates 5–6 white eggs for 27–29 days and broods the nestlings until the youngest is about 19 days old while male brings food.

Feeding: mainly nocturnal; hunts from a perch; eats small rodents, plus beetles, grasshoppers and small birds, especially in migration.

Voice: male gives an easily imitated, evenly spaced, vaguely 2-syllabled whistled song, repeated fairly rapidly, often for long periods.

Similar Species: *Boreal Owl* (p. 206): slightly larger; black-bordered paler face; white-speckled forehead; pale bill; juvenile has browner underparts and indistinctly streaked belly.

Best Sites: Saddle Mountain SP; Larch Mt.; Timothy L.; Lake Selmac CP; Cascades Lakes; Crater Lake NP; Langdon L. (Tollgate); Wallowa Lake SP; Elkhorn Mts.

COMMON NIGHTHAWK
Chordeiles minor

B y day, the Common Nighthawk is mild-mannered and largely unnoticed, but it is a conspicuous, spectacular flier at dusk. The male's seemingly death-defying display dive terminates in a hard braking action of the wings, which produces a deep, hollow *vroom* sound. • Despite its name, the Common Nighthawk is often visible at its daytime roost site on a tree limb or on the ground, and it is most active at dusk and dawn. It sits along the length of a tree branch rather than across the branch the way most perching birds do. This bird often migrates in loose flocks. • As with other members of the nightjar family, the Common Nighthawk's gaping mouth is surrounded by feather shafts that funnel airborne insects inside.

ID: cryptic, mottled white-buff-and-brown upperparts; brown barred, whitish underparts on male and buffy on female; large, dark eyes; long tail extends to folded wing tips; throat is white on male, pale buff on female. *In flight:* narrow, pointed, dark wing with prominent white "wrist" patch; long, notched, barred tail, with white subterminal band on male; erratic, darting flight; male does impressive diving display.
Size: *L* 8–10 in; *W* 23–26 in.
Status: common breeding summer resident and migrant; most common east of the Cascades; state-listed as sensitive.
Habitat: *Breeding:* coastal dunes; chaparral; grassy hills; sagebrush and juniper deserts, mountain forest clearings; canyons; urban buildings. *In migration:* valleys and rivers; open woodlands; meadows and grasslands; sagebrush flats; urban areas.

Nesting: flat city roof or on the ground, in sand or gravel, without making a nest; female incubates 2 heavily speckled white or pale gray eggs for 19–20 days; the young fledge at 21–23 days.
Feeding: hunts by twilight, sometimes cooperatively with several birds; catches flying insects, mainly queen ants, beetles and bugs, in midair.
Voice: male repeats a nasal *peent peent;* also, male makes a deep, hollow *vroom* with his wings during courtship flight.
Similar Species: *Common Poorwill* (p. 209): smaller; generally paler; bristles around mouth are more obvious; rounded wings; shorter, broader, rounded tail with white-tipped outer feathers (most prominent on male); no white patch on wing; roosts on ground.
Best Sites: *Summer:* sagebrush-covered hills and canyons east of the Cascades. *In migration:* widespread, even in settled areas of western Oregon.

COMMON POORWILL

Phalaenoptilus nuttallii

In 1946, the scientific community was surprised by the discovery of a Common Poorwill that appeared to be hibernating through winter in a rock crevice. Cold to the touch, it had no detectable breath or heartbeat. Apparently, poorwills that choose not to migrate to warmer climates enter a short-term torpor in which their temperature drops as low as 43°F and oxygen intake is reduced by over 90 percent, but it is not true mammal-style hibernation. This trait was known to the Hopi Indians, who named the bird *Holchoko*, "the sleeping one," and to Meriwether Lewis of the Lewis and Clark Expedition, who, in 1804, found a mysterious goatsucker "to be passing into the dormant state." • Another characteristic shared with few other birds is a tendency to carry eggs and young to a safer location after disturbance.

ID: cryptic upperparts are mottled gray, white and black; pale throat band; finely barred underparts; large head; dark eyes; prominent bristles around mouth. *In flight:* short, rounded wings; brown-barred cinnamon primaries; broad, rounded tail with white-tipped outer feathers (most prominent on male); flights usually short and close to ground.

Size: *L* 7–8 in; *W* 16–17 in.

Status: locally fairly common breeding summer resident east of the Cascades and in Jackson Co. and Josephine Co.

Habitat: dry, open habitats, including sagebrush-covered hills and rocky country; oak, juniper and chaparral hillsides; open ponderosa pine forests; isolated buttes.

Nesting: nests on bare ground, gravel, flat rock or bed of pine needles, usually partially shaded by a bush, log or rock; pair incubates 2 white, sometimes pink-tinged and dark-spotted eggs for 20–21 days; young fledge at 20–23 days; both parents feed the young regurgitated insects.

Feeding: sallies from a low perch or the ground, mostly at night, for large insects, such as moths and beetles.

Voice: male, and sometimes the female, utters the familiar *poor-will* call, often adding an additional syllable.

Similar Species: *Common Nighthawk* (p. 208): larger; long, pointed wings with white "wrist" patches; longer, narrower, notched tail, with broad white subterminal band on male; dark barring on underparts continues onto tail.

Best Sites: Roxy Ann Butte (near Medford); Prineville Reservoir; Fort Klamath; Fort Rock SP; Hart Mt.; Malheur NWR; Alvord Basin; Succor Creek SP.

BLACK SWIFT
Cypseloides niger

The fast-flying Black Swift is the largest of the North American swifts. • Few observers are lucky enough to see a Black Swift nest. Not only are these birds limited by their distribution, but they prefer to nest on steep, vertical walls well concealed behind the sheets of cascading spray of inland waterfalls. Only one Oregon nest site has so far been confirmed. • Black Swifts forage high in the air when skies are clear, and periods of rain or low overcast weather bring them closer to the ground. They hunt insects on the wing for much of the day, but, as the sun sets, the birds rocket back to their nests. • Swifts cast a characteristic boomerang silhouette in flight. They are shaped much like swallows—long, tapering wings, small bills, wide gape and long, sleek bodies—but these genuses are not closely related.

ID: black overall; slender, sleek body; whitish tipped feathers around forehead; very small legs.
Juvenile: thin, white barring on underparts.
In flight: long, tapering wings angle backward; fairly long tail can appear slightly forked; often glides in broad circles.
Size: *L* 7 in; *W* 18 in.
Status: very local summer resident; rare migrant from mid-May through early June and from late August to mid-October; state-listed as sensitive.
Habitat: *Breeding:* steep, usually wet cliffs in interior canyons and along ocean coasts. *Foraging* and *in migration:* over forests, woodlands, canyons, valleys, grasslands and even cities.
Nesting: semicolonial; on a cliff, in a crevice, in a cavity or on a ledge, often near or behind a waterfall; nest is made of moss, mud and algae; pair incubates 1 white egg for 24–27 days; both adults feed the young.
Feeding: feeds in flight; eats flying insects, especially stoneflies, caddisflies and mayflies; often seen feeding high in the sky by day.
Voice: high-pitched *plik-plik-plik-plik* near the nest site.
Similar Species: *Vaux's Swift* (p. 211): much smaller; lighter color overall; pale throat and rump; short, stubby, comblike tail. *White-throated Swift* (p. 212): white underneath from "chin" to vent; white flank patches; white tips on secondaries.
Best Sites: *Summer:* Salt Creek Falls, Lane Co. *In fall migration:* often along the coast.

VAUX'S SWIFT

Chaetura vauxi

Soon after their arrival in April and May, and again in late August and September, increasingly larger flocks of Vaux's Swifts circle above towns and cities. They plunge collectively into chimneys to roost—a habit shared with the Chimney Swift (*C. pelagica*) of the eastern United States. Roosting is very important for swifts year-round, so they favor habitats with suitable cavities. Rather than perching like most birds, they use their small, strong claws to grab onto vertical surfaces. • Among America's most aerial birds, Vaux's Swifts can be forced close to the ground by fogbanks or low cloud. • The Vaux's Swift was named for William Sansom Vaux, an eminent mineralogist, member of Philadelphia's Academy of Natural Sciences and friend of John Kirk Townsend, who first described this bird in 1839 from specimens collected on the Columbia River.

ID: brownish gray overall; lighter at throat and rump. *In flight:* paler below than above; long, swept-back, scimitar-shaped wings; shallow, rapid wingbeats and glides; comblike points on short tail; rarely leaves the air.
Size: *L* 5 in; *W* 12 in.
Status: locally common breeding summer resident from sea level to around 4500 ft in western Oregon; locally uncommon east of the Cascades in summer and migration.
Habitat: *Breeding:* cities; open country; mixed and coniferous old-growth forests. *In migration:* cities, roosting in chimneys; forests and open areas with tree cavities, particularly in grand fir; desert oases; mountain ridges.
Nesting: open half-circle of loosely woven twigs is glued together and to the inside of a hollow tree or chimney with the bird's own sticky saliva; pair incubates 6–7 white or creamy white eggs for 18–19 days; 3rd adult may feed the young, which fledge at 30 days.
Feeding: hawks in midair for flying ants, true bugs, flies, moths, spiders and aphids.
Voice: several high-pitched *chips* followed by an insectlike trill in flight; uses its wings to produce a booming sound in midair and at the nest, perhaps to discourage predators.
Similar Species: *White-throated Swift* (p. 212): larger; black with white areas, mainly on underparts; long, forked tail. *Black Swift* (p. 210): much larger; black overall; tail often forked; variable wingbeats; often soars. *Swallows* (pp. 260–66): relatively shorter, broader wings, not swept back; notched or forked tails; usually whiter below; darting, fluid flight.
Best Sites: widespread.

WHITE-THROATED SWIFT

Aeronautes saxatalis

This avian marvel certainly earns its wings as a true *aeronautes* ("sky sailor"). During its lifetime, the average White-throated Swift will likely travel more than a million miles—enough to take it around the world more than 40 times! Only brief, cliff-clinging rest periods and annual nesting duties keep the White-throated Swift grounded, because it feeds, drinks, bathes and even mates while flying. This scimitar-winged aerial insectivore also lives up to its family common name, having been timed at up to 200 miles per hour, which is fast enough to avoid any Prairie Falcons wanting to devour it. • A familiar sight in mountainous areas and even some cities of the western United States, the White-throated Swift is easily recognized by its loud, sharp, scraping notes, black-and-white coloring and rapid, rather erratic flight.

ID: dark upperparts; white on throat tapers to undertail coverts; black flanks with white hind patches. *In flight:* long, tapering, back-angled wings; long, slightly forked tail is often held in a point.

Size: *L* 6–7 in; *W* 15 in.

Status: locally uncommon breeding summer resident east of the Cascades; very rare in spring and summer west of the Cascades.

Habitat: *Breeding:* high cliffs in open country; high desert fault blocks; river canyons; ranges widely in search of food. *In migration:* more likely to be seen at lower elevations.

Nesting: on a cliff or ridge; cup made from materials gathered on the wing, including feathers, grass, moss, cotton, straw and plant down, is stuck together with gluelike saliva; pair incubates 4–5 white or creamy eggs for 24 days; young fledge at 45 days and are expert fliers on leaving the nest.

Feeding: snatches insects and other arthropods in midair; eats almost anything edible carried aloft by wind currents.

Voice: gives a loud, shrill, descending *skee-jee-ee-ee-ee-ee-ee*.

Similar Species: *Vaux's Swift* (p. 211): smaller; brown above, paler below; stubby, comb-pointed tail. *Black Swift* (p. 210): slightly larger; black overall; tail often appears notched; variable wingbeats; often soars. *Violet-green Swallow* (p. 262) and *Tree Swallow* (p. 261): smaller; all-white underparts; blue, green or olive brown upperparts.

Best Sites: Smith Rock SP; Prineville Reservoir; Picture Gorge (John Day Fossil Beds NM); Fort Rock SP; Abert Rim; Imnaha; Hart Mt.; Steens Mt.; Alvord Basin; Succor Creek SP.

BLACK-CHINNED HUMMINGBIRD

Archilochus alexandri

The Black-chinned Hummingbird is the western counterpart of the Ruby-throated Hummingbird (*A. colubris*) of eastern North America, and the females are virtually indistinguishable in the field. • The most noteworthy thing about the Black-chinned Hummingbird is that it is an average hummingbird. This low-elevation species uses many different habitats, is in the middle size range of North American hummingbirds, has a fairly large breeding range and lacks defining colors. • The species name *alexandri* honors a doctor who collected specimens in Mexico. The genus name was chosen by naturalist and hummingbird taxonomist H.G.L. Reisenbach. Deeply influenced by Greek mythology, he named several hummingbird genera after Greeks, including the notable poet Archilochus.

ID: green crown, nape and upperparts; white breast; gray-mottled white underparts; green-washed flanks; long, thin, black bill; small white spot behind eye. *Male:* black throat with iridescent bluish violet gorget (may appear dark). *Female* and *immature:* gray-streaked whitish throat; blackish eye line. *In flight:* many-pointed black tail; white-tipped on female.

Size: *L* 3¾ in; *W* 4½–5 in.

Status: uncommon breeding summer resident and migrant east of the Cascades; rare spring and summer visitor to western Oregon.

Habitat: *Breeding:* lower mountain foothills and valleys; arid canyons; oak scrublands; open and riparian woodlands. *In migration:* desert oases; city and town feeders.

Nesting: on a branch or outer twig; female molds a nesting cup using her belly and bill to smooth out plant down mixed with spiderwebs and insect cocoon fibers; female incubates 2 white eggs for 16 days; young fledge at 21 days; family stays together throughout summer.

Feeding: sips sugar water from feeders and nectar from flowers; catches flying insects by hovering in midair; gleans insects from vegetation, spiderwebs, soil and crevices.

Voice: male has a soft, high-pitched, warbling courtship song, accompanied by wing-buzzing; buzzy and chipping alarm calls.

Similar Species: *Female Anna's Hummingbird* (p. 214): more gray and green on underparts; red-spotted throat; more rounded tail. *Female Broad-tailed Hummingbird* (p. 365): dark-spotted face and throat; buff-washed underparts; rounder tail with rufous patches.

Best Sites: *Summer:* Summer Lake WMA; Spring Creek; Grande Ronde Valley; feeders at Cove and Enterprise; Imnaha; Sumpter; Bear Valley, Grant Co. *In migration:* Burns–Hines area; Malheur NWR HQ feeders; Page Springs Campground (near Malheur NWR); feeders in Fields.

ANNA'S HUMMINGBIRD

Calypte anna

Oregon has seven hummingbird species that could arrive at a well-stocked sugarwater feeder station, but none can compare with the male Anna's Hummingbird for sartorial splendor. He may not have the rufous coat of a Rufous or Allen's male, but a male Anna's impresses with the rose-red "bib" that covers his head and neck. • Once restricted as a nesting species to the Pacific slope of northern Baja California and southern California, Anna's Hummingbird expanded its range northward along the coast after the 1930s. Using cultivated exotic plants and year-round hummingbird feeders, it has also expanded eastward as far as Texas. • By nesting from December to May, Anna's Hummingbird can take advantage of the abundant late-spring blooms.

ID: iridescent, emerald green upperparts; grayish underparts; long, black bill; partial white eye ring. *Male:* extensive rosy-pink of gorget includes crown; greenish wash across lower breast and belly. *Female* and *immature:* green crown; several rosy feathers on throat; light green flanks. *In flight:* many-pointed black tail, white-tipped on female.
Size: *L* 3–4 in; *W* 5–5½ in.
Status: locally common summer resident and breeding winter resident along the coast and in western interior valleys; locally uncommon summer resident in Klamath Basin and other parts of southern Oregon.
Habitat: oak woodlands; chaparral; riparian areas; coastal scrubland; farmlands; urban gardens with exotic flowers or sugarwater feeders.
Nesting: often on a tree or shrub branch; cup nest of plant down and spiderwebs is lined with downy material; female incu-

bates 2 white eggs for 16–17 days; young fledge at 15–16 days.
Feeding: hovers, sometimes perches, to sip flower nectar and sugar water; gleans insects from flowers and shrubbery; territorial but tolerates other hummingbirds if food is plentiful.
Voice: high, short call note; excited, chattering chase call; male's complex songs include a varied series of high, scratchy, dry notes from a perch and sharp squeaks to end the diving display.
Similar Species: *Female Black-chinned Hummingbird* (p. 213): smaller; whiter underparts; plainer throat. *Broad-tailed Hummingbird* (p. 365): green crown; male's gorget is less extensive; peach wash on female's belly and flanks.
Best Sites: Oregon Institute of Marine Biology feeders (Charleston); Azalea SP (Brookings); Tryon Creek SP and Mount Tabor Park (Portland); Stewart Park (Roseburg); Merlin Rest Area (near Grants Pass); Lower Table Rock (near Medford).

CALLIOPE HUMMINGBIRD

Stellula calliope

Glistening in the slanting rays of sunlight announcing dawn, the iridescent, streaked gorget of the male Calliope Hummingbird suggests nectar dripping from the bird's needlelike bill. • The Calliope Hummingbird is North America's smallest breeding bird and smallest long-distance migrant—individuals routinely travel up to 5000 miles annually to and from wintering territory in Mexico. • Although they feed among clusters of wildflowers, male Calliopes often perch high atop shrubs or small trees to flash their unusual, pinkish red gorgets and make dazzling, high-speed dips and dives to entice the females to mate.

• *Stellula* is Latin for "small star," and Calliopeia, "the fair voiced," was the muse responsible for epic poetry in ancient Greece.

ID: iridescent, green upperparts; slender bill. *Male:* narrow, pinkish red gorget streaks extend down white throat from bill; whitish breast and belly; light green flanks. *Female:* white underparts; peach-washed flanks; dark green throat spots. *In flight:* blackish tail is white-tipped on female.
Size: *L* 3 in; *W* 4–4½ in.
Status: common breeding summer resident in the Cascades and locally to the east; locally uncommon summer resident in the Siskiyou Mts.; uncommon migrant elsewhere east of the Cascades and rare migrant west of the Cascades.
Habitat: *Breeding:* mid-elevation open forests and riparian woodland edges, occasionally higher. *In migration:* coastal mountains and valleys in spring; higher elevations, valleys and desert oases east of the Cascades in fall.

Nesting: usually on a conifer branch under foliage; tiny cup nest of plant down, moss, lichen and spiderwebs is often reused; female incubates 2 white eggs for up to 16 days.
Feeding: hovers and probes flowers for nectar; takes sugar water at feeders; also eats small insects, often in short sallies from a perch.
Voice: utters high-pitched *chip* calls; male sings high-pitched, chattering *tsew* notes in his relatively short courtship display.
Similar Species: *Costa's Hummingbird* (p. 365): male has bright violet extended gorget and crown; female has grayish green flanks. *Anna's Hummingbird* (p. 214): and *Broad-tailed Hummingbird* (p. 365): slightly larger; longer, wider tails; males have red gorgets; Anna's female has greenish flanks.
Best Sites: *Summer:* Indian Ford Campground and Cold Springs Campground (Sisters); Ochoco Creek; Moss Springs Guard Station (Wallowa Mts.); Wallowa Lake SP; Starr Campground (Blue Mts.).

RUFOUS HUMMINGBIRD

Selasphorus rufus

The tiny Rufous Hummingbird may spend part of its year in tropical regions, but its wings take it as far north as southern Alaska in summer. The southern boundary of its breeding range lies in Oregon. • Male hummingbirds are aggressively territorial and do not tolerate other males of their own species. The feistiness of male hummingbirds is clearly demonstrated at feeder stations, with males unwilling to concede space to any of their own kind yet perfectly content to let females of any species feed alongside them. • At the onset of nesting, Rufous males abandon females and head inland or upslope to higher elevations to take advantage of early blooming flowers, with the females and juveniles following later. They all head to Mexico and beyond for winter.

ID: long, thin bill; rufous flanks. *Male:* mainly rufous upperparts with green on wings and brownish crown (crown and back may be green); iridescent, orangy red gorget; white breast. *Female:* green back; white underparts; reddish throat spot. *In flight:* multi-pointed tail; male performs high-speed, whirring, oval courtship display flight.

Size: *L* 3–4 in; *W* 4¼–4½ in.

Status: locally common breeding summer resident; first coastal migrants arrive in early February, 1 month later in the interior.

Habitat: *Breeding:* open forests, especially secondary succession and glades; meadows; brushy habitats. *In fall migration:* high-elevation montane meadows and disturbed areas for males; lower on mountains for females and immatures. *In spring migration:* through the lowlands, especially along the coast.

Nesting: in a tree or shrub; well-hidden cup is lined with soft, downy plant materials and decorated with lichens, moss or bark fragments; female incubates 2 white eggs for 15–17 days; young fledge at 21 days.

Feeding: darts and hovers to catch insects and sip flower nectar; outside the nesting season, also gleans for insects; visits sugar-water feeders.

Voice: gives a loud, emphatic *chip chip chip* warning call and a raspy *eeech* or rapid, repeated *eeeeeedidayer* notes.

Similar Species: *Allen's Hummingbird* (p. 217): green back; female and immature are often indistinguishable. *Black-chinned Hummingbird* (p. 213): green-and-white plumage with no rufous or peach.

Best Sites: Charleston; Rogue R.; Azalea SP (Brookings); Pittock Bird Sanctuary (Portland); Lower Sandy R.; Timothy L.; Foster Reservoir; Spencer Butte and Skinner Butte (Eugene); Ochoco Mts.

ALLEN'S HUMMINGBIRD

Selasphorus sasin

To defend his territory, the male Allen's Hummingbird has one of the most complex and spectacular dive displays of any hummingbird. He swings back and forth in symmetrical arcs, pausing at the top of each one to shake his body and utter a loud buzzing note. He then soars to 100 feet and launches into a steep dive, pulling out at the very last moment while emitting a loud, metallic shriek and confronting his opposition. If that doesn't get your blood pumping, nothing will! • Most Allen's Hummingbirds arrive along the coast in Curry County and Coos County in late February and early March, timing their arrival to coincide with the first flowering of native shrubs.

ID: iridescent, green crown and back; rufous flanks; white breast; long, dark bill. *Male:* bright, orangy red gorget. *Female:* reddish throat spot; white underparts. *In flight:* broad tail.

Size: *L* 3–4 in; *W* 4–4¼ in.

Status: common breeding summer resident in a 20-mi-wide coastal strip of Coos Co. and Curry Co.

Habitat: male uses coastal shrubs or riparian scrub; female uses denser vegetation with some trees.

Nesting: in small trees or shrubbery; cup nest consists of spiderwebs and downy material; female incubates 2 white eggs for 12–22 days; young fledge at 22–25 days.

Feeding: hovers to sip plant nectar and sugar water at feeders; sometimes perches.

Voice: male emits a metallic shriek during display flight.

Similar Species: *Rufous Hummingbird* (p. 216): male usually has rufous back and brownish crown; green-backed male, female and immature are often indistinguishable. *Black-chinned Hummingbird* (p. 213): green-and-white plumage with no rufous or peach; downcurved bill.

Best Sites: Cape Blanco SP; Rogue R. meadows east of Weddeburn; Azalea Park (Brookings); any sugarwater feeders in coastal Curry Co. and southern coastal Coos Co.

BELTED KINGFISHER

Ceryle alcyon

Never far from its beloved water, the stockily built Belted Kingfisher is generally found perched on a bare branch surveying the food prospects swimming below. With a precise headfirst dive, it can catch fish up to 2 feet beneath the water's surface. It can also launch itself from a hovering flight. • Easily identified by its outsized head and bill, shaggy, blue crest and distinctive, rattling call, this bird is territorial year-round. • During the breeding season, a kingfisher male and female will excavate their nest burrow using their bills to chip away at the soil. They then kick loose material out of the tunnel with their tiny feet.

ID: bluish upperparts; mostly white underparts; shaggy crest; bluish gray breast band; white collar; long, straight bill; short legs; small white area ahead of eye. *Female:* rusty flanks and "belt" (occasionally incomplete) below bluish breast band. *In flight:* dark and white bars on squarish tail; white underwing with bluish trailing edge; white-marked primaries on bluish upperwing; flies low over water; often hovers.
Size: *L* 11–14 in; *W* 20–21 in.
Status: common year-round breeding resident with some concentration at the coast in late fall and early winter.
Habitat: *Breeding:* rivers, large streams, lakes, marshes and beaver ponds, especially near exposed soil banks, gravel pits or bluffs; brackish and saltwater estuaries; tidal creeks. *In migration* and *winter:* coastal swamps, brackish lagoons, oxbows, reservoirs and rivers.
Nesting: near water; in a cavity at the end of a burrow in earth or soft rock, often up to 6 ft deep, dug by pair; pair incubates 6–7 white eggs for 22–24 days and feeds the young in the nest until fledging at 28 days.
Feeding: dives headfirst, either from a perch or from a hover above water; eats mostly small fish, aquatic invertebrates and tadpoles.
Voice: fast, repetitive, cackling rattle resembles a heavy teacup shaking on a saucer.
Similar Species: *Blue Jay* (p. 365) and *Steller's Jay* (p. 252): brighter blue plumage; smaller bill and head; backswept crest; longer legs; completely different behavior.
Best Sites: almost any site with water. *Winter:* along the coast.

LEWIS'S WOODPECKER

Melanerpes lewis

This green-and-pink woodpecker has taken itself out of the ordinary life of a woodpecker—Lewis's Woodpecker does much of its foraging in the manner of a tyrant flycatcher, catching insects on the wing. It is also the only woodpecker that often perches on wires, but it is most likely to be seen in semi-open country high in oaks or pines or atop poles or snags. • Competition with European Starlings for nesting holes and the loss of favored snag habitats for feeding have greatly diminished this bird's numbers. • The Lewis's Woodpecker is named for Meriwether Lewis of the Lewis and Clark Expedition of the early 1800s. Although not a formal naturalist, he recorded in his diary a great many concise and original natural history observations.

ID: glossy, dark green upperparts; dark red face; light gray breast and collar; pinkish belly; dark undertail coverts; sharp, stout bill. *In flight:* appears mostly dark, especially from above; long wings and tail; crowlike flight with flapping and gliding.
Size: *L* 11 in; *W* 21 in.
Status: rare to fairly common breeding summer resident and migrant; fairly common in winter in Jackson, Wasco and Josephine Counties, uncommon in the Rogue Valley and surrounding hills and rare in the Willamette Valley and the Umpqua Valley; state-listed as sensitive.
Habitat: open woodlands; prefers oak woodlands and, in western Oregon, lower-elevation mixed conifers or, east of the Cascades, riparian ponderosa pines and cottonwoods; favors snags by watercourses.

Nesting: male selects a dead stub of a live tree; pair incubates 6–7 white eggs for 13–14 days; young fledge in 28–34 days.
Feeding: sallies from a perch to catch flying insects; also eats acorns and other nuts, pine seeds and berries; caches acorns and nuts in natural crevices for use in the non-breeding season and defends stores from other woodpeckers.
Voice: quiet away from the nest site; utters a wheezy contact call and harsh churring notes.
Similar Species: *Other woodpeckers* (pp. 220–30): none are dark green; only the Pileated Woodpecker (much larger) flies in a similar fashion.
Best Sites: Merlin; Lower Table Rock (near Medford). *Summer:* White River WMA; Deschutes R.; Tumalo SP (Bend); Cabin Lake Campground; Wildhorse Creek; Upper Wallowa Valley; Clyde Holliday SP.

ACORN WOODPECKER

Melanerpes formicivorus

♂

The highly social Acorn Woodpecker is well known for its communal lifestyle, which is unusual in its highly territorial family. During the breeding season, only one or two pairs in each group actually mate and produce eggs—nonbreeding members of the group help incubate the eggs and raise the young. • Communal groups place surplus acorns in one or two storage sites near the center of the group territory—dead trunks and limbs are studded with acorns jammed tightly into shallow holes. As many as 50,000 acorns have been stored in a single snag. All the woodpeckers in the group defend their acorns, which are often so tightly jammed that they cannot be removed without signaling that a robbery is in progress.

ID: glossy, black upperparts; pale underparts with heavily black-streaked breast; clownlike face with white and pale yellow areas and black "cheeks" and "chin"; pale eyes; red nape. *Male:* red crown. *Female:* black crown. *In flight:* black tail; white rump and upperwing patch; whitish underwing; flaps and glides.

Size: *L* 9 in; *W* 17½ in.

Status: locally common year-round resident in the Rogue Valley and foothills and in the Willamette Valley north to Forest Grove (mainly on the west side, north of Eugene).

Habitat: deciduous woodlands that include oaks.

Nesting: colonial; cavity in a deciduous snag, especially oak, or a pole, is lined with wood chips; helped by the young of previous years, the pair incubates 3–7 white eggs for 11–12 days; larger clutches result from laying by several females; young fledge at 30–32 days.

Feeding: eats large numbers of acorns and some fruit, sap and corn; gleans ants or other insects or catches them on the wing; occasionally drills into wood for insects.

Voice: very vocal; gives a nasal *wheka wheka* series and a raucous *jay-cup, jay-cup, jay-cup,* with all group members joining in.

Similar Species: *White-headed Woodpecker* (p. 226): white throat and head, except at back; black underparts and rump; solitary. *Male Williamson's Sapsucker* (p. 221): white-striped black face; red throat; yellow belly; white shoulder patch.

Best Sites: Lower and Upper Table Rocks (near Medford); Pacific University (Forest Grove); Baskett Slough NWR; Ankeny NWR; William L. Finley NWR headquarters area; Fern Ridge Reservoir; Eugene.

WILLIAMSON'S SAPSUCKER

Sphyrapicus thyroideus

Male and female Williamson's Sapsuckers are so radically different in appearance that naturalists long believed them to be separate species. The male is boldly patterned in black and white, but the female, with her barred back and wings, brown head and dark breast, resembles the juveniles of other sapsuckers. The male and female occupy separate winter territories. • Because each foot has two toes facing forward, another at a 90 degree angle and, on most species, a small, generally backward-pointing hind toe, woodpeckers can move vertically up and down trunks. The stiff tail helps brace the bird against the tree trunk when foraging or drumming. • Robert S. Williamson was a topographical engineer and U.S. Army lieutenant who led the Pacific Railroad Survey across Oregon during the mid-1800s.

ID: yellowish belly. *Male:* generally black; white "mustache" and "eyebrow"; broad, white wing patch; red "chin"; white-streaked blackish brown flanks. *Female:* dark brown and white bars on upperparts; blackish "bib" and upper breast; dark-barred flanks; brown head. *In flight:* white rump; white-barred dark underwing.

Size: *L* 9 in; *W* 17 in.

Status: uncommon to common breeding summer resident on the eastern slope of the Cascades and in the Blue, Wallowa and Warner Mts.; widespread east of the Cascades summit in migration; rare in the Siskiyou Mts. in summer; rare in the Klamath Basin in winter; state-listed as sensitive.

Habitat: coniferous forests, especially in pine or pine–aspen stands, usually at mid-elevation and higher; sometimes uses deciduous riparian areas.

Nesting: in a tree, often used over several years and riddled with cavities; cavity is lined with wood chips; pair incubates 5–6 white eggs for 12–14 days; young are almost immediately independent on fledging at 21–28 days.

Feeding: drills parallel lines of holes in hemlock, fir, pine and aspen for sap and insects; also gleans for ants; female eats more berries than does the male.

Voice: gives a loud, shrill *chur-cheeur-cheeur;* initially fast drumming slows, with lengthening pauses between the taps.

Similar Species: *Acorn Woodpecker* (p. 220): clownlike face; paler underparts; communal. *Other sapsuckers* (pp. 222–23): extensively red head and throat; heavily white-marked back; narrower white upper-wing area.

Best Sites: Indian Ford Campground (Sisters); Ochoco Mts.; Crater Lake NP; Klamath Forest NWR; Kimball SP (Fort Klamath); Spring Creek; Auburn; Starr Campground (Blue Mts.); Bear Valley, Grant Co.; Logan Valley.

RED-NAPED SAPSUCKER

Sphyrapicus nuchalis

Not having a reinforced skull like other woodpeckers, sapsuckers have evolved a successful variation of the typical woodpecker foraging strategy: they drill parallel lines of sap-wells in the bark of living trees and shrubs. The Red-naped Sapsucker, one of four species that have adopted this feeding method, is quick to make its rounds once the wells fill with sap, collecting trapped insects and oozing fluid as it goes. • Sapsuckers do not suck sap—they lap it up with a long tongue that resembles a frayed toothbrush. Most healthy trees and shrubs can withstand a series of sapsucker wells that also help sustain other woodpeckers, hummingbirds, waxwings, kinglets and warblers in times of need. • This species sometimes interbreeds with the Yellow-bellied Sapsucker (*S. varius*) and the Red-breasted Sapsucker.

ID: white-marked black back and wings; brown-chevroned pale underparts; yellow-washed upper breast; black "bib"; red throat, forehead and nape spot; black-and-white striped head. *Male:* red "chin." *Female:* "chin" is usually white. *In flight:* white upperwing patch; short, rapid flight.
Size: *L* 8 in; *W* 16 in.
Status: common breeding summer resident and migrant from the eastern slopes of the Cascades eastward; very rare in winter but more frequent in the Klamath Basin.
Habitat: aspen or cottonwood woodlands, riparian areas and residential woodlots; desert oases.
Nesting: makes a cavity in a live birch, cottonwood or aspen, often near water; pair

incubates 4–5 white eggs for 12–13 days; young fledge in 25–29 days.
Feeding: drills a series of parallel lines to drink sap or pine pitch and eats insects attracted to it; eats cambium, fruit and berries; also catches insects in flight.
Voice: common call is a catlike *neeah;* also utters a loud *kweear* on its territory and a series of wavering *wika* notes; drumming starts with several fast taps, then slower single and double taps.
Similar Species: *Red-breasted Sapsucker* (p. 223): redder head and breast, often with whitish stripes on worn female; generally blacker back. *Williamson's Sapsucker* (p. 221): male has red only on "chin," and all-dark back; female resembles juvenile Red-naped but has black upper chest, yellow belly and uniformly barred wings.
Best Sites: Indian Ford Campground and Cold Springs Campground (Sisters); aspens at Hart Mt.; cottonwoods at Spring Creek; Grande Ronde R.; Sumpter area; Starr Campground (Blue Mts.).

RED-BREASTED SAPSUCKER

Sphyrapicus ruber

Bold in appearance, yet shy and reclusive by nature, the Red-breasted Sapsucker is one of three species that used to be considered subspecies of the Yellow-bellied Sapsucker (*S. varius*). Especially in migration and winter, the Red-breasted Sapsucker is the most likely of the three species commonly found in Oregon to occur in urban areas. It is also more likely to be seen in dense coniferous forests, especially coastal rainforests, where it is the only regular one. The Red-breasted is known to interbreed with the Red-naped Sapsucker in the few places in inland mountains and valleys where their ranges overlap. • The wells that Red-breasted Sapsuckers drill also benefit other birds, such as other woodpeckers and warblers, and even chipmunks and squirrels.

ID: black-and-white back and wings; dark-streaked, yellow-washed pale belly and sides; red head, "chin," throat and breast; large, white "mustache." *In flight:* white upperwing patch.

Size: *L* 8 in; *W* 16 in.

Status: rare to fairly common year-round resident; rare summer visitor in the Blue Mts. and Wallowa Mts.; rare migrant in Harney Co.

Habitat: moist rainforests, interior conifers and broken, mixed woodlands, often close to riparian areas. *In migration* and *winter:* urban parklands, orchards and gardens.

Nesting: in a live alder, cottonwood, aspen, fir, riparian alder or willow (occasionally a snag); cavity is lined with wood chips; pair incubates 4–5 white eggs for 12–13 days; young fledge in 25–29 days and are fed fruit and insects while being instructed by parents.

Feeding: drills and strips bark to produce perennial sap wells; also eats insects, especially ants, and fruit; occasionally flycatches for insects.

Voice: loud, hoarse, descending *queeoh* spring call is often repeated several times; also utters a softer *cheer;* drumming starts with several fast taps, then becomes an irregular single- and double-tap series.

Similar Species: *Red-naped Sapsucker* (p. 222) and *Yellow-bellied Sapsucker:* black, red and white pattern on head, throat and "bib"; usually more white on back; Red-naped is mainly restricted to eastern Oregon, and Yellow-bellied is rare.

Best Sites: wooded hilly areas of the Willamette Valley, the western part of the Cascades and southwestern Oregon.

DOWNY WOODPECKER

Picoides pubescens

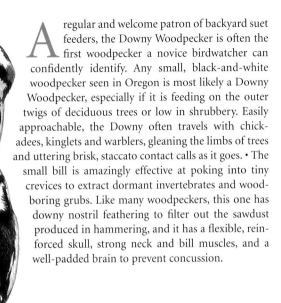

A regular and welcome patron of backyard suet feeders, the Downy Woodpecker is often the first woodpecker a novice birdwatcher can confidently identify. Any small, black-and-white woodpecker seen in Oregon is most likely a Downy Woodpecker, especially if it is feeding on the outer twigs of deciduous trees or low in shrubbery. Easily approachable, the Downy often travels with chickadees, kinglets and warblers, gleaning the limbs of trees and uttering brisk, staccato contact calls as it goes. • The small bill is amazingly effective at poking into tiny crevices to extract dormant invertebrates and wood-boring grubs. Like many woodpeckers, this one has downy nostril feathering to filter out the sawdust produced in hammering, and it has a flexible, reinforced skull, strong neck and bill muscles, and a well-padded brain to prevent concussion.

ID: black back with white patch; white or pale buffy underparts; white-striped black head; stubby bill; black tail with black-spotted white outer feathers. *Male:* small, red hind-crown patch. *In flight:* white-barred black wings with white linings; comparatively direct flight.

Size: *L* 6–7 in; *W* 12 in.

Status: common year-round resident at low to moderate elevations.

Habitat: deciduous and mixed woodlands; city woodlots and parks; prefers riparian willows, alders and cottonwoods.

Nesting: female selects a dead limb of a tree; pair excavates a hole, sometimes hidden in lichens or moss, and lines it with wood chips; mostly the male incubates 4–5 white eggs for 12 days; young fledge in 20–25 days but are dependent on the parents for up to 3 weeks.

Feeding: male prefers smaller branches, the upper canopy and angled limbs; female favors the trunk and upright limbs; eats mainly insects, especially wood-boring beetles and larvae, but also fruit, seeds and sap from sapsucker wells; uses suet feeders in winter.

Voice: calls include a long, unbroken trill, sharp *pik* or *ki-ki-ki* and whiny *queek queek;* drums more than the Hairy, usually at a higher pitch on smaller trees and dead branches.

Similar Species: *Hairy Woodpecker* (p. 225): larger; stockier; larger bill; unspotted white outer tail feathers; usually feeds on a tree trunk or large branches. *Three-toed Woodpecker* (p. 227): larger; finer white head stripes plus speckling; yellowish crown on male; muted wing barring; white-barred black back; three-toed foot.

Best Sites: open woodland habitats, including urban ones.

HAIRY WOODPECKER

Picoides villosus

Looking like an oversized Downy Woodpecker, the Hairy Woodpecker usually bullies its way to the forefront at a shared suet feeder. Too heavy to feed at a tree's outer extremities, the Hairy is often seen hammering away on the trunk or a large branch of a conifer or mature hardwood. It is proficient at opening up the shallow probings of a Black-backed Woodpecker or Three-toed Woodpecker and digging deeper into the huge excavations of Pileated Woodpeckers. • The secret to any woodpecker's success is its long tongue—in some cases more than four times the length of the bill. Stored in twin structures that wrap around the skull's perimeter, it uncurls like the proboscis of a butterfly. Its finely barbed, saliva-sticky tip helps ease out the most stubborn of wood-boring insects.

ID: black back with large white patch; white or dusky buff underparts; flanks may have dark streaks; black-and-white patterned head; heavy, straight bill; black tail with white outer feathers. *Male:* red hindcrown. *In flight:* black-and-white barred wings with white linings.

Size: *L* 8–9 in; *W* 15 in.

Status: uncommon to common year-round resident.

Habitat: evergreen, mixed and, less often, hardwood forests, especially burns, wooded swamps and alder woodlands with many dead trees.

Nesting: male selects a soft tree; pair makes a cavity and lines it with wood chips; pair incubates 4 white eggs for 11–15 days; young fledge at 28–30 days and are tended by both parents for several weeks; male brings most of the food, with the female staying within hearing range of the young.

Feeding: drills and expands holes in bark to reach wood-boring insects and larvae; also drinks sap in summer; winter diet of live and cached insects and nuts; male feeds higher on tree trunks than the female, especially in winter; occasionally visits suet feeders in winter.

Voice: calls include a loud, sharp *peek peek* and a long, unbroken *keek-ik-ik-ik-ik-ik* trill; drums less regularly than the Downy Woodpecker and at a lower pitch on tree trunks and large branches.

Similar Species: *Downy Woodpecker* (p. 224): smaller; daintier; shorter bill; prefers outer twigs or being close to the ground. *Black-backed Woodpecker* (p. 228): tiny, white "eyebrow" stripe; all-black back; muted wing barring; yellow crown patch on male and juvenile; black-barred white flanks and sides; 3-toed feet.

Best Sites: dense, older coniferous forests. *Winter:* feeders.

WHITE-HEADED WOODPECKER

Picoides albolarvatus

Unique among woodpeckers with its largely white head and throat, the White-headed Woodpecker is a reclusive specialty of ponderosa pine forests. Pine seeds are an important part of its diet, so the White-headed Woodpecker forages chiefly among old and mature forests of three- and five-needle pines. Such a dry diet means that a reliable nearby source of drinking water is a necessity. • Throughout most of the year, their habit of quietly tapping flaking, loose bark high on trunks and out on the limbs makes these woodpeckers harder to detect than their relatives, but pairs of White-headed Woodpeckers can be heard engaging in territorial drilling in spring. At other times, these birds are most likely to be seen flapping overhead from one foraging area to another.

ID: mostly black; largely white head and throat; brown eyes. *Male:* red nape patch. *Juvenile:* red crown. *In flight:* dark wing with white patch above and below; slow and lazy but direct flight.

Size: *L* 9 in; *W* 16 in.

Status: rare to common year-round resident in the Cascades and the Blue, Wallowa, Warner and Siskiyou Mts.; state-listed as sensitive.

Habitat: ponderosa pine forests, less often in mixed conifers with ponderosa pines.

Nesting: in a dying or dead pine, oak or aspen or a stump; pair excavates a cavity and lines it with wood chips; pair incubates

4–5 pitch-stained white eggs for 14 days; young fledge in 26 days.

Feeding: female forages in ponderosa pine and cedar stands in winter, but male feeds at higher elevations; drills less than other woodpeckers; eats wood-boring insects and larvae, plus large quantities of pine seeds and other plant material; diet requires drinking more water than other woodpeckers.

Voice: usual call is a sharp, rattling, sometimes extended *tea-deek* or *tea-dee-deek;* drumming sessions are long, with an uneven tempo.

Similar Species: *Acorn Woodpecker* (p. 220): black "chin"; yellowish throat; pale forehead; pale eyes surrounded by black; red head-patch on both genders; white rump; communal. *Pileated Woodpecker* (p. 230): much larger; longer, heavier bill; black-and-white head with red crest; dark-tipped white underwing feathers.

Best Sites: Indian Ford Campground (Sisters); Ochoco Mts.; Crater Lake NP; Klamath Forest NWR; Kimball SP (Fort Klamath); Spring Creek; Auburn; Starr Campground (Blue Mts.); Bear Valley, Grant Co.; Logan Valley.

THREE-TOED WOODPECKER

Picoides tridactylus

Evidence of its foraging activities often betrays the Three-toed Woodpecker long before it is seen. In its search for insects and their eggs, this resourceful bird flakes off bits of bark from old and dying conifers, exposing the red inner bark. Intent on extracting every last morsel from a tree, the Three-toed Woodpecker will return again and again. After months or years of serving as a foraging site, the tree takes on a conspicuous and distinctive reddish look and is skirted with bark chips. • A feeding bird's tapping and flaking noises can often be heard at short range, and its contact calls are often quite musical. Every so often, it will stop working to listen for the telltale sounds of grubs hidden beneath the bark or in the wood.

ID: black-and-white barring on back, with a mostly white patch on interior birds; white underparts with black-barred sides; white-striped and partly speckled black head; black tail with mostly white outer feathers; 3-toed feet. *Male:* yellow crown patch. *In flight:* black-and-white barring on wings, light below and dark above; typically short, fluttering flights.

Size: *L* 8–9 in; *W* 15 in.

Status: rare to uncommon year-round resident of the Blue Mts. and Wallowa Mts.; local resident in the Cascades; state-listed as sensitive.

Habitat: variety of higher-elevation sub-alpine forest types, especially lodgepole pine forests, burns and areas of insect outbreaks.

Nesting: partly colonial when food is plentiful; usually in a fir, but possibly a hardwood snag, especially near burns, or a pole; pair digs a cavity and lines it with wood chips; pair incubates 4 white eggs for 11–14 days; young fledge at 22–26 days and stay with the parents for much of summer.

Feeding: strips bark in search of wood-boring beetles; also eats other insects and drinks sap.

Voice: low *pik* or *teek* call; relatively noisy nestlings and fledglings; drums in a prolonged series of short bursts.

Similar Species: *Black-backed Woodpecker* (p. 228): slightly larger; glossy, black back; stronger call and drumming. *Hairy Woodpecker* (p. 225): mostly white or buff back; sides are white or black-streaked buff; thicker white (or buff) head markings; prefers hardwoods.

Best Sites: northern Cascades Lakes; Crater Lake NP; Tollgate area; Spring Creek; Bonny Lakes trail; Anthony Lakes; Starr Campground (Blue Mts.).

BLACK-BACKED WOODPECKER

Picoides arcticus

An uncommon resident of lodgepole pine and other higher-elevation forests in eastern Oregon, the Black-backed Woodpecker is most active in recently burned forest patches, where wood-boring beetles thrive under the charred bark. So focused are the birds on finding food that they can easily be approached and seldom fly far if disturbed. • Black-backed Woodpeckers and Three-toed Woodpeckers have only three toes and cannot perch like other woodpeckers, but they can nevertheless climb and descend tree trunks. • In years when food is scarce, a few birds may descend from high-elevation coniferous forests to foothill parks or even urban woodlots. At such times, they tend to remain in a relatively small area and can be found by locating their foraging tree, which is worked until no wood-boring beetles or larvae remain.

ID: glossy, black back; white underparts with black-barred sides; mainly black head with broad, white "mustache" stripe and tiny, white "eyebrow"; black tail with unmarked white outer feathers; 3-toed feet. *Male:* yellow crown. *In flight:* black-and-white barring on wings, light below and dark above.
Size: *L* 9–10 in; *W* 16 in.
Status: uncommon year-round resident east of the Cascades summit; state-listed as sensitive.
Habitat: moderate to high-elevation coniferous forests, especially recently burnt lodgepole pine and ponderosa pine areas.
Nesting: usually in a fir, with the nest entrance below a branch, or in a debarked snag; pair excavates a cavity and lines it with wood chips; pair incubates 4 white eggs for 12–14 days; young fledge in 25 days; family stays together until late fall.
Feeding: strips bark in search of wood-boring beetle larvae; also eats ants; prefers to forage in trees with easily stripped bark.
Voice: low *kik* call; prolonged drumming in a series of short bursts.
Similar Species: *Three-toed Woodpecker* (p. 227): slightly smaller; black-and-white barred back; weaker call and drumming. *Male Williamson's Sapsucker* (p. 221): red throat; yellow belly; all-black tail; large white upperwing patch.
Best Sites: northern Cascades Lakes; Crater Lake NP; Tollgate area; Spring Creek; Bonny Lakes trail; Anthony Lakes; Starr Campground (Blue Mts.).

NORTHERN FLICKER

Colaptes auratus

I f you want to watch a Northern Flicker foraging for food, check the ground. Flickers are partial to ants, which form a substantial part of their diet and serve as unwilling participants in flicker hygiene. After bathing in a dusty depression to remove oils and bacteria, a flicker will pick up ants and preen rigorously. Ants contain formic acid, which is lethal to small parasites on the skin and feathers. Many other birds use this method, but the Northern Flicker is the only one to eat ants in quantity. • Although the Red-shafted race is the widespread Northern Flicker breeding species in Oregon, some Yellow-shafts appear as migrants and winter residents. Hybridizing in other parts of their shared summer range produces many intermediate forms, any of which could show up in Oregon.

red-shafted

ID: neatly black-barred back and wings; heavily black-spotted pale buff underparts; long, straight bill; black "bib"; white rump; black-spotted white tail coverts; black tail. *Red-shafted:* mostly gray face; brown crown and nape. *Yellow-shafted:* mostly brown face; grayish crown; red nape patch. *Red-shafted male:* red "mustache." *Yellow-shafted male:* black "mustache." *In flight:* undertail and wings, especially below, are pinkish red on Red-shafted and yellow on Yellow-shafted.
Size: *L* 12–13 in; *W* 20 in.
Status: common year-round resident; Yellow-shafted race is a rare visitor from September to April.
Habitat: wide variety of habitats but rarely dense forests; prefers woodland edges, open forests, grasslands and deserts; favors farmlands and towns in winter.

Nesting: usually in dead wood in a tree, snag or pole, but possibly in a post, house, natural bank, haystack, nest box or usurped burrow of a Belted Kingfisher or Bank Swallow; cavity is usually unlined; pair incubates 5–8 white eggs for 11–14 days; young fledge at 25–28 days.
Feeding: gleans the ground, tree trunks, stumps and mounds for ants; also eats seeds, nuts and grain; visits feeders in winter.
Voice: male gives a loud, rapid, laughlike *kick-kick-kick-kick-kick-kick;* issues a *woika-woika-woika* during courtship; drums less often but more variably than other woodpeckers.
Similar Species: *Female Williamson's Sapsucker* (p. 221): smaller; all-brown head; yellow belly; fine white barring on black upperparts.
Best Sites: any suitable habitat. *Winter:* visits urban gardens.

PILEATED WOODPECKER

Dryocopus pileatus

With its flaming red crest, breathtaking flight and loud, maniacal call, this impressive deep-forest dweller is successful at stopping most hikers in their tracks. Considering its distinctive laugh, quirky looks and animated behavior, it is no surprise that the Pileated Woodpecker inspired a cartoon character. • Life is, however, a serious business for this crow-sized avian woodcarver. Using its powerful, dagger-shaped bill, the Pileated Woodpecker chisels out rectangular cavities in an unending search for grubs and ants. • A pair requires more than 100 acres of mature forest to survive and successfully raise its young. As a pair moves around its territory, it provides foraging sites for other woodpeckers, and the abandoned nesting cavities serve as bed-chambers for broods of tree-nesting ducks, falcons, owls and small mammals.

ID: mostly black plumage; flaming red crest; yellow eyes; stout, dark bill; white stripe from bill to shoulder; white "eyebrow" and "chin." *Male:* red "mustache" and forehead. *Juvenile:* pinkish crest; dark eyes. *In flight:* white wing lining and upperwing patch; distinctive crowlike flaps and glides.
Size: *L* 16–19 in; *W* 28–30 in.
Status: uncommon year-round resident; state-listed as sensitive.
Habitat: forests, including those dominated by conifers, maples, oaks or cottonwoods, and some urban woodlands; rare in or absent from open country, juniper forests and isolated pine and aspen stands east of the Cascades.
Nesting: in a conifer, with the hole often facing east or south and often on a bark-free surface; cavity is lined with wood chips; pair incubates 4 white eggs for 15–18 days; young fledge in 26–28 days.
Feeding: drills and excavates large, rectangular holes in search of insects; also eats fruit and nuts, especially in fall and winter, and drinks sap.
Voice: loud, fast, rolling, laughlike *woika-woika-woika-woika;* long series of *kuk* notes; loud, resonant drumming.
Similar Species: *Other woodpeckers* (pp. 219–29): much smaller; no crest.
Best Sites: widespread.

PASSERINES

Golden-crowned Kinglet

Passerines are also commonly known as songbirds or perching birds. Although these terms are easier to comprehend, they are not as strictly accurate, because some passerines neither sing nor perch, and many nonpasserines do sing and perch. In a general sense, however, these terms represent passerines adequately: they are among the best singers, and they are typically seen perched on a branch or wire.

It is believed that passerines, which all belong to the order Passeriformes, make up the most recent evolutionary group of birds. Theirs is the most numerous of all orders, representing about 43 percent of the bird species in Oregon, and nearly three-fifths of all living birds worldwide.

Passerines are grouped together based on the sum total of many morphological and molecular similarities, including such things as the number of tail and flight feathers and reproductive characteristics. All passerines share the same foot shape: three toes face forward and one faces backward, and no passerines have webbed toes. Also, all passerines have a tendon that runs along the back side of the bird's knee and tightens when the bird perches, giving it a firm grip.

Some of our most common and easily identified birds are passerines, such as the Black-capped Chickadee, American Robin and House Sparrow, but the passerines also include some of the most challenging and frustrating birds to identify, until their distinct songs and calls are learned.

Black-capped Chickadee

OLIVE-SIDED FLYCATCHER

Contopus cooperi

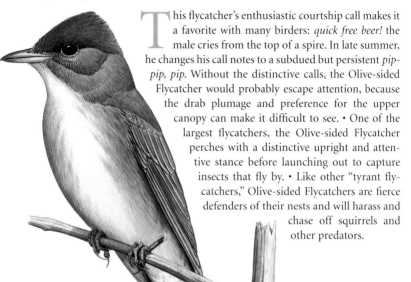

This flycatcher's enthusiastic courtship call makes it a favorite with many birders: *quick free beer!* the male cries from the top of a spire. In late summer, he changes his call notes to a subdued but persistent *pip-pip, pip*. Without the distinctive calls, the Olive-sided Flycatcher would probably escape attention, because the drab plumage and preference for the upper canopy can make it difficult to see. • One of the largest flycatchers, the Olive-sided Flycatcher perches with a distinctive upright and attentive stance before launching out to capture insects that fly by. • Like other "tyrant flycatchers," Olive-sided Flycatchers are fierce defenders of their nests and will harass and chase off squirrels and other predators.

ID: olive brown upperparts; olive gray "vest"; light throat and belly; white rump patches (often hard to see); barred undertail coverts; squared tail; dark eyes; large bill with largely pale lower mandible. *Juvenile:* mainly dark bill. *In flight:* wings paler below.

Size: *L* 7 in; *W* 13 in.

Status: fairly common to common breeding summer resident; uncommon migrant throughout May and from August to early September; federal species of concern and state-listed as sensitive.

Habitat: *Breeding:* coniferous or mixed forests with snags or tall trees with dead branches. *In migration:* woodlands of all types, including juniper and oak, riparian areas and desert oases.

Nesting: usually high in a conifer, on a horizontal branch far from the trunk; compact cup nest of twigs, rootlets, lichen and pine needles is firmly attached with cobwebs and lined with lichen, grass and rootlets; female incubates 3–4 brown-marked pale eggs for 14 days; young fledge in 21–23 days.

Feeding: sallies from a high perch to catch flying insects, especially honeybees where available.

Voice: utters a descending *pip-pip-pip* when excited; male gives a flat *quick free beer!*

Similar Species: *Western Wood-Pewee* (p. 233): smaller; more uniform coloration below; 2 faint gray wing bars; different calls. *Juvenile Cedar Waxwing* (p. 302): obvious crest; smaller bill; black "mask"; white facial lines; yellow-tipped tail.

Best Sites: coniferous forests with snags or trees that have high, dead branches.

WESTERN WOOD-PEWEE

Contopus sordidulus

Found mostly in forest clearings or edge habitats, this small, drab songster will sing persistently throughout the heat of a summer afternoon. Only by its down-slurred song can the Western Wood-Pewee be confidently distinguished from the nearly identical Eastern Wood-Pewee (*C. virens*) of eastern North America. • The Western Wood-Pewee will occasionally launch itself into aerobatic looping ventures in search of flying insects. It usually returns to the same perch. • The nest is a model of concealment—the completed structure resembles a bump on a horizontal limb. When cryptic concealment fails to provide enough protection against predators, this unassuming flycatcher will vigorously defend its nest, chasing away hawks, jays, squirrels and chipmunks. • The scientific name *sordidulus* refers to its dusky, "dirty" color.

ID: dark, olive brown upperparts; 2 faint gray wing bars; pale underparts with blurry, dark "vest"; pale throat; slightly peaked hindcrown; mainly dark bill; light undertail coverts; long, slightly notched tail. *Juvenile:* pinkish lower mandible.

Size: *L* 5–6 in; *W* 10½ in.

Status: common breeding summer resident and migrant; spring migrants appear in late April and may still be moving through by early June; fall migration peaks in late August and early September.

Habitat: *Breeding:* open deciduous and coniferous forests, orchards, riparian growth and residential woodlots. *In migration:* almost any woodland habitat.

Nesting: on a horizontal limb of a tree far from the trunk; fairly large, deep cup of plant fibers and down is bound to a branch with spiderwebs and lined with fine materials; female incubates 2–4 creamy white eggs marked with brown and purple for 12–13 days; young fledge at 14–18 days.

Feeding: sallies, hovers and gleans for insects and some berries.

Voice: whistles *sdree-yurr;* also utters other short, whistled and sneezy notes.

Similar Species: *Olive-sided Flycatcher* (p. 232): larger; white rump patches may be visible; explosive song and calls. *Empidonax flycatchers* (pp. 234–39): smaller; rounded heads; white eye rings; paler, often gray or yellow-tinged underparts; shorter wings; more contrast in underwing; some dip their tails.

Best Sites: woodland sites, including residential woodlots and farm homesteads.

WILLOW FLYCATCHER
Empidonax traillii

As the spring movement of songbirds wanes, Willow Flycatchers begin to appear in low-growth areas near water. Most of them continue onward to more northern latitudes, but many remain to nest in Oregon's lowland areas and locally in the mountains. • Similar plumages make the various *Empidonax* flycatchers the most difficult of any genera to distinguish—subtle differences in habitat preferences, calls and such difficult-to-observe details as mandible color and primary feather length provide better clues. Only since the 1970s has the Willow Flycatcher been recognized as separate from the more widespread Alder Flycatcher (*E. alnorum*) of eastern North America, based mainly on song and call characteristics. • The scientific name *traillii* honors Scotsman Thomas Stewart Traill, who helped John James Audubon secure a British publisher for his book *Ornithological Biography* in the 1830s.

ID: olive brown upperparts; 2 whitish wing bars; pale olive breast; yellowish belly; white undertail coverts; whitish throat; indistinct white eye ring; pink lower mandible. *Juvenile:* buffy wing bars. *In flight:* wings lighter below, with pale linings.
Size: *L* 5–6 in; *W* 8½ in.
Status: locally common breeding summer resident and migrant; migrants arrive in late spring; fall migration peaks from late August to early September; state-listed as sensitive; *brewsteri* ssp. is federal species of concern.
Habitat: *Breeding:* willow thickets at stream outlets; woodland edges; young alders; tall brush at field margins. *In migration:* brushy habitat, usually near water.
Nesting: female selects an upright or slanting fork of a deciduous sapling or bush; compact cup nest of bark, weed stems and grass is lined with grass, hair, plant down and feathers; pair incubates 3–4 brown-spotted buff eggs for 12–13 days; young fledge in 12–14 days.
Feeding: flies from a perch to hover and catch flying insects; also eats berries and some seeds.
Voice: call is a mellow *whit;* male (occasionally the female) sings a quick, sneezy *fitz-bew,* with emphasis on the 1st syllable and dropping off at the end; both genders have a more complex twilight flight song.
Similar Species: *Alder Flycatcher:* usually more olive green on back and rump; whiter wing bars; flatter *pip* call; song is usually *ree-bee-a. Other* Empidonax *flycatchers* (pp. 235–39): whiter eye rings and, generally, wing bars; less white throats; different calls and songs.
Best Sites: almost any brushy or riparian area; Sandy River delta; Blitzen R. at Malheur NWR.

HAMMOND'S FLYCATCHER

Empidonax hammondii

The retiring, diminutive Hammond's Flycatcher is easily confused with the very similar-looking Dusky Flycatcher. Strategies for telling the two species apart are based on subtle differences in habitat preferences and plumage. The Hammond's makes its home beneath the shady, dense canopy of mature mountain conifers throughout Oregon, whereas the Dusky prefers more open, sun-drenched forest edges, woodlands and brushy areas. The Hammond's slightly shorter bill and shorter, notched tail also help to distinguish it from the Dusky with it's longer bill and tail. • William Hammond was Surgeon-General of the U.S. Army during the Civil War. He sent scientific specimens from western North America to the Smithsonian Institution.

ID: olive gray upperparts; 2 white wing bars; yellowish underparts and undertail coverts; pale gray "vest"; slightly peaked head; distinct white eye ring; very small, darkish bill with partly orangy lower mandible; notched tail is comparatively short at rest. *Juvenile:* stronger colors. *In flight:* wings whitish below and dark above.
Size: *L* 5 in; *W* 8½–9 in.
Status: uncommon to common breeding summer resident on most mountains, though rare in the Coast Ranges; uncommon lowland migrant from mid-April to early June and from mid-August to early October.
Habitat: *Breeding:* dense, humid, mid- to high-elevation coniferous forests; rarely in more open forests. *In migration:* lowlands; sometimes along the coast.

Nesting: on a horizontal limb of a tall tree, usually a conifer; cup of leaves, bark and grass is lined with feathers, grass and hair; female incubates 3–4 unmarked creamy white eggs for 12–15 days; young fledge in 17–18 days.
Feeding: flycatches and hover-gleans for insects; usually in the mid-canopy; perches less in the open than similar flycatchers.
Voice: calls include a *pip,* a short *peek* and a mellow *weeoo;* male's song is a low and spiritless *dissup…wassup.*
Similar Species: *Dusky Flycatcher* (p. 237): longer bill and tail; pale-edged outer tail feathers; usually 2-phrased song; clearer whistles and *whit* call notes. *Gray Flycatcher* (p. 236): paler gray; longer, pale-based bill; dips tail persistently. *Other* Empidonax *flycatchers* (pp. 234–39): longer bills with conspicuous, pale lower mandibles.
Best Sites: Larch Mt.; Timothy L.; Santiam Flats (Detroit); Waldo L.; Davis L. (Cascades Lakes); Crater Lake NP; Tollgate; Moss Springs, Union Co.; Bonny Lakes trail.

GRAY FLYCATCHER

Empidonax wrightii

Distinctions between *Empidonax* flycatchers usually rely on subtle differences in plumage, vocalization and habitat, but the Gray Flycatcher can easily be identified by its habit of bobbing its pale-edged tail downward. Further clues are that it prefers low vegetation, tends to drop to the ground to pursue insects and makes its summer home in open sagebrush country, open pine forests, juniper forests and mountain mahogany woodlands at elevations up to at least 6000 feet. All other small flycatchers flick their tails quickly upward, flycatch from higher perches (except in migration) and tend to prefer less open habitat. • Spencer Fullerton Baird named this distinctly western species in honor of Charles Wright, who was a botanist with the North Pacific Exploring and Surveying Expedition of the mid-1800s.

ID: drab, grayish upperparts; 2 pale wing bars; whitish underparts; faint white eye ring; long, dark-tipped bill with pale lower mandible; long tail with thin, white border. *In flight:* gray underwing with pale yellow lining.
Size: *L* 5–6 in; *W* 8½–9 in.
Status: locally uncommon to fairly common breeding summer resident in southeastern, south-central and north-central Oregon and the Blue Mts. from late April to late September; rare migrant in western Oregon.
Habitat: *Breeding:* open sagebrush, juniper forests, mountain mahogany stands and local in ponderosa and lodgepole pines. *In migration:* low, brushy habitat, often well away from breeding habitats and mountains.
Nesting: in a crotch of a juniper or sage, or near the base of a thorny shrub; cup of

bark, plant down, weed stems and grass is lined with feathers and hair; female incubates 3–4 unmarked creamy white eggs for 14 days; young fledge at 16 days.
Feeding: sallies from a perch for flying insects; gleans in foliage and on the ground for insects and larvae.
Voice: *chawip seeahl* song is often followed by an aspirated *whea* or a liquid *whilp*.
Similar Species: *Dusky Flycatcher* (p. 237): usually darker, with more contrast; darker lower mandible; does not dip tail. *Hammond's Flycatcher* (p. 235): darker; darker "vest"; smaller bill with duskier lower mandible; often flicks wings and short, thin tail. *Willow Flycatcher* (p. 234): browner upperparts; does not dip tail; prefers wetter habitats.
Best Sites: Prineville Reservoir; Klamath Forest NWR; Ontario area; Fort Rock; Hart Mt.

DUSKY FLYCATCHER

Empidonax oberholseri

Many novice birdwatchers despair of trying to properly identify the very similar-looking Dusky, Hammond's and Gray flycatchers, so why not lump them together to make life a little easier? Prominent ornithologists did at one time consider the Dusky Flycatcher and the Gray Flycatcher to be one species, but closer inspection of collected specimens, DNA analysis and detailed studies of bird behavior and habitat requirements have revealed that these birds do deserve separate species status. • In the breeding season, Dusky Flycatchers favor mid- and high-elevation forests and other montane habitats. • The scientific name *oberholseri* honors renowned 20th-century ornithologist Dr. Harry C. Oberholser, who worked for the U.S. Fish and Wildlife Service and the Cleveland Natural History Museum.

ID: olive brown upperparts; 2 faint white wing bars; pale gray "vest"; pale yellow belly and undertail coverts; pale, elongated eye ring; rounded head; small, dark bill with orangy lower mandible; whitish throat; long, dark tail with lighter edges. *Juvenile:* yellow belly and undertail coverts; buffy yellow wing bars. *In flight:* pale-lined gray underwings.

Size: *L* 5–6 in; *W* 8–8½ in.

Status: uncommon to common breeding summer resident and uncommon to fairly common migrant in the Siskiyou Mts. and Cascades and all mountains to the east; rare migrant in western Oregon; scarce and local in the Coast Ranges.

Habitat: *Breeding:* montane chaparral; open conifers; higher sagebrush–aspen areas; mountain mahogany stands; juniper forests. *In migration:* riparian, deciduous and coniferous woodlands at lower elevations.

Nesting: in a crotch of a juniper or sagebrush, or near the base of a thorny shrub; cup nest of weed stems and grass is lined with feathers, grass and hair; female incubates 3–4 unmarked creamy white eggs for 12–15 days; young fledge at 18 days.

Feeding: flies from a perch to hover-catch flying insects; gleans for caterpillars and other larvae.

Voice: call is a flat *wit;* male's call is a quick, whistled *PREE-tick-preet,* rising at the end; summer song is a repeated *du...DU-hic.*

Similar Species: *Hammond's Flycatcher* (p. 235): smaller bill; shorter tail; prefers denser shade. *Gray Flycatcher* (p. 236): paler gray overall; dips tail persistently.

Best Sites: Santiam Flats (Detroit); Robert Sawyer Park (Bend); northern Cascades Lakes; Davis L.; Crater Lake NP; Upper Klamath NWR; Colvin Timbers (Abert Rim); Hart Mt.; Spring Creek; Rhinehart Canyon.

PACIFIC-SLOPE FLYCATCHER

Empidonax difficilis

Fortunately for birders, the song of the Pacific-slope Flycatcher is much more distinctive than its plumage. When you enter any moist woodland during spring, this small flycatcher's snappy, rising *pawee* or *tink* call is often one of the first sounds you'll hear. Nonetheless, the species name assigned to this bird, *difficilis*, is an appropriate designation given the difficulties of flycatcher identification. Until late in the 20th century, this common songbird and the Cordilleran Flycatcher were collectively known as "Western Flycatcher." • Like other members of the family, the Pacific-slope Flycatcher hunts primarily by "hawking": after launching from an exposed perch, it seizes a flying insect in midair and then loops back to alight on the same perch, ready for its next sally.

ID: olive brown upperparts; 2 pale wing bars; brownish rump; pale yellow underparts; brownish "vest"; yellowish throat; white eye ring; small crest; dark bill with orange lower mandible. *Juvenile:* buffier wing bars. *In flight:* pale-lined gray underwings.
Size: *L* 5 in; *W* 8 in.
Status: common breeding summer resident and migrant west of the Cascades; locally common summer resident and uncommon migrant east of the Cascades; present from late April to August.
Habitat: *Breeding:* moist deciduous or mixed forests in foothills and valleys. *In migration:* more varied habitats, but rarely away from treed areas.
Nesting: cavity in a stream bank, roots of an upturned tree, eaves, or a small tree; female constructs a nest of moss, lichen, rootlets, grass, leaves and bark that is lined with shredded bark, hair and feathers; female incubates 3–4 brown-spotted creamy eggs for 14–15 days; young fledge at 14–16 days.
Feeding: sallies from a perch and hover-catches flying insects; also gleans for insects and eats some berries and seeds.
Voice: male's call is a single, upslurred *sweeet* or *fe-oo-eeet!;* female's call is a brief, high-pitched *tink;* song is a series of high-pitched, repeated phrases *siLEEK...tup...P'SEET!*
Similar Species: *Cordilleran Flycatcher* (p. 239): almost identical plumage and voice, but usually browner on rump, and males utter a distinctive, upslurred *swee-dee. Gray Flycatcher* (p. 236) and *Dusky Flycatcher* (p. 237): pale gray throat; use more open sites.
Best Sites: Saddle Mountain SP; Charleston; Vernonia Log Pond; Sauvie I.; Pittock Bird Sanctuary (Portland); Foster Reservoir; Spencer Butte and Skinner Butte (Eugene); Lake Selmac CP; Tou Velle SP.

CORDILLERAN FLYCATCHER

Empidonax occidentalis

Because of differences in measurements and color, vocalizations, genetics and ecology, the Cordilleran Flycatcher and the Pacific-slope Flycatcher, previously both known as "Western Flycatcher," were distinguished as separate species in 1989. Not all ornithologists support this separation, though, and the species are often indistinguishable in the field.
• Research suggests that the Pacific-slope Flycatcher summers both in western and northeastern Oregon, whereas the Cordilleran Flycatcher nests largely in the extreme northeast. • *Empidonax* is a wonderful name for this confusing, but endearing, genus of small flycatchers—it means "king of the gnats," a reflection of these birds' amazing insect-catching abilities.

ID: olive brown upperparts; 2 pale wing bars; brown rump; pale yellow underparts; brownish "vest"; yellowish throat; elongated, white eye ring; small crest; dark bill with orange lower mandible. *Juvenile:* buffier wing bars. *In flight:* pale-lined gray underwing.
Size: *L* 5 in; *W* 8 in.
Status: locally uncommon breeding summer resident and migrant east of the Cascades from late April to mid-September.
Habitat: *Breeding:* moist canyons and mid- to upper-elevation forests, usually in valley bottoms or along watercourses. *In migration:* more varied habitats, including more open lowland forests and deciduous brush.
Nesting: in a cavity in a stream bank, the roots of an upturned tree, a cliff ledge or a small tree; female constructs a nest of moss, lichen, rootlets, grass, leaves and bark and lines it with shredded bark, hair and feathers; female incubates 3–4 brown-spotted creamy eggs for 14–15 days; young fledge at 14–16 days.
Feeding: sallies from a perch and hover-catches flying insects; also gleans for insects and eats some berries and seeds.
Voice: male's call is a chipper whistle: *swee-dee.*
Similar Species: *Pacific-slope Flycatcher* (p. 238): almost identical plumage and voice, but usually less brown on rump. *Gray Flycatcher* (p. 236) and *Dusky Flycatcher* (p. 237): pale gray throat; found in more open sites.
Best Sites: *Summer:* Ladd Marsh WMA; Moss Springs, Union Co.; Enterprise WMA; Powder River Valley. *In migration:* Malheur NWR; Page Springs Campground (near Malheur NWR); Alvord Basin.

BLACK PHOEBE

Sayornis nigricans

Small, dark and handsome—and highly animated—the Black Phoebe is the flycatcher of extreme southwestern Oregon's shady streamsides and river bridges. An expert insect hunter, this phoebe may look like it is lost in deep contemplation at times, but as soon as an insect zips past its perch, it is off and flying. Mostly, though, it makes short, fluttering sallies to the ground to capture its invertebrate prey. The Black Phoebe will even flycatch from boulders and cobblestones. • In cold weather, Black Phoebes concentrate in protected lowlands, often around houses and other buildings, and winter sees them around small lakes, ponds, parks and gardens in small towns. • Like other phoebes, the Black Phoebe frequently dips its tail, but it raises it higher between dips.

ID: blackish brown upperparts; white belly and undertail coverts; mildly peaked, black head; short, pointed, all-dark bill; short, dark legs; thin white edges to long, notched tail. *In flight:* short wings; long tail; blackish above; white belly and wing linings.

Size: *L* 7 in; *W* 11 in.

Status: locally common year-round resident in coastal Curry Co. and Coos Co., with small numbers recently breeding and wintering as far north as the northern part of the Willamette Valley; locally common breeding summer resident and rare in winter in the Rogue R. watershed.

Habitat: *Breeding:* coastal meadows and wet brushlands that have suitable nesting structures. *In migration* and *winter:* townsites and protected habitats at lower elevations.

Nesting: attached to, on or under a wall, ledge, bridge or other structure; cup nest of mud pellets, plant fibers and hair is lined with hair, rootlets, grass and bark; female incubates 3–6 (usually 4) mainly unmarked white eggs for 15–17 days; young fledge at 14–21 days.

Feeding: sallies from a low perch to catch flying insects, especially swarming flies; sometimes eats small fish.

Voice: song is an exclamatory *f'BEE, f'BEER!;* call is a penetrating *tsip!* or *tsee.*

Similar Species: *Male Slate-colored Dark-eyed Junco* (p. 337): stubbier, pale pinkish bill and legs; rounded crown; ground feeder.

Best Sites: Rogue R. meadows; Rogue Valley at Whitehorse CP; Mill Beach log ponds (Brookings); Kirtland Road sewage ponds, Jackson Co.; Ashland.

SAY'S PHOEBE

Sayornis saya

The Say's Phoebe, with its sandy brown and apricot plumage, is partial to dry environments. It thrives in sun-parched grassy valleys and hot, dry canyons, and it is particularly common where abandoned or little-used farm buildings provide a safe, sheltered nest site that can be reused every year and where livestock conveniently stir up insects. Waiting quietly on a fence post or other low perch, a Say's Phoebe can confidently sally forth to hawk an easy meal. • The Say's Phoebe is named for Thomas Say, a versatile naturalist known more for his expertise in the field of entomology. The name "phoebe" comes from an approximation of the call of a close relative, the Eastern Phoebe (*S. phoebe*), in much the same way as "pewee" is derived from the call of the Eastern Wood-Pewee (*Contopus virens*).

ID: pale gray head, throat, upperparts and breast; apricot buff undertail coverts and belly; stoutish, all-dark bill; dark eye line; dark legs; bobs long, squared, black tail frequently. *Juvenile:* buffy wing bars and pale lower mandible. *In flight:* pale underwings with dusky apricot buff linings.
Size: *L* 7 in; *W* 13 in.
Status: uncommon to common breeding summer resident and migrant east of the Cascades; rare migrant and winter visitor in western interior valleys and along the coast; spring migration starts in mid-February; the last fall birds usually leave in early November; may overwinter.
Habitat: *Breeding:* steep canyons, open country and foothills. *In migration:* streamsides and pond margins and open and semi-open habitats, even at higher elevations.
Nesting: attached to a wall or under the eaves or a bridge; cup nest of grass, forbs, moss and plant fibers is lined with fine materials, especially hair; female incubates 4–5 mostly unmarked white eggs for 14 days; young fledge at 14–16 days.
Feeding: sallies and hovers from a perch, often just above the water, to catch flying insects; eats some berries.
Voice: calls are low, mellow whistles; male's vireo-like song consists of 2 alternating 3-note phrases.
Similar Species: *Western Wood-Pewee* (p. 233): slightly smaller; pale yellow and brownish underparts; grayish wing bars; pale lower mandible; pointier wings; brown tail.
Best Sites: Deschutes R.; Smith Rock SP; Prineville Reservoir; Fort Rock SP; Virtue Flats (Pleasant Valley); Diamond area.

ASH-THROATED FLYCATCHER

Myiarchus cinerascens

The shrill, whistled calls of the Ash-throated Flycatcher are familiar summer sounds in the canyons and river valleys in much of Oregon. These infrequent, burry notes from somewhere in the shadows of the heat-hazed oaks are to many people the voice of the dry woodlands and tall chaparral. • The only Oregon representative of a large group of sub-tropical and tropical crested *Myiarchus* flycatchers with rufous tails, the Ash-throat is a paler version of the Great Crested Flycatcher (*M. crinitus*) familiar to eastern North America. • Although it spends summer in arid terrain, the Ash-throated Flycatcher requires a shaded cavity in which to nest. If a suitable tree cavity cannot be found, this opportunistic secondary cavity nester uses a bluebird box, a crevice in junked machinery or an unused mailbox.

ID: grayish brown upperparts; 2 indistinct pale wing bars; pale yellow underparts and undertail coverts; pale gray throat and breast; stout, dark bill; fluffy crest; dark brown tail with some rufous in central strip. *Juvenile:* smaller crest. *In flight:* rufous-tinged wing tips; pale yellow wing linings.
Size: *L* 8–9 in; *W* 12 in.
Status: uncommon to fairly common breeding resident from early May to September east of the Cascades and in interior southwestern Oregon; vagrant in the Willamette Valley and along the coast.
Habitat: *Breeding:* juniper woodlands; cottonwoods, willows and other deciduous trees in canyons and river valleys; oak and oak–ponderosa pine woodlands. *In migration:* variety of tree and shrub habitats.

Nesting: in a natural cavity, nest box or other suitable cavity; soft nest consists of hair, fur, feathers and grass, and sometimes snakeskin; female incubates 4–5 creamy eggs, marked with brown and lavender, for 15 days; young fledge at 14–16 days.
Feeding: hawks from a perch and searches on the ground for insects; also eats some small fruit and sips flower nectar.
Voice: common migratory call is a soft, purring *prrrt;* male's song sounds like repeated toots of a referee's whistle with occasional more musical phrases.
Similar Species: *Western Kingbird* (p. 243): uncrested, pale gray head; bright yellow below; darker, all-brown upperwing; thinly white-edged black tail.
Best Sites: Merlin Rest Area (near Grants Pass); Lower Table Rock and Roxy Ann Butte (near Medford); Smith Rock SP; Tumalo SP (Bend); Diamond area; Page Springs Campground (near Malheur NWR).

WESTERN KINGBIRD

Tyrannus verticalis

The male Western Kingbird's tumbling aerial courtship display is sure to enliven a tranquil spring scene. Twisting and turning all the way, he flies about 60 feet into the air, stalls, and then tumbles, flips and twists as he plummets to earth. • The Western Kingbird is often seen surveying for prey from fence posts, barbed wire and power lines. Once it spots a flying insect, especially a dragonfly, bee or butterfly, a kingbird will quickly give chase and pursue its prey for 40 feet or more if necessary. • Like any kingbird, the Western Kingbird will not hesitate to take on much larger birds that it considers a threat to its nest and young. • The scientific name *verticalis* refers to the small, hidden red crown patch that is flared in courtship and territorial displays.

ID: yellowish brown upperparts; yellow belly, sides and undertail coverts; pale gray head and breast; whitish "cheek" and throat; dark eye line; black bill; concealed orangy red crown patch; long, black tail with narrow white edges. *In flight:* yellow-lined brown wings; white-edged tail.

Size: *L* 8–9 in; *W* 15–16 in.

Status: common breeding summer resident east of the Cascades and in the Rogue Valley and the Umpqua Valley; rare to uncommon migrant and very rare breeder in the Willamette Valley; rare to uncommon coastal migrant; mainly present in April and May.

Habitat: *Breeding:* open country near ranch buildings, towns, isolated groves and cottonwood-lined stream courses.

In migration: almost any open habitat, even in suburbs.

Nesting: usually on a horizontal tree branch, against or near the trunk, or on an artificial structure; cup nest of available materials is well lined with hair, cotton and plant down; female incubates 3–4 heavily mottled white to pinkish eggs for 18–19 days; young fledge at 16–17 days.

Feeding: darts out from a perch to pounce on insects; also eats some berries.

Voice: chatty, twittering *whit-ker-whit;* also *pkit-pkit-pkeetle-dot;* feisty and argumentative.

Similar Species: *Ash-throated Flycatcher* (p. 242): browner upperparts and crested head; rufous in tail and wings; paler yellow underparts.

Best Sites: Crow Creek and Imnaha areas; Virtue Flats (Pleasant Valley); Diamond area; Malheur NWR; Succor Creek SP.

EASTERN KINGBIRD

Tyrannus tyrannus

When you think of a tyrant, an image of a ruthless despot might spring to mind. Most people wouldn't think of a small bird, except maybe those who are familiar with the exploits of the tyrant flycatchers, of which the Eastern Kingbird is North America's most widespread representative. This black-and-white kingbird is a bold brawler, a street fighter willing to attack crows, hawks and even humans audacious enough to invade its territory. Intruders are often vigorously pursued and pecked, and their feathers plucked for some distance, until the kingbird is satisfied that no further threat exists. • Fiercely argumentative on its breeding habitat, the Eastern Kingbird can be quite gregarious in migration, when birds can be seen spaced out on power lines and fencelines.

ID: dark gray to blackish upperparts; white underparts; grayish breast; white "bib"; stout, black bill; concealed, reddish crown patch; dark tail with conspicuous white tip. *Juvenile:* pale wing edges. *In flight:* gray wing with a white streak below; stiff-winged, fluttering flight.
Size: *L* 8 in; *W* 15 in.
Status: locally common breeding summer resident and migrant east of the Cascades; rare migrant from spring through early September in the Klamath Basin and western Oregon.
Habitat: *Breeding:* irrigated valleys, open or riparian woodlands and woodland edges. *In migration* and *winter:* any fairly open habitat.

Nesting: halfway up a tree on a horizontal limb or on a fence post or stump; bulky cup of weed stems, grass and plant down is lined with fine grass, rootlets, hair and feathers; female incubates 3–4 dark-mottled white to pinkish eggs for 16–18 days; young fledge at 16–18 days.
Feeding: perches in the open and flycatches aerial insects; also swoops to the ground and hovers to catch other invertebrates; infrequently eats berries in migration.
Voice: utters quick, loud, chattering *kit-kit-kitter-kitter* and buzzy *dzee-dzee-dzee* calls in flight and when perched.
Similar Species: *Black Phoebe* (p. 240): smaller; all-blackish upperparts, neck, breast and tail. *Olive-sided Flycatcher* (p. 232): paler, grayish brown upperparts and flanks.
Best Sites: Umatilla, Wallowa, Union and Baker Counties; along the lower Deschutes R.; Central Patrol Rd. (Malheur NWR).

LOGGERHEAD SHRIKE

Lanius ludovicianus

Patient and skilled hunters, Loggerhead Shrikes are often seen perched atop shrubs or small trees, using their keen vision to search for prey, which is quickly dispatched in a swift swoop and added to a storage cache of food impaled on thorns or barbs. Shrikes have been known to return to these caches up to eight months later. • Although the Loggerhead Shrike looks somewhat like the Northern Mockingbird, it differs greatly in its hunting techniques, dietary preferences and habitat requirements. • Pesticide use, from which the Loggerhead Shrike has been slow to recover, and habitat destruction have caused population declines across North America. • This "masked" songbird is named "Loggerhead" because of its large head.

ID: gray crown and back; white-marked black wings and tail; gray flanks; pale gray underparts; white throat; black "mask" extends above short, dark, hooked bill. *In flight:* white "wrist" patch and outer tail feathers; quick wingbeats; short glide to perch.
Size: *L* 9 in; *W* 12 in.
Status: fairly common breeding summer resident and rare winter lingerer east of the Cascades; very rare from winter to spring west of the Cascades; most migrants depart by late September and return in March; state-listed as sensitive.
Habitat: open country with short vegetation, open juniper woodlands and rangelands.
Nesting: usually well hidden in a crotch or on a large branch of a tree, occasionally in a vine tangle; bulky, woven cup of twigs,

forbs and bark strips is lined with finer materials; female incubates 5–6 grayish buff eggs marked with brown and gray for 16–17 days; young fledge at 17–21 days.
Feeding: perches for long periods and then stoops down to the ground or actively pursues prey in flight; eats mostly large insects, but also some small birds, rodents, frogs and lizards.
Voice: male's call in summer is a bouncy hiccup, *hugh-ee hugh-ee;* infrequently a harsh *shack-shack*.
Similar Species: *Northern Shrike* (p. 246): narrower "mask"; longer bill; lightly barred underparts; in Oregon only in winter. *Northern Mockingbird* (p. 297): slimmer bill; brownish yellow eyes; narrow, black eye line; longer legs; different behavior.
Best Sites: Prineville Reservoir; Summer Lake WMA; Warner Valley; Hart Mt.; Umatilla NWR; Diamond Craters; Malheur NWR; Alvord Desert.

245

NORTHERN SHRIKE

Lanius excubitor

When the Loggerhead Shrikes retreat to warmer climates for winter, the small rodents, reptiles and amphibians of open country might expect a break. Unfortunately for them, and for small wintering songbirds, the respite is brief, because Northern Shrikes soon arrive from their subarctic breeding grounds. Each winter, a small number of these predatory songbirds migrate into Oregon, where they perch hawklike to survey semi-open hunting grounds. • *Lanius* is Latin for "butcher," and *excubitor* is Latin for "watchman" or "sentinel." "Watchful butcher" does seem a good description of the Northern Shrike's tactics, and the macabre habit of impaling its prey on thorns and barbs has earned it the name of "Butcher Bird" throughout its range in the Northern Hemisphere.

ID: gray forehead, crown and back; white-marked black wings and tail; pale, gray-barred underparts; white throat; black "mask" extends no higher than all-dark, hooked bill. *Juvenile:* initial overall brownish tinge; "scaly" underparts. *In flight:* white "wrist" patch and outer tail feathers; quick wingbeats; short glide to perch; often hovers.
Size: *L* 10 in; *W* 14½ in.
Status: uncommon winter resident; arrives in October and departs in March or early April.
Habitat: semi-open country; scrub; areas with scattered trees at lower elevations, including orchards, farmlands and ranches; migrants often appear among dunes or in scrub along the coast.
Nesting: does not nest in Oregon.
Feeding: perches on a small tree, bush or wire and swoops to the ground or pursues prey in flight; eats small mammals and birds and large insects; impales prey on plant spines or barbed wire for later consumption.
Voice: usually silent; calls are usually harsh and nasal; infrequently gives a long, grating, laughlike *raa-raa-raa-raa;* male may utter a high-pitched, hiccupy *hee-toodle-toodle-toodle* song before leaving in spring.
Similar Species: *Loggerhead Shrike* (p. 245): slightly smaller; grayer underparts; white throat; more extensive "mask"; shorter bill; juvenile has barred back and crown and less heavily barred underparts; present from March to September, rarely until November. *Northern Mockingbird* (p. 297): slimmer bill; brownish yellow eyes; narrow, black eye line; longer legs; different behavior.
Best Sites: Clatsop Spit; Coos Bay North Spit; Sauvie I.; Baskett Slough NWR; Ankeny NWR; William L. Finley NWR; Foster Reservoir.

CASSIN'S VIREO

Vireo cassinii

Distinct white "spectacles" set against a gray head mark the Cassin's Vireo, a compact yet nimble forest songbird. This western breeder, the brighter colored Blue-headed Vireo (*V. solitarius*) of eastern and northern North America and the duller Plumbeous Vireo (*V. plumbeous*), which breeds in the mountains and deserts of the Southwest and Mexico, and rarely visits Oregon, were all formerly considered subspecies of the Solitary Vireo (*V. solitarius*). • Some birders report that the Cassin's Vireo is a fearless nester, often allowing brief close-range observations during incubation. It is one of the most likely vireos to be seen accompanying migrating warblers in fall. • The Cassin's Vireo is named for John Cassin, a well-traveled Pacific Coast ornithologist of the 19th century.

ID: olive gray back and rump; 2 white wing bars; white throat and underparts; yellowish sides and flanks; grayish head; bold white "spectacles"; fairly heavy, slightly hooked bill. *In flight:* pale gray wing linings; pale yellow "wing pits."
Size: *L* 5–6 in; *W* 9–9¹/₂ in.
Status: fairly common breeding summer resident throughout Oregon, but rare breeder and common migrant in the southeast and rare in summer on the north coast; first spring birds arrive in late March; southbound birds may remain until early October.
Habitat: open woodlands, especially mixed coniferous–deciduous woodlands; prefers drier situations, especially pine–oak and oak woodlands and riparian growth.

Nesting: in an oak or conifer, suspended from a forked twig and attached by spiderwebs and cocoon silk; deep basket of grass, forbs, shredded bark and plant fibers is lined with fine grass and hair; pair incubates 4 dark-spotted white eggs for 14–15 days; young fledge at 14–15 days.
Feeding: slowly and deliberately, with frequent pauses, gleans foliage and bark for insects, spiders and berries; sometimes hawks or hovers to catch insects.
Voice: harsh *ship* and *shep* call notes are often followed by a rising *zink* note; male's song is a series of high-pitched phrases: *See me...Detroit...Surreal.*
Similar Species: *Hutton's Vireo* (p. 248): more uniform yellowish olive brown overall; incomplete "spectacles"; smaller bill. *Warbling Vireo* (p. 249): more uniform overall coloration; creamy white "eyebrow" and lores; plain upperwings; warbling song.
Best Sites: Timothy L.; Detroit Reservoir; Waldo L.; Lake Selmac CP; Santiam Pass; Indian Ford Campground and Cold Springs Campground (Sisters).

HUTTON'S VIREO
Vireo huttoni

In late winter and early spring, the male Hutton's Vireo may wage continuous vocal battles throughout the day to defend his nesting territory. • This early nesting species is underrepresented in breeding bird surveys. With coloration and size so similar to those of the Ruby-crowned Kinglet, it is often overlooked, but the odds of seeing a Hutton's are good. It is far more numerous than inexperienced birders might imagine. • A persistent "pishing" or a convincing rendition of a Northern Pygmy-Owl call (a series of low-pitched *toot* notes) will attract this year-round sprite of deep woodland shadows. Its lazier feeding style helps distinguish it from any small flycatchers and fall-plumaged warblers that resemble it. • John Cassin was persuaded by Spencer F. Baird to name this bird for his friend, William Hutton, a field collector who first obtained this bird for scientific study in the 1840s.

ID: olive brown upperparts; 2 white wing bars; olive tan underparts; incomplete, pale "spectacles"; short, slim, hook-tipped bill. *Juvenile:* buffy wing bars. *In flight:* olive gray wings with pale linings.
Size: *L* 4–5 in; *W* 8 in.
Status: locally common year-round resident west of the Cascades crest; vagrant east of the Cascades.
Habitat: lowland mixed forests, especially coastal rainforests; valley foothills; Douglas-fir and western hemlock mixed with oak, maple or madrone.
Nesting: usually in a tree or bush, suspended in a twig fork; deep, round cup of tree lichens is bound with spiderwebs and lined with fine, dry grass; pair incubates 4 brown-spotted white eggs for 14 days; young fledge at 14–15 days.
Feeding: hops from twig to twig; gleans foliage and twigs for insects, spiders and berries.
Voice: call is a rather chickadee-like *reeee-dee-ree;* male's monotonous song is a nasal, buzzy series of tirelessly repeated 2-syllable notes: *zuWEEM, zuWEEM, zuWEEM.*
Similar Species: *Cassin's Vireo* (p. 247): whiter throat and underparts; gray head; complete white "spectacles." *Ruby-crowned Kinglet* (p. 285): slightly smaller; thinner bill; dark area between wing bars; shorter, notched tail; thinner, darker legs with yellowish feet; very active feeder.
Best Sites: *Summer:* Coffenbury L.; Saddle Mountain SP; Cape Blanco SP; Pittock Bird Sanctuary (Portland); Larch Mt.; Scoggins Valley Park; Foster Reservoir; Spencer Butte (Eugene); Merlin; Whitehorse CP; Roxy Ann Butte (near Medford).

WARBLING VIREO
Vireo gilvus

This vireo lives up to its name—its velvety voice has a warbling quality not present in the songs of other vireos. In eastern North America, the varied phrases end on an upbeat, as if asking a question, but songs heard in the West frequently have a dropping, fuzzy ending. • Common and widespread in Oregon, the Warbling Vireo prefers the upper canopy of deciduous woodlands to dense, mature evergreen forest, so its range has probably been expanding over the years. It is the most likely vireo to be found in deciduous habitats and residential areas. Seeing one requires a lot of patience, however, because its rather drab plumage and slow, deliberate foraging make it difficult to spot among the dabbled shadows of its wooded background.

ID: olive gray upperparts; unbarred wings; dull whitish or pale yellowish underparts; yellowish wash on flanks; dark eyes; creamy white "eyebrow" and lores; shortish, hook-tipped bill. *In flight:* olive gray wings with pale linings.
Size: *L* 5½ in; *W* 8½ in.
Status: common breeding summer resident throughout most of Oregon, from late April until late September.
Habitat: *Breeding:* riparian wooded areas; open oak forests; mixed forests. *In migration:* almost any woodlands; prefers deciduous stands and residential areas.
Nesting: usually high in a deciduous tree or shrub, suspended from the prongs of a forked twig and secured by spiderwebs or cocoon silk; well-made, compact, deep cup nest of bark strips, leaves, plant fibers and grass; pair incubates 3–4 dark-spotted white eggs for 13–14 days; young fledge at 14–16 days.
Feeding: feeds mostly in trees; gleans foliage, often from underneath, and makes hovering flights for insects; also eats spiders, berries and flower buds.
Voice: male's song is a squeaky but appealing musical warble: *I love you I love you Ma'am!* or *iggly wiggly piggly iggly eeek!*
Similar Species: *Red-eyed Vireo* (p. 250): slightly larger; greener upperparts; black-edged bluish gray "cap"; dark eye line; red eyes; larger bill. *Cassin's Vireo* (p. 247): 2 white wing bars; gray head; bold white "spectacles"; stouter bill.
Best Sites: Sauvie I.; Pittock Bird Sanctuary (Portland); Lewis and Clark SP (Lower Sandy R.); Cascade Gateway Park (Salem); Indian Ford Campground and Cold Springs Campground (Sisters); Robert Sawyer Park (Bend).

RED-EYED VIREO

Vireo olivaceus

The male Red-eyed Vireo is North America's undisputed champion of vocal endurance—in early spring and summer he sings throughout the day and well into the night before taking a well-earned break until sunrise. One patient ornithologist estimated that a male Red-eye may well sing his well-rehearsed phrases up to 21,000 times a day. The bird utters his robinlike song while hopping diagonally along branches and twigs, not from a perch. • Ornithologists do not yet agree about the reason for this vireo's eye color. Most other vireos, as well as young Red-eyed Vireos, have brown irises. Very uncharacteristic among songbirds, red eyes tend to be more prevalent in such nonpasserines as accipiters, grebes and herons.

ID: olive green upperparts and "cheeks"; white underparts; yellow-washed flanks and undertail coverts; black-edged, bluish gray "cap"; white "eyebrow"; red eyes. *In flight:* longish wings, greenish and gray with pale linings.

Size: *L* 6 in; *W* 10 in.

Status: locally common breeding summer resident in the northeast, the Ontario area, the Willamette Valley and the Columbia R. lowlands near Portland and rare elsewhere, from late May until early September.

Habitat: *Breeding:* favors riparian woodlands, especially with large cottonwoods. *In migration:* prefers deciduous woodlands.

Nesting: in a tree, suspended from a forked twig and secured by spiderwebs; dainty, deep cup of bark, grass, wasp-nest paper and other materials is lined with finer materials; female incubates 2–4 white eggs, spotted with reddish brown, for 11–15 days; young are fed snails and spiders and fledge at 10–12 days.

Feeding: hops along branches to glean upper-canopy foliage, hovers and fly-catches; eats insects, especially caterpillars, plus small fruits, especially berries, in late summer and fall.

Voice: gives short, scolding *neeah* calls; male's song is a continuous, variable run of quick, short phrases separated by pauses: *Look-up, way-up, in-tree-top, see-me, here-I-am, there-you-are.*

Similar Species: *Warbling Vireo* (p. 249): paler overall; grayer upperparts; unbordered crown; dark eyes; shorter bill; warbling song. *Hutton's Vireo* (p. 248): smaller; yellowish olive brown overall; 2 white wing bars; whitish eye ring; shorter bill; sings earlier in the year.

Best Sites: Virginia L. area (Sauvie I.); Lewis and Clark SP (Lower Sandy R.); Foster Lake Campground; Red Bridge SP (Grande Ronde R.); Enterprise WMA; Crow Creek, Wallowa Co.; near Union Creek Campground (Powder R.).

GRAY JAY

Perisoreus canadensis

Few birds in Oregon rival Gray Jays for boldness. Outwardly unspectacular, they are inquisitive, endearing, gregarious and individualistic by nature, always ready to seize any opportunity. Birds in small family groups glide slowly and unexpectedly out of coastal and mountain coniferous forests, attracted by the slightest commotion or movement and willing to show themselves to any passersby, especially if food is available. • Gray Jays build their well-insulated nests, lay their eggs and begin incubation as early as late February, allowing them to supply their nestlings with the first foods of spring. • Gray Jays often store food for future use. Coating it with a sticky mucus from specialized salivary glands both preserves it and renders it unappetizing to other birds and forest mammals.

ID: fluffy, light gray plumage, darker and browner above and paler below; dark "hood"; pale forehead; white nape and "cheeks"; short, black bill; long, rounded, white-tipped tail. *Juvenile:* more uniform grayish brown overall; gray bill. *In flight:* distinctive, bouncy flight with alternating fast flaps and short glides, usually close to the ground.
Size: *L* 11 in; *W* 18 in.
Status: locally common year-round resident in the mountains and along the coast.
Habitat: montane coniferous forests; a few found at sea level in spruce habitat.
Nesting: usually on a horizontal conifer branch near the trunk or in a crotch; bulky, well-woven cup of sticks, bark strips, moss and grass is fastened together with spider silk and insect cocoons and lined with feathers, bark strips, grass and fur; female incubates 3–4 finely spotted grayish white eggs for 16–18 days; young fledge at 15 days.
Feeding: gleans foliage and searches for food on the ground; eats mostly insects, fruit and carrion; caches partly digested food in conifers; steals or accepts food at campsites and picnic areas.
Voice: complex vocal repertoire includes a soft, whistled *quee-oo*, a chuckled *cla-cla-cla* and a *churr*; also imitates other birds.
Similar Species: *Clark's Nutcracker* (p. 255): mostly pale gray; much longer bill; black-and-white wings and tail. *Shrikes* (pp. 245–46): slightly smaller; black "mask"; larger, hooked bill; black-and-white wings and tail; favor open country.
Best Sites: Cape Meares SP; Saddle Mountain SP; Larch Mt.; Waldo L.; Lost L. (Santiam Pass); northern Cascades Lakes; Crater Lake NP; Tollgate; Bonny Lakes trail; Anthony L.; Starr Campground (Blue Mts.).

STELLER'S JAY
Cyanocitta stelleri

Normally noisy and pugnacious, the stunning Steller's Jay suddenly becomes silent, cautious and elusive at its nest, sitting tight on its eggs until action is required. • Most common in dense coniferous and evergreen hardwood forests, Steller's Jays regularly visit backyards in the foothills and lowlands, especially in winter, often descending upon feeders in search of peanuts and sunflower seeds. Inquisitive and bold like all jays, these crested opportunists are not averse to raiding the picnic sites and campgrounds of inattentive occupants for food scraps, but they rarely allow hand-feeding the way Gray Jays do. • When George Wilhelm Steller, the naturalist on Vitus Bering's ill-fated expedition to Alaska in 1740–42, saw his first Steller's Jay, the similarity to paintings of the Blue Jay convinced him he had arrived in North America.

ID: largely glossy, deep blue upperparts, with finely brown-barred wings and tail; medium blue underparts; blackish brown back, nape, head and prominent, shaggy crest; dark eyes; stout, black bill. *Juvenile:* slightly paler. *In flight:* grayish underwings with blue linings; round-tipped blue tail; leisurely flight with short glides and little upward lift.
Size: *L* 11 in; *W* 19 in.
Status: uncommon to common year-round resident in much of Oregon.
Habitat: *Breeding:* mixed woodlands; coastal and mountain conifers to timberline. *In migration* and *winter:* mostly coniferous woodlands.
Nesting: usually on a horizontal conifer branch or in a crotch, occasionally in a deciduous tree or shrub; bulky cup of twigs and dry leaves is cemented with mud and lined with rootlets, pine needles and grass; female incubates 4 brown-marked, pale greenish blue eggs for 16 days.
Feeding: gleans foliage and searches the ground for acorns, seeds, fruit, small invertebrates, bird eggs and nestlings.
Voice: varied; harsh, far-carrying *shack-shack-shack;* grating *kresh, kresh.*
Similar Species: *Western Scrub-Jay* (p. 253): sky blue upperparts, except for grayish brown back; pale grayish brown underparts; no crest; blackish "cheeks"; prefers open woodlands and brush. *Blue Jay* (p. 365): sky blue upperparts with white wing and tail markings; pale gray breast, blue crest; thin, black "collar"; smaller; grayish white face; prefers oak and other deciduous woodlands.
Best Sites: widespread in summer; during extreme winters, large numbers may gather in lowland towns such as Baker City and La Grande.

WESTERN SCRUB-JAY

Aphelocoma californica

The slender, uncrested Western Scrub-Jay is often seen foraging among leaf litter or surveying its tree-dotted habitat from a perch atop a tall shrub. • Each fall, these open-country jays gather fallen acorns and store them individually in holes they have dug in the ground with their strong bills. When it's time to eat the acorns, which form a staple of the winter diet, these intelligent birds often use a rock or concrete slab as an anvil to assist in cracking open the hard covering to get at the edible part inside. Because Western Scrub-Jays do not retrieve all of their hidden hoard, many acorns germinate, thus renewing the stand and keeping the resident scrub-jays supplied for life—a clear case of good forest management.

ID: sky blue upperparts with grayish brown back; pale grayish brown underparts; faintly streaked white throat bordered with blue "necklace"; dark, pointed bill; blackish "cheeks"; white "eyebrow"; long, unmarked blue tail. *Juvenile:* plain, grayish brown head and neck. *In flight:* tail and wings are bluish gray below.

Size: *L* 11 in; *W* 15½ in.

Status: common year-round resident in western interior valleys and from Lake Co. and Klamath Co. northward to Bend; uncommon along the southern coast, in the Hood River Valley and Wasco Co.; expanding range.

Habitat: open deciduous habitats, including agricultural and residential areas, brushy hillsides, oak woodlands and juniper forests.

Nesting: in a shrub or small conifer; platform of twigs and some moss supports a grass cup lined with fine rootlets and hair; female incubates 3–6 dark-spotted, pale green eggs for 15–17 days; young fledge at 18–19 days.

Feeding: mostly a ground feeder; in summer, largely eats insects, plus other invertebrates and small vertebrates, including bird eggs, nestlings and fledglings; winter diet is mostly acorns, seeds and fruit.

Voice: perch call is a harsh, repetitive *wenk wenk wenk* series or a rough, frequently repeated *quesh quesh quesh.*

Similar Species: *Pinyon Jay* (p. 254): lighter blue overall; shorter tail; stiff wingbeats and quick, direct flight; often in large flocks. *Blue Jay* (p. 365): all-blue back; blue crest; thin, black "collar"; white-marked wings and tail.

Best Sites: Willamette Valley; Hood River Valley; lower Columbia R.; central Wasco Co.; Rogue Valley; coastal Curry Co.; Umpqua Valley; southern Lake Co. and Klamath Co. northward to Bend.

PINYON JAY

Gymnorhinus cyanocephalus

Behaving much like American Crows, Pinyon Jays are loud and highly gregarious. Outside the breeding season, these all-blue birds forage in large flocks of up to several hundred that consist of many smaller family groups. Each group member has a specific duty—some birds take turns acting as lookouts, others act as food scouts, and all know their place. Even when nesting, Pinyon Jays maintain a tight social structure. • In the breeding season, colonies of up to 150 Pinyon Jays gather in pines and junipers, with some trees supporting several nests. By supplementing freshly harvested foods with cached seeds and nuts, adults can nest in late winter. If the year's pine seed crop is good, a second brood may be raised in late summer; if not, these jays become nomadic and disperse widely in search of food.

ID: pale blue plumage; whitish throat streaks; long, dark, pointed bill; long legs; short tail. *Juvenile:* grayer. *In flight:* grayish flight feathers; comparatively short, round-tipped tail; flies like other blue-colored jays, but faster and usually in flocks.
Size: *L* 9½–11 in; *W* 18–19 in.
Status: fairly common year-round resident in central Oregon.
Habitat: juniper forest. *Breeding:* transition zone between yellow or ponderosa pines and junipers. *Fall* and *winter:* semi-open country.
Nesting: colonial; in a juniper or pine tree; bulky outer platform of twigs and bark supports a cup of shredded bark, plant fibers, rootlets, paper and hair; female incubates 4–5 brown-marked, bluish, greenish or grayish white eggs for 16–17 days; young fledge at 21 days.
Feeding: searches the ground, gleans foliage and hawks; eats seeds of pines and other plants, fruits, insects, bird eggs and nestlings; caches pine seeds for winter consumption.
Voice: warning call is a low *krawk-krawk-krawk;* flight call is a high, piercing *mew* or laughing *hah-hah.*
Similar Species: *Western Scrub-Jay* (p. 253): darker blue on wings and tail; grayish brown back; pale underparts; blue "necklace"; blackish "cheeks"; longer tail. *Mountain Bluebird* (p. 288): smaller; male is slightly brighter blue; female is grayer; short bill; forked tail; whitish underwing flight feathers.
Best Sites: Lake, Deschutes, Jefferson and Crook Counties; Prineville Reservoir; Boonesboro area and airport at Bend; Cabin Lake Campground, Lake Co.; Summer Lake WMA.

CLARK'S NUTCRACKER

Nucifraga columbiana

Observations indicate that the Clark's Nutcracker can be either left-footed or right-footed when handling pine seeds, but research has yet to determine whether this preference is learned or innate. Like other corvids, this jay, which inhabits the higher ridges of the mountain chains, stores food for winter in ground caches that may be spread miles apart and hidden under deep snow. Clark's Nutcracker has, like some of its cousins, learned that a quick meal can be expected in campgrounds and day-use areas. • When explorer Captain William Clark of the Lewis and Clark Expedition saw the large, straight bill, he thought this raucous and gregarious bird was a woodpecker, so he placed it in the new genus *Picicorvus*, meaning "woodpecker-crow."

ID: light gray back, underparts and head; long, straight, black bill. *Juvenile:* shorter tail. *In flight:* small, white secondary patch on black wing; white tail with black center strip above; direct flight, usually to high location in pines.
Size: *L* 12 in; *W* 24 in.
Status: uncommon to common year-round resident of high mountain forests, with some movement to lower elevations east of the Cascades in fall and winter.
Habitat: high-elevation conifers; ponderosa pine and juniper forests at lower elevations.
Nesting: on a horizontal conifer limb; platform of twigs, secured with bark strips, supports an inner cup of fine bark strips, grass, conifer needles, hair and feathers; pair incubates 2–4 pale green eggs with brown, olive or gray markings for 16–18

days; young fledge at 18–21 days and travel with the parents.
Feeding: searches the ground and gleans foliage for pine nuts and other seeds, fruit, insects, bird eggs and nestlings; carries pine seeds in its throat pouch and caches them in the ground during summer and fall for winter consumption.
Voice: quite varied; usual call is a rather unpleasant, grating *skraaaaaaa*, usually delivered from a high perch; other calls are higher pitched or yelping.
Similar Species: *Gray Jay* (p. 251): smaller; generally brownish gray, with pale belly and dark "hood"; stubby bill; forages more in lower canopy of dense coniferous forests. *Northern Mockingbird* (p. 297): much smaller; lighter underparts; small bill; dark eye line; white "wrist" patch in flight; much longer tail.
Best Sites: Waldo L.; Big L. (Santiam Pass); northern Cascades Lakes; Davis L.; Crater Lake NP; Tollgate; Moss Springs, Union Co.; Wallowa L.; Bonny Lakes trail; Anthony L.

BLACK-BILLED MAGPIE

Pica hudsonia

Magpies are among the more strikingly plumaged of North America's birds, but their habits leave a little to be desired. Many magpies specialize in stealing the eggs of other birds, and some have taken to the widespread corvid habit of scavenging roadkills—Black-billed Magpies will even eat the remains of their own kind. • Until recently, the Black-billed Magpie, which is largely confined to western North America, was considered to be the same as the widespread magpie (*P. pica*) of many parts of Europe, North Africa and Asia. • A magpie's nest is an elaborate dome of sticks held together with mud, offering excellent protection to the young. Magpies will search high and low for decorative touches—many a wedding ring or gemstone has ended up in a nest, and brightly colored material of any kind is highly prized by this interior decorator.

ID: iridescent, blackish blue wings; black back, breast and head; white shoulders and belly; stout, black bill; long, black legs; black "leggings" and undertail coverts; long, dark-tipped, iridescent, green-and-blue tail. *Juvenile:* shorter tail. *In flight:* rounded wings with large white areas near tips.

Size: *L* 18–22 in; *W* 24–26 in.

Status: very common year-round resident east of the Cascades; rare visitor to western Oregon.

Habitat: sagebrush–juniper areas and agricultural areas with scattered trees, less often in dense juniper stands or treeless open country.

Nesting: in a tall shrub or conifer; large, conspicuous, domed platform of heavy, often thorny sticks contains a bowl of mud or cow dung lined with rootlets, fine plant stems and hair; female incubates 5–8 brown-marked greenish gray eggs for 16–21 days; young fledge in 25–29 days.

Feeding: searches the ground, gleans foliage and hawks; eats carrion, invertebrates, small vertebrates, fruit and seeds; fall and winter diet is largely cached seeds and carrion.

Voice: loud, nasal, frequently repeated *queg-queg-queg*; also many other vocalizations.

Similar Species: none.

Best Sites: Deschutes, Jefferson, Klamath and Lake Counties; foothills and valleys east of Ashland in Jackson Co.; northern Malheur Co.; Alvord Basin; Catlow Valley; Malheur NWR.

AMERICAN CROW

Corvus brachyrhynchos

American Crows are wary, intelligent birds that have flourished despite considerable efforts by humans to reduce their numbers. Much of their survival strength lies in their ability to adapt to a variety of habitats, food resources and environmental conditions. Crows remain year-round in coastal and moist lowland areas, preferring farmlands and urban areas; populations breeding at higher elevations usually flock together and migrate to warmer locations for winter. • Crows are highly gregarious birds with a complex social structure. Flocks can be composed of hundreds of birds, and these impressive, often noisy groups were once known as "murders." The purpose of flocking, however, is merely to prepare for evening roosts or migration.

ID: all black, typically with some iridescent, green or purple back feathers; sleek head and throat; stout, black bill; rounded tail. *Juvenile:* brownish black with pale areas on wings until fall molt. *In flight:* usually flies in pairs or flocks.
Size: *L* 17–21 in; *W* 3–3½ ft.
Status: common year-round resident west of the Cascades; locally common in summer and very local and sporadic in winter east of the Cascades.
Habitat: interior valleys, urban areas, agricultural lands and ranches, open country forests, coastal mountains and along the coast.
Nesting: partly colonial; in a deciduous or coniferous tree or shrub, rarely on the ground; cup of branches, twigs and bark is lined with shredded bark, moss, grass, feathers, hair and leaves; pair incubates 4–6 bluish green or olive green eggs with brown or gray markings for 18 days; young fledge at 28–35 days.
Feeding: ground feeder; eats insects and other invertebrates, carrion, bird eggs and nestlings, seeds (especially corn), fruit and nuts; coastal birds break mollusk shells by dropping them onto rocks (probably learned by watching gulls).
Voice: utters a distinctive, loud, repetitive *caw-caw-caw;* other calls are somewhat hoarse and hollow-sounding.
Similar Species: *Northwestern Crow:* virtually identical. *Common Raven* (p. 258): larger and much heavier; rough wedge shape to tail; heftier bill; throat looks shaggy; glides with wings held flat; often soars and engages in spectacular courtship and bonding flights.
Best Sites: widespread.

COMMON RAVEN

Corvus corax

Whether stealing food from a flock of gulls or a Bald Eagle, harassing a Great Horned Owl or Golden Eagle, or scavenging from a carcass miles from its nest site, the Common Raven substantiates its reputation as a clever bird. Glorified in many cultures, including those of many American Indians, as a magical being, the largest member of the crow family exhibits behavior that people often think of as exclusively human. It executes tumbling acrobatic feats that put the current crop of extreme sports practitioners to shame, and it performs everything with an individuality and practiced complexity that goes far beyond the instinctive behavior of most other birds. • Few birds boast the Common Raven's wide distribution, from the bitter winter cold and darkness of the arctic tundra to the hottest and most arid deserts, and few others demonstrate such an apparent enjoyment of life and such a loyalty to their mate.

ID: iridescent, purplish, all-black plumage; large head; heavy, black bill; shaggy-looking throat; powerful talons. *Juvenile:* grayish at neck; shorter bill. *In flight:* rough diamond shape to tail; soars and performs acrobatics.

Size: *L* 24 in; *W* 4½ ft.

Status: uncommon to common year-round resident, except in much of the northern part of the Willamette Valley.

Habitat: mountains, open country, cattle ranches, large freshwater marshes, sage–juniper scrubland, coastal habitats. *Winter:* lowlands.

Nesting: on a cliff ledge or in a conifer (occasionally in a hardwood); bulky cup of branches and twigs is lined with shreds of bark and hair; female incubates 4–6 brown- or olive-marked greenish eggs for 18–21 days; young fledge at 38–44 days.

Feeding: searches for food from the air; eats mainly carrion and also small vertebrates, bird eggs and nestlings (especially at seabird colonies), invertebrates, seeds and fruit; some birds scavenge in garbage.

Voice: gives a deep, loud, guttural, repetitive *craww-craww* or *quork quork* and many other vocalizations, including remarkably varied songs heard only at close range.

Similar Species: *American Crow* (p. 257): smaller and slimmer; smaller bill; rounded tail; smooth throat; higher pitched calls; more often seen in urban locations.

Best Sites: cattle ranches of Harney Co. and Lake Co.; Blue Mts.; Wallowa Mts.; locally in the Willamette, Umpqua and Rogue Valleys; Malheur L. is the site of a large winter roost.

HORNED LARK

Eremophila alpestris

Found from the Arctic south to central Asia and Mexico, with remnant populations in Morocco and Colombia, the Horned Lark nests in the mountains and on open grasslands. Until the mid-1980s, when taller grasses resulted from dune stabilization programs, a few pairs also nested on Oregon's coastal sand spits and dunes. A widespread migrant along the coast and freshwater shorelines, this small, uniquely patterned ground bird is nearly always encountered in open country. • Horned Larks rely on their disruptive light-and-dark coloring, their mouselike foraging technique and a low profile among scattered grass tufts to escape the eye of predators. Flushed flocks scatter in all directions and reassemble later. • Linnaeus, who encountered the species in Europe, named it *Alauda alpestris*, "lark of the mountains."

ID: mostly light brown above; white underparts; yellow face and throat; bluish gray bill; dark legs. *Male:* small, black "horns"; tapered black mark from bill to "cheek"; black breast band; rufous tints common, especially at nape. *Female:* duller brown replaces rufous and black; paler yellow. *In flight:* yellowish white wing linings; white-edged, brown-centered black tail.

Size: *L* 7 in; *W* 12 in.

Status: common year-round resident and migrant east of the Cascades; locally uncommon year-round at lower elevations in the west; locally uncommon breeding summer resident above timberline in the Wallowa Mts. and Cascades and on Steens Mt.; *strigata* ssp. is state-listed as sensitive.

Habitat: *Breeding:* bare arctic–alpine sites, short-grass habitats, deserts and farmlands. *In migration* and *winter:* open grasslands, beaches, dunes and salt marshes; forages on roadsides, feedlots and fields.

Nesting: in a natural cavity in the ground, usually protected by rocks or grass tufts; woven nest of grass, small roots and shredded cornstalks is lined with soft materials; female incubates 3–4 cinnamon-spotted gray eggs for 11–12 days; young leave the nest at 10 days and fledge at 27 days.

Feeding: forages mainly on the ground, especially in bare fields and short grass, for insects and seeds.

Voice: delicate song is a lilting, upward-spiraling tinkle of soft notes: *TEEP, tip, TOOP-pit-tip-pit-tip-pit-ittle-EEE;* flight call is a thin *seet* or *see-dirt*.

Similar Species: *American Pipit* (p. 300): buffier, often streaked breast and underparts; muted facial colors; wider white tail edges. *Lapland Longspur* (p. 338): streaked upperparts are brown, white and black; chestnut nape; stout, paler bill; breeding male has mostly black head and throat.

Best Sites: Willamette Valley; near Baskett NWR; open country east of the Cascades.

259

PURPLE MARTIN

Progne subis

At scattered locations across Oregon, the Purple Martin, the largest of our swallows, attempts to hold its own against pushy Eurasian immigrants—mostly European Starlings and House Sparrows that begin nesting before the martin returns in spring. • In 1831, John James Audubon noted that pub owners were placing nest boxes above tavern signs to encourage Purple Martins to nest and bring good luck. Less than 70 years later, almost all Eastern birds were using nest boxes, but in the later-colonized West, most birds still use natural cavities and woodpecker holes, although new colonies are more often in open boxes placed over water. • The scientific name *Progne* refers to Procne, a daughter of Pandion; according to Greek mythology, she was transformed into a swallow.

ID: small bill. *Male:* glossy, dark bluish black overall. *Female:* dusky blue back; brown-smudged grayish white forehead, forecrown, collar, throat and underparts. *In flight:* long, broad, pointed wings; notched tail; relatively slow wingbeats; often soars to 500 ft in sunny weather.
Size: *L* 7–8 in; *W* 18 in.
Status: rare to uncommon breeding summer resident and migrant west of the Cascades; possible current local breeding summer resident in Klamath Co.; rare migrant in eastern Oregon; state-listed as sensitive.
Habitat: *Breeding:* clear-cuts, ridges and open woodlands near rivers and estuaries; forages over water and open country. *In migration:* various habitats, including urban parklands and ponds.

Nesting: colonial; usually in a woodpecker hole in a snag or old log piling or a nest box; male helps female incubate 4–5 pure white eggs for 15–18 days; young fledge at 28–29 days.
Feeding: hawks for flying insects; occasionally gleans from foliage, picks off the ground or skims from the water's surface.
Voice: rich, fluty, robinlike *pew-pew* is often uttered in flight; song is a vibrant, congested warble, often uttered high in the sky.
Similar Species: *European Starling* (p. 299): longer bill; wedge-shaped tail; green-and-purple gloss; pale spotting. *Barn Swallow* (p. 266): smaller; glossy, blue upperparts; orangy to pale underparts; red forehead, throat and neck; longer tail.
Best Sites: along the coast and in the Willamette Valley from April to August; Nehalem Meadows; Bay City sewage ponds; Siuslaw R. estuary; Coos Bay; Sauvie I.; Marine Drive (Portland); Fern Ridge Reservoir; Sutherlin log ponds; Roseburg.

TREE SWALLOW

Tachycineta bicolor

Anyone with Tree Swallows nesting in the vicinity appreciates this bird's enormous appetite for flying insects, especially mosquitoes, which it brings back to its nestlings as often as 20 times per hour. Cavity nesters such as Tree Swallows benefit greatly when landowners and progressive foresters allow some dead trees to remain standing. In areas where natural tree cavities are scarce, the number of nest boxes available may well determine the size of the Tree Swallow (and mosquito) population. • The back of a male Tree Swallow appears steely blue in bright spring sunshine but looks much greener in late summer and fall. Unlike our other swallows, a female Tree Swallow does not acquire full adult plumage until her second or third year.

ID: small bill; folded wings do not project beyond short, forked tail. *Male:* iridescent, bluish green upperparts and "cap" that extends below eyes; white throat and underparts; mostly dark rump. *Female:* slightly duller than male, or drab brown above with darker mask. *In flight:* brown wings and tail.

Size: *L* 5–6 in; *W* 14–15 in.

Status: common breeding summer resident and migrant; arrives in mid- to late winter; fall migration is from August until early October; some birds may remain in the Willamette Valley until early winter.

Habitat: open areas, usually near water, including urban lawns. *Breeding:* requires nesting cavities. *In migration:* freshwater bodies; open habitats.

Nesting: loosely colonial; in a natural cavity, old woodpecker hole or nest box; nest of weeds, grass, feathers, rootlets and other plant materials is lined with fine grass, feathers and sometimes pine needles; fed by male, female incubates 4–7 white eggs for 14–15 days; young fledge at 18–22 days.

Feeding: hawks for flying insects low over land or water; requires insects in spring but, unlike other swallows, can subsist for extended periods on seeds and berries.

Voice: gives a liquid *buli-dulu-dulit* contact call and a metallic, buzzy *klweet* alarm call; male's song is a liquid, chattering repetition of 2- or 3-note phrases.

Similar Species: *Violet-green Swallow* (p. 262): male has green back, "cap" and nape, plus purplish wings, rump (white sides) and tail; female is often duller, with smudgy head pattern; white on face extends above eyes; wing tips extend past tail at rest.

Best Sites: throughout Oregon.

VIOLET-GREEN SWALLOW
Tachycineta thalassina

Demonstrating a greater aptitude for taking advantage of Oregon's diverse habitats than the Tree Swallow, the Violet-green Swallow is found around cliffs and treeless open areas far more than its cousin and is less reliant on riparian habitats. It often travels to higher altitudes to feed with swifts. The Violet-green nests in cliff crevices, sandbanks, stream banks or old Cliff Swallow or Barn Swallow nests. • Swallows occasionally eat mineral-rich soil, eggshells and shellfish fragments, possibly to renew the minerals lost during egg formation. • *Tachycineta* is from Greek words that mean "I move fast," and *thalassina* is Latin for "sea green," a reference to the color of the upper plumage, especially the male's, which is reminiscent of shallow inshore waters.

ID: white underparts; white-sided rump; tiny bill; long, pointed wings extend short, notched tail at rest. *Male:* iridescent, green "cap," nape and back; purplish wings, rump and tail; white underparts; white on face extends above and behind eyes. *Female:* duller; can be more bronze brown, with dark-barred "cheeks." *In flight:* purplish brown wings and tail.
Size: *L* 5 in; *W* 13½ in.
Status: common breeding summer resident and migrant; begins arriving in late winter, peaking in early spring; southbound flocks form in late July and leave by early October.

Habitat: *Breeding:* open woodlands, wooded canyons, towns and open areas near water. *In migration:* any open area.
Nesting: loosely colonial; in a cavity in a tree, cliff or bank, or in a nest box or old swallow nest; cup of grass stems, small twigs, rootlets and straw is topped with feathers; female incubates 4–6 white eggs for 14–15 days; young fledge at 23–24 days.
Feeding: hawks for flying insects, especially leafhoppers, leaf bugs, flies and ants.
Voice: exuberant, irregular chatter: *ch-ch-ch-ch-chairTEE, chairTEE-ch-ch;* male's song is a squeaky series of single notes and rapid *tsip* repetitions.
Similar Species: *Tree Swallow* (p. 261): blue or bluish brown above; white on face stops abruptly below eyes; folded wings do not project beyond tail.
Best Sites: throughout Oregon.

NORTHERN ROUGH-WINGED SWALLOW
Stelgidopteryx serripennis

The Northern Rough-winged Swallow is the cool-temperate representative of a group of swallows that wear almost the same colors as the earthen banks in which they live. These low-flying, semi-colonial aerialists nest in burrows alongside streams and roadcuts, often making use of the abandoned diggings of other birds and rodents. Usually seen in small numbers, they frequently join mixed flocks of swallows hawking insects over rivers or lakes. • In 1819, at a Louisiana Bank Swallow colony, John James Audubon was the first to scientifically record Northern Rough-wings. Noticing the curved barbs along the outer edges of the primary wing feathers, he named them *Stelgidopteryx* (Greek for "scraper-wing") *serripennis* (Latin for "saw-feathered").

ID: plain, earthy brown upper-parts, darkest on wings; light brown throat; pale underparts; wings extend just beyond tail at rest. *Juvenile:* 2 reddish wing bars. *In flight:* broad wings; square tail, often spread when soaring; less erratic flight than other swallows.
Size: *L* 5–6 in; *W* 14 in.
Status: common breeding summer resident and migrant; first appears in early April; fall migration is from July until early September.
Habitat: *Breeding:* open areas with earthen banks, especially gorges, roadcuts, railroad embankments, gravel pits, stream margins and coastal ridges. *In migration:* with other swallows over fairly open forest and grassland areas, freshwater lakes, marshes and lagoons.

Nesting: usually near water, in a cavity or crevice in a cliff or bank, such as a swallow, kingfisher or rodent excavation, or a gutter, culvert, drainpipe or a hole in a wall; nest is a pile of various materials with a neat inner cup of softer materials, rarely feathers; female incubates 5–7 white eggs for 16 days; young fledge at 19–20 days.
Feeding: hawks at low levels over land, and especially water, for flying insects, particularly flies and beetles; occasionally picks floating insects off the water's surface.
Voice: generally quiet; gives an occasional quick, short, squeaky *brrrtt.*
Similar Species: *Bank Swallow* (p. 264): paler rump and lower back; white at throat continues up behind dark ear patch; complete, distinct brown breast band. *Female* and *juvenile Purple Martin* (p. 260): much larger; broader wings; whitish underparts indistinctly marked with gray and brown; narrow, forked tail.
Best Sites: throughout Oregon.

BANK SWALLOW

Riparia riparia

A Bank Swallow breeding colony seems to be in a constant flurry of activity as the dark, sandy brown adults fly back and forth delivering mouthfuls of insects to their insatiable young. All this activity tends to attract predators, yet few birds are caught, because the adults are swift and agile fliers, and the entrances to the nest holes are placed in such a way that reaching them from above or below is very difficult. • In medieval Europe, it was believed that swallows overwintered in mud at the bottom of swamps, because the huge flocks seemed to disappear overnight after breeding. • *Riparia* is from the Latin word for "riverbank," which remains the preferred nest site for this bird.

ID: brown upperparts, head and complete breast band; white underparts, throat and foreneck; small, thin bill; short, dark legs. *In flight:* dainty wings; long, narrow, forked tail; fluttering wingbeats; sudden direction changes; almost always in flocks.
Size: *L* 5 in; *W* 13 in.
Status: locally common breeding summer resident and uncommon migrant east of the Cascades; very local breeder and rare migrant in the west; state-listed as sensitive.
Habitat: *Breeding:* stabilized banks, usually at lower elevations; feeds mostly over wetlands, riparian woodlands, farmlands and shrub lands. *In migration:* open areas near water.
Nesting: colonial; in a burrow to 4 ft in length, close to the top of a cliff face or bank; flat platform is made of grass, feathers, small twigs, straw, rootlets or leaves; male helps female incubate 3–5 white eggs for 13–15 days; young fledge at 20–25 days.
Feeding: captures insects in the air; feeds on the ground in insect infestations.
Voice: both genders utter a *speed-zeet speed-zeet* twittering chatter; quite noisy at nesting colonies; male's song is a repeated series of short, clear notes.
Similar Species: *Female* and *juvenile Violet-green Swallow* (p. 262) and *Tree Swallow* (p. 261): greenish, bluish or smudgy brown upper head; partly white sides of rump; broader, less-forked tail; indistinct breast band on juvenile Tree Swallow. *Northern Rough-winged Swallow* (p. 263): paler head and back; brownish underparts, fading from breast to belly.
Best Sites: Tumalo SP; Hatfield L. (Bend); Fort Klamath; Summer L. WMA; Cold Springs NWR; Ladd Creek (Grande Ronde Valley); Thief Valley Reservoir; Burns–Hines area; Malheur NWR.

CLIFF SWALLOW
Petrochelidon pyrrhonota

Silvestre Vélez de Escalante of Spain saw and described nesting colonies of Cliff Swallows in Utah in 1776. If these birds had been named more recently, they would probably have been named "Bridge Swallows," because many bridges seem to have Cliff Swallow colonies underneath. Dramatic clouds of stocky, square-tailed swallows will suddenly swirl up along either side of the bridge, and a close inspection of the underside will reveal dozens to hundreds of gourd-shaped mud nests stuck to the pillars and structural beams. Some Cliff Swallows forego the tedium of raising young by dumping eggs in the nests of neighbors, who treat them as a gift and give them the same attention as their own eggs.

ID: bluish black back with 2 white stripes; dark brownish gray wings and tail; rusty rump; white underparts; brown spots on undertail coverts; pale buff breast and nape joined by thin "necklace"; bluish black "cap" and throat; white forehead; rusty "cheeks." *In flight:* broad-based, triangular wings; dark, square-ended tail; fairly direct flight.
Size: *L* 5 in; *W* 13 in.
Status: common breeding summer resident and migrant; first migrants appear in early spring; fall migration is from July until mid-September.
Habitat: *Breeding:* various upland and riparian habitats, especially canyons and artificial structures; foraging habitats include stream edges and wetlands, grasslands and other open country and towns, though less often cities.
Nesting: colonial; attached to a rock face or rough wall of a building with mud gathered by the pair and applied together with saliva; gourd-shaped nest of mud and some grass is lined with dry grass stems, very rarely feathers; pair incubates 3–4 finely marked whitish eggs for 11–16 days; young fledge at 22–24 days and fly to a "nursery" site up to several miles away.
Feeding: catches flying insects on the wing; ingests gravel, probably to help in digestion.
Voice: a *nyew* alarm call and thin, high notes; also makes twittering *churrr-churrr* chatter; male's song sounds creaky and rattly.
Similar Species: *Barn Swallow* (p. 266): brighter, more extensively blue upperparts; orangy to pale underparts; longer, deeply forked tail.
Best Sites: throughout Oregon.

BARN SWALLOW

Hirundo rustica

The much-loved Barn Swallow is the world's most widespread and well-known swallow. In Europe, 2000 years of association with humans have resulted in a preference for nesting on buildings, and a swallow's nest is universally considered a good luck omen. • Pairs often raise two broods in heavy traffic areas without any problem. Not everyone appreciates the craftsmanship of the Barn Swallow's mud nest or the mess left behind, though, and many Barn Swallow lives are extinguished each summer before they have begun. Such a course of action is all the more regrettable given that this natural pest controller is more effective at keeping insect populations under control than any insecticide. • The scientific name means simply "rural swallow."

ID: blue-glossed upperparts; blue "necklace"; rusty throat and forehead; short, dark bill; short, blackish legs; long, deeply forked tail with white inner edges. *Male:* buff to orange red underparts; longer tail streamers. *Female:* whitish to buff underparts. *In flight:* underwing has bluish flight feathers and orangy or pale lining; leisurely, measured flight, rarely to any height.
Size: *L* 6–7 in; *W* 15 in.
Status: common breeding summer resident and migrant; first spring birds appear in early April; most fall migrants pass through between mid-August and mid-October.
Habitat: open country near water, including farmlands, freshwater wetlands and suburban areas. *Breeding:* needs cliffs or artificial structures for nesting.
Nesting: on a vertical wall, occasionally on a crossbeam or ledge, attached by a mixture of mud gathered by both birds and saliva; half-cup if attached to a wall without support, or a full cup if supported, is lined with fine grass stems, horsehair and many large feathers; male helps female incubate 3–5 creamy white eggs, dotted and streaked with brown, for 13–15 days; young fledge at 19–24 days.
Feeding: opportunistic; hawks for various flying insects over land and water; sometimes collects dead and dying insects on the ground in cold or wet weather.
Voice: utters continuous *zip-zip-zip* twittering chatter and a *kvick-kvick* call; male gives a husky, squeaky but pleasant, lilting song with intermittent rattles.
Similar Species: none.
Best Sites: throughout Oregon.

BLACK-CAPPED CHICKADEE

Poecile atricapilla

Throughout the Northern Hemisphere, titmice and chickadees are among the friendliest and most cheerful of woodland inhabitants. The well-known and widespread Black-capped Chickadee reaches its southwestern range limit just south of the northern California border. • Black-caps travel in family groups throughout summer and then band together in flocks that have both regular members and "floaters" that move between flocks. These flocks of fall and winter often attract other chickadees, woodpeckers, nuthatches, creepers, kinglets, vireos and warblers. • When foraging, chickadees often swing upside down on the tips of twigs, gleaning insects or plucking berries. • The closest relative of the Black-capped Chickadee may well be the Mountain Chickadee, and not the Carolina Chickadee (*P. carolinensis*), which looks most like it.

ID: grayish olive back and rump; gray wings with white-edged feathers; white underparts, becoming pale buff or light rufous on sides and flanks; black "cap" and "bib"; white "cheeks" and foreneck; stubby, dark bill; dark, bluish gray legs. *In flight:* whitish wing linings; rounded tail.

Size: *L* 5 in; *W* 8 in.

Status: common year-round resident west of the Cascades and locally common east of the Cascades.

Habitat: deciduous and riparian woods, orchards; parks, residential areas and urban woodlots, especially those with maple and alder.

Nesting: in a cavity, typically in a dead snag or rotten branch, or in a woodpecker hole or nest box; moss foundation is lined with rabbit fur or hair; female incubates 6–8 brown-dotted white eggs for 12–13 days; young fledge at 14–16 days; pair feeds young for additional 3–4 weeks.

Feeding: gleans foliage in summer, mostly for caterpillars and small bugs; in winter, probes in bark, and sometimes on the ground, for insects, spiders, seeds and berries; takes seeds at urban feeders from fall until early spring.

Voice: clear *chip* contact call, usually extended into familiar *chick-a-dee-dee-dee;* song is a clear, whistled, easily imitated *fee-bee* with lower 2nd note, sometimes with a 3rd note.

Similar Species: *Mountain Chickadee* (p. 268): white "eyebrow"; pale gray below, with less buff; harsher calls; longer song. *Chestnut-backed Chickadee* (p. 269): rufous brown back, flanks and sides; dark brown "cap"; shorter tail; buzzier calls; song is a *chip* series.

Best Sites: almost any deciduous habitat; easiest to find at feeders in fall and winter.

MOUNTAIN CHICKADEE

Poecile gambeli

This year-round resident of high-elevation forests spends much of its time feeding on seeds and insects high in conifers. The Mountain Chickadee breeds at higher elevations than any other chickadee and usually only meets up with other chickadee species outside the nesting season. • Mountain Chickadee parents show considerable individuality in prey selection when feeding their young, generally choosing whatever is easiest to catch. Mountain Chickadees cache conifer seeds in fall and defend the sites in winter territories. In seed-poor years, juveniles are forced to leave for lowland habitats. • The scientific name *gambeli* honors William Gambel, a 19th-century ornithologist who was very active on the West Coast but died of typhoid fever at a very young age.

ID: plain gray back; pale-edged gray wing and tail feathers; grayish white belly; light gray or pale buff flanks and undertail coverts; black "cap" split by white "eyebrow"; white "cheeks" and foreneck; black "bib." *In flight:* white wing linings, often faintly yellowish; rounded tail.

Size: *L* 5 in; *W* 8½ in.

Status: common year-round resident in mountainous areas, except the Coast Range; winters at lower elevations east of the Cascades but very rarely in the west.

Habitat: *Breeding:* pine, fir, spruce–fir, mountain hemlock and juniper forests; rare in Douglas-fir. *Winter:* any forests east of the Cascades; rarely western Oregon.

Nesting: in a cavity, typically in a tree, but possibly on the ground, under roots or in a nest box; base of rotten wood chips is topped with loose fur from mammal scats and owl pellets; female incubates 5–8 red-spotted white eggs for 12–14 days; young fledge at 18–23 days.

Feeding: mainly gleans in conifer foliage for insects, especially moths, sawflies, beetles and aphids, plus spiders, augmented by conifer seeds in winter; sometimes hawks insects in midair.

Voice: call is a drawling *chick a-day, day, day;* song is a sweet, clear, whistled *fee-bee-bay.*

Similar Species: *Black-capped Chickadee* (p. 267): back is usually more olive or brown; buff or rufous sides and flanks; larger "bib"; black "cap" extends below eye; longer tail; prefers hardwoods.

Best Sites: Waldo L.; Indian Ford Campground and Cold Springs Campground (Sisters); Ochoco Campground (near Prineville); northern Cascades Lakes; Crater L. NP; Kimball SP; Tollgate; Moss Springs; Wallowa L. SP; Bonny Lakes trail; Anthony L.

CHESTNUT-BACKED CHICKADEE

Poecile rufescens

The smallest of the North American chickadees, the colorful Chestnut-backed Chickadee inhabits the denser forests of the Pacific Northwest. Its habit of foraging widely within the forest canopy—from the lowermost boughs to the crown tips—allows it to survive in smaller ranges than most other forest birds. Like the Black-capped Chickadee, the Chestnut-back forms winter flocks that attract kinglets, vireos, nuthatches, creepers and lingering warblers. Preferring to stay in denser cover than its cousin, the Chestnut-back is less regular at feeders away from its evergreen nesting habitats, but, in severe winters, small parties may join other wintering songbirds in urban areas. • The tree cavities favored by chickadees in search of a nest site occasionally also attract insects. Bumblebees intent on establishing a new hive have been known to invade a chickadee cavity and chase the small birds from their nest.

ID: rufous brown back and sides; dark brownish gray wings and tail; whitish underparts; dark brown "cap" and darker "bib"; white "cheeks"; stubby, dark bill; darkish legs. *In flight:* pale gray wing linings; rounded tail.
Size: *L* 4½–5 in; *W* 7½ in.
Status: common year-round resident from the crest of the Cascades to the coast; locally uncommon in the Blue Mts. and Wallowa Mts.
Habitat: moist coniferous forests, especially Sitka spruce, western hemlock and Douglas-fir; some downslope movement and dispersal in winter.

Nesting: excavated cavity in a soft, rotting trunk or stub, natural cavity or abandoned woodpecker nest is lined with fur, feathers, moss and plant down; male helps female incubate 6–7 rufous-marked white eggs for up to 15 days.
Feeding: gleans foliage, bark and twigs for insects, larvae, spiders, seeds and small fruits; visits seed and suet feeders near protective cover.
Voice: gives higher, buzzier call notes than other chickadees; song is a *chip* series.
Similar Species: *Black-capped Chickadee* (p. 267): grayish back; paler, buffier flanks; black "cap" and "bib"; whistled song; prefers hardwoods.
Best Sites: along the coast; dense forests on the western slopes of the Cascades; wetter parts of the Blue Mts. and Wallowa Mts.

269

OAK TITMOUSE
Baeolophus inornatus

The Oak Titmouse and the Juniper Titmouse were formerly considered to be the same species, the Plain Titmouse (*Parus inornatus*). However, careful study revealed differences in several genetic, plumage, voice and ecological characteristics. To some people, the Oak Titmouse seems ordinary, but, to others, an oak forest would seem empty without it. • The Oak Titmouse nests in natural cavities, rotten stumps and abandoned woodpecker nests, preferring these sites over nest boxes whenever they are available. Nesting cavities are lined with a variety of soft materials and may be reused by the same pair for several years. • The pair bond is much stronger among titmice than among the closely related chickadees; they often breed with the same mate throughout their short lives, which seldom exceed five years.

ID: grayish brown back, tail and wings; grayish underparts with hint of buff; crested, brownish gray head; large, dark eyes; stubby, slightly bluish bill; bluish gray legs. *In flight:* pale gray wing linings; rounded tail.

Size: *L* 5 in; *W* 9 in.

Status: common year-round resident in the Rogue Valley watershed and surrounding hills of Jackson, Josephine and southern Klamath Counties.

Habitat: prefers pure and mixed oak woodlands but will use other woodland types.

Nesting: in a cavity or tree stump or a nest box or other artificial site; nest is made of grass, moss, hair and feathers; female incubates 6–7 largely unmarked white eggs for 14–16 days; young fledge at 16–21 days and are independent at 5 weeks.

Feeding: usually gleans and probes for food high in the canopy but will retrieve food on the ground; eats mostly seeds and acorns and land invertebrates.

Voice: song is a clear, whistled *teewee teewee teewee* or *weety weety weety;* chickadee-like calls include *tsik-a-dee-dee* or *tsik-a-deer.*

Similar Species: *Juniper Titmouse* (p. 271): almost identical; medium gray upperparts; little or no brown in plumage; heavier bill; prefers junipers and pines; range differs.

Best Sites: Merlin area; Lower Table Rock and Roxy Ann Butte (near Medford); Tou Velle SP.

JUNIPER TITMOUSE

Baeolophus ridgwayi

The Oak Titmouse contents itself largely with oak habitats, but the grayer Juniper Titmouse prefers dry juniper situations. One of Oregon's least colorful songbirds, the Juniper Titmouse nevertheless always seems bright and cheerful by nature, and, like all members of its family, inquisitive. • Juniper Titmice spend much of their time as arboreal acrobats, dangling upside down to examine the underside of every twig and leaf and clinging to a trunk or branch to pry out any tiny morsel lodged beneath the bark, but they also do a lot of pecking on the ground for fallen tidbits and tiny pieces of food. If winter food supplies are scarce, Juniper Titmice will visit feeders, accepting with relish any offers of sunflower or safflower seeds. • *Baeolophus,* which comes from Greek words, means "small crest."

ID: gray (with little or no brown) back, tail and wings; grayish underparts; crested; gray head; large, dark eyes; stubby, bluish gray bill; bluish gray legs. *In flight:* pale gray wing linings; rounded tail.

Size: *L* 5 in; *W* 9 in.

Status: locally uncommon year-round resident in eastern Klamath Co. and Lake Co.

Habitat: juniper woodlands, juniper woods and associated brushy habitats.

Nesting: in a cavity or tree stump or a nest box or other artificial site; nest is made of grass, moss, hair and feathers; female incubates 6–7 largely unmarked white eggs for 14–16 days; young fledge at 16–21 days and are independent at 5 weeks.

Feeding: usually gleans and probes for food high in the canopy but will retrieve food on the ground; eats mostly seeds and land invertebrates.

Voice: song is a clearly whistled *witt-y witt-y witt-y;* call is a chickadee-like *tsick-a-dee-dee.*

Similar Species: *Oak Titmouse* (p. 270): almost identical; more olive brown upperparts; underparts are usually darker and browner; prefers oaks; range differs.

Best Sites: Bullard Canyon Park (Lakeview); Warner Valley.

271

BUSHTIT

Psaltriparus minimus

A fastidious perfectionist when it comes to nests, the Bushtit will test every fiber to ensure that the structure fulfills all tenets of Bushtit architecture, and it will desert both nest and mate if its sanctity is violated. • Hyperactive in everything they do, these tousled, fluffy, gregarious birds are constantly on the move in roaming bands of up to 40 members. They bounce from one shrubby perch to another, examining everything of interest, filling the neighborhood with charming, bell-like, tinkling calls, and doing it all with panache. In cold weather, flocks will huddle together in a tight mass to reduce heat loss. • *Psaltriparus* is derived from Greek and Latin roots that mean "a harpist" and "titmouse."

ID: dull gray back, wings and tail; pale buff wash on grayish underparts; gray head (with brown "cap" in coastal birds); tiny, dark bill; long tail; black legs. *Male:* dark eyes. *Female:* pale yellow eyes. *In flight:* pale gray wing linings; rounded tail.

Size: *L* 4–4½ in; *W* 6 in.

Status: common year-round resident from moderate elevations of the western Cascades and Coast Range to interior valleys and locally along the coast; locally common east of the Cascades, mostly in central Oregon.

Habitat: brushy habitats and chaparral; juniper, oak and mountain mahogany woodlands; riparian brushlands; residential plantings.

Nesting: in a shrub; pair builds a socklike hanging nest, intricately woven with moss, lichen, cocoons, spider silk, fur and feathers; pair incubates 5–7 white eggs for 12 days; young fledge at 14–15 days.

Feeding: gleans lower vegetation for insects, small fruits and seeds; foraging flocks stay within visual and auditory distance at all times.

Voice: flocks keep in contact with a series of short, high, buzzy notes that often resemble the calls of kinglets and titmice; a high, falling series of notes indicates an aerial predator.

Similar Species: *Oak Titmouse* (p. 270) and *Juniper Titmouse* (p. 271): larger; crested head; heavier bill; large, dark eyes; paler legs; broader tail. *Chickadees* (pp. 267–69): slightly larger; faces mostly white; dark "bibs" and "caps"; heavier bills; different calls.

Best Sites: throughout Oregon.

RED-BREASTED NUTHATCH

Sitta canadensis

Red-breasted Nuthatches often announce their presence with distinctive nasal calls. They are easily "pished" into view, where their bright colors, chubby bodies and headfirst movement down trunks set them apart from their traveling companions. Differing foraging techniques help to identify the three nuthatch species roaming Oregon's woods in fall and winter. The result of this specialization is a thorough haul of what the forest has to offer without over-extending any particular resource. • Nuthatches are unique among tree-climbing songbirds in that they use one foot to brace themselves while the other holds onto the bark—woodpeckers and the Brown Creeper use their tails for stability.

ID: bluish upperparts and flank feathers; black eye stripe; white "eyebrow" and "cheek"; dark eyes; pointed, slightly upturned bill; blackish legs. *Male:* rusty underparts; black "cap." *Female:* orangy buff belly; bluish "cap." *In flight:* broad wings; gray underwing with buff lining and whitish area near tip; short, gray tail with white diagonal stripes.
Size: *L* 4½ in; *W* 8½ in.
Status: common year-round resident; irregular common migrant and winter resident in much of Oregon.
Habitat: *Breeding:* almost any coniferous forest from sea level to timberline. *In migration* and *winter:* almost any woodlands.
Nesting: in a natural cavity or old woodpecker nest in a tree; entrance is smeared

with sap or pitch to catch insects; lined with bark, grass and fur; female incubates 5–6 rufous-marked, white or pinkish white eggs for 12 days; young fledge at 14–21 days.
Feeding: creeps along boughs or moves headfirst down a trunk while probing under loose bark for wood-boring beetles and larvae and other invertebrates; switches to pine and spruce seeds and visits feeders in winter.
Voice: gives a slow, continually repeated, nasal *yank-yank-yank* or *rah-rah-rah-rah* or short *tsip*.
Similar Species: *White-breasted Nuthatch* (p. 274): larger; plain white head with dark crown stripe; grayish white underparts with rufous brown upper legs and undertail coverts; longer bill; longer wings; prefers hardwoods. *Pygmy Nuthatch* (p. 275): stockier; paler underparts; more gray on flanks; brown "cap" descends to eye line; stouter bill; gray wing linings.
Best Sites: throughout Oregon.

WHITE-BREASTED NUTHATCH

Sitta carolinensis

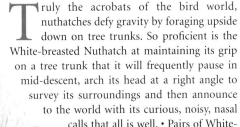

Truly the acrobats of the bird world, nuthatches defy gravity by foraging upside down on tree trunks. So proficient is the White-breasted Nuthatch at maintaining its grip on a tree trunk that it will frequently pause in mid-descent, arch its head at a right angle to survey its surroundings and then announce to the world with its curious, noisy, nasal calls that all is well. • Pairs of White-breasted Nuthatches remain in permanent, year-round territories in open pine stands or mature oak and other deciduous woodlands and store their gathered food items in cache sites, each containing just one type of food. Stored foods are supplemented by regular visits to any bird feeders in the territory, lasting just long enough to select a seed, pick it up and then flutter off.

ID: grayish blue back, wings (with white-edged primaries) and tail; black shoulders; white throat and breast; gray flanks and sides; rufous behind legs and on undertail coverts; black nape and "cap"; white face; uptilted, gray-and-black bill. *In flight:* broad wings; gray underwing has conspicuous white area near tip; prominent white flashes on short, rounded, gray tail.

Size: *L* 5½–6 in; *W* 11 in.

Status: uncommon to common permanent resident in much of Oregon.

Habitat: open woodlands, preferring oak woodlands in western Oregon and ponderosa pine forests on the eastern slopes of the Cascades.

Nesting: in a natural cavity or old woodpecker hole, in a deciduous tree or perhaps a ponderosa pine, and lined with bark, grass and rootlets and possibly fur, hair and feathers; female incubates 5–9 chestnut-spotted whitish eggs for 12 days; young fledge at 26 days.

Feeding: hops across trunks and main branches, exploring everywhere for various insects; also eats fallen beechnuts, acorns, grain and seeds.

Voice: utters *tuck* location calls and *quark* alarm calls; song is a simple repetition of 6–10 persistent, high, whining notes.

Similar Species: *Red-breasted Nuthatch* (p. 273): smaller; buffy or orangy underparts and underwings; black eye stripe; smaller bill; prefers conifers; more direct, buzzing flight. *Pygmy Nuthatch* (p. 275): smaller; brown "cap"; stouter bill; warm buff breast and undertail coverts.

Best Sites: western valleys; Hood River Co. and Wasco Co.; eastern slopes of the Cascades; Siskiyou, Blue and Wallowa Mts.; eastern foothills and drier valleys of the Coast Ranges.

PYGMY NUTHATCH

Sitta pygmaea

When you're as small as the Pygmy Nuthatch and live high in the mountains year-round, a lot of your time is spent finding food. During daylight hours, this energetic Oregon resident hops along the limbs and twigs of pines, probing and calling incessantly. With a body designed mainly for foraging among clumps of needles, the Pygmy Nuthatch seems barely capable of keeping itself airborne as it flutters awkwardly between adjacent trees. • Like the larger nuthatches, the Pygmy is gregarious by nature, usually forming flocks in fall and winter. At night, when the temperature drops, this resourceful bird seeks the shelter and warmth of communal roosts in tree cavities—as many as 100 birds have been recorded in a cavity.

ID: grayish blue back; dark-and-white edges to wings; pale buff underparts; grayish blue flanks; brown "cap"; black eye line; white "cheeks" and throat; uptilted, stout, black-and-gray bill; dark legs. *In flight:* gray, rounded wing with white arc below; white flashes on gray tail; short, fluttering flights.

Size: *L* 4 in; *W* 7½–8 in.

Status: common year-round resident eastward from the eastern slopes of the Cascades, uncommon on the western slope in Jackson Co.; rare in the Rogue Valley and Siskiyou Mts.; state-listed as sensitive.

Habitat: ponderosa pine forests and adjacent areas; rarely leaves breeding areas.

Nesting: uses an old woodpecker cavity or excavates its own hole; lining is soft plant material, wood chips, fur and feathers; female incubates 6–8 sparsely red-spotted white eggs for 15–16 days; up to 3 unmated males may assist with nesting duties.

Feeding: forages in outer limbs for adult and larval insects and other invertebrates, including spiders; also eats pine seeds and suet at feeders.

Voice: varied, persistent, loud chipping and squeaking notes.

Similar Species: *Red-breasted Nuthatch* (p. 273): larger; orangy buff or rusty underparts; black eye stripe; smaller bill; nasal calls. *White-breasted Nuthatch* (p. 274): larger; white head with dark "cap"; grayish and white underparts with rufous confined to above legs and undertail coverts; nasal calls; usually in pairs.

Best Sites: Indian Ford Campground and Cold Springs Campground (Sisters); Ochoco Campground; Robert Sawyer Park (Bend); Klamath Forest NWR; Kimball SP (Fort Klamath); Cabin Lake Campground; Hart Mt.; Spring Creek; Auburn; Starr Campground (Blue Mts.); Bear Valley, Grant Co.; Logan Valley; Idlewild Campground (Burns).

BROWN CREEPER

Certhia americana

Various nearly identical creeper species inhabit Europe and Asia, but the Brown Creeper is one of a kind in North America. Found in sizable stands of large trees most of the year, this small, fragile-looking bird usually goes unnoticed until what looks like a flake of bark suddenly comes alive. The camouflage is so effective that even when a creeper is detected, it may once again blend into the background until it moves again. Completely at home among the flaking bark, the Brown Creeper even builds its nest there. • The Brown Creeper usually spirals methodically up a tree trunk until it reaches the upper branches and then darts down to the base of a neighboring tree to begin again—the opposite of what nuthatches do. The long, stiff, pointed tail feathers and long claws help to stabilize this bird against the trunk much like a woodpecker does.

ID: upperparts are mottled, gray, brown and white with dark streaks; white underparts and throat; pointed, downcurved bill; white "eyebrow"; buffy undertail coverts; long, spiked tail. *In flight:* buffy arc on wing; undulating, often short flights.

Size: *L* 5 in; *W* 7½ in.

Status: common year-round resident; also a migrant from early March to early June and from late September to mid-November.

Habitat: *Breeding:* coniferous and deciduous woodlands, except juniper. *In migration* and *winter:* low-elevation woodlands, including small woodlots, parklands and coastal forests.

Nesting: suspended under loose bark; nest of grass and conifer needles is woven together with spider silk; female incubates 5–6 faintly marked white eggs for 14–17 days; young fledge at 13–16 days.

Feeding: ascends trunk in a spiral or straight course and then drops down to another trunk; most prey is picked from beneath loose bark.

Voice: gives a high *tseee* call; also utters faint, very high *zip* notes in flight; male's song is a faint, high-pitched *trees-trees these-trees, see the trees.*

Similar Species: *Several wrens* (pp. 277–82): upraised, barred tails; forage on the ground, in woodpiles and foliage; harsh calls and powerful songs.

Best Sites: mature woodlands.

ROCK WREN

Salpinctes obsoletus

This endearing, mysterious bird with dull, cryptic markings is not always easy to find in its rocky habitat. It doesn't help that the male Rock Wren expertly bounces his songs off surrounding rocks to maximize their effectiveness. One of western North America's best songsters, he might use up to 100 or more song types. • Hidden in cracks and crevices, Rock Wren nests typically have their entrances "paved" with a few (or up to 1500!) small pebbles, bones, shells and other flat items. This "welcome mat" may be intended to protect the nest from moisture, make it easier to find in confusing rocky terrain or reduce the risk of marauding ants. • *Salpinctes*, from the Greek word for "trumpeter," refers to this genus's loud calls.

ID: white-speckled brownish gray upperparts; light buff belly and flanks; finely gray-streaked white throat and breast; cinnamon rump; pale "eyebrow"; long, slightly downcurved bill; black-barred white undertail coverts. *In flight:* more direct, less fluttering flight than woodland wrens.

Size: *L* 6 in; *W* 9 in.

Status: common breeding summer resident and uncommon in winter east of the Cascades; locally uncommon to fairly common breeding summer resident in the Cascades and Siskiyou Mts.; rare year-round resident in the Rogue Valley; most migrants arrive in late April and May and leave in September and October.

Habitat: arid or semi-arid rocky areas, including rock outcroppings, rimrock, canyons, talus slopes, gravel quarries and recent rock-strewn clear-cuts.

Nesting: in a cavity or crevice, with a "paved" entranceway; female incubates 5–6 brown-spotted white eggs for 14–16 days; young fledge at 14–16 days.

Feeding: gleans from the surface, probes in cracks and crevices (often entering cavities) and flycatches for insects and other arthropods.

Voice: gives buzzy calls; male's song consists of loud, buzzy, trilled phrases, each repeated 3–6 times: *tra-lee tra-lee tra-lee.*

Similar Species: *Canyon Wren* (p. 278): largely cinnamon rufous with brown barring; white throat; longer, more downcurved bill; cascading song. *House Wren* (p. 280): smaller; plainer, browner upperparts; duskier underparts; shorter bill; bubblier song; prefers woodland edges.

Best Sites: Lower Table Rock (near Medford); Deschutes River SP; Fort Rock SP; Smith Rock SP; Diamond Craters; Malheur NWR; Steens Mt.; Succor Creek SP.

CANYON WREN

Catherpes mexicanus

Visitors to western North America's broad, steep-sided canyons have probably heard the song of the male Canyon Wren without catching sight of the bird itself. In fact, most people are surprised to discover that the songster is a small bird. The song, which echoes off the canyon walls, ripples and cascades downward in pitch as if it were recounting the action of tumbling boulders. • If you are lucky enough to catch sight of a Canyon Wren as it squeezes its somewhat flattened body into nooks and crevices in a tireless search for hidden insects and spiders, it may look like a small rodent until it quickly raises and lowers its tail and hindquarters, which it does every few seconds. • *Catherpes* is the latinized form of the Greek word *katherpein,* meaning "to creep."

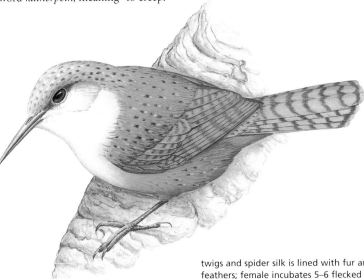

ID: brown-barred, cinnamon rufous back, wings, tail and underparts; gray-streaked "cap"; clean white throat and upper breast; very long, downcurved bill. *In flight:* direct flight with quick, whirring wingbeats.

Size: *L* 5–6 in; *W* 7½ in.

Status: locally common breeding summer resident east of the Cascades (likely as common in winter); locally rare year-round resident in Jackson Co. and Douglas Co.

Habitat: steep, often vertical, rocky canyon walls and open-country rimrock.

Nesting: in a crevice under rocks, on a ledge or on a cave shelf; cup nest of moss, twigs and spider silk is lined with fur and feathers; female incubates 5–6 flecked white eggs for up to 18 days; young fledge at 15–17 days and forage with parents.

Feeding: gleans rocks, exposed ground and vegetation for insects and spiders.

Voice: gives high-pitched, far-carrying calls; male's song is a startling cascade of descending 1- and 2-note whistles: *dee-ah dee-ah dee-ah dah-dah-dah.*

Similar Species: *Rock Wren* (p. 277): brownish gray upperparts; unbarred underparts; lightly streaked throat and breast; shorter bill; buzzy, trilling song. *House Wren* (p. 280): plainer, browner upperparts; much shorter bill; more bubbly song; prefers woodland edges.

Best Sites: Lower Table Rock (near Medford); Smith Rock SP; Prineville Reservoir; Abert Rim; Diamond Craters; Malheur NWR; Page Springs Campground (near Malheur NWR); Succor Creek SP.

BEWICK'S WREN

Thryomanes bewickii

Bewick's Wren investigates all the nooks and crannies of its territory with endless curiosity and exuberant animation. As this charming resident briefly perches to scan its surroundings for food, its long, narrow tail flits and waves from side to side, occasionally flashing with added verve as the bird scolds an approaching intruder. • The songs of western males are simpler than those of eastern ones, perhaps because a scattered distribution in the East (resulting from habitat loss) has made mating more competitive than among stabler western populations. • The first scientific specimen, collected in Louisiana in 1821, was identified by John James Audubon and named for his friend Thomas Bewick, a talented British wood engraver who wrote and illustrated *History of British Birds*.

ID: brown or grayish brown upperparts; pale underparts; dark-barred undertail; white throat; white "eyebrow"; downcurved gray bill; long, banded tail.

Size: *L* 5 in; *W* 7 in.

Status: common year-round resident west of the Cascades, along the upper Columbia R. and its tributaries and in the Klamath Basin and locally uncommon eastward.

Habitat: woodland edges, urban woodlots, shrubbery and chaparral; dense riparian oak and ash understory; late-summer dispersal to timberline in the Cascades.

Nesting: in a cavity or structure, such as a brush pile, rock crevice or outbuilding; open cup of fine plant materials is lined with feathers and fine materials; female incubates 3–8 dark-marked white eggs for 14–16 days; young fledge at 14–16 days.

Feeding: gleans invertebrate eggs, larvae and adults from trees and shrubs, mostly close to the ground.

Voice: bold and clear *chick-click, for me-eh, for you;* alarm call is a *dzeeeb* or *knee-deep.*

Similar Species: *Marsh Wren* (p. 282): stockier; rufous-tinged plumage; white-streaked black back. *Winter Wren* (p. 281): compact; darker brown; more mottling and barring; smaller bill and tail.

Best Sites: brushy areas in western Oregon; in eastern Oregon, limited to the Columbia River Basin, including Umatilla NWR, McNary Wildlife Park, Cold Springs NWR, McKay Creek NWR, Wildhorse Creek and the lower Deschutes R.

HOUSE WREN

Troglodytes aedon

With their bubbly singing and spirited disposition, House Wrens enhance any neighborhood. All it usually takes to attract these feathered charmers is some shrubby cover, plus a small cavity in a dead tree or a nest box. Sometimes even an empty flowerpot, vacant drainpipe, abandoned vehicle or forlorn shoe will serve as a nest site. • Male House Wrens, like several of their relatives, build a number of "dummy" nests for potential partners to inspect and complete. An offering rejected by one female may become another's "dream home." • In Greek mythology, Zeus transformed Aedon, the Queen of Thebes, into a nightingale—it says much for the appeal of the House Wren's song that an early ornithologist used such a heady comparison.

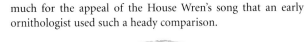

ID: grayish brown upperparts, barred on wings and tail; grayish underparts; brown rump and undertail coverts; faint buff "eyebrow" and eye ring; whitish throat; long, downcurved bill with yellow lower mandible; pale pink legs and feet.
Size: *L* 4½ in; *W* 6 in.
Status: uncommon to common breeding summer resident.
Habitat: semi-open habitats, including lodgepole pine forests, montane conifer parklands, oak and oak–fir forests, cottonwood and aspen woodlands, oak–juniper hillsides and riparian woods.
Nesting: in a tree cavity, often an old woodpecker hole, also uses a nest box or various artificial objects; female completes nest started by male; female incubates 4–8 chestnut-marked whitish eggs for 12–13 days; young fledge at 15–17 days.

Feeding: more arboreal than other wrens, gleaning small invertebrates from the lower tree canopy, shrubs, low vegetation and the ground.
Voice: call is a harsh, scolding rattle; male's song is a rapid, chattering, unmusical 2–3 second series of notes: *tsi-tsi-tsi oodle-oodle-oodle-oodle*.
Similar Species: *Marsh Wren* (p. 282): rustier plumage; white-streaked black back; shorter tail; strong "eyebrow"; prefers aquatic vegetation. *Winter Wren* (p. 281): stockier; more mottling and barring; stubby tail; shorter bill; prefers moist woodlands; long, tumbling, warbling song.
Best Sites: Sauvie I.; Lower Sandy R.; William L. Finley NWR; Roseburg; Merlin; Whitehorse CP; Lower Table Rock (near Medford); Indian Ford Campground (Sisters); Robert Sawyer Park (Bend).

WINTER WREN

Troglodytes troglodytes

Wrens are tiny, combative bundles of energy, and the males have vocal abilities unmatched by most other songbirds. The loudest singer of his size, the male Winter Wren has one of the most vibrant songs of any species. Long and melodious, the bubbly song stands out both by its length and its sheer exuberance. • Males build several "dummy" nests prior to egg laying. They deliver food to their nesting mates but sleep apart in unfinished nests. Outside of the breeding season, several Winter Wrens may huddle together in a nest or sheltered crevice, but usually each bird lays claim to a patch of moist coniferous forest, defending it against other wrens, and makes its home among the soft moss and upturned roots of decomposing trees carpeting the forest floor. They are widespread and easy to locate in Oregon's wetter forests.

ID: barred, dark brown upperparts (migrants are paler); lighter brown underparts; barred flanks and undertail coverts; pale "eyebrow"; short, upraised, barred tail. *In flight:* low, whirring flight.

Size: *L* 4 in; *W* 5½ in.

Status: uncommon to common breeding summer resident and uncommon migrant in early spring and from September to November, common in winter in lowlands and foothills west of the Cascades and locally uncommon in the east.

Habitat: lowland forests, woodlands and thickets.

Nesting: in a natural cavity or old woodpecker hole, under bark or in an artificial item; bulky nest of twigs, moss, grass and fur; female incubates 5–8 chestnut-flecked creamy or pinkish white eggs for 12–14 days; young fledge in 19 days.

Feeding: forages on the ground, around tree trunks and in woodpiles and tangles for invertebrates; also picks aquatic insects and larvae from small pools.

Voice: calls include a sharp *chat-chat* and occasional churring; male's song is an outpouring of rapid trills and twitters, lasting several seconds and repeating.

Similar Species: *House Wren* (p. 280): paler brown overall; longer tail; paler legs; shorter song; prefers drier and more open habitats. *Marsh Wren* (p. 282): more rufous; largely unstreaked with white-streaked black back; longer tail; rattling song; inhabits aquatic vegetation.

Best Sites: Saddle Mt. SP; Tahkenitch L., Douglas Co.; Charleston; Larch Mt.; Starr Campground (Blue Mts.).

281

MARSH WREN

Cistothorus palustris

The energetic but often reclusive Marsh Wren keeps a low profile by staying hidden in the dense aquatic vegetation of its marsh home. However, the male is one of the most aggressive and noisy songbirds. John J. Audubon wrote the song off as sounding like "the grating of a rusty hinge," but many birders appreciate the reedy, gurgling outpouring of emotion. Although some notes are harsh, competing males use as many as 200 riffs in complex songfests to attract mates. • A male will build as many as a dozen nests, and a successful male may mate with several females. Additional nests are often used for a second brood or roosting, but unsuccessful males—and even females—often destroy the nests of their neighbors.

Habitat: freshwater and brackish marshes; aquatic vegetation bordering ponds, lakes and rivers.

Nesting: in cattails, reeds or sedges; dome-shaped nest of reeds, grass and aquatic plant stems is lined with fine materials and has a side entrance; female incubates 4 or more brown eggs for 14–15 days; young fledge at 13–15 days.

Feeding: forages near the water's surface, on aquatic vegetation, for insects, spiders and snails; hawks for flying insects.

Voice: calls are harsh and blackbirdlike; male's song is a rapid-fire series of *zig* notes and squeaking and rattling notes.

Similar Species: *Bewick's Wren* (p. 279): plain brown back; longer, banded tail; prefers drier habitats; simpler, trilled song. *House Wren* (p. 280): paler; brown overall; faint "eyebrow"; prefers drier habitats; bubbly, warbling song.

Best Sites: Fern Ridge Reservoir; Upper Klamath NWR; Lower Klamath NWR. *Summer:* Klamath Forest NWR; Summer L. WMA; Ladd Marsh WMA; Umatilla NWR.

ID: rusty brown nape, shoulders and rump; white-striped black back; banded wings; buffyish underparts; brown crown; white "eyebrow"; long, downcurved, yellow-based bill; white "chin"; near-upright, banded tail.

Size: *L* 5 in; *W* 6 in.

Status: common breeding summer resident and uncommon migrant in early spring and from late August to November; common on the coast and locally uncommon inland in winter.

AMERICAN DIPPER
Cinclus mexicanus

The unusual, wrenlike American Dipper (also known as "Water Ouzel") is often seen standing on an exposed boulder in the middle of a raging torrent performing deep knee-bends before plunging into the frigid water. Below the surface, this songbird may use its wings to dive and maintain its position in the water and its long legs and claws to walk along the streambed of rocks and gravel in search of hidden aquatic insect larvae. Suddenly, it pops back into view, returns to the midstream boulders and emits a series of loud calls or flies to another watery perch. Fitted with scaly nose plugs, strong claws, dense plumage, "eyelids" to protect against water spray and an oil gland to protect its feathers, the American Dipper can survive a lifetime of ice-cold forays. No other songbird has a similar combination of plumage, foraging technique and song.

ID: slate gray overall; brownish head; short, wrenlike tail, often raised; straight, dark bill; long, pale legs. *In flight:* low, whirring flight following streams.

Size: *L* 7½ in; *W* 11 in.

Status: locally common year-round resident.

Habitat: fast-flowing, rocky streams and rivers with cascades, riffles and waterfalls.

Nesting: usually on a cliff ledge, behind a waterfall or on a midstream boulder, but possibly in tree roots or a hollow tree stump close to water; domed or ball-like nest, with a side entrance; nest made of moss, grass and leaves; female incubates 4–5 white eggs for 13–17 days; young fledge at 24–26 days.

Feeding: forages in streams by walking, swimming and diving for aquatic insects and other invertebrates and their larvae and fish fry and eggs; picks small prey from snow or flycatches for flying insects.

Voice: gives high-pitched, buzzy call notes; both genders sing loud, clear, repetitive, high whistles most of the year.

Similar Species: *Gray Catbird* (p. 296): leaner; rusty undertail coverts; dark "cap"; long tail; inhabits thickets.

Best Sites: Scoggins Valley Park; Wallowa Lake SP; Bonny Lakes trail; Anthony Lakes; Multnomah Falls.

283

GOLDEN-CROWNED KINGLET

Regulus satrapa

With its calls and song beyond the hearing of many people, the tiny Golden-crowned Kinglet often goes unnoticed. • What this little jewel of the coniferous forest canopy lacks in size—it is North America's smallest songbird—it more than makes up for in its friendliness and approachability. In winter's mixed foraging flocks, the first bird to be "pished" out of cover is often a kinglet. • The Golden-crowned Kinglet is able to withstand colder winter temperatures than the Ruby-crowned Kinglet and is found as far north as coastal Alaska in winter. Winter is seldom a problem for a bird that is so efficient at finding wintering insect eggs and other small items. Even if some birds die over winter, the normally large clutches help maintain population sizes.

ID: grayish olive back; gray-and-yellow wings with blackish bar and white bar; gray-washed underparts; black-bordered crown; white "eyebrow"; white below eye and on throat; dark eye stripe; tiny bill. *Male:* orangy crown. *Female:* yellow crown.

Size: *L* 4 in; *W* 7 in.

Status: locally common breeding summer resident and migrant; common in winter at lower elevations in, and west of, the Cascades; uncommon to fairly common in winter in the mountains and at lower elevations east of the Cascades; fall migration starts in late August.

Habitat: *Breeding:* dense subalpine spruce, hemlock and fir forests and localized conifer stands, occasionally in Douglas-fir and riparian woodlands. *In migration and*

winter: forests, particularly coastal ones, riparian areas and desert oases.

Nesting: in the upper tree canopy, usually well out on a twig; squarish nest attached by spider silk, cottongrass bristles and thin bark is lined with fine materials; female incubates 8–9 whitish eggs, speckled with brown and gray, for 15 days.

Feeding: gleans foliage and bark for insect adults and eggs, frequently hanging upside down; sometimes hovers; also eats spiders, berries and tree sap.

Voice: male's song is a faint, high-pitched accelerating *I...am...not...a...CHEST-nut-backed CHICK-a-dee;* call is a very high-pitched *tsee tsee tsee.*

Similar Species: *Ruby-crowned Kinglet* (p. 285): buffier flanks; plain head, with normally hidden red crest on male; harsh calls and powerful song. *Hutton's Vireo* (p. 248): 2 white wing bars; olive brown head and back; pale eye ring.

Best Sites: most woodland habitats.

RUBY-CROWNED KINGLET

Regulus calendula

The female Ruby-crowned Kinglet lays the largest egg clutches of any North American songbird her size. The male, with a voice second in power-to-weight ratio only to the Winter Wren's, sings a loud, rollicking song that enlivens many a walk past the lowland thickets in spring or upper-elevation conifers in summer. Normally quite drab, he adds to the effect by raising his red crest as he sings to impress a prospective mate or chase off a rival. • This tiny, hyperactive woodland sprite continuously flicks both tail and wings, which is enough to distinguish it from similar looking Hutton's Vireos and small *Empidonax* flycatchers in roving bands of mixed passerines.

ID: olive green upperparts; prominent white wing bar; buffy olive underparts; white eye ring; pale lores; tiny bill. *Male:* ruby red crest, usually hidden.

Size: *L* 4 in; *W* 7½ in.

Status: common breeding summer resident at higher elevations in the Cascades and the Warner, Blue and Wallowa Mts.; common migrant throughout Oregon; common winter resident west of the Cascades, uncommon in eastern Oregon.

Habitat: *Breeding:* spruce–fir, mountain hemlock, Douglas-fir and lodgepole pine forests. *In migration* and *winter:* forests, streamside willows and suburban backyards.

Nesting: in a tree, protected by overhanging foliage; outside structure of materials such as moss, spiderwebs, bark pieces, twigs and conifer needles is lined with feathers, fine grass, plant down and fur; female incubates 5–9 lightly brown-speckled white or buffy eggs for 13–14 days; young fledge at 16–18 days.

Feeding: eats small arthropods and berries.

Voice: gives harsh *tit* calls; male's song is a loud, spirited combination of clear notes and whistles, such as *see si seeseesee here-here-here ruby ruby ruby see.*

Similar Species: *Golden-crowned Kinglet* (p. 284): grayer underparts; black-bordered orangy or yellow crown; black-and-white face. *Hutton's Vireo* (p. 248): 2 white wing bars; plain olive brown back and face; thicker bill. Empidonax *flycatchers* (pp. 234–39): larger; larger bills; longer tails; no red in crown; perch upright; dark toes; simple songs.

Best Sites: woodland habitats.

BLUE-GRAY GNATCATCHER

Polioptila caerulea

The tiny Blue-gray Gnatcatcher belongs to a largely subtropical genus, yet is a true migrant that has been expanding northward into temperate North America on both coasts since the 1960s. • Gnatcatchers are restless inhabitants of woodlands and brushy areas, flitting from shrub to shrub with their long tails held upraised and moving from side to side. The scratchy, banjolike twanging calls announce progress and keep pairs close together. • During courtship, a male gnatcatcher follows his prospective mate around his territory. Paired birds are inseparable, and males take a greater part in nesting and raising the young than in closely related species. • Although these birds undoubtedly eat gnats, they are not the major part of a gnatcatcher's varied diet.

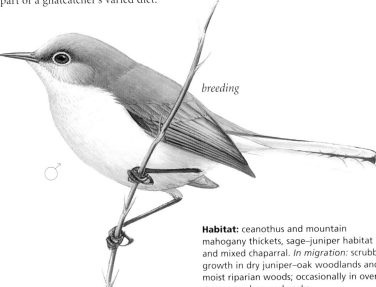

breeding

ID: gray upperparts; pale gray underparts; white eye ring; thin, dark (breeding) or pale (nonbreeding) bill; dark legs; long, thin, flexible tail, dark above with white outer feathers, mostly white below. *Breeding male:* bluish gray upperparts; black forehead patch. *Female:* upperparts often brownish.
Size: *L* 4½ in; *W* 6 in.
Status: locally uncommon breeding summer resident in the Rogue Valley, southern Klamath Co. and Lake Co., and irregularly in southern Harney Co.

Habitat: ceanothus and mountain mahogany thickets, sage–juniper habitat and mixed chaparral. *In migration:* scrubby growth in dry juniper–oak woodlands and moist riparian woods; occasionally in overgrown gardens and parks.
Nesting: on a limb in a deciduous tree; concealed, neat cup of fibers and bark, is lined with stems, bark, fungi, plant down, hair and feathers; female incubates 4–5 spotted eggs for 11–15 days; young fledge at 19–21 days.
Feeding: moves quickly through foliage to flush small insects and spiders; also gleans twigs and flycatches.
Voice: gives thin, high-pitched single *see* notes or a short series of "mewing" or chattering notes; very accomplished mimic of several species.
Similar Species: none.
Best Sites: Rogue Valley watershed (April to August); Merlin area; Lower Table Rock and Roxy Ann Butte (near Medford); Tou Velle SP; Page Springs Campground (near Malheur NWR).

WESTERN BLUEBIRD

Sialia mexicana

The blue on feathers of the Western Bluebird, as on most blue birds, is not the result of a pigment but of each feather's microscopic structure. Shiny blues are produced by iridescence and dull blues result from the same effect that makes the sky blue. • Oregonian Western Bluebird pairs usually manage to raise two broods of young by starting a second clutch of eggs when the first brood leaves the nest. Both parents may maintain another mate to help raise their young. Almost every brood has uncles, aunts, nieces, nephews and cousins on hand to lessen the load. • In fall and winter, Western Bluebirds may join Yellow-rumped Warblers or waxwings around good crops of winter berries.

ID: short, dark bill; dark legs. *Male:* deep blue upperparts and head; deep rusty breast, shoulder patches and flanks; blue-washed white belly and undertail coverts. *Female:* paler than male; brownish gray upperparts, pale blue mostly on tail and wings; partial whitish eye ring. *Juvenile:* white-spotted brownish gray overall; pale blue on wings and tail.

Size: *L* 7 in; *W* 13½ in.

Status: locally common year-round resident west of the Cascades, preferring low elevations in winter; locally common breeding summer resident and migrant east of the Cascades; state-listed as sensitive.

Habitat: open Douglas-fir and pine forests, wooded riparian areas, oak woodlands, areas with snags; forest edges and farmlands.

Nesting: in a rotted or excavated cavity in a tree or snag, beneath the bark of a pine or riparian hardwood or in a nest box; nest consists of available natural and artificial material; female incubates 5 pale blue eggs for 13–14 days; young fledge at 20–21 days.

Feeding: forages from a perch or from hovering; flycatches and gleans insects in summer; picks small fruits from trees and shrubs; takes seeds from beaches in winter.

Voice: calls are a low, chippy warble, a *chuk* and dry chatter; male's song is a harsh but upbeat *cheer cheerful charmer.*

Similar Species: *Mountain Bluebird* (p. 288): male is sky blue overall; grayer female may have pale rufous buff breast. *Male Lazuli Bunting* (p. 341): smaller; white wing bars; whiter underparts; sturdy bill; shorter wings.

Best Sites: clear-cuts outside Vernonia; Scoggins Valley Park; William L. Finley NWR; Roxy Ann Butte (near Medford). *Summer:* Sumpter area; Bear Valley, Grant Co.; Logan Valley; Fort Klamath; White River WMA.

MOUNTAIN BLUEBIRD

Sialia currucoides

The Mountain Bluebird differs from most thrushes in that it prefers more open terrain, nests in cavities, frequently hovers and eats more insects. • Few birds rival male Mountain Bluebirds for good looks, cheerful disposition and boldness—it is not surprising that bluebirds are viewed as the "birds of happiness." • Bluebirds have profited from the clearing of forests, raising of livestock and installation of nest boxes, but they have suffered from land management schemes that include fire suppression and from the introduction of European Starlings and other aggressive competitors. • During migration and winter, it is common for flocks of 100 or more Mountain Bluebirds to travel and forage together.

ID: short, dark bill; dark legs. *Male:* sky blue upperparts, slightly paler below; whitish undertail coverts. *Female:* bluish gray head and back; gray underparts, sometimes pale rufous buff on breast; white eye ring; pale "chin." *Juvenile:* brownish gray overall; white-spotted underparts; pale blue on wings and tail.

Size: *L* 7 in; *W* 14 in.

Status: common breeding summer resident and migrant and uncommon winter resident east of the Cascades; uncommon breeding summer resident and migrant in the Cascades and Siskiyou Mts.; fall migration peaks in September and October.

Habitat: pine forests. *Breeding:* short-grass prairies with groves of trees, juniper woodlands, burns and clear-cuts, farms and meadow edges. *In migration* and *winter:* junipers, sagebrush and hedgerows.

Nesting: in a natural cavity, stump or artificial shelter, rarely in a nest box; male displays at several sites and the female selects one; female incubates 5–6 pale blue eggs for 13 days; young fledge at 18–21 days.

Feeding: pounces from a perch on the ground or above; also flycatches, hovers and hawks; eats mainly insects, especially caterpillars, in summer; small fruits and seeds mostly in winter.

Voice: varied calls include a *chik,* a whistled *cheeeer* and a *turf;* male's song is a series of low, churring whistles, less mellow than for other bluebirds.

Similar Species: *Western Bluebird* (p. 287): rusty breast; male is deeper blue; female's back is usually buffier; juvenile's spotting includes back.

Best Sites: Crater Lake NP; Hoodoo Butte area (Santiam Pass); Wickiup Reservoir (Cascades Lakes); Spring Creek; Wallowa Mts.; Smith Rock SP; Fort Rock SP; Grande Ronde Valley.

TOWNSEND'S SOLITAIRE

Myadestes townsendi

Few birds characterize the upper-elevation mountain forests better than Townsend's Solitaires. Slim and elegant but generally inconspicuous, these thrushes will drop to the ground to snatch food in the manner of bluebirds. They nest in open coniferous forests within the zone of winter snows, where undergrowth is sparse and the ground lies exposed. During the colder months, Townsend's Solitaires move southward and to lower elevations, defending feeding territories among junipers and mistletoe-bearing trees. They are often found with Mountain Bluebirds in open areas in eastern Oregon. • Generally quiet, the male may suddenly burst into a bout of sustained song. • The Townsend's Solitaire was named for John Kirk Townsend. He found the first specimen in the Willamette Valley in 1835.

ID: warm gray overall; whitish undertail coverts; bold white eye ring; shortish, dark bill; dark legs. *In flight:* broad, triangular, white-edged dark gray tail; peach stripe on dark wing.
Size: *L* 8 in; *W* 14½ in.
Status: common breeding summer resident and migrant and locally common in winter at high elevations east of the Cascades; locally common breeding summer resident on the western slope of the Cascades and in the Siskiyou Mts. and Coast Ranges.
Habitat: *Breeding:* high-elevation conifers, clear-cuts, burns and open forests. *In migration* and *winter:* juniper forests; interior foothills and valleys; riparian woodlands; suburban areas.

Nesting: in a concealed hollow on the ground or in a cavity in dead wood; nest of twigs and pine needles is lined with plant materials; female incubates 3–4 blotched pale eggs for 11–14 days; pair feeds young by regurgitation; young fledge at 13–14 days.
Feeding: forages at lower levels for insects and spiders caught in midair, picked off trunks or on the ground; mostly in winter, eats berries and female juniper cones.
Voice: whistled calls; male's often long (10–30 seconds) and rambling song is a mixture of whistled and mumbled notes.
Similar Species: *Northern Mockingbird* (p. 297): slightly larger; paler underparts; longer, often upraised tail; bold white wing patches in flight; inhabits lowlands.
Best Sites: *Summer:* high elevations in eastern Oregon and locally in the Coast Ranges and on the western slope of the Cascades. *Winter:* Smith Rock SP; Prineville Reservoir; Wallowa Fish Hatchery (Enterprise).

VEERY

Catharus fuscescens

The male Veery's voice, like a musical waterfall, descends through thick undergrowth in liquid ripples. Even more reclusive than other *Catharus* thrushes, the Veery is the one that spends the most time on the ground—it nests and forages among tangled vegetation and gets around in short, springy hops. Its reddish plumage distinguishes it from other thrushes in Oregon, except the rare and heavily spotted Wood Thrush and some Swainson's Thrushes. • The Veery was first described by Alexander Wilson in 1831 as "Wilson's Thrush" or "Tawny Thrush"; its present name is an interpretation of the male's song. *Catharus* is a latinized version of the Greek *katharos*, which means "pure," referring to the songs of the thrush family, and *fuscescens* means "dusky."

ID: reddish brown upperparts; white underparts; brown-spotted breast; gray flanks; streaked "cheeks"; thin, buff eye ring; straight, pale bill; pale throat; pale pink legs.

Size: *L* 7 in; *W* 12 in.

Status: common breeding summer resident in the mountains and valleys of northeastern Oregon and Crook Co.

Habitat: moist woodlands with deciduous trees and shrubs next to watercourses.

Nesting: on or near the ground, in a bush or small tree; nest of dead leaves, bark, weed stems and moist leaf-mold is lined with rootlets and fibers; female incubates 4–5 bluish green eggs for 10–14 days; pair feeds the fledged young for a few days before abandoning them.

Feeding: insects and fruit eaten in summer are mostly taken on the ground, but insects are sometimes gleaned from foliage or taken in short flycatching sallies.

Voice: call is a high, whistled *feeyou*; male's song is a fluty, descending series of whistled notes: *da-vee-ur, vee-ur, vee-ur, veer, veer, veer.*

Similar Species: *Swainson's Thrush* (p. 291): red-tinged olive brown upperparts and flanks; pale "spectacles"; rising, flutelike song. *Hermit Thrush* (p. 292): rufous tints are limited to tail, back and wings; darker breast spotting; flutelike song has ascending and descending phrases.

Best Sites: locally in the Blue, Wallowa and Ochoco Mt. watersheds; Ochoco Creek; Grande Ronde River Valley; Enterprise WMA; Crow Creek; Imnaha area; Powder River Valley.

SWAINSON'S THRUSH

Catharus ustulatus

The word "ethereal," often applied to thrush songs, is particularly appropriate when referring to the Swainson's Thrush. One of the last forest songsters to be silenced by nightfall, the male Swainson's sings well into spring evenings. He can often be seen in silhouette against the colorful sunset sky as he perches atop the tallest tree in his territory. His phrases rise ever higher and then disappear as if he had run out of air or inspiration. • Migrating Swainson's Thrushes, preferring the understory, skulk about the ground under low shrubs and tangles, occasionally visiting backyards and neighborhood parks. Ever alert to potential danger, they often vanish after giving a sharp warning call. • The Swainson's Thrush was named for 19th century English zoologist and illustrator William Swainson.

ID: olive brown to reddish brown upperparts and flanks; pale gray underparts; brown-spotted breast; pale "spectacles"; streaked "cheeks"; straight bill; brown-bordered pale throat; pale pink legs.

Size: L 7 in; W 12.

Status: uncommon to common breeding summer resident and common migrant; migrants arrive as early as mid-April; fall migration is from August to early October; especially common along the coast.

Habitat: *Breeding:* coniferous and mixed forests with dense undergrowth, riparian thickets and aspen woodlands. *In migration:* low-elevation woodlands or thickets, including moist and riparian woodlands, canyon bottoms and city parks.

Nesting: in the understory, usually in a fork of a deciduous shrub or conifer sapling; outer layer of plant materials is lined with fine materials; female incubates 4 greenish blue eggs with brownish speckles for 10–14 days; young fledge at 12–14 days.

Feeding: gleans vegetation and forages on the ground for invertebrates, including spiders; eats berries and other small fruits.

Voice: gives a single, sharp *whit* but also issues generic harsh calls; male's flutelike song, heard mostly at dusk or dawn, spirals upward and ends quickly.

Similar Species: *Veery* (p. 290): more reddish overall; white belly; gray flanks; indistinct eye ring; descending song. *Hermit Thrush* (p. 292): rufous tints are limited to tail, back and wings; song has ascending and descending phrases.

Best Sites: *In migration:* residential areas and urban parks. *Summer:* widespread in mid-level conifers and mixed woods.

HERMIT THRUSH

Catharus guttatus

True to its name, the generally very quiet and unobtrusive Hermit Thrush spends much of its time hidden in the lower branches of the undergrowth or on the forest floor. If seen, it is most likely to be perched close to the ground, quickly raising and slowly lowering its tail, or flitting off to cover. This all changes in spring and early summer, when the male Hermit Thrush takes up a prominent perch and sings his beautiful, flutelike song in the choruses of dawn and dusk. • Like many *Catharus* thrushes, the Hermit Thrush shows noticeable regional differences in plumage and size. Coastal birds are smaller and darker, whereas interior mountain birds are larger, paler, grayer and more heavily spotted.

ID: brown to grayish upperparts, reddish on wings and tail; heavily dark-spotted breast; faint spots on white underparts; grayish brown flanks; thin, white eye ring; streaked "cheeks"; dark-tipped pale bill; pale pink legs.

Size: *L* 6–7 in; *W* 11–12 in.

Status: uncommon to common breeding summer resident and common migrant in early spring and early fall; uncommon in western Oregon in winter, though fairly common along the coast.

Habitat: *Breeding:* mountain coniferous forests, bogs and watercourses. *In migration* and *winter:* coniferous and deciduous woodlands with dense undergrowth; forest edges; towns and ranches with berry-bearing trees and bushes.

Nesting: on a conifer branch or in a snag or tree roots; bulky nest of grass, leaves and hair; female incubates 3–4 light blue eggs for 11–13 days.

Feeding: forages on the ground or gleans vegetation; eats mostly insects, earthworms and spiders, but also small salamanders; small fruits are important in winter.

Voice: gives a low *chup* or fluty *treeee;* male sings a series of ethereal, flutelike notes, some rising and others falling, in no set order, from a high, exposed perch at twilight or on a cloudy day.

Similar Species: *Swainson's Thrush* (p. 291): bold "spectacles"; buff-washed lower "cheeks" and breast; tail colored like back; ascending song. *Veery* (p. 290): reddish brown with white belly and gray flanks; indistinct eye ring; descending song.

Best Sites: *Summer:* high-elevation forests. *Winter:* western Oregon residential areas.

AMERICAN ROBIN

Turdus migratorius

The well-loved American Robin, the most widespread and commonest North American thrush, is one of the easiest birds to recognize. It is well known for seeking worms in gardens and grassy areas, yet it occurs in more habitats and has a more varied diet than most Oregon songbirds. • Many American Robins form flocks, move to lower elevations and seek berries over winter. Check these flocks, which attract waxwings, starlings and other thrushes, for any rare species caught up in the crowd. • A hunting American Robin that appears to be listening for prey is actually looking for movements in the soil— with eyes on the sides of its head, a robin must tilt its head sideways to look down.

ID: *Male:* gray upperparts and tail; reddish orange underparts; white undertail coverts; blackish head and white-streaked throat; broken white eye ring; yellow bill; dark legs. *Female:* generally paler than male; whiter throat; white-mottled rusty underparts. *Juvenile:* dark-spotted whitish breast.
Size: *L* 10 in; *W* 17 in.
Status: common to abundant year-round resident and migrant in late winter, especially along the coast, and early fall.
Habitat: *Breeding:* deciduous and coniferous forests, including juniper forests, farmlands, chaparral, riparian oases and residential areas. *In migration:* open grassy areas. *Winter:* sites with berries, especially juniper forests.

Nesting: in a tree or shrub, possibly in a building or on a ledge; twig-and-grass platform has an inner cup of mud and grass with moss and shredded bark; female incubates 4 pale blue eggs for 12–14 days; young are fed insects, especially caterpillars, and fledge at 14–16 days.
Feeding: forages on the ground and among vegetation for insects, earthworms, snails and other small invertebrates; eats small fruits in fall and winter.
Voice: typical thrush calls and unique ones, such as a rapid, clucking *tut-tut-tut;* male sings a series of low whistles with long pauses and repeated or alternated phrases, such as *cheerily cheer-up cheer-up cheerio.*
Similar Species: *Varied Thrush* (p. 294): orangy breast, sides (gray "scales"), throat, eyebrow and wing stripes; black to gray breast band. Catharus *thrushes* (pp. 290–92): smaller; dark-spotted pale breasts; buff underwing bars.
Best Sites: *Winter:* berry bushes. *Spring:* residential lawns.

VARIED THRUSH

Ixoreus naevius

Among migrant and wintering American Robins in urban parks and gardens, the Varied Thrush hardly gets a second glance from most observers, yet this bird is among the most attractive of North America's many thrushes. • The whistling tones of the male's long, drawn-out song easily penetrate the dense vegetation and drifting mist enshrouding his forest habitat, with each one at a different pitch and seeming to come from a different location. When finally revealed, the songster shows a plumage pattern unmatched by any other North American bird. • The Varied Thrush does well in cold, humid conditions, but severely cold spring storms can dampen its plumage and kill it just before summer's warm days and abundant food arrive.

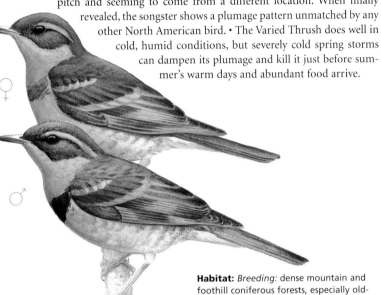

ID: dark bill; dark eyes; pinkish orange legs. *Male:* dark gray upperparts; orange wing bars; orange belly and upper breast; black breast band; gray "scaling" on flanks; dark head; orangy throat and "eyebrow." *Female:* paler than male, especially on head and breast band. *Juvenile:* paler than female; gray-barred breast and white belly. *In flight:* long, buffy orange wing stripe above and below.
Size: *L* 9 in; *W* 16 in.
Status: common breeding summer resident, primarily in the mountains, and migrant in early spring and early fall; common in winter in western foothills and valleys and uncommon east of the Cascades.

Habitat: *Breeding:* dense mountain and foothill coniferous forests, especially old-growth; damp coastal hemlock, red cedar and spruce forests. *In migration* and *winter:* Douglas-fir forests, riparian woodlands, juniper forests, madrone stands, lowland suburbs and orchards.
Nesting: near the trunk or branch tip of a conifer; loose, open cup of twigs, bark, leaves and lichen is filled with rotten wood and lined with grass, leaves and moss; female incubates 3–4 light blue eggs for 12–13 days; young fledge at 13–15 days.
Feeding: forages on the ground and gleans vegetation for small invertebrates; eats fruits, seeds and acorns in winter.
Voice: call is a *chup;* male's unique song is a series of whistles of different pitches, often about 10 seconds apart.
Similar Species: *American Robin* (p. 293): orangy-lined, plain gray wings; plain breast; juvenile is more heavily spotted, with no peach on wings or head.
Best Sites: Portland Audubon Sanctuary; Cape Meares SP; Skinner Butte; Finley NWR; Crater Lake NP; Wallowa Mts.

WRENTIT

Chamaea fasciata

The secretive Wrentit has a wrenlike, skulking nature and a long, flexible tail, often held upraised, as well as the large head and sturdy bill of a titmouse. • The Wrentit prefers to remain concealed within dense tangles of brush and scrub, rarely crossing open areas and only occasionally gleaning the confines of the small territory each pair defends. The wrenlike trilling song of the male Wrentit is often the only indication that a pair, which mates for life, is in residence—unless the birds are scolding away an intruder. • A nonmigratory specialty of North America's Pacific Coast, the Wrentit occurs only as far north as Oregon's northern border.

ID: plain brown, sometimes gray-ish upperparts; lightly streaked grayish to brownish underparts, often pink-tinged to orangy; yellow eyes with dark pupils; small, slightly down-curved bill; long, brownish tail, often held upraised.

Size: *L* 6 in; *W* 7 in.

Status: common breeding permanent resident along the coast and in southwestern interior valleys; uncommon along the western slope of the southern Cascades and along the eastern slope of the Coast Ranges to Yamhill Co.; locally uncommon in southern Klamath Co.

Habitat: heavy brush and chaparral along the coast; brushy habitats and chaparral inland.

Nesting: in a shrub, close to the ground; compact, open cup of bark strips, lichen and spiderwebs is lined with soft plant fibers and hair; pair incubates 4 pale green-ish blue eggs for 15–16 days; pair feeds the young, which fledge at 15–16 days.

Feeding: actively gleans from bark, low branches, twigs and foliage, occasionally hanging titlike, for insects and spiders; feeds heavily on small fruits in fall and winter; occasionally visits feeders to take sugar water and soft foods, such as raisins.

Voice: call is a purring rattle; male's song is a short series of accelerating whistled notes ending in a trill.

Similar Species: *Bushtit* (p. 272): smaller; grayer overall; unstreaked underparts; brown cap; only female has yellow eyes. *Bewick's Wren* (p. 279): brown back; light gray underparts; white eyebrow; dark eyes; long, downcurved bill; less skulking nature.

Best Sites: Coffenbury L. (Clatsop Spit); Ecola SP; Bayocean Spit; Cape Meares SP; Yaquina Bay SP; Siuslaw R. estuary; Cape Arago and Shore Acres SP; Chetco Point (Brookings); Whitehorse CP; Tou Velle SP; Roxy Ann Butte (near Medford).

GRAY CATBIRD
Dumetella carolinensis

Sometimes revealed only by its mewing call, the Gray Catbird prefers to remain concealed in shrubbery. The male does come out in the open, however, to perform a most unusual "mooning" courtship display: he raises his long, slender tail to show off his bright rusty undertail coverts. As with other members of the mimic thrush family, the male Gray Catbird can counter-sing by using each side of his syrinx separately. • The Gray Catbird vigorously defends its nesting territory, often to the benefit of neighboring warblers, towhees and sparrows. Although this species is one of the few that can distinguish cowbird eggs from its own, confused individuals have been seen expelling their own eggs in error. • *Dumetella*, Latin for "small thicket," reflects the Gray Catbird's favorite habitat.

ID: medium gray overall; darker "cap" and tail; rusty undertail coverts; dark eyes; thin, straight bill; dark legs. *Juvenile:* dark brown; "scaly" appearance; heavily buff-spotted, especially on underparts.
Size: *L* 8 in; *W* 11 in.
Status: locally common breeding summer resident in the valleys and foothills of northeastern Oregon; vagrant elsewhere.
Habitat: *Breeding:* deciduous growth along watercourses, forest edges and clearings, roadsides, dense shrubbery and vine tangles; rarely found in suburban areas.

In migration: tangles and thickets, even in residential areas.
Nesting: in a shrub, sapling, small tree or vine; bulky open cup, usually in 3 layers, with a lining of rootlets and tendrils; female incubates 3–4 turquoise green eggs for 12–14 days; young fledge at 10–15 days.
Feeding: forages on the ground and in vegetation, largely for insects and spiders; also eats berries; sometimes visits feeders.
Voice: usual call is catlike; male's song, sung at a slow, uneven pace, is an unstructured babble of whistles, chattering notes, squeaks and limited mimicry.
Similar Species: *Townsend's Solitaire* (p. 289): peach wing bars; gray undertail coverts; shorter bill; large eyes; white eye ring; prefers mountain areas in summer.
Best Sites: restricted to valleys of the Wallowa Mts. and eastern Blue Mts., including the Grande Ronde River Valley, Rhinehart Canyon, Enterprise WMA, Crow Creek and Powder River Valley.

NORTHERN MOCKINGBIRD
Mimus polyglottos

Well known for its vocal dexterity, the Northern Mockingbird has been designated the state bird in several states. The male can sing more than 400 different song types, and he can imitate other birds, barking dogs and even musical instruments. His mimicry is so accurate that computer analysis is often unable to distinguish it from the original source. No one has yet determined the purpose of this mimicry—perhaps being able to mimic so many different sounds suggests that the singer is more attuned to the environment and, therefore, a fitter mate. The female mockingbird also sings, though not as skillfully, and only unmated males will continue to sing after sunset. • The scientific name *polyglottos* is Greek for "many tongues."

VAGRANT

ID: gray upperparts; dark wing with 2 white bars; light gray underparts; brownish yellow eyes; blackish eye line; dark bill; long, black tail, often held parallel to ground, with white outer feathers.

Size: *L* 10 in; *W* 14 in.

Status: rare year-round west of the Cascades, with breeding not yet proven; rare from spring to fall east of the Cascades and very rare in winter.

Habitat: open woodlands, farmlands and 2nd-growth at lower elevations; especially mowed grass in suburban situations.

Nesting: not known to nest in Oregon.

Feeding: gleans vegetation and walks, runs and hops on the ground to catch insects, worms and small lizards; swoops from a perch and occasionally hawks flying insects; eats small fruits; visits feeders for suet and dried and overripe fruit.

Voice: gives a harsh *chuk* call note; male's song repertoire consists of musical and nonmusical phrases acquired through imitation, repeated in series; female sings a shorter version with less mimicry.

Similar Species: *Shrikes* (pp. 245–46): thicker, hooked bill; black "mask"; feed almost entirely from a perch. *Townsend's Solitaire* (p. 289): gray overall; peach wing markings; white eye ring; shorter legs and tail. *Sage Thrasher* (p. 298): heavily streaked underparts; indistinct wing bars; prefers drier scrub habitats.

Best Sites: listen to Portland Audubon Society's weekly Rare Bird Alert; the Rogue Valley in spring and summer; Malheur NWR and Alvord Basin in spring; along the coast in winter.

SAGE THRASHER

Oreoscoptes montanus

The Sage Thrasher, which is heavily dependent on the open sagebrush flats east of the Cascades, is the smallest and plainest of the thrashers. However, the male redeems himself by performing both a melodious song that can last several minutes and an exaggerated, undulating courtship flight. Because of these two attributes, this species is considered a closer relative to mockingbirds than to other thrashers—it was even originally named "Mountain Mockingbird." Other mockingbird-like mannerisms include slowly raising and lowering its tail while perched and holding its tail high while running along the ground.
• *Oreoscoptes* is Greek for "mimic of the mountains," a misnomer for this bird, because its range is mostly not in the mountains.

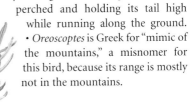

ID: pale grayish brown upper-parts; 2 thin, white wing bars; brown-streaked buffy-ish underparts; yellowish eyes; short, slim, straight bill; dark legs; plumage fades by late summer. *In flight:* long, rounded tail with mostly white tip.

Size: *L* 8 in; *W* 12 in.

Status: common breeding summer resident and migrant east of the Cascades and rare in winter; very rare in spring and fall in western Oregon.

Habitat: *Breeding:* sagebrush, low grease-wood flats and dry areas with scattered junipers. *In migration* and *winter:* dry, open-country areas, especially with scrub or sagebrush; grassland with scattered bushes; open pine–juniper woodlands.

Nesting: in sagebrush, occasionally in a juniper or on the ground; bulky structure of coarse twigs is lined with grass, rootlets and fur; pair incubates 3–5 boldly spotted, rich blue eggs for 11–13 days; young fledge at 10–11 days.

Feeding: gleans sagebrush for insects and spiders; also eats berries and other fruits, especially in winter.

Voice: utters a low *tup;* male's song is a sustained, complex, mellow warble with repeated phrases and little change in pace or pitch; often sings at night.

Similar Species: *Northern Mockingbird* (p. 297): plainer underparts; blackish eye line; large, white wing patches in flight; longer, darker tail with white outer feathers. *Swainson's Thrush* (p. 291) and *Hermit Thrush* (p. 292): stockier; browner upper-parts; spotted breast; unmarked belly; dark eyes; pinkish legs; prefer forest habitats.

Best Sites: *Summer:* sagebrush areas at Prineville Reservoir; Fort Rock SP; Summer Lake WMA; Abert Rim; Hart Mt.; Thief Valley Reservoir; Diamond Craters; Malheur NWR; Alvord Desert.

EUROPEAN STARLING
Sturnus vulgaris

European Starlings were released into New York's Central Park in 1890–91 as part of the local Shakespeare society's plan to introduce all the birds mentioned in the author's works. Starlings quickly spread across North America. In spite of their attractive, iridescent plumage, their ability to mimic almost any other bird and their appetite for insects and other pests, many ornithologists dislike European Starlings because they have outcompeted many native birds for cavity nest sites. Their success is largely a result of their association with urban areas (buildings and other structures provide them with plenty of nesting and roosting habitats), their flocking tendency (which reduces the chance of predation) and a unique bill muscle structure (which helps detect and expose hidden prey).

breeding

ID: generally shiny black; orangy edges to wing feathers; dark eyes; straight, pointed bill; orangy pink legs; blunt tail. *Breeding:* greenish back; pinkish buff spots on upperparts and undertail coverts; glossy purple head, neck and breast; bright yellow bill. *Nonbreeding:* white-spotted back and underparts; finely white-streaked head; black bill. *Juvenile:* uniformly dull brown.
Size: *L* 8 in; *W* 16 in.
Status: abundant introduced year-round resident; fall and winter flocks and communal roosts up to thousands or hundreds of thousands.
Habitat: favors urban areas, farmlands and open forests up to 7000 ft.
Nesting: in cavity or crevice; messy nest of grass, twigs and straw; female incubates 4–6 brown-marked bluish or greenish

white eggs for 12–14 days; young fledge at 18–21 days; raises 2–3 broods a year.
Feeding: omnivorous and opportunistic; searches the ground and gleans foliage for insects, berries, seeds and human scraps; flycatches for flying termites and ants; picks off small invertebrates behind farm machinery; scavenges from garbage.
Voice: common call is harsh chatter; flight call is typically buzzy; male sings a mixture of mellow whistles, squeaks and mimicked sounds of other birds.
Similar Species: *Male Brewer's Blackbird* (p. 347): unmarked, shiny, greenish black plumage, purplish on head and breast; yellow eyes; stouter black bill; black legs; rounded wings; longer tail; usually in looser flocks. *Male Brown-headed Cowbird* (p. 348): smaller; shiny, black plumage, often greenish; brown head; sturdier bill; more rounded wings.
Best Sites: almost anywhere except dense forests and mountaintops.

AMERICAN PIPIT

Anthus rubescens

I n Oregon, American Pipits breed only in open, treeless, alpine environments. Many birds are already paired when they reach the breeding territories, having gone through the preliminaries of courtship and pair formation at lower elevations. • In fall migration, flocks of American Pipits carpet open areas, especially short grasslands, barren fields, park lawns and lowland shorelines. Pipits can often be seen with flocks of shorebirds on salt marshes and grasslands. Their plain wardrobe and habit of continuously bobbing their white-sided tails make American Pipits instantly recognizable. Tail-wagging, a common feature of the Northern Hemisphere pipits and wagtails, may help to stir up hidden prey.

nonbreeding

ID: weakly streaked grayish brown upperparts; large, dark eyes; pale "eyebrow"; white eye ring; grayish "ear" patch. *Dark morph:* pale buff lower face and underparts, strongly dark-streaked, particularly on breast, with breeding bird showing white areas and darker streaking. *Light morph:* buff parts are cinnamon-tinged, unmarked (with smaller "ear" patch) in breeding plumage and lightly streaked otherwise.
Size: *L* 6–7 in; *W* 10¹/₂ in.
Status: locally common breeding summer resident in alpine areas; common migrant at lower elevations throughout Oregon in spring and from late August to November; uncommon in farmlands in winter.
Habitat: *Breeding:* open, windswept alpine meadows and slopes. *In migration* and *winter:* shorelines and other areas with low or no vegetation.

Nesting: concealed in grass, a bank or a burrow; base of dried grass and sedges is lined with finer grass and hair; female incubates 3–7 brown-spotted pale eggs for 14–15 days; young fledge at 13–15 days and are fed for another 2 weeks.
Feeding: forages on the ground and pecks or gleans land and aquatic invertebrates in summer; eats plant seeds in fall and winter.
Voice: high, thin calls are often repeated; male's courtship song is a high, repeated *tiwee.*
Similar Species: *Sparrows* (pp. 321–38): stouter bills; shorter legs; plainer tail coloration. *Nonbreeding* or *female Lapland Longspur* (p. 338): rusty neck, back and wing bar; darkish breast band; conical pinkish bill; shorter legs. *Sage Thrasher* (p. 298): larger; yellowish eyes; tail often upraised; mostly in sagebrush habitats.
Best Sites: *Summer:* alpine areas of the Cascades and Wallowa Mts. and Steens Mt. *Winter and in migration:* coastal, interior western, central and northeastern Oregon; Klamath Basin.

BOHEMIAN WAXWING

Bombycilla garrulus

A flock of waxwings swarming over a suburban neighborhood is guaranteed to dispel even the most severe winter blues. Faint, quavering whistles announce an approaching flock, which may swoop down to perch and then take turns to strip berries from mountain ashes, junipers and other trees and bushes. • Bohemian Waxwings normally breed in Canada and Alaska, and the only summer sighting and nesting record for Oregon was in Clatsop County in 1958. Somewhat larger than any Cedar Waxwings among them, these birds usually arrive just in time to be tallied in reasonable numbers on Christmas bird counts and depart for their boreal homes before most songbirds arrive back in Oregon. • Waxwings get their name from the "waxy" red spots on their secondary feathers. Actually enlargements of the feather shafts, these spots get their color from the berries the birds eat. • This nomadic avian wanderer is named for Bohemia, once considered the ancestral home of the Gypsies.

ID: grayish brown upperparts and breast; darker wing tip with yellow stripe, "waxy" red spot and 2 white areas; black throat; prominent, rear-pointing brown crest; reddish forehead and "cheeks"; black "mask" with white line below; short, gray bill; rufous undertail coverts; grayish rump and upper tail; black band and yellow tip on tail.
Size: *L* 8 in; *W* 14½ in.
Status: erratic winter resident, particularly in northeastern Oregon, from mid-November until late March or April, and irruptive elsewhere.
Habitat: open or juniper woodlands; townsites, cities and suburbs with berry-bearing trees and shrubs.
Nesting: not known to nest in Oregon.
Feeding: forages in flocks; eats mostly berries, other fruits and some tree seeds in winter; gleans vegetation or catches flying insects on the wing.
Voice: usual call is a series of high notes, slightly lower than those of accompanying Cedar Waxwings.
Similar Species: *Cedar Waxwing* (p. 302): smaller; tawnier; only a red spot on wing tip; yellowish belly; white undertail coverts.
Best Sites: Pendleton; Grande Ronde R.; Ladd Marsh WMA; Enterprise; Crow Creek; Imnaha; Sumpter.

CEDAR WAXWING
Bombycilla cedrorum

Cedar Waxwings, unlike the larger, winter-only Bohemian Waxwings, inhabit Oregon year-round. In cold winters, most breeding birds migrate southward, but, if food is plentiful in warm winters, they will remain to join flocks of other Cedar Waxwings and Bohemian Waxwings from boreal breeding locations. • Waxwings gorge themselves on fruit left hanging on tree and shrub branches in fall and winter, occasionally eating themselves to flightless intoxication on fermented fruit. In summer, Cedar Waxwings add insects to their diet, capturing them by gleaning or by flycatching near streams and ponds. • Flocks show little site loyalty, and Cedar Waxwings nest later than most songbirds.

ID: tawny brown upperparts and breast; wing is grayer and darker toward tip and has "waxy" red spot; black throat; prominent, rear-pointing brown crest; white-bordered black "mask"; short, gray bill; white under-tail coverts; grayish rump and upper tail; black band and yellow tip on tail.

Size: *L* 7 in; *W* 12 in.

Status: fairly common breeding summer resident and migrant from mid-May to early June and from late August to early November; locally uncommon in winter in western interior valleys and east of the Cascades.

Habitat: *Breeding:* deciduous and mixed forests, woodland edges, fruit orchards, young pine plantations and riparian hardwoods among conifers. *In migration* and *winter:* open woodlands and brush, often near water; desert watercourses and oases; residential areas; any habitat near a source of berries.

Nesting: in a fork of a branch or trunk, in a vine or on a branch; bulky, open cup is lined with fine plant materials, spider silk and hair; female incubates 3–5 sparsely dark-spotted, very pale blue eggs for 11–13 days; young fledge at 14–18 days.

Feeding: forages in branches of fruit trees and shrubs for fruits, flowers and insects; sallies from high, exposed branches near fresh water; gleans bark for insects.

Voice: high-pitched purrs and trills that intensify in large flocks; simple song is similar.

Similar Species: *Bohemian Waxwing* (p. 301): larger; grayer; gray belly and rufous undertail coverts; white areas and yellow stripe on wing; reddish face.

Best Sites: woodland edges and berry-bearing trees throughout Oregon.

ORANGE-CROWNED WARBLER

Vermivora celata

Unlike many birds, the Orange-crowned Warbler is best identified by its lack of field marks—no wing bars, no flashing rump, no visible color patch, not even a memorable song—and the male's telltale orange crown is hidden most of the time. Its plain appearance is all the more surprising considering that most of the 109 New World wood-warblers, of which 56 species occur north of Mexico, boast at least one of those features, even in their confusing fall plumages. • Some fall migrants of the boreal-nesting Taiga race—with grayish olive on the back, gray on the head and yellow confined to the undertail coverts—can easily be confused with Nashville Warblers or Tennessee Warblers. • *Vermivora* is Latin for "worm-eating," and *celata* is derived from the Latin word for "hidden," a reference to the inconspicuous crown patch.

ID: olive green to dull yellow overall; faintly greenish-streaked under-parts; yellow undertail coverts; broken yellow eye ring; faint dark eye line; faint yellow "eyebrow"; dusky legs. *Male:* orange crown patch (usually hidden).

Size: *L* 5 in; *W* 7½ in.

Status: common breeding summer resident and migrant and rare in winter west of the Cascades; locally common breeding summer resident east of the Cascades; migration is from mid-March to early June and from late August to mid-October.

Habitat: *Breeding:* brush, understories of dense forests, chaparral, oak woodlands and aspen, willow and mountain mahogany stands. *In migration* and *winter:* deciduous and brushy habitats, especially berry-bearing thickets.

Nesting: on the ground or low in a shrub; well-hidden nest of coarse grass and bark strips is lined with finer materials; female incubates 4–5 russet-marked white eggs for 12–14 days; young fledge at 8–10 days.

Feeding: gleans foliage for invertebrates and berries; feeds on flower nectar; visits sapsucker "wells" and hummingbird feeders.

Voice: high-pitched, chippy calls; male's faint trill song breaks downward at midpoint.

Similar Species: *Nashville Warbler* (p. 304): greener back and wings; yellower below; grayer head; prominent white eye ring. *Female Yellow Warbler* (p. 305): brighter yellow underparts and head; 2 yellow wing bars; larger eyes; narrow, complete eye ring; yellow tail flashes.

Best Sites: Ankeny NWR; W.L. Finley NWR; Foster Reservoir; Indian Ford Campground (Sisters).

NASHVILLE WARBLER

Vermivora ruficapilla

The male Nashville Warbler has plenty to sing about: his plumage is a bright mixture of green, yellow and bluish gray, with splashes of rufous and white thrown in for good measure. Fortunately for beginning birdwatchers, this species retains the same plumage from juvenile to adult, though only the breeding male has the kingletlike crown patch. • Nashville Warblers prefer drier, more open woodlands and brush more than most other warblers. Quite conspicuous in summer, in migration they are much more retiring and can easily slip by unnoticed. • The Nashville Warbler—like the Tennessee, Cape May and Connecticut warblers—bears a name that reflects where it was first collected in migration and not its breeding or wintering range. • *Ruficapilla* refers to the hidden red crown patch of the male.

ID: thin, dark bill; dusky legs. *Male:* plain, olive green back; brownish green wings and tail; yellowish green rump; yellow throat and underparts; bluish gray head; rufous crown patch (often hidden); prominent white eye ring. *Female:* like male, but whitish throat and lower belly; paler head with gray crown.
Size: L 4 in; W 7½ in.
Status: common breeding summer resident in southwestern and northeastern Oregon and locally in the Cascades; uncommon migrant, except along the northern coast, from mid-April to early May and from August to mid-September.
Habitat: *Breeding:* dry, brushy areas and foothills; high elevation brushy wetlands.
Nesting: on the ground; well-hidden nest of coarse materials and moss is lined with fur and fine materials; female incubates 4–5 white eggs wreathed in reddish brown for 11–12 days; young fledge at 11 days.
Feeding: gleans foliage for insects, such as caterpillars, flies and aphids; occasionally hover-gleans or feeds on the ground.
Voice: usual call is a rather sharp *twit;* male's song is a 2-part descending trill.
Similar Species: *MacGillivray's Warbler* (p. 313): larger; gray "hood" extends to upper breast; broken eye ring; pink bill; pink legs; longer tail. *Wilson's Warbler* (p. 315): yellow head; black or olive "cap."
Best Sites: Davis L. (Cascades Lakes); Crater Lake NP; Hart Mt.; Rhinehart Bridge; Bonny Lakes trail; Anthony Lakes; Roxy Anne Butte (Medford).

YELLOW WARBLER

Dendroica petechia

ctive and inquisitive, flitting from branch to branch in search of plant-eating insects, this small warbler is the home gardener's perfect house guest. With golden plumage and a cheerful song, it is easy to see why the Yellow Warbler is a welcome addition to any neighborhood. • The Yellow Warbler is also popular with the Brown-headed Cowbird, which deposits an egg or two of its own into this warbler's nest. Unlike most forest songbirds, the Yellow Warbler recognizes the foreign eggs and either abandons the nest or builds over the clutch. Some persistent pairs build over and over, creating bizarre, multilayered high-rise nests. Despite this vigilance, the Yellow Warbler is in decline, with the trend toward exotic ornamental plants and undergrowth removal in residential areas also being responsible.

ID: large, black eyes; small, black bill. *Male:* yellowish green back, rump, nape, crown and "cheeks"; bright lemon yellow underparts; reddish streaks on breast and sides. *Female:* drabber than male; white-edged inner flight feathers; smudgy olive streaks on breast and flanks.

Size: *L* 5 in; *W* 7½ in.

Status: common breeding summer resident and migrant (mid-April to late May and mid-August to early October).

Habitat: *Breeding:* riparian willows, cottonwoods and deciduous thickets; aspen groves; shade trees in residential areas. *In migration:* 2nd-growth or shrubby habitats, including urban ones.

Nesting: in a fork of a deciduous tree or small shrub; female builds a neat, compact nest of weed stalks, shredded bark and lichen and lines it with plant down, spider silk and other fine materials; female incubates 4–5 variably marked off-white eggs for 11–12 days; young fledge at 9–12 days.

Feeding: gleans foliage, bark and vegetation for invertebrates, especially caterpillars and cankerworms, beetles and aphids; also hawks and hover-gleans for insects.

Voice: lackluster chipping call is sometimes repeated; male's song is a fast, repeated *sweet-sweet-sweet summer sweet*.

Similar Species: *Wilson's Warbler* (p. 315): greener upperparts; plain yellow underparts; dark crown; smaller bill; chipping, trilled song. *Orange-crowned Warbler* (p. 303): olive green to dull yellow overall; faintly greenish-streaked underparts; unbarred wings; dry, dull trilling song.

Best Sites: widespread in most edge and 2nd-growth habitats; Malheur NWR headquarters.

YELLOW-RUMPED WARBLER

Dendroica coronata

The Yellow-rumped Warbler is North America's most abundant and widespread warbler. Even though it is a common sight for most birdwatchers, its energetic behavior and the male's attractive breeding plumage make it welcome at all times, especially during the cold, sometimes misty days of fall and early winter. • Other warblers also seem to appreciate the Yellow-rump's company and its alertness, and they tag along with it in fast-moving foraging flocks. • Although all breeding Yellow-rumps in Oregon are of the western "Audubon's Warbler" race, migrants and wintering birds are equally likely to be of the more widespread "Myrtle Warbler" race, which commonly migrates down the Pacific Coast from breeding sites in northwestern Canada and Alaska.

breeding
"Audubon's"

ID: 2 white wing bars, merging in "Audubon's"; yellow rump and side patch. *Breeding male:* heavily streaked gray back; black breast; white underparts; black-streaked flanks; yellow crown patch; throat yellow ("Audubon's") or white ("Myrtle"); black "mask"; white "eyebrow"; gray tail. *Breeding female:* like male but drabber, with more streaking below; all-gray crown.
Size: *L* 5½ in; *W* 9–9½ in.
Status: common breeding summer resident and migrant from mid-March to early June and from mid-September to mid-November; uncommon winter resident west of the Cascades and rare in eastern Oregon.
Habitat: *Breeding:* any coniferous or mixed forests. *In migration* and *winter:* deciduous

and mixed thickets and woodlands along the coast and in interior valleys.
Nesting: in a conifer; female constructs a compact nest of shredded bark, weed stalks, twigs and rootlets and lines it with fine materials; female incubates 4–5 brown-marked creamy white eggs for 12–13 days; young fledge at 10–12 days; may raise a 2nd brood.
Feeding: hawks, hover-gleans or gleans vegetation for insects; also feeds on the ground, fencelines, and structures; eats mostly berries in fall and winter.
Voice: "Myrtle" gives a sharp, dry *kep* call; "Audubon's" utters a more liquid, rising *swip;* male's song varies from a tinkling trill to a more varied warble.
Similar Species: *Townsend's Warbler* (p. 308) and *Hermit Warbler* (p. 309): greenish rump; mostly yellow face, often with darker markings and black on throat; buzzy songs.
Best Sites: widespread in woodlands, especially during migration.

BLACK-THROATED GRAY WARBLER

Dendroica nigrescens

The Black-throated Gray Warbler is one of the very few western warblers that rarely crosses the continental divide. • The male's shrill, buzzy song is very similar to the songs of his relatives. Once seen, however, the Black-throated Gray Warbler is instantly recognizable—it looks like a yellow-challenged Townsend's Warbler, with the male darker than the female. It is a close relative of the Townsend's Warbler and the Hermit Warbler, but these two species both have a moderate amount of yellow in their plumages in contrast to the small facial spot on the Black-throated Gray. Another distinction is that the Black-throated Gray Warbler frequents the transition zone between lower oak–deciduous woodlands and higher conifer forests, whereas the other two warblers exploit the higher conifers.

breeding

ID: yellow spot ahead of eye; blackish legs. *Male:* black-marked gray nape and upperparts; 2 white wing bars; white underparts; black-streaked breast and sides; black throat and head; white "eyebrow" and "mustache." *Female:* black markings less pronounced than male's; white or black throat; paler, usually unstreaked back.
Size: *L* 5 in; *W* 7¾ in.
Status: common breeding summer resident and migrant west of the Cascades and locally uncommon east of the Cascades, except in the northeast; migration is from late March to early May and from mid-August to mid-October.
Habitat: deciduous and mixed forests, 2nd-growth clear-cuts and juniper woodlands. *In migration:* towns and riparian areas.
Nesting: usually far out on a horizontal conifer branch; small cup nest of weed stalks, grass and plant fibers; female (and perhaps male) incubates 3–5 brown-marked white eggs for about 12 days; young leave the nest 8–10 days after hatching.
Feeding: hawks, hover-gleans and gleans for insects.
Voice: usual call is a low *tep;* male's song is a series of wiry musical notes with a loud final flourish.
Similar Species: *Black-and-white Warbler* (p. 366): white streaking on back; white crown stripe; yellowish feet. *"Myrtle" Yellow-rumped Warbler* (p. 306): white throat; yellow rump and side patch; less white in tail. *Townsend's Warbler* (p. 308): yellow on head and breast; olive green back.
Best Sites: Mt. Tabor Park (Portland); Pittock Bird Sanctuary (Portland); Dabney SP (Lower Sandy R.); Larch Mt.; Lake Selmac CP; Robert W. Sawyer Park; Tumalo SP (Bend); Page Springs Campground.

TOWNSEND'S WARBLER

Dendroica townsendi

Hardier than many of its close relatives, the stripe-headed Townsend's Warbler reaches its southernmost nesting range in Oregon. As the male utters his wheezy song from the tip of a conifer branch in the upper canopy, he is difficult to locate amidst the dense, dark foliage. In winter, however, when the Townsend's joins other cold-hardy warblers in dense cover along the coast and in sheltered valleys in western Oregon, it sometimes offers a much better look at its attractive plumage as it forages at suet feeders. • Some Townsend's Warblers bear evidence of hybridization with the yellow-headed Hermit Warbler, which occurs in some of the same mountainous areas, but usually at slightly higher elevations.

♂

♀

breeding

ID: small, black bill; blackish legs. *Male:* dark olive green back and rump; bluish gray wing with 2 bold white bars; yellow breast with heavy black streaks; white belly, flanks and undertail coverts; yellow face with black crown, "cheek" patches and throat; yellow below eye. *Female:* black largely replaced by dark olive; white throat.
Size: *L* 5 in; *W* 8 in.
Status: common breeding summer resident in northeastern mountains and uncommon from the central Cascades northward; common migrant throughout Oregon from early April to mid-June and from mid-August to mid-October; uncommon at lower elevations west of the Cascades in winter.
Habitat: *Breeding:* mountain fir forests and other coniferous forests. *In migration*

and *winter:* coniferous and mixed woods, urban parks and coastal thickets.
Nesting: far out on a horizontal branch of a fir; shallow nest of grass, moss, cedar bark, fir twigs and plant fibers is lined with moss, feathers and hair; male helps female incubate 4–5 brown-marked white eggs for 12 days; young fledge at 8–10 days.
Feeding: gleans vegetation and hawks for invertebrates; eats seeds and plant galls in winter; occasionally visits suet feeders.
Voice: utters a chippy call; male's song consists of wiry *zee* and *zoo* notes in an uneven pattern with a final flourish.
Similar Species: *Hermit Warbler* (p. 309): more streaked, grayish back; unmarked white underparts; all-yellow (male) or gray-smudged (female) face.
Best Sites: *Summer:* Blue, Wallowa and Ochoco Mts. *Fall:* lowland areas in eastern Oregon. *Winter:* along the coast and at lower elevations inland in the west.

HERMIT WARBLER

Dendroica occidentalis

Upon arriving on his nesting territory, the male Hermit Warbler begins patrolling the crowns of the tall conifers marking its boundaries. Each tree-top offers a superb singing perch and a vantage point from which to welcome potential mates or thwart the intrusions of other males. • Sightings are mostly of pure Hermit Warblers, but Townsend's Warbler x Hermit Warbler hybrids are regularly reported; some of them resemble the Black-throated Green Warbler (*D. virens*), a rare vagrant in Oregon. Because the male Hermit Warbler's song is similar to that of the Townsend's Warbler, misidentifications can occur. • Hermit Warblers travel in mixed-species flocks during migration.

breeding

ID: small, black bill; dark eyes; blackish legs. *Male:* heavily black-streaked gray nape, back and rump; bluish black wing with 2 bold white bars; unmarked white underparts; cleanly defined black throat and upper breast; bright yellow face and crown. *Female:* smudgy throat patch, crown, "ear" patch and lores.

Size: *L* 5 in; *W* 8 in.

Status: locally common breeding summer resident and migrant in mid-spring and from late August to mid-October on the slopes of Cascades, in the Siskiyou Mts. and Coast Ranges and along the coast.

Habitat: coniferous forests.

Nesting: on a horizontal conifer branch, far from the trunk; deep, compact cup of weed stems, pine needles, fine twigs, moss, spider webs and lichen; male helps female incubate 4–5 brown-flecked creamy white eggs for about 12 days; young fledge at 8–10 days.

Feeding: forages on branches, gleaning and hawking for insects and larvae; male usually feeds higher in the canopy than the female.

Voice: call is a sharp *tsik* or *te;* male's song is a series of buzzes in one note, often with a final flourish of higher or lower notes.

Similar Species: *Townsend's Warbler* (p. 308): yellow breast with heavy, dark streaks continuing onto white flanks; dark crown and ear patch; plainer, greener back.

Best Sites: Saddle Mountain SP; Larch Mt.; Timothy L.; Detroit Reservoir; Green Peter Reservoir; Waldo L.; Big Lake Campground.

PALM WARBLER

Dendroica palmarum

O ne of the habitual "tail-waggers," the Palm Warbler can easily be picked out in mixed-species foraging flocks, even when its plumage details are hard to observe. This tail-wagging continues when the bird is at rest on a perch or hopping on the ground in search of food. • The Palm Warbler's name is based on the location where this species was first collected in winter, but it actually breeds in tamarack and spruce bogs in boreal Canada, the Great Lakes states and the northern part of the Eastern Seaboard. It is also a regular migrant along the Oregon coast, with the number of birds varying considerably from year to year. Although the great majority of Palm Warblers seen in Oregon are of the western race, there are a few records of individuals of the eastern race.

nonbreeding

ID: dark-streaked grayish brown upperparts; dark eye line; yellow undertail coverts; white corners to tail; constantly pumps tail at rest and when feeding. *Breeding:* dark-streaked whitish belly; yellow throat; rufous crown. *Nonbreeding:* paler, smudgy underpart streaking; grayish brown crown.

Size: *L* 5 in; *W* 8 in.

Status: rare to uncommon fall migrant and rare in winter and spring along the coast; vagrant to inland western Oregon and east of the Cascades; locally common during irregular irruptions from mid-September to early November.

Habitat: shrubby growth, especially on wet woodland edges, and coastal scrub.

Nesting: does not nest in Oregon.

Feeding: forages mostly on the ground for insects and seeds; gleans foliage and hawks for insects; eats some berries in fall.

Voice: call is a clipped *chik;* male's song is a monotonous, insectlike trill, more uneven than a Swamp Sparrow's or a Dark-eyed Junco's.

Similar Species: *Yellow-rumped Warbler* (p. 306): chunkier; grayer; localized yellow patches; 2 white wing bars; brighter yellow rump; white undertail coverts. *Female Blackpoll Warbler:* 2 white wing bars; olive green rump; white undertail coverts.

Best Sites: Mark O. Hatfield Marine Science Center in Yaquina Bay; Clatsop Spit; Nehalem Meadows; Barview Jetty CP (Tillamook Bay); Siuslaw R. estuary; Pony Slough woodlands (North Bend); Harris Beach SP (Brookings).

AMERICAN REDSTART

Setophaga ruticilla

Many species exhibit sexual dimorphism, but male and female American Redstarts are so different that it seems impossible that they are the same species. • American Redstarts are always in motion. It is as if they are eager to show off their contrasting plumage, which is continually displayed in an enthusiastic series of flutters, twists, turns and feather-spreading. They behave the same way on their Central American wintering grounds, where they are called *candelitas*—"little candles." • The song of the American Redstart is so variable that even experienced birders who are faced with an unknown warbler song will exclaim, "It must be a Redstart!"

ID: dark eyes; small, dark bill; blackish legs. *Male:* black upperparts, throat and head; orangy red (yellow on juvenile) sides of breast, wing bar and tail patch; white belly and undertail. *Female:* olive gray upperparts; yellow wing bar, upper sides and tail patch; light gray underparts; gray head; pale "spectacles."

Size: *L* 5 in; *W* 7½ in.

Status: locally uncommon breeding summer resident in the Blue Mts. and Wallowa Mts.; very local and rare breeder on the eastern slope of the southern Cascades; rare migrant, mostly east of the Cascades, from mid-May to early June and from mid-August to early October.

Habitat: *Breeding:* riparian and lake-edge deciduous woods, often with ponderosa pine and Douglas-fir forests. *In migration:* coastal thickets, woodlots, 2nd-growth along streams and desert oases.

Nesting: in the fork of a low tree or shrub, occasionally on the ground; compact cup of plant fibers, grass and rootlets is lined with fine materials; female incubates 4 brown-wreathed white eggs for 12 days; young fledge at 9 days.

Feeding: actively gleans foliage and hawks for insects and spiders; occasionally consumes flower nectar, seeds and berries.

Voice: call is a sharp, sweet *chip;* male's song is a highly variable series of *tseet* or *zee* notes, often at different pitches.

Similar Species: *Virginia's Warbler:* smaller; grayer overall; yellow on mid-breast, undertail coverts and rump.

Best Sites: Grande Ronde R. area; Rhinehart Bridge; Enterprise Wildlife Area; Wallowa Lake SP; Imnaha and Sumpter areas; Odell Creek at Davis L. *In migration:* Malheur NWR; Alvord Basin desert oases.

NORTHERN WATERTHRUSH

Seiurus noveboracensis

Not a thrush but resembling one, the tail-bobbing Northern Waterthrush has a stronger affinity for wet habitats than do most ground-feeding warblers. Like many waterside foragers, it teeters along like a slightly out-of-practice Spotted Sandpiper. • The male's song is so loud and raucous that the earlier name of "New York Warbler" almost seems justified. • Generally a vagrant here, the Northern Waterthrush maintains a small breeding population in riparian thickets along Crescent Creek and the Little Deschutes River in Klamath County and along Salt Creek in Lane County. Birds have also been found in summer at Lost Lake in Linn County and Clear Creek in Wasco County, and a few are usually seen from mid-May to mid-June and from early August to early October, mostly at Harney County sites and at Hart Mountain National Wildlife Refuge.

ID: plain, dark brown upperparts and tail; heavily black-streaked white or yellow-washed underparts; white or yellow undertail coverts; brown crown and eye line; narrow, white or pale yellow "eyebrow"; pink bill and legs; pumps tail; distinctive song.
Size: *L* 6 in; *W* 9½ in.
Status: very local breeding summer resident; rare migrant, mostly in southeastern Oregon.
Habitat: wooded swamps; riparian thickets in coniferous and deciduous forests; flooded scrubby growth.
Nesting: on the ground, hidden among the roots of a fallen tree, under an overhanging bank or on a broken stump or branch; small, concealed cup of moss, leaves, twigs and inner bark is lined with fine materials; female incubates 4–5 variably marked white eggs for 12–13 days; young fledge at 10–12 days.
Feeding: feeds mostly on the ground, frequently tossing aside leaves with its bill in a search for invertebrates; also gleans foliage and dips into shallow water for invertebrates and small fish.
Voice: gives a brisk *chip* or *chuck* call; male's song is a loud, 3-part *sweet sweet sweet, swee wee wee, chew chew chew*, usually down the scale and speeding up, with an ending flourish.
Similar Species: *Ovenbird* (p. 366): warm brown above; black-bordered rusty crown; bold white eye ring; distinctive song.
Best Sites: brushy areas near the Little Deschutes R. and nearby areas in the Cascades; Malheur NWR; Alvord Basin desert oases.

MACGILLIVRAY'S WARBLER

Oporornis tolmiei

The MacGillivray's Warbler is a difficult bird to get to know—birders often have difficulty viewing this understory skulker, even when its loud, rich *chip* appears to be less than a binocular-view away. • Multiple wood-warbler species can coexist in one habitat by using different foraging niches and nest sites. Some species inhabit the upper canopy, with a few feeding and nesting along the outer branches and others restricting themselves to inner branches and trunks. MacGillivray's Warbler claims the dense understory shrubbery and bushy tangles in conifer glades, deciduous woodlands or even residential parks. • The best time of year to look for this shy species is in spring, when the males ascend tall shrubs to impress the females with their parlor songs.

breeding

ID: plain, olive green upperparts; unmarked lemon yellow underparts; brownish flanks; dark eyes; broken white eye ring; slightly downcurved, pinkish bill; pink legs. *Male:* grayish blue "hood," darkest on breast, forehead and eye line. *Female:* paler, more uniform "hood"; whitish throat; longer tail.
Size: *L* 5 in; *W* 7½ in.
Status: common breeding summer resident and migrant from late April to early June and from mid-August to early October.
Habitat: *Breeding:* stream- and lakeside deciduous brush; forest understory; early clear-cut and burn regeneration. *In migration:* any dense vegetation.
Nesting: usually close to the ground in thick shrubbery; small cup nest of weed stems and grass is lined with fine materials; female incubates 4 brown-marked creamy

white eggs for 11 days; young fledge at 8–9 days.
Feeding: gleans bark, low vegetation and the ground for beetles, bees, leafhoppers, insect larvae and other invertebrates; rarely moves higher than the understory.
Voice: call is a typical *chik;* male's song is a somewhat buzzy *sweeter sweeter sweeter sugar sugared* with less clear final notes.
Similar Species: *Nashville Warbler* (p. 304): smaller; yellow throat and breast; complete white eye ring; may have white belly. *Wilson's Warbler* (p. 315): smaller; yellow head; dark "cap"; finer bill.
Best Sites: *Summer:* Larch Mt.; Ankeny NWR; Foster Reservoir; Indian Ford Campground and Cold Springs Campground (Sisters); Hart Mt.; Spring Creek; Rhinehart Bridge; Union Creek Campground (Sumpter). *In migration:* any brushy areas.

COMMON YELLOWTHROAT

Geothlypis trichas

Other warblers avoid getting their feet wet by frequenting drier areas or climbing high in the forest canopy, but the Common Yellowthroat muddles around in the mud and muck of marsh and lakeshore vegetation. At home in the world of cattails and tules, the male fires off his salvo of loud, repetitive songs as his mate gets down to the job of raising a family—often including some "donated" Brown-headed Cowbird eggs. • Common Yellowthroats do not spend all their time hidden away in the dense, wet vegetation. When the job of nesting is over, they can be found in almost any damp, scrubby habitat. Here they fuel up for a short winter trip south, often no farther than California.

ID: greenish brown nape and upperparts; bright yellow throat, breast and undertail coverts; dusky flanks; dark eyes; dark bill; pink or orangy legs. *Male:* black "mask" from forehead to shoulder, white-bordered above. *Female:* greenish brown face; indistinct pale eye ring.

Size: *L* 5 in; *W* 6½ in.

Status: locally common breeding summer resident and common migrant from late March to early May and from late August to mid-October.

Habitat: *Breeding:* marshes; damp, lush vegetation, especially wet areas with willow or brush; overgrown fields and hedgerows. *In migration* and *winter:* wet thickets, dense brush and weedy fields.

Nesting: in low, scrubby growth or shrubs; bulky, loosely made nest of weed stems, grass, bark, dead leaves and ferns is lined with fine material; female incubates 3–5 dark-marked creamy white eggs for 12 days; young fledge at 10 days.

Feeding: gleans vegetation and bark, hover-gleans and flycatches for invertebrates; also eats some seeds, usually picked from the ground.

Voice: gives a sharp *tcheck* or *tchet* call; male's song is a clear, oscillating *witchety witchety witchety-witch* or other repetitions of 3 (rarely 2) syllables.

Similar Species: *MacGillivray's Warbler* (p. 313): deeper olive green upperparts; underparts more yellow; gray "hood"; prominent broken white eye ring.

Best Sites: *Summer:* Fern Ridge Reservoir; Indian Ford Campground and Cold Springs Campground (Sisters); Umatilla NWR; McNary Wildlife Park; Wallowa Fish Hatchery; Malheur NWR.

WILSON'S WARBLER

Wilsonia pusilla

Even a casual glance into a streamside thicket is sure to reveal an energetic Wilson's Warbler flickering through tangles of leaves and branches in pursuit of its food as if every moment is precious. With more energy than many a larger bird, the Wilson's Warbler is also quick to jump to the defense of its hidden brood should an intruder come too close. • Often intensely golden over much of its plumage, this tiny warbler could be confused with the Yellow Warbler, but a closer look will usually reveal that error, especially if the Wilson's flashes its black crown. • The Wilson's Warbler bears the name of birding pioneer Alexander Wilson—his energetic devotion to ornithology in the early 1800s inspired many careful studies of North American birds.

ID: yellowish green upperparts; yellow underparts; small, pink-and-dark bill; large, black eyes; pink legs. *Male:* black crown; bright, golden yellow face; broad, yellow "eyebrow." *Female:* olive forehead and crown (sometimes light-spotted black instead).
Size: *L* 4 in; *W* 7 in.
Status: common breeding summer resident and migrant from mid-April to mid-June and from early August to mid-October west of the Cascades summit and locally common eastward.
Habitat: *Breeding:* dense deciduous understory and brush, usually near fresh water. *In migration:* conifers, deciduous brush and residential parks and gardens.

Nesting: on the ground in the mountains, or low in a shrub or vine tangle along the coast; bulky nest of dead leaves, grass and moss is lined with fine grass and hair; female incubates 4–6 brown-marked creamy white eggs for 10–13 days; young fledge at 8–11 days.
Feeding: gleans vegetation and bark, hover-gleans and hawks for adult and larval insects; eats berries in winter and sometimes visits feeders.
Voice: utters a flat, low *chet* or *chuck* call; male's song is a rapid 2-part chatter that drops in pitch and speeds up at the end.
Similar Species: *Yellow Warbler* (p. 305): plainer face; heavier bill; male has yellow crown, reddish orange breast streaks and is bright yellow overall. *MacGillivray's Warbler* (p. 313): larger; gray "hood"; prominent broken white eye ring.
Best Sites: *Summer:* deciduous and mixed woodlands, clearings and forest edges. *In migration:* Tahkenitch L., Douglas Co.; Oxbow Park (Lower Sandy R.); Foster Reservoir; Sutherlin-Winchester area; Deschutes River SP; Rhinehart Bridge.

YELLOW-BREASTED CHAT

Icteria virens

In some ways, the Yellow-breasted Chat is a typical wood-warbler—its bright yellow breast and intense curiosity are typical warbler traits. Yet it seems too large, a trifle too clumsy and has a most unwarbler-like song. Although its inclusion in the wood-warbler family has been questioned, molecular studies seem to support this grouping. • The Yellow-breasted Chat is sorely taxed when it tries to find a summer home. The riparian buffer zones of scrubby and brushy habitat that it likes are being degraded by livestock grazing and are becoming scarce as a result of urban sprawl, but some suitable protected areas remain where you can still enjoy this unique songbird. • The scientific name refers to the yellow underparts and olive green upperparts respectively.

ID: unmarked olive green upperparts; rich yellow (sometimes orange) breast and throat; buffy flanks; white belly and undertail coverts; white "spectacles" and "mustache"; heavy, dusky bill; long tail, often held upraised wrenlike.

Size: *L* 7 in; *W* 10 in.

Status: locally uncommon breeding summer resident and migrant from mid-April to late May and from late August to early October on the south coast, in western interior valleys and east of the Cascades; state-listed as sensitive.

Habitat: *Breeding:* dense streamside and bottomland willows and brush; open-country thickets; understory in open deciduous and mixed woodlands. *In migration:* almost any brushy habitat, including urban parks and overgrown gardens.

Nesting: low in a shrub or small tree; well-concealed, bulky nest of leaves, straw, weed stems and vine bark is thinly lined with fine weed stems and grass; female incubates 3–4 large, brown-marked creamy white eggs for 11 days; young fledge at 8 days.

Feeding: gleans vegetation for insects and berries; usually feeds low in thicket growth.

Voice: calls include *whoit, chack* and *kook;* male's song is an assorted series of whistles, squeaks, grunts, rattles and mews; male often sings after dusk and before dawn.

Similar Species: *Common Yellowthroat* (p. 314) and *MacGillivray's Warbler* (p. 313): much smaller; no white "spectacles" or "mustache"; finer bill; shorter tail.

Best Sites: Vernonia Log Pond; Sutherlin-Winchester area; Smith Rock SP; John Day Fossil Beds NM; McKay Creek NWR; Whitehorse CP, Josephine Co.; Grande Ronde R.; Rhinehart Bridge; main road between Frenchglen and Page Springs Campground; Succor Creek SP.

WESTERN TANAGER

Piranga ludoviciana

Few birds can match the tropical splendor of the tanagers. Four species of this Central and South American family have expanded northward into the United States. The Western Tanager, the most northerly breeding species, is the only one regularly seen in Oregon. • The male Western Tanager brings a splash of color to Oregon's foothills and lower mountain slopes. His difficult-to-learn song closely parallels the phrases of an American Robin's song, but the notes are somewhat hoarser, as if the bird had a sore throat, and it ends with a distinctive, hiccuplike *pit-a-tik*. • Female tanagers are more cryptically colored than males, and the female Western Tanager is no exception.

breeding

ID: stout, dull orangy bill; dark eyes; bluish gray legs. *Breeding male:* deep yellow overall with black back, wings and tail; 1 yellow wing bar and 1 white one; orangy red face and throat. *Nonbreeding male:* duller yellow; duller back; dusky wash on head and flanks; orangy only on forehead, lores and "chin." *Female:* like nonbreeding male, but with dusky back, paler upper wing bar, white belly and less orange on face.
Size: *L* 7 in; *W* 11½ in.
Status: common summer breeding resident and migrant from late April to mid-June and from late July to early October.
Habitat: *Breeding:* coniferous and mixed forests, locally in ponderosa pines. *In migration:* deciduous and riparian woodlands.
Nesting: usually in a fork of a horizontal conifer branch, well out from the trunk; loose cup nest of twigs, rootlets and moss is lined with hair and rootlets; female incubates 3–5 brown-marked blue eggs for 13 days; young fledge at 13–15 days.
Feeding: gleans vegetation and catches flying insects on the wing; eats wasps, beetles and other insects; also eats flower buds and small fruits.
Voice: soft, whistled calls are usual, but utters fast, rattling notes when agitated; male's song is a robinlike series of somewhat hoarse, slurred whistles.
Similar Species: *Female Bullock's Oriole* (p. 349): larger; gray wings; whitish belly; bright yellow head and breast; bluish bill. *Summer Tanager* and *Scarlet Tanager:* wing bars absent or vague; Summer has much heavier bill; females are more uniform greenish above and yellowish below.
Best Sites: Dabney SP; Larch Mt.; Scoggins Valley Park; Spencer Butte and Skinner Butte (Eugene); Waldo L.; Lake Selmac CP; Big Lake Campground; Tollgate; Spring Creek.

GREEN-TAILED TOWHEE

Pipilo chlorurus

The cryptically colored Green-tailed Towhee often goes unrecognized as a close relative of the Spotted Towhee, which sports a striking plumage of red, white and black. Yet, a few moments of observation reveals the Green-tailed Towhee's classic towhee foraging style: leaping back and forth in the dappled shade of the forest floor, it scratches away loose leaf litter and debris with both feet in its search for insects and hidden seeds. • Green-tailed Towhees rarely venture far from the dense, low understory of forest openings. When startled, they prefer to run for cover or flutter off, often "mewing" their annoyance, and nesting females scurry away mouselike if approached. In spring, male towhees gradually emerge from cover to produce a series of clear, whistled notes and raspy trills from an exposed woody perch.

ID: dull yellowish green back, wings and tail; bright yellowish edge on wings and tail; sooty gray neck and underparts; whitish belly; greenish undertail coverts; orangy rufous crown; gray stripe on white throat; gray face; conical, gray bill. *Juvenile:* brown-streaked whitish overall; yellowish green wings and tail.

Size: *L* 7 in; *W* 9½ in.

Status: rare to uncommon breeding summer resident on the lower eastern flanks of the Cascades and eastward, though very scarce north of Jefferson Co., and locally rare in the Siskiyou Mts.; uncommon migrant east of the Cascades in mid-spring and late summer.

Habitat: *Breeding:* dry foothills and canyons; open and brushy slopes; ponderosa pine–juniper forests with dense brush cover; mountain mahogany; riparian areas in dry, open country. *In migration:* brushy areas, including residential ones.

Nesting: on the ground or low in a bush; large, thick-walled nest of grass, bark, twigs and weed stems is lined with fine material; female incubates 3–4 heavily brown-spotted white eggs for 11 days; young fledge at 7–8 days.

Feeding: scratches the ground for insects, seeds and berries; drinks morning dew from leaves; occasional, flighty visits to feeders.

Voice: calls are thin and wheezy, sometimes mewing; male's song consists of several clipped notes, then a variable trill, such as *swee-too weet chur cheee-churr.*

Similar Species: none.

Best Sites: *Summer:* Indian Ford Campground and Cold Springs Campground (Sisters); Robert Sawyer Park and Tumalo SP (Bend); Cabin Lake Campground; Summer Lake WMA; Hart Mt.; Idlewild Campground; Fort Rock SP.

SPOTTED TOWHEE

Pipilo maculatus

Scratching for food on the forest floor, a Spotted Towhee puts both feet to use, its long claws revealing anything hidden in the leaf litter. It makes such a ruckus that most people hearing it expect to find a squirrel and are surprised to see a bird not much larger than a sparrow. • Towhees like tangled thickets and overgrown gardens, especially if blackberries or other small fruits are ripe for the taking. Many pairs nest in urban neighborhoods, where they take turns to scold the family cat or check out any suspicious sounds. • The male Spotted Towhee will often select a prominent perch to spit out his curious, trilled song, puffing out his chest and exposing his striking rufous flanks.

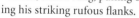

ID: bright rufous sides and flanks; white belly; buffy pink undertail coverts; red eyes; dark bill; pinkish legs; long claws. *Male:* white-spotted black back and wings; all-black head; black tail. *Female:* paler, with brown replacing black in plumage. *Juvenile:* buff-spotted upperparts; dark-streaked brownish underparts; pale-marked throat.

Size: *L* 7–8 in; *W* 10½ in.

Status: common year-round resident west of the Cascades; locally common breeding summer resident and locally uncommon migrant and winter resident east of the Cascades; migrants arrive from early March to mid-April; fall migration is from early September to late October.

Habitat: *Breeding:* wide variety of brushy habitats, especially in valleys and coastal lowlands. *In migration* and *winter:* brushy areas and scrub, including residential areas.

Nesting: low in a shrub or in a scratched depression on the ground; neat cup of leaves, grass, bark, twigs and rootlets is lined with fine grass and hair; male helps female incubate 3–4 brown-wreathed white eggs for 12–13 days; young fledge at 10–12 days.

Feeding: scratches the ground vigorously to uncover seeds and insects; also eats berries and acorns, especially in winter; occasionally visits feeding stations.

Voice: call note is a growling *to-heeeeee;* male's song starts with a few simple notes and then accelerates into a fast, raspy trill.

Similar Species: *Male Rose-breasted Grosbeak* (p. 366): all-dark back; white rump and underparts; triangular, rosy red breast; large, conical whitish bill; more white and red in wing.

Best Sites: widespread; Fern Ridge Reservoir; Lower Table Rock (near Medford); Thief Valley Reservoir; Powder R. Valley.

CALIFORNIA TOWHEE

Pipilo crissalis

Of the three very similar, mainly brown towhees that breed in parts of California, the recently distinguished California Towhee is the only species that has made it as far north as Oregon. In our state, this bird usually frequents brushy chaparral and canyon floors, but it is sometimes found in densely vegetated backyards and coastal scrub. • California Towhees are highly territorial, and males have even been known to attack their own reflections in low-mounted windows and shiny hubcaps. Yet California Towhees are ready to accept whatever their human neighbors have to offer. They regularly forage under picnic tables and around campsites, even approaching to within a few feet of an observer if they don't feel threatened. • If a pair becomes separated while foraging, one of the birds squeals atop a bush until its partner returns to view.

ID: brown or grayish brown overall; bright rufous undertail coverts; cinnamon patches around eyes and throat; pale, often bluish bill; pale pink legs; long claws; long, blackish brown tail. *Juvenile:* weakly streaked underparts.
Size: *L* 8½–9 in; *W* 11½ in.
Status: locally common year-round resident in the Rogue Valley and lower Klamath R. canyon and rare near Klamath Falls; very local year-round resident in southern Douglas Co.
Habitat: chaparral, especially oak–buckbrush woodlands; sagebrush–bitterbrush

hillsides; some brushy fields and farmyards; sometimes in towns.
Nesting: low in a shrub or bush; bulky, open cup of stems, twigs, grass and strips of inner bark is lined with hair, grass and rootlets; female incubates 3–4 bluish white eggs marked with brown and purple for 11 days; young are fed by both parents and fledge at 8 days.
Feeding: forages on the ground, scratching at leaf litter or soil in shaded cover; eats seeds and insects, with some berries and small fruits in fall and winter.
Voice: call is a high *peek;* male's song is a metallic, accelerating *tik-tik-tik-tiktiktitktitk.*
Similar Species: *Green-tailed Towhee* (p. 318): smaller; yellowish green upperparts; greenish undertail coverts; orangy rufous crown. *Juvenile Spotted Towhee* (p. 319): some spotting and streaking.
Best Sites: Merlin area; Tou Velle SP; "Lower Table Rock and Roxy Ann Butte (near Medford).

AMERICAN TREE SPARROW
Spizella arborea

You know winter is near when you start to find more than the occasional American Tree Sparrow among the local sparrow flocks. Quietly arriving from the north, this bird is easily identified by its two-tone bill and the central breast spot on its otherwise clear underparts. The American Tree Sparrow finds its place in brushy and shrubby areas alongside summering species and remains after many other species have moved on. By March, the lengthening days encourage a few birds to leave, and by mid-May every American Tree Sparrow has headed to its summer home in the arctic vegetation of Canada and Alaska. • Although both its common and scientific names (*arborea* means "tree") imply that it is a forest-dwelling bird, this sparrow prefers semi-open areas where trees are at a premium—a more appropriate name might be "Arctic Shrub Sparrow."

ID: mottled, brown and chestnut upperparts; 2 prominent white wing bars; chestnut shoulder line; buff sides; gray underparts; dark central breast spot; creamy undertail coverts; chestnut or rufous crown and eye line; gray face; white eye ring; gray-and-yellow bill; whitish throat; long, gray tail.
Size: *L* 6 in; *W* 9–9½ in.
Status: uncommon winter resident in northeastern Oregon from late October to mid-May; rare elsewhere east of the Cascades; very rare in western Oregon.
Habitat: riparian growth and low-elevation meadow brush.
Nesting: does not nest in Oregon.
Feeding: forages on the ground and in low shrubs; eats insects, spiders, seeds, buds, catkins and berries.

Voice: call is 3-note *tsee-dle-eat*; male's song of late winter and spring migration is a high, whistled *tseet-tseet,* then a short, sweet, musical series of slurred whistles.
Similar Species: *Nonbreeding Chipping Sparrow* (p. 322): smaller; streaked brown crown; long, pale buff "eyebrow"; thin, blackish eye line; yellowish pink bill; all-gray breast and underwings. *White-crowned Sparrow* (p. 335): slightly larger; all-pink or all-yellow bill; unmarked breast; brownish rump; black and white head stripes.
Best Sites: Umatilla NWR; Cold Springs NWR; Wildhorse Creek (Pendleton); McKay Creek NWR; Ladd Marsh WMA; Grande Ronde Valley; Crow Creek; Alvord Basin.

CHIPPING SPARROW

Spizella passerina

The Chipping Sparrow and the Dark-eyed Junco obviously do not share the same tailor, but they must have had the same song stylist. The subtle differences between their two songs are not easy to learn. The rapid trill of the Chipping Sparrow is slightly faster, drier and more mechanical, but the distinction is small. • Habitat preferences are often the best means of distinguishing unseen singers. The Chipping Sparrow is more likely to be found in open or semi-open woodlands, whereas the junco prefers darker, denser forests once it has left its wintering flocks. • Commonly nesting at eye level, the Chipping Sparrow offers the opportunity to study its courtship and nest-building rituals at close range. • The common name refers to this bird's call, and *passerina* is Latin for "little sparrow."

breeding

ID: dark eyes; dark eye line; pink legs; long tail. *Breeding:* dark-mottled brown back and wings; 2 white wing bars; gray "cheeks," nape, rump and underparts; chestnut "cap"; white "eyebrow"; white throat with thin, grayish "mustache." *Nonbreeding:* less distinct brown "cap"; buffy "eyebrow"; pink bill.
Size: *L* 5½ in; *W* 8½ in.
Status: common to scarce breeding summer resident and migrant throughout much of the state, though rare in migration along the coast, from late March to early November.
Habitat: *Breeding:* grassy clearings in forests; open or semi-open grassy woodlands. *In migration* and *winter:* open grasslands with brushy cover, chaparral, sagebrush scrub and residential woodlots and parks.

Nesting: low to mid-level in a conifer or oak, occasionally in a vine tangle; compact cup of grass, forb stalks and rootlets is lined with fur or hair; female incubates 2–5 blackish-marked bluish green eggs for 11–14 days; young fledge at 10 days.
Feeding: forages on the ground but also gleans in low foliage and trees for insects and seeds, especially those of grasses, dandelions and clovers.
Voice: usual call is a short, clipped *chip;* male's song is a simple, long, dull trill.
Similar Species: *Clay-colored Sparrow* (p. 366): streaked brown crown with white central stripe; pinkish or orangy bill; brownish rump; nonbreeding adult and 1st-winter bird have buff breast band and flanks. *American Tree Sparrow* (p. 321): slightly larger; dark central breast spot; usually redder crown and eye line; gray-and-yellow bill; buff wing linings.
Best Sites: widespread in any open woodland or brushy cover.

BREWER'S SPARROW

Spizella breweri

The Brewer's Sparrow is the ultimate in sparrow design—its plumage is so nondescript and its song so insectlike that it would go completely unnoticed in a brushy woodland filled with bird songs. Fortunately for birders, the Brewer's Sparrow favors treeless sagebrush plains and brushy habitats, where it is constantly in sight. The male's song, which usually lasts over 10 seconds, is a remarkable outburst of rapid, buzzy trills that constantly change in speed, pitch and quality. • Ranging east of the Cascades, the Brewer's Sparrow starts to form migrant flocks late in summer, and it is one of the commonest species in open-country flocks until its departure in midfall. • This bird's name honors Dr. Thomas Brewer, who made significant contributions to understanding the breeding behavior of North American birds in the 19th century.

breeding

ID: small, pink bill; unbroken white eye ring; pink legs; long tail. *Breeding:* streaked brown upperparts; light brown to whitish underparts; light throat; "cheek" patch with dark brown border. *Nonbreeding:* paler upperparts; faint head and throat stripes.
Size: *L* 5½ in; *W* 7½ in.
Status: locally common breeding summer resident east of the Cascades from mid-April to late September; very rare migrant in western Oregon.
Habitat: sagebrush; rocky, brushy breaks in lodgepole pine forests; greasewood flats; grassland shrubbery.
Nesting: in a low, dense shrub, usually sagebrush, or a small tree; small, compact cup of grass, forbs and rootlets is lined with fine materials and fur; pair incubates 3–4 bluish green eggs with brown marks for 11–13 days; young fledge at 8–9 days.
Feeding: usually forages on the ground and in low vegetation for insects, spiders and seeds; can eat seeds without water for up to 3 weeks.
Voice: usual call is a high-pitched *psst;* male's long song of interspersed buzzes and trills changes in speed and pitch.
Similar Species: *Clay-colored Sparrow* (p. 366): unstreaked rump; unstreaked gray nape; white "eyebrow"; grayer and more heavily patterned in breeding plumage; buffier, especially on underparts, in non-breeding plumage. *Chipping Sparrow* (p. 322): chestnut on crown and upperparts; grayer rump; black eye line; plainer "cheeks."
Best Sites: Prineville Reservoir; John Day Fossil Beds NM; Lower Klamath NWR; Fort Rock SP; Summer Lake WMA; Hart Mt.; Virtue Flats (Pleasant Valley); Diamond Craters; Malheur NWR; Ontario area.

VESPER SPARROW

Pooecetes gramineus

For birders who live on flat grasslands and shrub lands that teem with confusing little brown sparrows, the Vesper Sparrow offers welcome relief—its white-edged tail and deeply undulating flight are reliable identification features. The Vesper is also known for its bold and easily distinguished song, which is often heard in the evening (*vesper* means "evening" in Latin). • The Vesper Sparrow's nest is usually in a grassy hollow at the base of a low shrub, thus providing camouflage, a windbreak and an umbrella. Unfortunately, changing agricultural practices have reduced the amount of preferred habitat to a point where the Vesper Sparrow is becoming rare in much of its breeding range, particularly west of the Cascades in Oregon.

ID: streaked brown upperparts; whitish underparts and undertail; pink bill; white eye ring; pink legs; white-edged tail. *Breeding:* chestnut shoulder patch; dark-streaked breast; faintly streaked flanks; pale "cheek" patch with brown border; dark "mustache." *Nonbreeding:* paler; buff sides.

Size: *L* 6 in; *W* 10 in.

Status: common breeding summer resident and migrant from early March to April and from August to early October east of the Cascades and in the mountains of the Rogue Valley watershed, and locally uncommon in the Willamette Valley, Umpqua Valley and coastal Curry Co.; *affinis* ssp. is state-listed as sensitive.

Habitat: grasslands and farmlands. *Breeding:* sagebrush; dry, grassy hillsides. *In migration:* low desert brush areas, open grassy areas and fields.

Nesting: in an excavated depression; well-concealed, bulky, loose nest of grass, forbs and rootlets; pair incubates 3–4 brown-marked creamy or greenish white eggs for 11–13 days; young fledge at 7–14 days; 1–2 broods per year.

Feeding: walks or runs to catch grasshoppers, beetles and cutworms; picks up seeds; not known to drink or bathe in water.

Voice: short, hard *chip* call; male's song, usually from an elevated perch or in a brief song flight, begins with 4 low notes, with the 2nd higher in pitch, then a bubbly trill of *here-here there-there, everybody-down-the-hill.*

Similar Species: *Savannah Sparrow* (p. 328): pale "eyebrow"; stronger flank streaking; tail dark below, with brown or pale edges; weak, buzzy song. *Lark Sparrow* (p. 325): chestnut head pattern; heavier bill; dark tail with white-tipped outer feathers; slow-paced, uneven song.

Best Sites: widespread in grassland habitats.

LARK SPARROW

Chondestes grammacus

Singing atop small bushes or low rock outcrops in their rural haunts, male Lark Sparrows reminded early naturalists of the famed Sky Lark (*Alauda arvensis*) of Eurasia and North Africa. Lark Sparrow males do occasionally indulge themselves in short display flights, but they do not fly as high or as skillfully as the Sky Lark. • Typically seen in dry scrubland, open oak woodlands and edge habitats, Lark Sparrows occasionally venture into meadows, grassy forest openings and other wooded areas, where they sometimes join Vesper Sparrows and Savannah Sparrows. Their unique tail pattern easily identifies them in such situations and during migration, when small flocks of Lark Sparrows are regularly seen foraging alongside juncos, sparrows and towhees in suburban parks and gardens.

ID: brown-streaked back and wings; dark spot on pale breast; buffy gray sides and flanks; chestnut "cheeks" and white-striped crown; black eye line and "mustache"; heavy, grayish bill; grayish brown rump and tail with white-tipped darker outer feathers.

Size: *L* 6½ in; *W* 11 in.

Status: locally common breeding summer resident and migrant east of the Cascades from late March to early October; uncommon year-round resident in the Rogue Valley; scarce local breeding summer resident in the Umpqua Valley; rare visitor to the coast and the remainder of western Oregon.

Habitat: grasslands with scattered bushes and open woodlands. *Breeding:* farmlands, open pine and juniper forests and sagebrush.

Nesting: in a depression in the ground, or in a shrub or rock crevice; bulky, twig-based shrub nest is covered with a cup of grass and forbs and lined with fine materials; female incubates 4–5 dusky-marked, creamy or grayish white eggs for 11–12 days; young fledge at 9–10 days.

Feeding: walks or hops on the ground to find seeds; also eats grasshoppers and other invertebrates.

Voice: utters a finchlike *pik* flight call and a loud, high alarm call; male's song, occasionally given on the wing, has a variable pace and rhythm with rattling trills.

Similar Species: *Vesper Sparrow* (p. 324) and *Savannah Sparrow* (p. 328): heavily streaked breast and sides; plainer face; thinner bill; less white on upper tail.

Best Sites: Warner Valley; Hart Mt.; Thief Valley Reservoir; Virtue Flats (Pleasant Valley); Diamond Craters; Malheur NWR; Alvord Basin.

BLACK-THROATED SPARROW

Amphispiza bilineata

The Black-throated Sparrow shares with the Sage Sparrow the arid, sagebrush-dominated habitats of eastern Oregon, where they often forage together for seeds and insects. Quite different and easily distinguished as adults, they are almost identical in juvenile plumage. • In its hot, dry habitat, the Black-throated Sparrow is usually without any source of standing or flowing water. To survive without drinking water, it has evolved a super-efficient physiology that allows it to extract and recycle moisture obtained from its food. • Because Black-throated Sparrows nest on the ground, the nestlings and eggs often fall prey to a variety of lizards, snakes, ground squirrels and other terrestrial predators.

ID: grayish brown back and crown; dark brown wings; plain, pale gray underparts; black face with broad, white "eyebrow" and "mustache"; heavy, bluish bill; buff undertail coverts. *Juvenile:* faintly streaked back; indistinct wing bars; gray throat; faintly streaked band across breast; weaker head pattern.
Size: *L* 5½ in; *W* 7¾ in.
Status: locally uncommon breeding summer resident and migrant in southeastern Oregon from mid-April to early September; rare nonbreeding spring and summer resident elsewhere east of the Cascades; very rare stray in western Oregon; state-listed as sensitive.
Habitat: barren and brushy hillsides; brush and scrub; open, brushy flatlands.

Nesting: on the ground sheltered by tall weeds, in a shrub or cactus, or in a rocky cliff crevice; sturdy nest of grass and plant fibers is lined with fine grass, rootlets and hair; female incubates 3–4 bluish white eggs for up to 12 days.
Feeding: forages on the ground for seeds; gleans foliage and flycatches for insects; survives without water in winter and spring by eating green vegetation and insects.
Voice: calls and song consist of high, tinkling notes and phrases.
Similar Species: *Sage Sparrow* (p. 327): back is usually streaked; dark-bordered white throat; dark breast spot; gray head; short "eyebrow"; straight-ended tail; juvenile has heavily streaked underparts; runs with tail held high.
Best Sites: Alvord Rim; Diamond Craters, near Coyote Buttes (Malheur NWR); along the gravel road west of Fields.

SAGE SPARROW

Amphispiza belli

Oregon's Sage Sparrows are almost entirely of the pale *nevadensis* subspecies, which forages and nests in areas dominated by sagebrush. Each year, males return to the same breeding site, which they defend by singing from exposed perches. Breeding pairs often raise two broods per year, usually producing three or four young per brood. The production of so many young may be in response to high predation. • The Sage Sparrow can often be distinguished from other sparrows by its habits of wagging and twitching its tail when perched and holding it upward in wrenlike fashion during short runs. • John Cassin of the Philadelphia Academy of Natural Sciences chose the scientific name for the Sage Sparrow in honor of John Graham Bell, the taxidermist who collected the first scientific specimen of this bird in the mid-1800s.

ID: streaked, pale brown upperparts and wings; white underparts; dark "V" patch on breast; buff gray flanks; gray blue head; short, white "eyebrow"; unbroken white eye ring; white "mustache" and dark-bordered throat; stubby, bluish bill; long, dusky legs.
Size: *L* 5–6 in; *W* 8–8½ in.
Status: locally common breeding summer resident and rare in winter east of the Cascades, with birds mostly arriving as early as late February and leaving by October; very rare stray in western Oregon; state-listed as sensitive.
Habitat: arid sagebrush and greasewood, occasionally in grasslands with scattered shrubs.

Nesting: low in sagebrush, occasionally on the ground; bulky nest of twigs, grass, forbs and bark is lined with grass, plant down and sometimes hair; female incubates 2–4 dark-spotted bluish white eggs for 13–16 days; young fledge at 9–11 days.
Feeding: forages on the ground and gleans foliage for insects, spiders and seeds.
Voice: calls are usually in a series of high, tinkling notes; male's song is a mechanical, uninspired mixture of notes: *slip, slip freeee slip-slip free you.*
Similar Species: *Black-throated Sparrow* (p. 326): unstreaked back and underparts; stronger facial pattern; shorter legs; buff undertail coverts; more white in undertail; runs with tail held flat.
Best Sites: Diamond Craters; Malheur NWR; Alvord Desert.

SAVANNAH SPARROW

Passerculus sandwichensis

Anyone wanting to study songbird plumage variations might well consider choosing the Savannah Sparrow as a model. At least seven subspecies visit California at various times of year, and the situation is not that different in Oregon. • Savannah Sparrows are common in open, grassy country, where their plumage conceals them perfectly among tall grasses. They like to remain hidden, often scurrying like feathered voles low in cover or making short, low flights to clumps of concealing grass. • Savannah Sparrows roost on the ground in short grass in small, compact groups. Disturbed migrating or wintering flocks will scatter, flushing from the ground one by one like miniature quails, and rejoin later.

ID: grayish brown head and dark-streaked back; medium to reddish brown wings; dark-streaked white breast and white or buffy flanks; white belly and undertail coverts; dark "V" spot on breast; pale throat; dark eye line and "mustache"; pale "eyebrow"; pink bill.
Size: *L* 5–6 in; *W* 6–7 in.
Status: common breeding summer resident and locally uncommon winter resident in the Willamette Valley, along the coast and east of the Cascades, very local in the Rogue Valley; common migrant throughout Oregon from March to early June and from August to October.
Habitat: *Breeding:* most grassy habitats, including open forest glades. *In migration and winter:* grasslands and farmlands;

lakeshores, coastal dunes and salt marshes; residential parks.
Nesting: on the ground, usually in a natural or excavated depression; small, well-concealed cup of coarse grass is lined with finer materials; pair incubates 3–5 brown-marked pale greenish blue eggs for 12–13 days; young fledge at 7–10 days.
Feeding: forages on the ground for insects, spiders and grass seeds; also eats small snails.
Voice: gives a high, thin *tsit* call; male's song is a high-pitched, clear, buzzy *tea tea tea teaaa today.*
Similar Species: *Vesper Sparrow* (p. 324): chestnut shoulder patch; tail is white below and prominently white-edged above; undulating flight to a high perch. *Lincoln's Sparrow* (p. 332): buffier overall, particularly on breast; gray or olive face; all-brown tail; prefers scrubby cover.
Best Sites: widespread in grassy habitats, especially along the coast in migration.

GRASSHOPPER SPARROW

Ammodramus savannarum

The Grasshopper Sparrow is one of Oregon's most enigmatic summer songbirds. Its loose colonies are forever shifting from one place to the next in search of the optimal grassland nesting and foraging sites. • This species is named not for its diet, which consists largely of insects much smaller than grasshoppers, but for its buzzy, insectlike perch singing. The flight song that the male Grasshopper Sparrow uses in pursuit of females, however, is so high pitched as to be inaudible to humans. • The Grasshopper Sparrow prefers to run from danger rather than fly or hide, so the genus name *Ammodramus*— Greek for "sand runner"—is appropriate, and so is *savannarum*, in reference to the bird's grassland habitat.

ID: chestnut-streaked nape and back; dark-centered wing feathers with rusty and white tips; plain buff underparts; brown "cap" with whitish middle stripe; sloping forehead; buffy face; large, dark eyes; thick, pale bill; pale pink legs.

Size: *L* 4–5 in; *W* 7–7½ in.

Status: irregular and local breeding summer resident, mainly in north-central, east-central and southwestern Oregon and at a few Willamette Valley locations; rare migrant anywhere; state-listed as sensitive.

Habitat: open grasslands, particularly dry, ungrazed ones in foothills, but also on prairies and old fields with scattered bushes.

Nesting: semi-colonial; in a low depression well concealed by overhanging grass and forbs; nest of dried grass, arched or domed at the back, is lined with fine materials;

female incubates 4–5 russet-marked white eggs for 11–12 days; young fledge at 9 days.

Feeding: forages on the ground and in low vegetation for insects, other invertebrates and the seeds of grasses and forbs.

Voice: calls are high-pitched and thin; male's *tea-tea-tea zeeeeeeeeee* song is 1–3 high, thin, whistled notes followed by a high, faint, buzzy trill.

Similar Species: *Brewer's Sparrow* (p. 323): grayer overall; less patterned back; streaked crown; rounder head; dark "mustache"; smaller bill; prefers sagebrush.

Best Sites: foothills of the Blue Mts.; eastern Columbia River Basin, especially in Morrow, Umatilla and Gilliam Counties, including along OR 74 just west of Nye Junction and in the Blackhorse Canyon area near Heppner; Baskett Slough NWR; near Fern Ridge Reservoir.

FOX SPARROW

Passerella iliaca

Scratching away leaf litter and duff to expose seeds and insects, the Fox Sparrow forages much like a towhee. • Several races of the Fox Sparrow, which is one of North America's largest sparrows, occur in Oregon. The only birds that breed in Oregon are the gray-and-rusty ones that nest in the mountains of the east and the southwest. The medium brown birds commonly seen wintering or in migration in western Oregon spend their summers on the Pacific Coast of Canada and Alaska, and there are also a few records of the widespread, more easterly race that has a reddish coloration like that of a red fox. Each race has a different version of beautiful, warbled song.

ID: rufous-and-gray or brown upperparts; mostly white underparts with lines of black, gray, brown or rufous spots; thick, gray or yellowish bill; dark eyes; pinkish legs.

Size: *L* 7 in; *W* 10½ in.

Status: uncommon breeding summer resident eastward from the western slope of the Cascades and in desert mountains; common migrant and winter resident west of the Cascades, uncommon migrant and rare winter resident in eastern Oregon; migration from March to early May and from early September to late October.

Habitat: *Breeding:* dense brush and riparian thickets, in open ponderosa pine forests. *In migration* and *winter:* dense brush in open and forested habitats, including residential areas and coastal thickets.

Nesting: on the ground, low in a shrub, rarely in a tree; bulky nest of grass, moss, lichen, rootlets, shredded bark, leaves and twigs; female incubates 2–5 russet-marked pale green eggs for 12–14 days; young fledge at 9–11 days.

Feeding: scratches the ground to uncover seeds, berries and invertebrates; feeds largely on small fruits, especially blackberries, in fall and early winter; visits feeders in winter and in migration.

Voice: calls are explosive *tak* notes; burry, whistled songs of coastal males sound patchy and uninspired; interior birds have a purer, ringing song with noticeable trills.

Similar Species: *Song Sparrow* (p. 331): streaked upperparts; breast and sides more streaked than spotted; brown-striped grayish face; slimmer bill.

Best Sites: widespread in brushy habitats and low 2nd-growth, best seen in winter.

SONG SPARROW
Melospiza melodia

When amateur birdwatcher Margaret Morse Nice began studying plumage variations in the widespread Song Sparrow in the 1920s, she had no idea how much interest she would eventually trigger among professional ornithologists. We now know that the dowdy Song Sparrow probably has the greatest variation in plumage of any North American songbird, which suggests that it has readily adapted to differences in factors such as climate, soil coloration and food selection. Given time and some separation, these subspecies could become so different that they would one day become reproductively incompatible and thus distinct species.

• Other sparrows may have more beautiful songs, but the complexity, rhythm and sweetness of the male Song Sparrow's springtime rhapsodies justify the name.

ID: streaked, rufous-and-brown upperparts; thickly brown-streaked gray or brown flanks and breast with smudgy spot; whitish belly; grayish face; brown or rufous crown (with pale center stripe) and eye line; thick, gray bill; pinkish legs.

Size: *L* 5–6 in; *W* 8–8½ in.

Status: common permanent resident; some migratory movement and withdrawal from higher elevations in winter.

Habitat: *Breeding:* deciduous brush in forests and open country; near water or in lush vegetation in chaparral, riparian willows, marshy habitats and residential areas.

Nesting: usually beneath a grass tuft or in a shrub or brush pile; bulky nest of twigs, bark strips, grass, forbs and leaves; female incubates 3–4 russet-marked, pale blue or green eggs for 12–14 days; young fledge at 9–12 days; frequent 2nd brood.

Feeding: gleans the ground and foliage for insects and seeds; coastal birds eat crustaceans and mollusks; eats berries in winter; may visit feeders for seeds.

Voice: calls include a short *tsip* and nasal *tchep;* male's song is 1–4 bright introductory notes, such as *sweet, sweet, sweet,* followed by a buzzy *towee* and a short, descending trill.

Similar Species: *Fox Sparrow* (p. 330): plainer upperparts and head; lines of spots rather than streaks. *Lincoln's Sparrow* (p. 332): daintier; gray or olive back and face; brown-streaked buffy breast and flanks; more white on belly; buffy "mustache," finer bill.

Best Sites: widespread, including residential areas.

LINCOLN'S SPARROW

Melospiza lincolnii

The subtle beauty of a Lincoln's Sparrow's plumage is greater than the sum of its feathers. The colors are not spectacular, yet they match and give the bird a distinctive, well-groomed look lacking in most other sparrows. • The Lincoln's Sparrow usually skulks among tall grasses and dense, brushy growth, but when the male sings, he sheds his shy nature and issues territorial challenges from a prominent perch. • Lincoln's Sparrows prefer wetter conditions than most sparrows, and most Oregon breeders occupy eastern mountain territories, often freshly emerged from melting snow and swollen streams. In fall, these birds generally move downslope or leave the state; meanwhile, others travel south from Alaska and Canada to join wintering sparrow flocks in our area.

ID: dark-streaked gray upperparts, often with rufous on wings and tail; lightly brown-streaked, buff-washed breast and flanks; white belly; peaked, dark brown "cap" with gray median stripe; gray or olive nape and "eyebrow"; brown facial lines.

Size: *L* 5 in; *W* 7½ in.

Status: locally common breeding summer resident in the Cascades, Blue Mts. and Wallowa Mts.; common migrant and uncommon winter resident west of the Cascades; common migrant and rare in winter in eastern Oregon; migration throughout spring and from late August through October.

Habitat: *Breeding:* wet meadows with willow patches; streamside marshes; deciduous brush. *In migration* and *winter:* tall grass and dense brush in wet areas; coastal brush; salt-marsh margins.

Nesting: in a grass tussock or a shallow depression in moss; well-hidden nest of grass or sedges is lined with fine grass and hair; female incubates 4–5 russet-marked pale green eggs for 12–14 days; young fledge at 9–12 days.

Feeding: scratches on the ground for insects, spiders, millipedes and seeds; occasionally visits feeders.

Voice: calls include a buzzy *zeee* and a *tsup;* male sings a musical mixture of buzzes, trills and warbled notes, often at night.

Similar Species: *Song Sparrow* (p. 331): stockier; untidier and coarser streaking; central breast spot; heavier bill; less bubbly song; prefers more open, shrubby areas by wetlands. *Brewer's* (p. 323), *Clay-colored* (p. 366) and *Chipping* (p. 322) *sparrows:* paler upperparts; unstreaked underparts; yellowish or pinkish bill; simpler, buzzy or trilling songs.

Best Sites: *Summer:* mountain habitats. *In migration:* widespread in wet, brushy sites.

SWAMP SPARROW
Melospiza georgiana

In eastern and northern parts of North America, the Swamp Sparrow is one of the most common wetland inhabitants, sharing its habitat with blackbirds, wrens and yellowthroats. It is perfectly suited to life around water. Because it eats mostly insects and fewer hard seeds than other sparrows, its bill and associated muscles are comparatively small. • The male Swamp Sparrow's song would not win any awards, but in this bird's open habitat, a simple, dry, rattling trill is all that is required to gain the necessary attention from females. • The first state record of this eastern species was in 1955, and few representatives were seen until the early 1970s. Since then, the Swamp Sparrow has been recorded in small numbers, especially at coastal locations.

nonbreeding

ID: black and buff stripes on back; rusty brown wings and tail; grayish breast; buffy chestnut flanks; dark-bordered whitish throat; small, grayish bill with yellow base; dark stripe behind eye; pink legs. *Breeding male:* chestnut crown with pale median stripe; largely gray face and nape. *Breeding female:* like breeding male, but with dark brown crown. *Nonbreeding:* weaker brown crown; olive tinge on face; buffier gray on breast.
Size: *L* 5–6 in; *W* 7–7½ in.
Status: locally uncommon migrant and winter resident along the coast from early October to early April; rare migrant and winter resident at lower elevations in western Oregon; very rare east of the Cascades.

Habitat: marshy river mouths; wet grass–sedge meadows; cattail marsh edges; brushy habitats.
Nesting: does not nest in Oregon.
Feeding: forages on the ground, on mud and in low marshland vegetation for insects and seeds; rarely visits feeders.
Voice: gives an emphatic *tchip* call; male's simple, trill song has separated notes.
Similar Species: *White-throated Sparrow* (p. 334): larger; indistinct white wing bars; black or dark brown crown; more clearly defined white throat; yellow lores; white or light buff "eyebrow." *White-crowned Sparrow* (p. 335): larger; unmarked buffy gray underparts; yellowish to pinkish bill; black and white crown stripes.
Best Sites: Lower Coquille Valley; Milicoma Wetlands (near Coos Bay); near river mouths that empty into Tillamook Bay.

WHITE-THROATED SPARROW

Zonotrichia albicollis

L isten to almost any film soundtrack that features a woodland setting, and you are almost sure to hear the unmistakable, whistled song of the White-throated Sparrow, even though this forest songbird's breeding range is limited largely to Canada and only reaches into the United States around the Great Lakes and the northern Eastern Seaboard. • In Oregon, a few White-throated Sparrows join the overwintering flocks of White-crowned Sparrows and Golden-crowned Sparrows in the lowlands. Most of these White-throats stay in the brushy fields and hedgerows, but a few venture away from these open habitats to visit bird feeders, where they are often the first "rare birds" to be identified by novice birders. • The especially handsome white-striped White-throated Sparrows are about as common as the tan-striped ones, and the two morphs often mate with each other.

tan-striped morph

ID: 2-tone patterned brown back; rufous-marked brown wing with 2 indistinct white bars; pale brown rump and tail; finely streaked grayish brown breast and flanks; whitish belly; pale gray bill; dark eye line; pink legs. *White-striped morph:* sharply defined white throat patch; black crown with bold white median stripe and "eyebrow"; bright yellow lores. *Tan-striped morph:* brown-tinged neck and flanks; divided white throat patch; smudgier facial markings; light tan "eyebrow" and median crown stripe; fainter yellow lores.
Size: *L* 6–7 in; *W* 9 in.
Status: uncommon migrant and winter resident, especially in the west, from mid-September to late May.

Habitat: woodlands with brush, brushy patches in open country and residential areas; often associates with Golden-crowned Sparrows.
Nesting: does not nest in Oregon.
Feeding: scratches the ground for insects, spiders, millipedes, snails and seeds; also eats small fruits; occasionally visits feeders.
Voice: call is a distinctive, sharp *chink;* foraging flocks keep in touch with low, chuckling calls; male's song, seldom heard here, is a series of clear and distinct whistles.
Similar Species: *White-crowned Sparrow* (p. 335): duller rufous on wings; brown flanks; yellowish to pinkish bill; more peaked head; uniformly gray face, throat and breast; buzzy, trilled song. *Golden-crowned Sparrow* (p. 336): partly yellow crown; dull gray face and underparts; broad, black "eyebrow."
Best Sites: *Winter:* Sauvie I.; Portland area; Forest Grove; Cascade Gateway Park (Salem); William L. Finley NWR; Fern Ridge Reservoir; Alton Baker Park (Eugene); Roseburg; Whitehorse CP, Josephine Co.

WHITE-CROWNED SPARROW

Zonotrichia leucophrys

The ubiquitous White-crowned Sparrow is highly visible and audible at its breeding grounds and is a common member of sparrow flocks that winter in the lowlands. One of the most common of the wintering sparrows, the White-crown enlivens dull situations in brushy expanses and suburban parks and gardens with its perky attitude and bright song. • The White-crown is one of North America's most studied sparrows. It has given scientists an intriguing, and somewhat confusing, insight into avian speciation and the geographic variation in song dialects. • Most breeders east of the Cascades are of the black-lored interior race, *Z.l. oriantha*, whereas those nesting in western Oregon are of the pale-lored coastal Pacific race, *Z.l. pugetensis*.

ID: black-striped brown back; lightly rufous-marked brown wing with 2 white bars; buff or brown flanks; brownish rump; clear gray underparts; pale undertail coverts; black stripe on each side of white crown stripe; broad, white "eyebrow"; black eye line; pinkish to yellow bill and legs; black, white or gray lores.

Size: *L* 7 in; *W* 9½ in.

Status: common breeding summer resident and migrant; locally common winter resident; spring migration is from late March to mid-May; fall migrants arrive from early September to late October.

Habitat: *Breeding:* shrubby areas, especially along the coast and in the mountains. *In migration* and *winter:* brushy areas, sometimes residential ones.

Nesting: on the ground or in a shrub or small conifer; neat nest is lined with fine materials; female incubates 3–5 russet-marked pale greenish blue eggs for 11–14 days; young fledge at 7–12 days; male feeds young after the female starts a 2nd brood.

Feeding: forages on the ground for seeds and insects; gleans foliage and hawks for insects; also eats plant buds and similar items; visits feeders.

Voice: high *seet* and crisp *pink* calls; male's song is a repeated *I gotta go see-see now;* coastal birds sing a cleaner and more rapid 4-part song than interior birds.

Similar Species: *Golden-crowned Sparrow* (p. 336): yellow crown stripe; gray or gray-and-yellowish bill; no white on head. *White-throated Sparrow* (p. 334): more rufous in wings; clearly defined white throat; pale gray bill; yellow lores.

Best Sites: widespread.

GOLDEN-CROWNED SPARROW
Zonotrichia atricapilla

Shortly before Golden-crowned Sparrows leave their winter quarters in Oregon's roadside hedgerows, residential parks and neighborhoods to head north, they acquire the bold, black "eyebrow" and bright golden crown of their breeding plumage and fine-tune their songs. Unlike many wintering birds, male Golden-crowns regularly sing throughout the colder months. • While foraging for seeds and invertebrates, these sociable sparrows team up with other ground-feeding birds, especially White-crowned Sparrows and Dark-eyed Juncos, as they scour shrubby open ground, dense brush and backyards. • This largest of the *Zonotrichia* sparrows nests in the weather-beaten subalpine meadow-edges and tundra of the western Canadian mountains and Alaska, where its dreamy, whistled song is often the last sound snowline campers hear at night, as well as their morning wake-up call.

nonbreeding

ID: buff and black streaks on brown back; rufous-tinged brownish wing with 2 white bars; light brown rump; gray underparts; pale rufous or tan streaking on sides and flanks; gray face. *Breeding:* broad, black "cap" with median stripe of yellow and white; yellow-ish lower mandible. *Nonbreeding:* black in crown patch mostly absent.

Size: *L* 7 in; *W* 9½ in.

Status: common migrant and winter resident from mid-September to mid-May west of the Cascades; locally common migrant east of the Cascades, except rare in the northeast; uncommon winter resident in central Oregon and rare to the east.

Habitat: brush patches; brushy woodland edges at lower elevations; willows and forest edges at higher elevations.

Nesting: does not nest in Oregon.

Feeding: scratches the ground for insects and seeds; also eats berries and other small fruits, moss capsules, buds, blossoms and fresh leaves; visits bird feeders, often with White-crowned Sparrows.

Voice: gives a sharp, loud *seek* call; male's usual song is a 3-note whistle, but birds from the Canadian Rockies add a slow trill.

Similar Species: *White-crowned Sparrow* (p. 335): black and white stripes on head; pinkish to yellow bill. *White-throated Sparrow* (p. 334): clearly defined white throat; black and white (or tan) head stripes; yellow lores.

Best Sites: widespread in western Oregon.

DARK-EYED JUNCO
Junco hyemalis

The Dark-eyed Junco is a widespread sparrow with easily recognizable subspecies, several of which are found in Oregon. The brownish-sided, black-headed "Oregon Junco" is the common nesting and year-round resident in Oregon, and the mostly gray "Slate-colored Junco," sporting its black "mask," is an uncommon migrant and winter resident. Other subspecies can be expected in Oregon as well. • Juncos are nervous and flighty. The scissorlike flash of their white outer tail feathers is a familiar sight along rural roadsides and mountain trails. When they aren't nesting, they are gregarious, flocking in shrubby openings that offer open ground on which to search for seeds. These birds are routine visitors to backyard feeders, where they typically form the center of large, mixed-species sparrow flocks.

"Oregon Junco"

♂

ID: white belly and undertail coverts; pink bill; large, dark eyes; pinkish legs; gray or brownish rump and tail with prominent white outer feathers. *"Oregon" male:* reddish brown back with paler sides and flanks; gray-and-brown wings; black "hood" and breast. *"Oregon" female:* gray instead of black.
Size: *L* 6 in; *W* 9–9½ in.
Status: common breeding permanent resident, increasing in lowlands in winter; several races are often present in winter.
Habitat: *Breeding:* coniferous and deciduous forests; riparian areas within forests and in open country; residential parks and woodlots. *In migration* and *winter:* brushy, open country, towns and forest edges at lower elevations.

Nesting: usually on the ground, in a depression, or low in a shrub or tree; deep cup of coarse grass, moss, rootlets, bark and twigs; female incubates 3–5 chestnut-marked pale blue eggs for 12–13 days; young fledge at 9–13 days, leaving the nest early if disturbed.
Feeding: gleans on the ground and in low vegetation for seeds, insects and spiders; also hawks for flying insects; eats berries and visits feeders in fall and winter.
Voice: call is a high, often-repeated, clicking *stip;* wintering flocks keep up a constant ticking chorus; male's song is a brief trill.
Similar Species: *Spotted Towhee* (p. 319): much larger; red eyes; white-dotted black (male) or brown (female) back and wings; brilliant rufous sides and flanks; buff undertail coverts.
Best Sites: widespread in most woodland habitats.

LAPLAND LONGSPUR

Calcarius lapponicus

Longspurs are small songbirds of mostly treeless country that breed on extensive plains or tundra. Of the four North American species, only the Lapland Longspur occurs in any numbers in Oregon. It is best found by inspecting roaming flocks of Horned Larks, Snow Buntings and American Pipits. • A Lapland Longspur's extremely long claws aid it in finding food, but they are not suited to gripping branches, so this bird prefers perches such as flat-topped boulders, logs or posts on which it can spread its toes. • Males arriving here in fall have long since molted out of their spectacular breeding plumage, and most birds leave again by March, but a few later males may already be sporting their unmistakable black-and-rufous breeding colors.

nonbreeding

ID: back and wings are mottled with black, white and brown; rufous patch and 2 thin, white bars on wing; streaked gray rump; white underparts; blackish legs; long claws. *Breeding male:* boldly dark-streaked flanks; black crown, face, throat and mid-breast; white (often partly yellow) "L" stripe from eye to upper breast; chestnut nape; yellow bill. *Female* and *nonbreeding male:* like breeding male, but nape and black areas on head and breast look "washed out," and white areas on head and flanks may be buffy; pinkish bill. **Size:** *L* 6 in; *W* 11½ in. **Status:** uncommon migrant from early September to early November along the coast and then rare until early May; locally uncommon in the Klamath Basin from October to March. **Habitat:** dunes, estuary edges and plowed and fallow farmlands. **Nesting:** does not nest in Oregon. **Feeding:** forages on the ground in flocks for seeds, such as waste grain, and invertebrates, including spiders. **Voice:** mellow, whistled contact calls; rattled *tri-di-dit* and descending *teew* flight calls; male's flight song is a rapid, slurred warble.

Similar Species: *Vesper Sparrow* (p. 324): less contrasting facial pattern than nonbreeding Lapland Longspur; pink bill and legs; broader wings; perches in trees and bushes. *Chestnut-collared Longspur:* smaller; breeding male has black belly and pale buff throat; other plumages show little color.

Best Sites: Clatsop Spit; Nehalem Meadows; Bayocean Spit; North Spit (Coos Bay); Klamath WMA; Lower Klamath NWR.

SNOW BUNTING

Plectrophenax nivalis

When late fall frosts settle on Oregon's northeastern grasslands and northern coastal dunelands, Snow Buntings are surely close behind. They arrive in fall and endure winter in tight, wandering flocks, often with a few Lapland Longspurs mixed in, using their long hind claws to scratch away the snow in a search for seeds and waste grains scattered beneath. • As spring approaches, the warm rufous tones of the winter plumage fade to leave the male with a decidedly formal black-and-white look. • One bird took the trek to its breeding grounds in the Arctic a little too far. It was reported close to the North Pole, thus setting a record not known to have been beaten or matched by any other songbird.

nonbreeding

ID: stubby bill; dark eyes; black legs. *Breeding male:* brilliant white with black back, wing tips, "wrist" patch and bill. *Breeding female:* dark areas browner than on male; white mottling on back, and more extensive on wing; faint dark streaking on crown, "cheeks" and nape; dark gray bill. *Nonbreeding:* dark-streaked rufous back and rump; warm, golden rufous crown, "cheeks" and partial breast band; yellow bill.
Size: *L* 6–7 in; *W* 14 in.
Status: irruptive winter resident in northeastern Oregon; rare winter resident

elsewhere, mainly along the coast, from early October to mid-April.
Habitat: open country, especially farmlands and grasslands; coastal sand dunes and beaches.
Nesting: does not nest in Oregon.
Feeding: forages on the ground in large flocks; diet includes insects, spiders, seeds and buds; spring migrants eat fresh leaves.
Voice: call is a whistled *tew;* flocks keep up a constant twittering on the ground and especially in flight.
Similar Species: *McKay's Bunting* (only one Oregon record): more white on back, wings and head for each plumage.
Best Sites: Clatsop Spit; Bayocean Spit; North Spit (Coos Bay); OK Gulch (Crow Creek).

BLACK-HEADED GROSBEAK

Pheucticus melanocephalus

Almost any spring or summer visit to deciduous woodlands will reveal Black-headed Grosbeaks. Between late April and early July, the first sign is often the robinlike songs of the males as they advertise their territories with extended bouts of complex, accented caroling. Meanwhile, the females forage and conduct the household chores within dense foliage cover, frequently betraying their presence with sharp, woodpecker-like calls that reassure the males. • Characteristic of deciduous habitats, even ones within broken conifer forests, Black-headed Grosbeaks are sometimes found alongside Steller's Jays in campgrounds and picnic sites; during migration, they also visit feeders.

ID: heavy, conical, bluish gray bill; pinkish lower mandible; pale bluish legs. *Breeding male:* white-streaked dark brown back; dark brown wing with 2 white bars; orangy chestnut neck, breast, flanks and rump; yellowish belly; brownish black head. *Breeding female:* paler upperparts than male; buffy to whitish neck and underparts; white "eyebrow" and "mustache."

Size: *L* 7–8 in; *W* 12–13 in.

Status: common breeding summer resident and migrant from mid-April through May and from early August to mid-September.

Habitat: deciduous and mixed forests, including bottomland willows and cottonwoods, riparian and lakeshore woodlands, maple forests and high-elevation aspen groves.

Nesting: in a tall shrub or deciduous tree, often near water; loosely built, bulky nest is lined with finer stems and rootlets; pair incubates 3–4 bluish green eggs with brown and purple marks for 12–13 days; young fledge at 11–12 days.

Feeding: gleans upper-canopy for invertebrates, seeds, buds and fruit; occasionally visits feeders for seeds and small fruits.

Voice: contact call is a high, woodpecker-like *pik;* male's song is a leisurely, whistled warble with a robinlike cadence, but huskier and less measured.

Similar Species: *Male Bullock's Oriole* (p. 349): slimmer bill; brighter underparts; orange face with dark eye line; 1 large white patch on upperwing. *Male Hooded Oriole* (p. 367): smaller; orangy "hood"; slim, downcurved bill; long, black tail.

Best Sites: Sauvie I.; Pittock Bird Sanctuary (Portland); Scoggins Valley SP; Whitehorse CP, Josephine Co.; Deschutes River SP; Hagelstein CP, Klamath Co.; Cold Springs Reservoir; Wildhorse Creek (Pendleton); Page Springs Campground.

LAZULI BUNTING

Passerina amoena

Small flocks of Lazuli Buntings work their way northward into Oregon in spring, bringing a splash of color to feeders and desert oases. They do not demand much of their environment, making use of dry brushlands and woodland edges and often sharing their quarters with Black-headed Grosbeaks in the upper canopy. • From May to early July, the brightly colored male's crisp and varied songs punctuate the hot "siesta hours" during which only a handful of other species regularly vocalize. Singing intensity diminishes as broods are fledged. • By late August, most Lazuli Buntings appear to have deserted their summer homes. They undergo a partial molt before they leave, completing their change of plumage at their wintering grounds.

ID: whitish belly and undertail coverts; pale, stubby, conical bill; dark legs; bluish tail. *Breeding male:* bright blue head, back and rump; dark, gray-and-blue wing with 2 prominent white bars; orangy chestnut breast; pinkish buff sides. *Nonbreeding male:* tan-mottled blue head, back and wings; duller breast. *Female:* dull, grayish brown upperparts with 2 paler wing bars; off-white underparts; buffy breast; buffy eye ring.
Size: *L* 5½ in; *W* 9 in.
Status: common breeding summer resident and migrant from mid-April to May and from mid-August to mid-September at low- to mid-level elevations east of the Cascades, in western interior valleys and foothills and in the coastal valleys of Curry Co.; rare along the coast north of Curry Co.
Habitat: open, wooded bottomlands; weedy fields with brushy margins; streamside or high-elevation willows; brushy slopes and chaparral. *In migration:* also sagebrush and desert oases.
Nesting: in a crotch in a shrubby tangle; coarsely woven nest of dried grass and forbs is lined with fine grass and hair; female incubates 3–5 pale bluish white eggs for 12 days; young fledge at 10–12 days; female defends nest against other females.
Feeding: feeds on the ground; gleans low shrubs; eats invertebrates and seeds; visits feeders.
Voice: utters buzzy, trilling flight calls and woodpecker-like *pik* notes; male's song is a brief, varied warbling note series.
Similar Species: *Breeding Indigo Bunting* (p. 367): male is blue overall; female has faintly streaked underparts and vaguer wing markings; hybrids are relatively regular.
Best Sites: Lewis and Clark SP; Plat Island Reservoir (Sutherlin); Merlin; Roxy Anne Butte (near Medford); Deschutes River SP; Smith Rock SP; Hagelstein CP, Klamath Co.; McKay Creek NWR; Page Springs Campground.

BOBOLINK

Dolichonyx oryzivorus

The male Bobolink is unlike any other North American bird in his plumage and breeding strategies. Roger Tory Peterson described him as "wearing a backward tuxedo," but his courting tactics are very forward as he flashes his yellow nape and white wing patches at any female within view. If that doesn't work, he launches into a bubbly, zestful song in a trembling song-flight or atop a low bush. • Once his early summer duties have been performed, the male Bobolink acquires the same cryptic coloring as his mate and gets ready for fall migration. • "Bobolink" may be an abbreviation of "Robert O. Lincoln," the subject and title of a poem by William Cullen Bryant that used the phrase in its interpretation of the bird's song, but the name could have originated earlier.

breeding

ID: pink legs; sharp-tipped tail feathers. *Breeding male:* mostly black plumage; buffy nape; white shoulder patch and rump; black bill. *Breeding female:* sparrowlike, brown-striped back and wings; sandy brown rump; pale buff underparts and head; pink bill; black crown and line behind eye. *Nonbreeding:* like breeding female, except yellower overall.

Size: *L* 6–8 in; *W* 11–12 in.

Status: locally uncommon breeding summer resident and August to early September migrant east of the Cascades; vagrant migrant in western Oregon; state-listed as sensitive.

Habitat: *Breeding:* grassy meadows interspersed with sedges and shrubs; alfalfa meadows and tall grass. *In migration:* mainly habitats close to breeding colonies.

Nesting: colonial; depression in the ground, in dense plant cover; coarse nest is lined with fine materials; female incubates 5–6 purple-marked, gray to pale rufous eggs for 10–13 days; young fledge at 10–14 days.

Feeding: gleans the ground and low vegetation for adult and larval invertebrates, including spiders, and for seeds.

Voice: gives a *pink* flight call; male's song, often issued in flight, is a series of bubbly notes and banjolike twangs: *bobolink bobolink spink spank spink.*

Similar Species: *Lark Bunting* (p. 366): very similar breeding male has black nape and rump; female and nonbreeding male are browner, with a dark central breast spot and unevenly streaked underparts.

Best Sites: near "P" Ranch at the south end of Malheur NWR; Ladd Marsh WMA; Burns–Hines area.

RED-WINGED BLACKBIRD
Agelaius phoeniceus

The male Red-winged Blackbird's bright red shoulder patches and raspy song are his most important tools in the often intricate strategy he uses to defend his territory. A richly voiced male who has established a high quality territory can attract several mates to his cattail kingdom. His main role during summer is to defend his hard-won territory against encroaching males, usurping Yellow-headed Blackbirds and marauding Marsh Wrens (which may destroy the eggs and young, though not often for food). That done, he becomes just another member of a large flock of foraging blackbirds roaming agricultural fields, grasslands and marshes. These flocks, augmented by other species and by northern immigrants, can number in the hundreds, and sometimes thousands, and are a regular feature of Oregon winters.

ID: *Male:* all-black, nonglossy plumage; orangy red shoulder patch with partly hidden, lower border. *Female:* variable brown overall; heavily streaked, especially on belly and flanks; usually some rufous on upperparts.
Size: *L* 7–9 in; *W* 12–13 in.
Status: common breeding summer resident; common in winter west of the Cascades and locally uncommon in eastern Oregon.
Habitat: *Breeding:* freshwater bodies with standing aquatic vegetation, including ditches and flooded fields. *In migration* and *winter:* dry agricultural fields and marshes.
Nesting: usually in cattails, reeds or other vegetation; woven nest of sedges, dried cattails and grass; female incubates 3–4 dark-marked pale bluish green eggs for 10–12 days; young fledge at 11–14 days.
Feeding: gleans the ground and vegetation for seeds, including waste grain, and

invertebrates; catches insects in flight; eats fruit in fall and winter; sometimes visits feeders.
Voice: calls include a harsh *check* and high *tseert;* female may give a *che-che-che chee chee chee;* male's song is a loud, raspy *konk-a-ree* or *ogle-reeeee.*
Similar Species: *Tricolored Blackbird* (p. 344): male has glossier plumage and white lower border to shoulder patch, different song; female's plumage is darker, with less contrast and no rufous.
Best Sites: *Summer:* wetland areas below 6000 ft elevation; Fern Ridge Reservoir; Malheur NWR; Ladd Marsh; Finley NWR; Upper Klamath Lake. *Winter:* western interior valleys; Klamath Basin; coastal areas, especially Tillamook Co.

TRICOLORED BLACKBIRD

Agelaius tricolor

The Tricolored Blackbird is found only along the Pacific coast of the U.S. and northern Mexico. • Birders should study any dense colony of nesting blackbirds for Tricolors, which are strictly colonial and nonterritorial. In Oregon, colonies are small compared to the colonies composed of hundreds, sometimes thousands, of birds per acre found in California. • After the breeding season, males and females go their separate ways in nomadic, gender-specific flocks that later merge into large, mixed-species flocks that include cowbirds, starlings, grackles and other blackbirds. • The draining of productive marshlands has accelerated the decline of this species, which lacks the nesting versatility of the Red-winged Blackbird.

ID: *Male:* glossy, all-black plumage; small, dark red shoulder patch, with buffy or white lower border. *Female:* dark brownish gray; streaked and mottled, especially on belly; pale "eyebrow" and throat.

Size: *L* 7–9 in; *W* 13–14 in.

Status: local breeding summer resident and migrant in the eastern Rogue Valley, in southern Klamath Co. and at isolated colonies, mainly in north-central Oregon and irregularly near Portland; a few birds winter in the Rogue Valley and Klamath Basin and in central Oregon; federal species of concern; state-listed as sensitive.

Habitat: *Breeding:* cattail and tule marshes. *In migration* and *winter:* more widespread in farmlands with other blackbirds.

Nesting: colonial; in reeds, cattails or willows, near or over water, rarely in crop fields; bulky, woven nest of marsh vegetation and grass; female incubates 3–4 brown-marked pale green eggs for 11–13 days; young fledge at 11–14 days.

Feeding: forages in flocks on the ground; gleans the foliage of trees and shrubs; eats insects, snails, seeds and waste grain.

Voice: gives calls similar to the Red-winged Blackbird's, but less accomplished; male's song is a poorly refined, less bubbly, short, falling *a green carrrr-ot.*

Similar Species: *Red-winged Blackbird* (p. 343): flat black plumage; shoulder patch has yellowish lower border; female is paler and crisper looking, often with rufous in plumage.

Best Sites: *Summer:* Klamath WMA; Lower Klamath NWR; northeastern Portland (check birding hotline); near Clarno and Wamic, Wasco Co.; John Day Fossil Beds NM; near Stanfield, Umatilla Co.

WESTERN MEADOWLARK

Sturnella neglecta

The Western Meadowlark, Oregon's state bird, displays a combination of cryptic coloration on the upperparts and bright courtship elegance on the underparts. To show off his plumage and vocal abilities, the male finds a prominent perch or indulges in a brash display flight. • When the female needs to draw predators away from her nest, she flashes her yellow-, black-and-white plumage in a fast-moving blur. As soon as the nest is safe, she folds away her white tail flags, and her well-camouflaged back allows her to return to the nest undetected. • Western Meadowlarks have benefited from the grazing, plowing and spraying of sagebrush, but numbers have declined wherever monoculture crops, overgrazing or asphalt have replaced large expanses of grassland.

breeding

ID: long, sharp, pale bill; short, banded tail. *Breeding:* dark-mottled, pale sandy brown overall; yellow throat, lower breast and belly; black "V" breast band; boldly black-streaked whitish flanks and undertail coverts. *Nonbreeding:* paler, with indistinct breast band.
Size: *L* 8–10 in; *W* 14–15 in.
Status: common breeding summer resident and uncommon winter resident in eastern Oregon; locally uncommon breeding summer resident and more widespread in winter in western inland valleys; common migrant from late February to early April and from August to November; state-listed as sensitive.
Habitat: grasslands, rough pastures and deserts; also sandspits and airports in winter.
Nesting: in a natural or scraped depression on the ground; domed canopy with a side entrance, of grass, bark and plant stems interconnected with surrounding vegetation; female incubates 3–7 white eggs marked with purple and brown for 13–15 days; young fledge at 12 days.
Feeding: walks and runs on the ground, gleaning grasshoppers, crickets, sowbugs, snails and spiders; also eats seeds and probes the soil for grubs, worms and insects.
Voice: issues a *bluk* and a rattling call; male's song is a rich series of flute-like warbles.
Similar Species: *Juvenile European Starling* (p. 299): resembles juvenile meadowlark, but without white on tail or yellow on face or underparts.
Best Sites: southeastern and north-central Oregon. *Winter:* Sauvie I; Baskett Slough NWR.

YELLOW-HEADED BLACKBIRD
Xanthocephalus xanthocephalus

The arrival of the male Yellow-headed Blackbird with his raw, rasping song is one of the first signs of spring in many freshwater marshes. Standing head and shoulders above his Red-winged Blackbird neighbors, the later-arriving male Yellow-headed Blackbird bullies his way to the choicest areas, forcing the Red-wings to the outskirts, where predation is highest. • Once the males have staked out their territories, the females arrive. From their nest sites, pairs forage a mile or more into croplands and pastures. The bright yellow heads of the males make large colonies resemble fields of mustard. After the colony completes its breeding season, flocks gather to feed with other blackbirds. Most birds depart before winter's chill, but a few occasionally remain with wintering flocks of other blackbird species.

ID: *Male:* black body; orangy yellow head and breast; black lores; white wing patches.
Female: dark brown overall; dull yellow breast and face.
Size: *L* 8–11 in; *W* 13–15 in.
Status: locally abundant breeding summer resident and migrant east of the Cascades, locally rare in winter; locally uncommon breeding summer resident and migrant west of the Cascades, particularly in the Willamette Valley, and very rare in winter; migration is from late March to mid-May and from August to late September.
Habitat: *Breeding:* large freshwater marshes. *In migration:* agricultural areas.

Nesting: colonial but territorial; over water in cattails or shoreline shrubs; bulky nest is firmly woven with wet vegetation and lined with dried grass; female incubates 4 greenish or grayish white eggs with gray and brown markings for 11–13 days; young fledge at 9–12 days.
Feeding: gleans vegetation and probes the ground for seeds and invertebrates; also opens cattail heads for larval invertebrates.
Voice: calls are harsher than those of the Red-winged Blackbird, except for a whistled trill and soft *kruk* or *kruttuk* flight call; song is a strained, metallic grating similar to the sound of an old chainsaw.
Similar Species: none.
Best Sites: Klamath, Lake and Harney Counties; Fern Ridge Reservoir; Danebo Pond (Eugene); Umatilla NWR; Ladd Marsh WMA; Grande Ronde Valley; Diamond area.

BREWER'S BLACKBIRD

Euphagus cyanocephalus

Even in some residential areas, male Brewer's Blackbirds in their glossy plumage can easily be seen strutting their stuff to impress the dowdy females. Rather than gathering in large colonies, Brewer's Blackbirds nest in small groups or as widely dispersed pairs. For this reason, they are more widespread in summer than colony-nesting blackbirds. Following nesting, adults and juveniles form small flocks, which then team up with roving mobs of other blackbirds, Brown-headed Cowbirds and European Starlings that spread out over lowland fields and wetlands throughout winter. • Our network of highways provides a bounty of vehicle-struck insects for Brewer's Blackbirds, which exploit this "roadkill resource" niche better than any other songbird.

ID: walks with a head-up strut, with head nodding at each step. *Male:* all-black plumage, glossed green on back, wings and tail and purple on breast and head; pale yellow eyes. *Female:* dull grayish brown; eyes usually dark.
Size: *L* 8–9 in; *W* 15–15½ in.
Status: common year-round resident in coastal lowlands and inland valleys west of the Cascades; abundant breeding summer resident and uncommon winter resident in eastern Oregon; common migrant from late February to May and from August to October.
Habitat: *Breeding:* open areas near wetlands and farmlands; grasslands; sagebrush–greasewood deserts. *Winter:* agricultural areas, roadsides and suburbs.

Nesting: loosely colonial; in a tree, on the ground, in a shrub or in marsh vegetation; sturdy basket of twigs and grass is cemented with mud or cow dung and lined with grass, rootlets and hair or fur; female incubates 4–6 brown-marked grayish eggs for 12–14 days; young fledge at 13–14 days.
Feeding: picks, gleans or chases food items; eats a wide variety of invertebrates, seeds and fruit; often wades in shallow water to feed.
Voice: unusually quiet for a blackbird; gives a plain *chek* call; male's song is a creaking, 2-note *k-sheee*.
Similar Species: *Brown-headed Cowbird* (p. 348): smaller; stouter bill; dark eyes; male has brown head; sandy brown female has some streaking on underparts; juvenile has strongly streaked underparts and "scaly" back.
Best Sites: farmlands.

BROWN-HEADED COWBIRD
Molothrus ater

The male Brown-headed Cowbird's song is a bubbling, liquid gurgle that could well be interpreted by nesting songbirds as "Here comes trouble!" This species once followed the great bison herds across the Great Plains and Prairies of central North America. With its nomadic lifestyle making building and tending nests impractical, it learned to lay its eggs in the nests of other birds, thus passing on the parental responsibilities. • Some warblers and vireos recognize the odd eggs, but many birds simply incubate cowbird eggs along with their own. Often hatching earlier than the host's young, nestling cowbirds get most of the food provided by the often smaller foster parents. Because ranching expansion, forest fragmentation, urbanization and an increase in transportation corridors have allowed the cowbird's range to dramatically increase, more species, unable to discern the stranger in their midst, have been victimized.

ID: stout bill; dark legs. *Male:* green-glossed black body; brown head. *Female:* grayish brown overall, typically with fine-streaked underparts. *Juvenile:* like female, but with clearer streaking and "scaly" back.
Size: *L* 6–8 in; *W* 12 in.
Status: common breeding summer resident and migrant from mid-April to mid-May and from August to early October; uncommon in winter west of the Cascades and in the Klamath Basin.

Habitat: *Breeding:* arid sagebrush and juniper country, farmlands, marshes, grasslands, conifers and deciduous woodlands.
Nesting: female lays up to 40 eggs singly in other birds' nests; brown-marked grayish eggs hatch in 10–13 days; young fledge at 10–11 days.
Feeding: gleans the ground for seeds, waste grain and invertebrates, especially grasshoppers and beetles, often those flushed by livestock; gleans tree foliage for caterpillars and other items in summer.
Voice: issues squeaky, high-pitched *seep*, *psee* and *wee-tse-tse* calls, often given in flight; also gives a fast chipping note series; male's song is a high, liquidy, gurgling *glug-ahl-whee* or *bubbloozeee*.
Similar Species: *Brewer's Blackbird* (p. 347): larger; longer bill and tail; male has purple-glossed head and yellow eyes; female is darker brown and unstreaked.
Best Sites: farmland and suburban areas, plus woodlands in summer; often near livestock and feed pens.

BULLOCK'S ORIOLE

Icterus bullockii

Even though the Bullock's Oriole is common and widespread in much of Oregon, most residents are unaware of its existence. The plumage of the male blends remarkably well with the sunlit and shadowed upper-canopy summer foliage where he spends much of his time. Finding the drab female oriole is even more difficult, especially for predators in search of an easy meal. Protection and shelter for the offspring come from very elaborate hanging nests. • The Bullock's Oriole is a good example of the sometimes vacillating nature of avian nomenclature. Considered a separate species for more than a century, this oriole was then for a time lumped with the Baltimore Oriole (*I. galbula*), as the Northern Oriole.

ID: bluish gray bill; dark eyes; bluish gray legs. *Male:* black upperparts, crown and throat patch; large, white wing patch; bright orange underparts, rump and face; black eye line. *Female:* gray back and wings; 2 white wing bars; whitish underparts; yellow head and breast; yellowish orange rump and tail.

Size: *L* 7–9 in; *W* 11–12 in.

Status: common breeding summer resident east of the Cascades, in the Rogue Valley and Umpqua Valley and locally common to uncommon in the Willamette Valley and lower Columbia R. lowlands; common migrant throughout spring and in late summer in these areas.

Habitat: riparian cottonwoods and willows; semi-open oak and madrone woodlands; ranches and towns with shade trees; rarely in juniper forests.

Nesting: attached to a high, deciduous, drooping branch; woven nest of plant fibers is lined with fine grass, plant down, string and hair; female incubates 4–5 dark-marked, grayish or bluish white eggs for 12–14 days; young fledge at 12–14 days.

Feeding: gleans upper canopy foliage and shrubs for caterpillars, wasps and other invertebrates; also eats small fruits and plant nectar; sometimes visits feeders.

Voice: 2-note whistles and dry chatters; male's song is a rich, sharply punctuated series of 6–8 whistled and guttural notes.

Similar Species: *Hooded Oriole* (p. 367): longer, downcurved bill; black tail; male is yellower, has less black on head and has 2 separate wing bars; female has more yellow on underparts.

Best Sites: Sauvie I.; Lewis & Clark SP; William L. Finley NWR; Fern Ridge Reservoir; Tou Velle SP; White River WMA; Smith Rock SP; Hagelstein CP, Klamath Co.; Wildhorse Creek (Pendleton).

GRAY-CROWNED ROSY-FINCH
Leucosticte tephrocotis

The remarkable Rosy-finches spend the summer around the summits and higher slopes of mountains with permanent snowfields and glaciers. During the nesting season, they conserve energy by taking slow, measured steps across patches of snow as they inspect crevices for chilled or weakened insects and other small invertebrates. At the end of summer, family groups assemble into larger flocks, which remain in the alpine zone until driven into the lowlands by the first major winter storms. • Three fairly distinct races of this species appear in Oregon: the gray-crowned nominate race (*L.t. tephrocotis*), which occurs here in winter, sometimes in huge flocks from breeding areas farther north, the gray-headed Wallowa Rosy-Finch (*L.t. wallowa*) and the gray-hooded Hepburn's Rosy-Finch (*L.t. littoralis*).

breeding

ID: conical bill; dark eyes; blackish legs. *Breeding male:* brown back, wings and underparts; rosy wing coverts, flanks and rump; gray "cap" or "hood" with dark forehead and throat; black bill; dark tail. *Female* and *nonbreeding male:* generally paler, with less pink in plumage; yellow bill.
Size: *L* 6 in; *W* 13 in.
Status: locally common breeding summer resident above timberline in the Cascades and Wallowa Mts.; irregular to abundant in winter east of the Cascades and rare in western Oregon.
Habitat: *Breeding:* near summer snowfields, alpine glaciers and barren rocky areas above timberline. *Winter:* snowfields above timberline; open fields and exposed hillsides at lower elevations.

Nesting: typically among rocks; bulky nest of moss, grass and lichen; female incubates 4–5 white eggs for 12–14 days; young fledge at 16–22 days; adults bring insects to the young in special pouches opening from the floor of the mouth.
Feeding: walks and hops on the ground or snow (and on the edge of water, ice or snow) gleaning small seeds and insects.
Voice: flight call is a soft *chirp;* song is a long, goldfinchlike warble.
Similar Species: *Black Rosy-Finch* (p. 351): gray-mottled blackish back and underparts; less pink on belly; male has very dark "cheeks"; grayer female shows less pink.
Best Sites: *Hepburn's:* breeds on the highest peaks at Crater Lake NP and near Timberline Lodge on Mt. Hood. *Wallowa:* breeds above timberline in the Blue Mts. and Wallowa Mts.; overwinters at lower elevations, including OK Gulch (Crow Creek) and the Imnaha area.

BLACK ROSY-FINCH
Leucosticte atrata

Black Rosy-finches prefer the highest mountain peaks, except when fierce winter storms drive them downslope to join other rosy-finches. Where they nest in the same areas as Gray-crowned Rosy-finches, they sometimes hybridize, producing confusingly plumaged offspring. This interbreeding makes searching winter flocks for Black Rosy-finches more difficult, at a time when they are restless and much less obliging than when they are picking along the edges of ice and snow for insects on their nesting grounds. • The Black Rosy-Finch has only recently been designated as a separate species, and its wintering grounds have yet to be fully determined. The breeding male is much blacker than the Gray-crowned Rosy-Finch, and the female and nonbreeding male Black Rosy-Finch can be distinguished by their frosted gray appearance. Juveniles of the two species are indistinguishable.

breeding

ID: conical bill; dark eyes; blackish legs. *Breeding male:* gray-mottled black back and underparts; rosy flush on flanks and rump; blackish wings with rosy coverts; black head with gray hindcrown and well-defined dark forehead; black bill; dark tail. *Female* and *nonbreeding male:* paler; less pink in plumage; yellow bill.
Size: *L* 6 in; *W* 13 in.
Status: uncommon breeding summer resident on Steens Mt. and historically in the Wallowa Mts., remaining until at least mid-October; state-listed as sensitive.
Habitat: snowfields and barren, rocky areas above timberline.

Nesting: on the ground or among rocks; bulky nest consists of moss, grass, plant stems and lichen; female incubates 4–5 white eggs for 12–14 days; young fledge at 16–22 days; adults bring insects to the young in special pouches opening from the floor of the mouth.
Feeding: walks and hops on the ground or snow (and on the edge of water, ice or snow), gleaning small seeds and insects.
Voice: flight call is a soft *chirp;* wintering flocks sound like Evening Grosbeaks arriving at a feeder; song is a long, goldfinch-like warble.
Similar Species: *Gray-crowned Rosy-Finch* (p. 350): browner back and underparts; more pink on belly; breeding male has gray "cap" or "hood," dark forehead and throat.
Best Sites: *Summer:* Steens Mt.

351

PINE GROSBEAK

Pinicola enucleator

Pine Grosbeaks favor the solitude of mountain forests and timberline scrub. Here they feed leisurely on insects, seeds, buds and berries and occasionally introduce themselves with a distinctive, loud whistling call uttered from the highest point they can find. Every now and again, an early summer hiker might be surprised by what seems to be the song of a robin high atop a mountain, only to find that the songster is a particularly beautiful finch. Anyone fortunate enough to have Pine Grosbeaks visiting their feeder in winter may also get to hear this quiet, warbled song from a bird that has adorned many a Christmas card. • The Latin term *enucleator* refers to the bird's method of obtaining seeds hidden in protective cones.

ID: dark, conical bill with down-curved tip; dark eyes, legs and tail; dark wing with 2 white bars. *Male:* rosy red head, back, rump and underparts; grayish sides, belly and undertail coverts. *Female:* generally gray; yellowish olive or russet crown, face and rump.

Size: *L* 8–9 in; *W* 14–15 in.

Status: locally uncommon year-round resident in the northeastern mountains, often moving to lower elevations in winter; very rare stray in the Cascades; rare in winter elsewhere in eastern Oregon.

Habitat: *Breeding:* coniferous forests above the ponderosa pine zone. *In migration* and *winter:* coniferous and mixed forests; rarely in lowland wooded areas and towns.

Nesting: in a conifer or tall shrub; loosely built, bulky nest of moss, twigs, grass and lichen; female incubates 4 heavily marked bluish green eggs for 13–15 days; young fledge at 13–20 days; family stays together for most of the year.

Feeding: forages on the ground for seeds; gleans foliage for insects; fond of crab apples, mountain-ash berries, pine seeds and maple buds; visits gardens and feeders in winter and spring.

Voice: call is a 3-note *tew* whistle with a higher middle note; often gives a short, muffled trill in flight; male's song is a short, sweet musical warble.

Similar Species: *White-winged Crossbill* (p. 367): much smaller; longer, crossed bill; bolder wing patches.

Best Sites: *Summer:* Wallowa Mts., Blue Mts. and the Cascades, especially Bonny Lakes trail. *Winter:* Moss Springs Campground; Enterprise–Joseph area; Wallowa Lake SP; Auburn (Sumpter); Anthony Lakes.

PURPLE FINCH

Carpodacus purpureus

Take a walk along forested lower mountain slopes or in riparian or mixed-oak woodlands, and you are almost certain to hear, emanating from the highest branch, the continuous, bubbly warble of a male Purple Finch. • Roger Tory Peterson described this finch best when he said it looked like a "sparrow dipped in raspberry juice." Not all singing birds will appear this color—first-year males practice their songs before they get their adult coats, and some males are an aberrant yellow or orange, much like the more widespread House Finch. • Unlike Purple Finches in the east and House Finches in the west, western Purple Finches show no affinity for highly developed urban and residential areas.

ID: dusky, conical bill; dark eyes. *Male:* brown sides and flanks; whitish belly; weakly streaked reddish back; raspberry red head with color "dripping" down the body. *Female:* drab greenish brown upperparts; blurred streaking on breast and flanks.

Size: *L* 5–6 in; *W* 9–10 in.

Status: common year-round resident from the western slope of the Cascades to the coast; rare to locally common in Klamath Co.; uncommon breeding summer resident in Lake Co.; very rare migrant and winter resident elsewhere east of the Cascades.

Habitat: *Breeding:* mid-elevation conifers and mixed forests; riparian and oak-containing woodlands. *In migration and winter:* mostly in interior valleys, in riparian areas, deciduous forests and towns.

Nesting: on a horizontal tree branch far from the trunk; neat, shallow cup of twigs, fine roots and grass is lined with rootlets, hair, moss and lichen; female incubates 4–5 heavily dark-marked, pale green or blue eggs for 13 days; young fledge at 14 days.

Feeding: gleans the ground and canopy foliage for seeds and insects; eats fruit in summer and tree buds and blossoms in winter and spring; visits seed feeders in winter.

Voice: call is a single metallic *cheep* or *weet;* male's song is a bubbly, rambling, continuous warble.

Similar Species: *Cassin's Finch* (p. 354): pale "spectacles"; male has bright red forecrown; female's streaks are darker and clearer.

Best Sites: widespread in western Oregon; Ft. Steven SP; Finley NWR; Pittock Bird Sanctuary (Portland); Oregon Caves NM; McDonald State Forest.

CASSIN'S FINCH

Carpodacus cassinii

Cassin's Finch inhabits the mountains within the range of the ponderosa pine, but it also favors firs, lodgepole pines and cottonwoods. Traveling in small flocks, it would probably go unnoticed except for its characteristic calls. • Purple, Cassin's and House finches are all present in Oregon. Having three *Carpodacus* finches to contend with makes Christmas bird counts even more interesting, but these birds generally go their separate ways in summer. Cassin's Finches claim the eastern mountain ranges, Purple Finches nest mostly at lower elevations west of the Cascades, and House Finches are the common open-country and lowland species. The variability in the plumage of immature males, which may be orange or yellow in all three species, and their tendency to intermix in winter, add up to inevitable confusion.

ID: heavily dark-streaked grayish brown upperparts; pale, conical bill; dark eyes; pale spectacles. *Male:* pinkish wash on wings and back; whitish sides, flanks and belly; pinkish red on rump, breast and head; bright red crown. *Female:* distinctly dark-streaked white underparts.

Size: *L* 6–6½ in; *W* 11–12 in.

Status: common year-round resident in the Cascades and eastward; rare in the Siskiyou Mts.; very rare winter visitor to western Oregon.

Habitat: *Breeding:* mid- to high-elevation forests, especially ponderosa and lodgepole pines; aspen groves close to conifers. *In migration* and *winter:* moves to lower foothills and valleys, sometimes to desert oases.

Nesting: near the end of a large conifer limb, rarely in a shrub; nest consists of grass, moss, bark shreds, rootlets and lichen; female incubates 4–5 dark-spotted bluish green eggs for 12–14 days; young fledge at 13–14 days.

Feeding: gleans foliage and the ground for conifer seeds, buds, berries and insects; often visits winter feeders.

Voice: flight call is a warbling *kiddileep;* male's rich, warbling song is higher and livelier than that of the Purple Finch.

Similar Species: *Purple Finch* (p. 353): no "spectacles"; pink on male is more widespread; female has less clear, browner streaks and unstreaked undertail coverts.

Best Sites: Tumalo SP (Bend); Indian Ford Campground (Sisters); Ochoco Campground; Crater Lake NP; Kimball SP (Fort Klamath); Tollgate; Wallowa Lake SP; Starr Campground (Blue Mts.).

HOUSE FINCH

Carpodacus mexicanus

Originally a bird of the arid Southwest and Mexico, the House Finch has, with the help of humans, spread across all the lower 48 states and into southern Canada. Introductions in the eastern U.S. and the urbanization of much of California have both helped to establish this bird. • As recently as 1940, the House Finch was a common permanent resident in Oregon only east of the Cascades and in the southwest. Since then, it has colonized all the valleys and coastal lowlands west of the Cascades. • The male's cheerful song may be heard year-round, and no berry bush, grassy patch or weedy shrub is beyond the interest of family parties in late summer and fall.

ID: gray, conical bill; dark eyes; dark legs. *Male:* reddish orange (sometimes yellow) crown, throat, breast and "cheeks"; blurry brown streaking on whitish sides, flanks and belly; weakly streaked back. *Female:* drab brown overall; blurry streaking; pale eye ring.
Size: *L* 5–6 in; *W* 9–10 in.
Status: common year-round resident at lower elevations.
Habitat: disturbed areas, including farms, ranches, towns, residential areas, open fields and woodlands; often visits feeders in winter.
Nesting: in a cavity, building, dense shrub or abandoned nest; nest of twigs, grass, leaves, rootlets and hair; female incubates 4–5 bluish eggs for 12–14 days; young fledge at 11–19 days.

Feeding: forages on the ground and in shrubbery for small insects, seeds and juniper berries; fond of maple sap and deciduous buds; eats dirt and gravel for minerals and salts.
Voice: gives a sweet *cheer* flight call singly or in a series; male's song is a bright, disjointed warble lasting about 3 seconds, often ending with a harsh *jeeer* or *wheer.*
Similar Species: *Cassin's Finch* (p. 354): pale "spectacles"; male has bright red crown; streaks on underparts are limited to flanks and undertail coverts; female's streaks are darker and clearer.
Best Sites: widespread, especially around farms and residential areas.

RED CROSSBILL

Loxia curvirostra

With crossed bill tips and nimble tongues, crossbills are uniquely adapted for extracting seeds from conifer cones. • Irregular cone distribution forces Red Crossbills into a nomadic existence. They can often be located by listening for their loud calls wherever the boughs of conifers are laden with ripe or ripening cones. If they discover a bumper crop, they might stay to breed regardless of the season (late winter or early spring is typical), and it is not unusual to hear Red Crossbills singing in midwinter or to find newly fledged juveniles begging for food in November or February. • Ongoing research, based on different vocalizations, bill sizes and seed preferences, suggests that the Red Crossbill may consist of up to eight (or more) "sibling species."

ID: dark brown wings; heavy, obviously crossed bill; dark eyes; dusky legs. *Male:* brick red overall; grayish bars on lower flanks; occasionally has 2 narrow buff wing bars. *Female:* yellowish to olive green overall.
Size: *L* 5–6 in; *W* 10–11 in.
Status: rare to common erratic year-round resident and winter visitor.
Habitat: coniferous forests statewide; occasionally in deciduous habitats as a nonbreeder; rarely at feeders.
Nesting: loosely colonial; on an outer conifer branch, usually high in the canopy; loose, bulky nest of twigs, grass, moss, rootlets and bark strips; female incubates

3–4 dark-spotted, pale blue or green eggs for 12–18 days; young fledge at 15–20 days.
Feeding: perches in conifers to extract seeds; sometimes feeds on the ground; eats insects, spruce buds, berries and seeds; licks salt, ash or minerals from the soil, roadsides, coastal mud or intertidal rocks.
Voice: issues a distinctive *jip-jip* call note, often in flight; song (similar to other finches) is a varied series of warbles, trills and chips.
Similar Species: *White-winged Crossbill* (p. 367): 2 prominent white wing bars; male is usually pinker; female has blurry underpart streaking. *Pine Grosbeak* (p. 352): larger; 2 prominent white wing bars; shorter, uncrossed bill; male is rosy red and gray; female has gray underparts and yellowish olive or russet head and rump.
Best Sites: Charleston; Lost L. and Hoodoo Butte, Linn Co.; Indian Ford Campground (Sisters); Ochoco Campground; Crater Lake NP; Umatilla NF (Tollgate); Moss Springs; Wallowa Lake SP; Anthony Lakes.

COMMON REDPOLL

Carduelis flammea

A predictably unpredictable winter visitor, the Common Redpoll might arrive in flocks of hundreds or in family groups of a dozen or fewer, depending on the year. • With their light, fluffy bodies, redpolls can "float" on the softest snowbanks to pick off fallen seeds without sinking beyond their bellies. These birds might seem to possess good winter survival skills, but they are in constant danger of running out of fuel and succumbing to hypothermia. Therefore, they must eat almost continuously, either waste grain from bare fields or seeds from weedy waste ground or winter feeders, and they seem remarkably fearless of humans, as long as you move slowly and quietly. Flocks will sometimes meet up with Pine Siskins in willows and alders, but, when the feeding is finished, the two species usually go their separate ways.

nonbreeding

ID: heavily streaked brown-and-white upperparts and flanks; white belly; 2 white wing bars; small, red "cap"; black lower forehead, lores and "chin"; tiny, stubby, yellow bill. *Male:* largely unstreaked, deep pink breast and sides; grayish face. *Female:* more extensive streaking on underparts and browner head than male.
Size: *L* 5 in; *W* 9 in.
Status: rare and irregular winter resident in northeastern Oregon; very rare elsewhere east of the Cascades and in western Oregon.
Habitat: fields and farmlands; conifer forests and forest edges; open brushy country.
Nesting: does not nest in Oregon.

Feeding: forages on the ground and in alders, willows and other small trees for seeds; eats insects in summer.
Voice: calls are a soft *chit-chit-chit-chit* and a faint *swe-eet;* male's song is a twittering series of trills.
Similar Species: *Hoary Redpoll:* looks "frosty" overall; male has less pink on breast; vagrant in Oregon. *Pine Siskin* (p. 358): more brown on upperparts; more profuse streaking below; brown crown; longer, dusky bill; male has 1 yellow and 1 white wing bar; yellow tail flashes.
Best Sites: McKay Creek NWR; Ladd Marsh WMA; Grande Ronde Valley; Enterprise–Joseph area; OK Gulch (Crow Creek); Wallowa Lake SP; Imnaha area; Auburn (Sumpter).

PINE SISKIN

Carduelis pinus

The abundance of Pine Siskins fluctuates seasonally and with the availability of favored food sources, so you can wait months or even years to see one unless you frequent conifer forests. • When plentiful, Pine Siskins consume seed in great quantities, and even a lingering small flock can necessitate daily feeder restocking—keep the seed dry and disinfect the feeder regularly to prevent salmonellosis outbreaks that may weaken or kill siskins and other feeder users. • Pine Siskins are often heard before they are seen, their distinctive calls confirming their presence high in the canopy. Restless winter flocks can often be observed flashing their yellow wing and tail patches as they move around their territories.

ID: dark-streaked brown upperparts; whitish belly; small, sharp, dusky bill. *Male:* brown-streaked white underparts; large yellow wing bar and small white one; may have overall yellow wash. *Female:* brown-washed sides and breast, brown lower border on "cheek" and white wing bars. *In flight:* yellowish wing stripe above and below; notched tail with yellow flashes, particularly on male.
Size: *L* 4–5 in; *W* 8–9 in.
Status: common year-round resident of coniferous forests; common erratic migrant and winter resident in other habitats.
Habitat: *Breeding:* coniferous forests, especially firs, spruces and hemlocks; rarely in pines. *In migration* and *winter:* also low-elevation woodlands, shrubbery and residential areas.
Nesting: loosely colonial; usually on an outer conifer branch; nest of twigs, rootlets and grass is lined with fine rootlets, moss, fur and feathers; female incubates 3–4 dark-spotted pale greenish blue eggs for 13 days; young fledge at 14–15 days and join foraging flocks.
Feeding: gleans the ground, shrubby vegetation and tree foliage for seeds, buds and insects; attracted to road salt, mineral licks and ashes; regularly visits feeders for niger seeds and sunflower seeds.
Voice: utters a distinctive, buzzy, ascending *zzzreeeee* call; male's song is a variable, bubbly mix of squeaky, metallic and raspy notes, sometimes resembling a jerky laugh.
Similar Species: *Female Carpodacus finches* (pp. 353–55): larger; longer tail; stouter bill; no yellow in wings or tail. *Sparrows* (pp. 321–37, 366): generally have thicker, stubbier bills, no yellow in wings or tail and pinkish or reddish legs.
Best Sites: *Summer:* widespread in conifers, except pines. *Winter:* often irrupts abundantly in residential areas.

LESSER GOLDFINCH
Carduelis psaltria

Lesser Goldfinches are often overlooked by people unfamiliar with their calls, but they enliven the margins of watercourses flowing through dry, weedy expanses—as well as various brushy or semi-open habitats at a wide range of elevations. • Despite their resemblance to American Goldfinches, Lessers breed early in the year and have young in their nests well before their late-nesting cousins produce their clutches. Family groups join up in fall and winter, congregating in weedy thickets, untilled gardens and meadows and at hillside seeps, sometimes flocking with American Goldfinches and Pine Siskins.

ID: greenish back and rump; black wing with prominent white bar and "wrist" patch; bright yellow underparts; thick, pale or grayish bill; dark eyes. *Male:* black "cap." *Female:* often drabber or paler than male; olive-and-yellow head.

Size: *L* 4½ in; *W* 8 in.

Status: common year-round resident in western interior valleys, rarer in the Willamette Valley and southern Klamath Co.; uncommon breeding summer resident in Lake, Harney and Malheur Counties; locally common year-round resident from north-central Oregon to the Columbia R.

Habitat: oak foothills; riparian woods and brushy valley floors; occasionally in high-elevation juniper forests. *In migration and winter:* residential areas.

Nesting: on an outer portion of a small tree or shrub; compact, woven nest of plant fibers, grass stems, bark and moss is lined with plant down; female incubates 4–5 pale blue eggs for 12 days; young fledge at 12–15 days and join family flocks.

Feeding: gleans foliage and fruit of deciduous trees, plants and grass; eats seeds and insects; attracted to salt-rich soil, seeps and mineral licks; visits birdbaths and sprinklers for water and feeders for niger seeds.

Voice: calls include high, thin notes and a coarse *shik shik shik* flight call; male sings a long, varied and unstructured series of trills, twitters and warbles.

Similar Species: *Breeding American Goldfinch* (p. 360): larger; whitish undertail coverts; orangy pink bill; yellow on male's upperparts is more extensive; female's back and head are browner.

Best Sites: Cascade Gateway Park (Salem); William L. Finley NWR; Fern Ridge Reservoir; Sutherlin–Winchester; Merlin; Whitehorse CP, Josephine Co.; Tou Velle SP; Roxy Ann Butte; Page Springs Campground.

AMERICAN GOLDFINCH

Carduelis tristis

As it swings over suburban parks and gardens in bounding, deeply undulating flight, uttering its familiar *po-ta-to-chip* call, the highly social American Goldfinch is hard to miss. • Seen along rural roads, at streamsides and in weedy fields and residential plantings most of the year, American Goldfinches concentrate in willow and cottonwood thickets to nest and raise their young. Afterward, family parties form larger flocks and roam the lowlands and foothills in search of weed seeds and other food, particularly thistle seeds, which they gather one by one, twisting and turning to extract the tiny morsels from the seedhead. Birds can be closely approached at such times, but, if someone comes too near, they will move a short distance or rise as one in a flock. • At feeders, American Goldfinches target niger seeds, the closest equivalent to their regular diet.

♀

♂

nonbreeding

ID: stout, orangy pink (breeding) or dusky (nonbreeding) bill. *Breeding male:* bright yellow overall; white rump; mostly black wing with narrow white bar; black "cap"; white-edged brown tail feathers. *Breeding female:* brownish back; dark wing with broad, yellowish wing bar and smaller white one; yellow underparts and throat; brownish head. *Nonbreeding:* brownish back and head; buffy gray underparts; male retains some yellow on wing and throat and around eye.
Size: *L* 5–5½ in; *W* 9–9½ in.
Status: common year-round resident, less widespread in winter.

Habitat: *Breeding:* open country with weedy fields; other low-vegetation areas. *Winter:* wanders from breeding areas, often using feeders as it visits residential areas, ranches and farms.
Nesting: in the fork of a bush, shrub or small tree; tightly woven nest of plant fibers, grass, cocoon silk and spider silk is lined with fur or plant down; female incubates 4–6 pale blue eggs for 10–12 days; young fledge at 11–17 days and join foraging flocks.
Feeding: gleans vegetation for thistle seeds, insects, flower buds and berries; visits feeders for sunflower and niger seeds.
Voice: calls include *po-ta-to-chip* or *per-chic-or-ee* (often in flight) and whistled *dear-me, see-me;* male's song is a long and varied series of trills, twitters and warbles.
Similar Species: *Lesser Goldfinch* (p. 359): smaller; unchanging plumage year-round; greenish back and rump; dark bill; male has black "cap"; female's head is mostly olive green.
Best Sites: widespread.

EVENING GROSBEAK

Coccothraustes vespertinus

Anyone with a bird feeder knows the appetite of Evening Grosbeaks—it doesn't take long for a flock to finish a tray of sunflower seeds. Scattering husks and unopened seeds, they often create an unplanned sunflower garden. If they don't like what's offered, these picky eaters are quick to look elsewhere. • Scattering in pairs to nest in coniferous forests in summer, Evening Grosbeaks appear scarce until after their young fledge. By late summer, flocks are assembling in the lowlands, ready to devour tender hardwood buds before launching an aerial assault on neighborhood feeders. • With their habit of appearing in large numbers in backyards and in flowering streetside trees, Evening Grosbeaks have sparked an interest in birds that few species can rival.

ID: pink legs; large, conical, pale yellowish bill. *Male:* brownish back and breast; black wings with white secondaries; yellow "shoulders," belly and undertail coverts; dark olive brown head and throat, yellow "eyebrow"; all-black tail. *Female:* dull gray overall; black wing with gray area; olive nape and flanks; black lores and vertical "chin" line; black tail with white tips and spots.

Size: *L* 7–8 in; *W* 13–14 in.

Status: uncommon year-round resident with erratic late-summer and spring movements, especially in western Oregon, where it can be abundant in some springs.

Habitat: *Breeding:* coniferous woodlands and mixed forests, at middle to high elevations. *In migration* and *winter:* lowland habitats, especially interior towns with big-leaf maples, sometimes desert oases; visits feeders in large flocks.

Nesting: normally well out on a conifer limb; flimsy nest of twigs, sticks, roots, plant fibers and grass is lined with fine materials; female incubates 3–4 dark-marked, blue or bluish green eggs for 11–14 days; young fledge at 13–14 days; usually attempts a 2nd brood.

Feeding: gleans the ground and foliage for seeds, insects and berries; fond of maple sap and the buds of deciduous trees and shrubs; eats dirt and gravel for minerals and salts; takes sunflower and safflower seeds at feeders.

Voice: call is a high, clear, whistled *teew;* flocks utter a low, dry, rattling buzz; repeated call constitutes the song.

Similar Species: *Goldfinches* (pp. 359–60): smaller; small bill; breeding males have yellow faces and black "caps." *Black-headed Grosbeak* (p. 340): female has browner upperparts, buffier underparts and more patterned face; male is orangy and dark brown, with no "eyebrow."

Best Sites: widespread; winter feeders; desert oases and mountain forests; towns in spring.

HOUSE SPARROW

Passer domesticus

Probably the most familiar songbird in the world—and one of the least prized—the House Sparrow is not a true sparrow but a weaver-finch from Eurasia and northern Africa. • Introduced to the U.S. in the 1850s to control insect pests, the House Sparrow immediately began to exploit human-modified habitats. Nonmigratory by nature, this bird nevertheless has a knack for colonizing far-flung settled areas and usurping territory from native species. The House Sparrow will nest in any nest box within practical flight distance of foraging sites. With its year-round breeding habits, it occupies nest boxes before most native cavity-nesting birds, such as bluebirds and swallows, have arrived. In a predator-scarce urban environment, the brazen and seemingly fearless House Sparrow is a survivor.

breeding

ID: conical bill is yellowish, pinkish or black (breeding male). *Breeding male:* buff-streaked chestnut brown upperparts; bright chestnut nape; pale gray underparts and "cheeks"; black "bib"; gray crown, rump and tail. *Nonbreeding male:* duller plumage; mostly white breast. *Female:* buff-striped brown upperparts; 2 indistinct wing bars; drab grayish brown underparts; grayish head; pale buff "eyebrow."

Size: *L* 6 in; *W* 9–10 in.

Status: common year-round resident near human settlements; rarely moves far from where it nests, even to forage.

Habitat: never far from human settlements, especially where grain is stored or where other human-originated food can be found.

Nesting: communal but territorial; normally in a nest box, natural cavity or artificial cavity; nest is a sprawling, untidy mass of loosely woven grass and other materials; female incubates 4–6 pale eggs marked with gray and brown for 10–13 days; young fledge at 14–17 days; 2–3 broods per year.

Feeding: gleans the ground, low foliage, livestock manure, grain stores and human environments for seeds, blossoms, insects, fruit and food scraps; visits feeders.

Voice: call is a hoarse *chirrup;* flocks chatter and squeak constantly; male's song is a series of similar chirps.

Similar Species: *Black-throated Sparrow* (p. 326): unstreaked, grayish brown upperparts; dark face with white stripes; found only in arid environments.

Best Sites: widespread in all settlements; absent only from dense woodlands.

RARE SPECIES

YELLOW-BILLED LOON
Gavia adamsii

The largest of the four loons seen in western North America, the
Yellow-billed Loon is a very rare winter visitor, mainly to
coastal estuaries but occasionally to larger inland lakes
and reservoirs. Most records are from late September to
April, but individuals have been seen every month of the year.

Yellow-billed Loon

EMPEROR GOOSE
Chen canagica

The small, stocky, but beautifully marked Emperor Goose is equally at home in salt- or freshwater habitats, feeding either on eelgrass, sea lettuce and barnacles or sedges and grasses. Single
birds and small groups or families have been seen at Sauvie Island, the Klamath Basin, and various locations in the Willamette Valley from October to March, and one group of 17 appeared
once at Gold Beach, Curry County, in early May.

GYRFALCON
Falco rusticolus

The Gyrfalcon is a rare winter visitor to Oregon, which makes its appearance all the more satis-
fying to those birders who catch a glimpse of the speedy falcon as it rockets by in hot pursuit of
an unfortunate duck or shorebird. Most birds reaching Oregon are dark morphs, but gray
morphs and white morphs can also be found if conditions farther north drive them southward.

UPLAND SANDPIPER
Bartramia longicauda

The Upland Sandpiper almost disappeared from North America when market gunners targeted it
in the 1880s. This unusual land-loving shorebird returns from Argentina year after year to the
same patch of open grassland each spring and summer. The male's unique courtship flight com-
bines an airy "wolf-whistle" song with shallow, fluttering wingbeats. This bird breeds in very small
numbers in northern Harney County and occasionally elsewhere east of the Cascades.

SEMIPALMATED SANDPIPER
Calidris pusilla

In late summer and fall, one or two Semipalmated
Sandpipers may be found hidden among large flocks of
Western Sandpipers staging along the coast and on inland
marshes and flats. The dull-plumaged adults appear from July into early
August, and the crisper-plumaged juveniles first arrive in mid-July, peak
between mid-August and mid-September, and leave by the end of the
month. One or two birds have been reported in spring, when more rufous
adults might be mistaken for Western Sandpipers.

*Semipalmated
Sandpiper*

BUFF-BREASTED SANDPIPER
Tryngites subruficollis

The plain but attractive, large-eyed Buff-breasted Sandpiper occurs in small numbers in fall
almost annually in Oregon, mostly along the coast on open coastal beaches, dry edges of estuaries, short grass and plowed fields, and flats behind coastal dunes and airports. All sightings
have been of juveniles, mostly from mid-August to mid-October. A few of these small shorebirds have been seen inland, and one bird was found in mid-April.

RUFF
Philomachus pugnax

Anyone who has had the pleasure of seeing a male Ruff in breeding plumage is likely to never forget the encounter. Unfortunately, this Eurasian vagrant is much more prone to turn up in fall when the larger males have lost their colored "ruffs" and resemble the smaller females (known as Reeves). Several adults have appeared in Oregon between late July and mid-August, with juveniles following until mid-October. There have been single winter, spring and summer records.

Ruff

LONG-TAILED JAEGER
Stercorarius longicaudus

The smallest and most graceful of the three tundra-nesting jaegers, the Long-tailed Jaeger prefers the open ocean along the margin of the continental shelf at least 25 miles from shore. Most Oregon sightings from land have been in late August and September, although birds have been observed from mid-July to mid-October and once at the end of May. A few birds, usually juveniles, stray inland, with records from late July to mid-September.

GLAUCOUS GULL
Larus hyperboreus

The arctic-nesting Glaucous Gull is a great wanderer until it reaches maturity. Though adults are rarely seen in Oregon, first- and second-winter birds are seen occasionally offshore, along the coast and in the Willamette Valley. These immature birds join other large gulls wherever they roost and feed, usually near large lakes and reservoirs, open ocean beaches, farmlands and garbage dumps.

ELEGANT TERN
Sterna elegans

First recorded in Oregon during the El Niño summer of 1983, the medium-sized, slender Elegant Tern appeared in record numbers that year, with as many as 225 birds at the mouth of the Rogue River in mid-September. All birds had departed by mid-October. Similar invasions have taken place since then, normally in warm-ocean years. When they arrive en masse, Elegant Terns fly back and forth high over the water in every direction.

YELLOW-BILLED CUCKOO
Coccyzus americanus

Yellow-billed Cuckoos are most frequently observed during June and July, often in places where they are unlikely to be nesting and usually east of the Cascades, but there is a recent record from southwestern Oregon. Historically, they were seen in the Columbia and Willamette River Valleys. Dense cottonwoods and willows bordering watercourses, such as those along the Grande Ronde, Umatilla, Owyhee and Snake Rivers, have been likely nesting locations, though such habitats have been severely altered in many areas where these birds may have formerly nested.

Yellow-billed Cuckoo

COSTA'S HUMMINGBIRD
Calypte costae

Considered to be the "dry desert hummingbirds," Costa's Hummingbirds leave the Sonoran Desert after the nesting season to visit flowers in other habitats for nectar and flying insects. Several birds have appeared in Oregon at coastal locations and in the interior on both sides of the Cascades, mostly at feeders. Although not as regular as other hummingbirds, they will grace feeders with brief visits and may return for several seasons.

Costa's Hummingbird

BROAD-TAILED HUMMINGBIRD
Selasphorus platycercus

The Broad-tailed Hummingbird's breeding season is characterized by a brief flowering season and often chilling nocturnal temperatures. Selection of the appropriate microclimate in which to nest and the ability to undergo torpor are necessary for survival in this bird's subalpine nesting range. A courting male performs spectacular aerial display flights, involving a series of high climbs, dives and hovers accompanied by a loud wing trill. The Broadtail is occasionally seen in southeastern Oregon, such as in the town of Fields.

PLUMBEOUS VIREO
Vireo plumbeus

This slow-moving, interior mountain vireo is an uncommon visitor to eastern Oregon, with reports and photographs from Harney County and possible nesting in Umatilla and Wallowa Counties. There have also been reports of the eastern Blue-headed Vireo (*V. solitarius*) from southeastern Oregon, which makes positive identification problematical, even when birds are singing. Plumbeous Vireos are, however, usually much less brightly colored—essentially gray and white—and have a larger, thicker bill.

BLUE JAY
Cyanocitta cristata

The Blue Jay embodies all the virtues of the corvid family—it is beautiful, resourceful and vocally proficient—but it is also loud and mischievous and not averse to stealing other birds' eggs and even killing adults and nestlings. Partly as a result of its ability to exploit human resources, the Blue Jay has expanded its range westward, taking advantage of forest clearing to establish new territories. Winter invasions have brought several parties and individuals to Oregon, although the Blue Jay remains a very rare visitor.

BROWN THRASHER
Toxostoma rufum

The most rufous of the mimic thrushes, the Brown Thrasher is also one of the most accomplished singers, with a repertoire of more than 3000 song variations. It is a reclusive bird with a preference for tangled thickets and is generally absent from suburban habitats. A few birds have appeared in Oregon in a number of locations and at different times of year, including several birds in winter.

Brown Thrasher

BLACK-THROATED BLUE WARBLER
Dendroica caerulescens

Although it generally inhabits eastern North America's broadleaf forests, the Black-throated Blue Warbler is a great wanderer. On the rare occasions when the male is seen in Oregon, mostly in mid- to late fall, observers are struck by its tameness and habit of creeping along branches in a slow, methodical manner. The male's rich blue-, black-and-white plumage contrasts strongly with the female's drab olive coloration.

BLACK-AND-WHITE WARBLER
Mniotilta varia

Behaving more like a nuthatch than a warbler, the Black-and-white Warbler creeps along branches, peers into cracks and crevices in the bark and probes for hidden insects, larvae and eggs. It is most likely to be seen in Harney County from early May to late June, with fewer birds from mid-August to late October. This warbler is better equipped than most to find food in winter, so the few overwintering records are not surprising.

Black-and-white Warbler

OVENBIRD
Seiurus aurocapillus

Named for its nest, which is shaped like a Dutch oven, the Ovenbird is best known for the male's explosive song, which starts out softly and then increases in intensity. Mostly a ground-dwelling bird, the Ovenbird creeps like a mouse among the leaf litter and turns everything over in search of food. Most often found at Harney County sites in late May and June, and from early September to early October, singing birds have been found in the Cascades in summer.

CLAY-COLORED SPARROW
Spizella pallida

The small and dainty Clay-colored Sparrow is a rare migrant and winter visitor to Oregon between mid-September and mid-June, though it is easily overlooked because of its close resemblance to the Brewer's Sparrow in spring and the Chipping Sparrow in fall and winter. Most birds are found along the coast in fall, but a few have lingered with wintering sparrows in western Oregon, and all but one of the spring records have been from east of the Cascades.

LARK BUNTING
Calamospiza melanocorys

The male Lark Bunting's butterfly-like courtship display and tinkling song is similar to the song flight of the Eurasian Skylark. Sightings of Lark Buntings have occurred throughout the year, mostly from western Oregon. One bird overwintered at a Portland feeder in 1972, and others were reported in January, mid-May to mid-June and mid-August to late September.

HARRIS'S SPARROW
Zonotrichia querula

Arriving in Oregon in late October to join other *Zonotrichia* sparrows in brush patches in open country or to enliven a winter feeder, the Harris's Sparrow is often the sole member of its species in the flock. As winter progresses, more black feathers appear on the face and the brown head gradually becomes gray as the bird gets ready to head north to breed in April or May.

ROSE-BREASTED GROSBEAK
Pheucticus ludovicianus

The Rose-breasted Grosbeak often goes unnoticed in its North American breeding range, because its song is like that of the American Robin and it spends much of its time in the upper canopy. The male's red breast and wing linings provide a distinctive contrast to this otherwise black-and-white bird. Most Oregon records are of adult males, and as with most eastern vagrants, the majority come from Harney County oases in late May and early June, but every year a few show up at feeders in widely scattered parts of the state. At least four birds have been seen in winter.

Rose-breasted Grosbeak

INDIGO BUNTING
Passerina cyanea

In poor light, a male Indigo Bunting can appear black, but given the right light conditions, the startling indigo coloring is obvious. The plain brown female is often overlooked. Indigo Buntings are most likely to be seen in the last week of May and the first week of June, with the Harney County desert oases providing the most records, although there have been widespread sightings.

Indigo Bunting

COMMON GRACKLE
Quiscalus quiscula

Where they occur regularly in North America, Common Grackles will take over a feeder by sheer numbers. In Oregon, however, most sightings are of one to three birds from May to July, although there have also been some late summer and fall records.

GREAT-TAILED GRACKLE
Quiscalus mexicanus

The largest of the North American grackles made its first recorded appearance in Oregon at Malheur National Wildlife Refuge in 1980. Since then, other Great-tailed Grackles have appeared in Harney County fairly regularly, and there have been sightings from Umatilla, Union, Jefferson and Curry Counties in spring and early summer. Nesting is a distinct possibility, given the recent northward expansion of the species from its breeding base in Texas, Arizona, Idaho and southern California.

HOODED ORIOLE
Icterus cucullatus

The beautiful, orange male Hooded Oriole seems perfectly at home in the ornamental palms that have been planted along the California coast. This colorful oriole's breeding range extends up the coast of California almost to the Oregon border, but it has not nested in Oregon because we do not have the long-fibered palm species it needs for nesting. About half the Oregon records are between mid-April and early June. It has also occurred in early fall, and there have been at least five reports of birds overwintering at hummingbird feeders—a regular event in its southwestern U.S. breeding range.

Hooded Oriole

WHITE-WINGED CROSSBILL
Loxia leucoptera

When news of an irregular winter invasion of these small, nomadic northern finches reaches the rare bird alerts, many birders quickly don their winter coats, thermal underwear, gloves and anything else that will keep out the cold. In Oregon, most White-winged Crossbills do not appear close to cities, but the ones that do usually justify a winter expedition to find them.

White-winged Crossbill

GLOSSARY

accipiter: a forest hawk (from the genus *Accipiter*), characterized by short, rounded wings and a long tail; feeds mostly on birds.

brood: *n.* a family of young from one hatching; *v.* to incubate the eggs.

buteo: a high-soaring hawk (from the genus *Buteo*), characterized by broad wings and a short, wide tail; feeds mostly on small mammals and other land animals.

cere: the fleshy area above the base of the bill on some birds.

clutch: the number of eggs laid by the female at one time.

corvid: a member of the crow family (*Corvidae*); includes crows, jays, magpies and ravens.

covey: a flock of partridges, quail or grouse.

crop: an enlargement of the esophagus; serves as a storage structure and also (in pigeons) has glands that produce secretions to feed the young.

cryptic: a coloration pattern that helps to conceal the bird.

dabbling: a foraging technique used by ducks in which the head and neck are submerged but the body and tail remain on the water's surface; dabbling ducks can usually walk easily on land, can take off without running and have brightly colored speculums.

diurnal: most active during the day.

drake: a male duck.

eclipse plumage: a cryptic plumage, similar to that of females, worn by some male ducks in autumn when they molt their flight feathers and consequently are unable to fly.

egg dumping: the laying of eggs in another bird's nest, leaving the "foster parent" to raise the young.

endangered: facing imminent extirpation or extinction.

extinct: no longer existing anywhere.

extirpated: no longer existing in the wild in a particular region but occurring elsewhere.

fledge: to grow the first full set of feathers.

hawking: attempting to capture insects through aerial pursuit.

Common Poorwill

lek: a place where males gather to display for females in spring.

mantle: the area covering a bird's back and wings.

morph: one of several alternate color phases displayed by a species.

peep: a sandpiper of the genus *Calidris.*

pelagic: open ocean habitat very far from land.

polyandrous: having a mating strategy in which one female breeds with several males.

riparian: along rivers and streams.

sensitive: likely to become threatened or endangered in all or part of its range (state listing).

sexual dimorphism: a difference in plumage, size or other characteristics between males and females of the same species.

species of concern: likely to become threatened or endangered in all or part of its range (federal listing).

stage: to gather in one place during migration, usually when birds are flightless or partly flightless during molting.

stoop: a steep dive through the air, usually performed by birds of prey while foraging or during courtship displays.

threatened: likely to become endangered in the near future in all or part of its range.

torpor: a temporary reduction in body temperature and metabolism in order to conserve energy, usually in response to low temperatures or a lack of food.

tubenose: an albatross, shearwater, petrel or storm-petrel.

vagrant: a transient bird found outside its normal range.

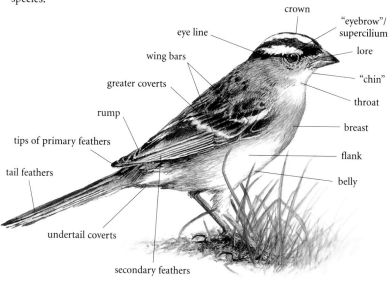

SELECT REFERENCES

American Ornithologists' Union. 1998. *Check-list of North American Birds*. 7th ed. (and its supplements). American Ornithologists' Union, Washington, D.C.

Choate, E.A. 1985. *The Dictionary of American Bird Names*. Rev. ed. Harvard Common Press, Cambridge, MA.

Contreras, A. 1997. *Northwest Birds in Winter*. Oregon State University Press, Corvallis.

Cox, R.T. 1996. *Birder's Dictionary*. Falcon Publishing, Helena, MT.

Ehrlich, P.R., D.S. Dobkin and D. Wheye. 1988. *The Birder's Handbook: A Field Guide to the Natural History of North American Birds*. Simon and Schuster, New York.

Evanich, J.E., Jr. 1990. *The Birder's Guide to Oregon*. Portland Audubon Society, Portland.

Gilligan, J., M. Smith, D. Rogers and A. Contreras, eds. 1994. *Birds of Oregon: Status and Distribution*. Cinclus Publications, McMinnville, OR.

Jones, J.O. 1990. *Where the Birds Are: A Guide to All 50 States and Canada*. William Morrow and Company, New York.

Kaufman, K. 1996. *Lives of North American Birds*. Houghton Mifflin Co., Boston.

Kaufman, K. 2000. *Birds of North America*. Houghton Mifflin Co., New York.

National Geographic Society. 2002. *Field Guide to the Birds of North America*. 4th ed. National Geographic Society, Washington, D.C.

Paulson, D. 1993. *Shorebirds of the Pacific Northwest*. University of British Columbia, Vancouver, B.C.

Sibley, D.A. 2000. *National Audubon Society: The Sibley Guide to Birds*. Alfred A. Knopf, New York.

Sibley, D.A. 2001. *National Audubon Society: The Sibley Guide to Bird Life and Behavior*. Alfred A. Knopf, New York.

Sibley, D.A. 2002. *Sibley's Birding Basics*. Alfred A. Knopf, New York.

Wassink, J.L. 1995. *Birds of the Pacific Northwest Mountains*. Mountain Press Publishing Company, Missoula, MT.

Wauer, R. H. 2000. *Birds of the Northwestern National Parks: A Birder's Perspective*. University of Texas Press, Austin.

CHECKLIST

The following checklist contains 477 species of birds that have been officially recorded in Oregon. Species are grouped by family and listed in taxonomic order in accordance with the A.O.U. *Check-list of North American Birds* (7th ed.) and its supplements.

Regularly appearing species are in plain text. Accidental species that have at least one record verified by photograph, specimen, or video or sound recording are in *italics*. Species in *italics* with an asterisk (*) are accidental species that have been identified by sight records only with no additional verification. A plus (+) indicates introduced species. In addition, the following Oregon state risk categories are noted: extirpated (ex), endangered (en), threatened (th) and sensitive (se).

We wish to express our appreciation to the Oregon Field Ornithologists for giving permission to use their Official Checklist of Oregon Birds as the basis for this checklist.

Loons (Gaviidae)
☐ Red-throated Loon
☐ *Arctic Loon*
☐ Pacific Loon
☐ Common Loon
☐ Yellow-billed Loon

Grebes (Podicipedidae)
☐ Pied-billed Grebe
☐ Horned Grebe (se)
☐ Red-necked Grebe (se)
☐ Eared Grebe
☐ Western Grebe
☐ Clark's Grebe

Albatrosses (Diomedeidae)
☐ *Shy Albatross*
☐ Laysan Albatross
☐ Black-footed Albatross
☐ *Short-tailed Albatross** (en)

Petrels & Shearwaters (Procellariidae)
☐ Northern Fulmar
☐ *Murphy's Petrel*
☐ *Mottled Petrel*
☐ *Streaked Shearwater**
☐ Pink-footed Shearwater

☐ Flesh-footed Shearwater
☐ Buller's Shearwater
☐ Sooty Shearwater
☐ Short-tailed Shearwater
☐ *Black-vented Shearwater**

Storm-Petrels (Hydrobatidae)
☐ *Wilson's Storm-Petrel**
☐ Fork-tailed Storm-Petrel (se)
☐ Leach's Storm-Petrel
☐ *Black Storm-Petrel*

Pelicans (Pelecanidae)
☐ American White Pelican (se)
☐ Brown Pelican (en)

Cormorants (Phalacrocoracidae)
☐ Brandt's Cormorant
☐ Double-crested Cormorant
☐ Pelagic Cormorant

Frigatebirds (Fregatidae)
☐ *Magnificent Frigatebird*

Herons (Ardeidae)
☐ American Bittern
☐ Least Bittern (se)
☐ Great Blue Heron
☐ Great Egret
☐ Snowy Egret (se)
☐ *Little Blue Heron*
☐ *Tricolored Heron*
☐ Cattle Egret
☐ Green Heron
☐ Black-crowned Night-Heron

Ibises (Threskiornithidae)
☐ *White Ibis*
☐ White-faced Ibis

Vultures (Cathartidae)
☐ Turkey Vulture
☐ *California Condor* (ex)

Waterfowl (Anatidae)
☐ *Fulvous Whistling-Duck*
☐ Greater White-fronted Goose
☐ Emperor Goose
☐ Snow Goose
☐ Ross's Goose
☐ Canada Goose

CHECKLIST

☐ Brant
☐ Trumpeter Swan
☐ Tundra Swan
☐ *Whooper Swan*
☐ Wood Duck
☐ Gadwall
☐ Eurasian Wigeon
☐ American Wigeon
☐ *American Black Duck*
☐ Mallard
☐ Blue-winged Teal
☐ Cinnamon Teal
☐ Northern Shoveler
☐ Northern Pintail
☐ *Garganey*
☐ *Baikal Teal*
☐ Green-winged Teal
☐ Canvasback
☐ Redhead
☐ Ring-necked Duck
☐ *Tufted Duck*
☐ Greater Scaup
☐ Lesser Scaup
☐ *Steller's Eider*
☐ *King Eider*
☐ Harlequin Duck (se)
☐ Surf Scoter
☐ White-winged Scoter
☐ Black Scoter
☐ Long-tailed Duck
☐ Bufflehead (se)
☐ Common Goldeneye
☐ Barrow's Goldeneye (se)
☐ *Smew*
☐ Hooded Merganser
☐ Common Merganser
☐ Red-breasted Merganser
☐ Ruddy Duck

Kites, Hawks & Eagles (Accipitridae)
☐ Osprey
☐ White-tailed Kite
☐ Bald Eagle (th)
☐ Northern Harrier
☐ Sharp-shinned Hawk
☐ Cooper's Hawk
☐ Northern Goshawk (se)
☐ Red-shouldered Hawk
☐ *Broad-winged Hawk*
☐ Swainson's Hawk (se)
☐ Red-tailed Hawk
☐ Ferruginous Hawk (se)
☐ Rough-legged Hawk
☐ Golden Eagle

Falcons (Falconidae)
☐ American Kestrel
☐ Merlin
☐ *Gyrfalcon*
☐ Peregrine Falcon (en)
☐ Prairie Falcon

Grouse & Allies (Phasianidae)
☐ Chukar +
☐ Gray Partridge +
☐ Ring-necked Pheasant +
☐ Ruffed Grouse
☐ Greater Sage-Grouse (se)
☐ Spruce Grouse (se)
☐ Blue Grouse
☐ *Sharp-tailed Grouse* (ex)
☐ Wild Turkey +

New World Quails (Odontophoridae)
☐ Mountain Quail (se)
☐ California Quail
☐ Northern Bobwhite +

Rails & Coots (Rallidae)
☐ Yellow Rail (se)
☐ Virginia Rail
☐ Sora
☐ *Common Moorhen*
☐ American Coot

Cranes (Gruidae)
☐ Sandhill Crane (se)

Plovers (Charadriidae)
☐ Black-bellied Plover
☐ American Golden-Plover
☐ Pacific Golden-Plover
☐ *Mongolian Plover*
☐ Snowy Plover (th)
☐ *Wilson's Plover*
☐ Semipalmated Plover
☐ *Piping Plover**
☐ Killdeer
☐ *Mountain Plover*
☐ *Eurasian Dotterel*

Oystercatchers (Haematopodidae)
☐ Black Oystercatcher

Stilts & Avocets (Recurvirostridae)
☐ Black-necked Stilt
☐ American Avocet

Sandpipers & Allies (Scolopacidae)
☐ Greater Yellowlegs
☐ Lesser Yellowlegs
☐ *Spotted Redshank*
☐ Solitary Sandpiper
☐ Willet
☐ Wandering Tattler
☐ Spotted Sandpiper
☐ Upland Sandpiper (se)
☐ Whimbrel
☐ *Bristle-thighed Curlew*
☐ Long-billed Curlew (se)
☐ *Hudsonian Godwit*
☐ *Bar-tailed Godwit*
☐ Marbled Godwit
☐ Ruddy Turnstone
☐ Black Turnstone
☐ Surfbird
☐ *Great Knot*
☐ Red Knot
☐ Sanderling
☐ Semipalmated Sandpiper
☐ Western Sandpiper
☐ *Red-necked Stint*
☐ *Little Stint*
☐ *Long-toed Stint*
☐ Least Sandpiper
☐ Baird's Sandpiper
☐ Pectoral Sandpiper
☐ Sharp-tailed Sandpiper

❑ Rock Sandpiper
❑ Dunlin
❑ *Curlew Sandpiper*
❑ Stilt Sandpiper
❑ Buff-breasted Sandpiper
❑ Ruff
❑ Short-billed Dowitcher
❑ Long-billed Dowitcher
❑ Wilson's Snipe
❑ Wilson's Phalarope
❑ Red-necked Phalarope
❑ Red Phalarope

Gulls & Allies (Laridae)
❑ South Polar Skua
❑ Pomarine Jaeger
❑ Parasitic Jaeger
❑ Long-tailed Jaeger
❑ *Laughing Gull*
❑ Franklin's Gull (se)
❑ *Little Gull*
❑ *Black-headed Gull*
❑ Bonaparte's Gull
❑ Heermann's Gull
❑ Mew Gull
❑ Ring-billed Gull
❑ California Gull
❑ Herring Gull
❑ Thayer's Gull
❑ *Slaty-backed Gull*
❑ Western Gull
❑ Glaucous-winged Gull
❑ Glaucous Gull
❑ Sabine's Gull
❑ Black-legged Kittiwake
❑ *Red-legged Kittiwake*
❑ *Ross's Gull*
❑ Caspian Tern
❑ Elegant Tern
❑ Common Tern
❑ Arctic Tern
❑ Forster's Tern
❑ *Least Tern* (en)
❑ Black Tern

Alcids (Alcidae)
❑ Common Murre
❑ *Thick-billed Murre*
❑ Pigeon Guillemot

❑ Marbled Murrelet (th)
❑ *Xantus's Murrelet*
❑ Ancient Murrelet
❑ Cassin's Auklet
❑ *Parakeet Auklet*
❑ Rhinoceros Auklet
❑ Horned Puffin
❑ Tufted Puffin

Pigeons & Doves (Columbidae)
❑ Rock Dove +
❑ Band-tailed Pigeon
❑ *White-winged Dove*
❑ Mourning Dove

Cuckoos (Cuculidae)
❑ *Yellow-billed Cuckoo* (se)

Barn Owls (Tytonidae)
❑ Barn Owl

Owls (Strigidae)
❑ Flammulated Owl (se)
❑ Western Screech-Owl
❑ Great Horned Owl
❑ Snowy Owl
❑ *Northern Hawk Owl*
❑ Northern Pygmy-Owl (se)
❑ Burrowing Owl (se)
❑ Spotted Owl (th)
❑ Barred Owl
❑ Great Gray Owl (se)
❑ Long-eared Owl
❑ Short-eared Owl
❑ *Boreal Owl* (se)
❑ Northern Saw-whet Owl

Nightjars (Caprimulgidae)
❑ Common Nighthawk (se)
❑ Common Poorwill

Swifts (Apodidae)
❑ Black Swift (se)
❑ Vaux's Swift
❑ White-throated Swift

Hummingbirds (Trochilidae)
❑ *Broad-billed Hummingbird*
❑ Black-chinned Hummingbird
❑ Anna's Hummingbird
❑ *Costa's Hummingbird*
❑ Calliope Hummingbird
❑ Broad-tailed Hummingbird
❑ Rufous Hummingbird
❑ Allen's Hummingbird

Kingfishers (Alcedinidae)
❑ Belted Kingfisher

Woodpeckers (Picidae)
❑ Lewis's Woodpecker (se)
❑ Acorn Woodpecker
❑ Williamson's Sapsucker (se)
❑ *Yellow-bellied Sapsucker*
❑ Red-naped Sapsucker
❑ Red-breasted Sapsucker
❑ *Nuttall's Woodpecker*
❑ Downy Woodpecker
❑ Hairy Woodpecker
❑ White-headed Woodpecker (se)
❑ Three-toed Woodpecker (se)
❑ Black-backed Woodpecker (se)
❑ Northern Flicker
❑ Pileated Woodpecker (se)

Flycatchers (Tyrannidae)
❑ Olive-sided Flycatcher (se)
❑ Western Wood-Pewee
❑ *Eastern Wood-Pewee*
❑ Willow Flycatcher (se)
❑ *Least Flycatcher*
❑ Hammond's Flycatcher
❑ Gray Flycatcher

CHECKLIST

❏ Dusky Flycatcher
❏ Pacific-slope Flycatcher
❏ Cordilleran Flycatcher
❏ Black Phoebe
❏ *Eastern Phoebe*
❏ Say's Phoebe
❏ *Vermilion Flycatcher*
❏ *Dusky-capped Flycatcher*
❏ Ash-throated Flycatcher
❏ *Tropical Kingbird*
❏ Western Kingbird
❏ Eastern Kingbird
❏ *Scissor-tailed Flycatcher*

Shrikes (Laniidae)
❏ Loggerhead Shrike (se)
❏ Northern Shrike

Vireos (Vireonidae)
❏ *Bell's Vireo**
❏ Cassin's Vireo
❏ *Blue-headed Vireo**
❏ Hutton's Vireo
❏ Warbling Vireo
❏ *Philadelphia Vireo*
❏ Red-eyed Vireo

Crows, Jays & Magpies (Corvidae)
❏ Gray Jay
❏ Steller's Jay
❏ Blue Jay
❏ Western Scrub-Jay
❏ Pinyon Jay
❏ Clark's Nutcracker
❏ Black-billed Magpie
❏ American Crow
❏ Common Raven

Larks (Alaudidae)
❏ Horned Lark

Swallows (Hirundinidae)
❏ Purple Martin (se)
❏ Tree Swallow
❏ Violet-green Swallow
❏ Northern Rough-winged Swallow

❏ Bank Swallow (se)
❏ Cliff Swallow
❏ Barn Swallow

Chickadees & Titmice (Paridae)
❏ Black-capped Chickadee
❏ Mountain Chickadee
❏ Chestnut-backed Chickadee
❏ Oak Titmouse
❏ Juniper Titmouse

Bushtits (Aegithalidae)
❏ Bushtit

Nuthatches (Sittidae)
❏ Red-breasted Nuthatch
❏ White-breasted Nuthatch
❏ Pygmy Nuthatch (se)

Creepers (Certhiidae)
❏ Brown Creeper

Wrens (Troglodytidae)
❏ Rock Wren
❏ Canyon Wren
❏ Bewick's Wren
❏ House Wren
❏ Winter Wren
❏ Marsh Wren

Dippers (Cinclidae)
❏ American Dipper

Kinglets (Regulidae)
❏ Golden-crowned Kinglet
❏ Ruby-crowned Kinglet

Gnatcatchers (Sylviidae)
❏ Blue-gray Gnatcatcher

Thrushes (Turdidae)
❏ *Northern Wheatear*
❏ Western Bluebird (se)
❏ Mountain Bluebird
❏ Townsend's Solitaire

❏ Veery
❏ *Gray-cheeked Thrush*
❏ Swainson's Thrush
❏ Hermit Thrush
❏ *Wood Thrush*
❏ American Robin
❏ Varied Thrush

Wrentits (Timaliidae)
❏ Wrentit

Mockingbirds & Thrashers (Mimidae)
❏ Gray Catbird
❏ Northern Mockingbird
❏ Sage Thrasher
❏ *Brown Thrasher*
❏ *California Thrasher**

Starlings (Sturnidae)
❏ European Starling +

Wagtails & Pipits (Motacillidae)
❏ *Black-backed Wagtail*
❏ American Pipit

Waxwings (Bombycillidae)
❏ Bohemian Waxwing
❏ Cedar Waxwing

Silky-flycatchers (Ptilogonatidae)
❏ Phainopepla

Wood-Warblers (Parulidae)
❏ *Blue-winged Warbler**
❏ *Golden-winged Warbler*
❏ Tennessee Warbler
❏ Orange-crowned Warbler
❏ Nashville Warbler
❏ *Virginia's Warbler*
❏ *Lucy's Warbler*
❏ *Northern Parula*
❏ Yellow Warbler
❏ *Chestnut-sided Warbler*
❏ *Magnolia Warbler*

- ☐ Cape May Warbler
- ☐ Black-throated Blue Warbler
- ☐ Yellow-rumped Warbler
- ☐ Black-throated Gray Warbler
- ☐ *Black-throated Green Warbler*
- ☐ Townsend's Warbler
- ☐ Hermit Warbler
- ☐ *Blackburnian Warbler*
- ☐ *Yellow-throated Warbler*
- ☐ *Pine Warbler**
- ☐ *Prairie Warbler*
- ☐ *Palm Warbler*
- ☐ *Bay-breasted Warbler*
- ☐ *Blackpoll Warbler*
- ☐ Black-and-white Warbler
- ☐ American Redstart
- ☐ *Prothonotary Warbler*
- ☐ *Worm-eating Warbler**
- ☐ Ovenbird
- ☐ Northern Waterthrush
- ☐ *Louisiana Waterthrush*
- ☐ *Kentucky Warbler*
- ☐ *Mourning Warbler**
- ☐ MacGillivray's Warbler
- ☐ Common Yellowthroat
- ☐ Hooded Warbler
- ☐ Wilson's Warbler
- ☐ *Canada Warbler*
- ☐ Yellow-breasted Chat (se)

Tanagers (Thraupidae)
- ☐ *Summer Tanager*
- ☐ *Scarlet Tanager*
- ☐ Western Tanager

Sparrows & Allies (Emberizidae)
- ☐ Green-tailed Towhee
- ☐ Spotted Towhee
- ☐ California Towhee
- ☐ American Tree Sparrow
- ☐ Chipping Sparrow
- ☐ Clay-colored Sparrow
- ☐ Brewer's Sparrow
- ☐ *Black-chinned Sparrow*
- ☐ Vesper Sparrow

- ☐ Lark Sparrow
- ☐ Black-throated Sparrow (se)
- ☐ Sage Sparrow (se)
- ☐ *Lark Bunting*
- ☐ Savannah Sparrow
- ☐ Grasshopper Sparrow (se)
- ☐ *Le Conte's Sparrow*
- ☐ Fox Sparrow
- ☐ Song Sparrow
- ☐ Lincoln's Sparrow
- ☐ Swamp Sparrow
- ☐ White-throated Sparrow
- ☐ Harris's Sparrow
- ☐ White-crowned Sparrow
- ☐ Golden-crowned Sparrow
- ☐ Dark-eyed Junco
- ☐ *McCown's Longspur**
- ☐ Lapland Longspur
- ☐ *Chestnut-collared Longspur*
- ☐ *Rustic Bunting*
- ☐ Snow Bunting
- ☐ *McKay's Bunting*

Grosbeaks & Buntings (Cardinalidae)
- ☐ *Rose-breasted Grosbeak*
- ☐ Black-headed Grosbeak
- ☐ *Blue Grosbeak*
- ☐ Lazuli Bunting
- ☐ *Indigo Bunting*
- ☐ *Painted Bunting*
- ☐ *Dickcissel*

Blackbirds & Allies (Icteridae)
- ☐ Bobolink (se)
- ☐ Red-winged Blackbird
- ☐ Tricolored Blackbird (se)
- ☐ Western Meadowlark (se)
- ☐ Yellow-headed Blackbird
- ☐ *Rusty Blackbird*

- ☐ Brewer's Blackbird
- ☐ *Common Grackle*
- ☐ *Great-tailed Grackle*
- ☐ Brown-headed Cowbird
- ☐ *Orchard Oriole*
- ☐ *Hooded Oriole*
- ☐ *Streak-backed Oriole*
- ☐ Bullock's Oriole
- ☐ *Baltimore Oriole*
- ☐ *Scott's Oriole**

Finches (Fringillidae)
- ☐ *Brambling*
- ☐ Gray-crowned Rosy-Finch
- ☐ Black Rosy-Finch (se)
- ☐ Pine Grosbeak
- ☐ Purple Finch
- ☐ Cassin's Finch
- ☐ House Finch
- ☐ Red Crossbill
- ☐ White-winged Crossbill
- ☐ Common Redpoll
- ☐ *Hoary Redpoll**
- ☐ Pine Siskin
- ☐ Lesser Goldfinch
- ☐ *Lawrence's Goldfinch*
- ☐ American Goldfinch
- ☐ Evening Grosbeak

Old World Sparrows (Passeridae)
- ☐ House Sparrow +

INDEX OF SCIENTIFIC NAMES

This index references only the primary species accounts.

INDEX OF COMMON NAMES

Page numbers in **boldface** type refer to the primary, illustrated species accounts.

ABOUT THE AUTHORS

Roger Burrows

Roger Burrows has traveled North America extensively. While completing his B.Sc., he worked as a naturalist, interpretive planner and avifaunal consultant and has since worked as a bird identification workshop provider, avifaunal surveyor and naturalist on cruise ships. He has also been a writer/photographer for, and then owner of, a rural lifestyle magazine. Roger has coauthored a number of Lone Pine nature guides.

Jeff Gilligan

An avid birder since he was 12 years old, Jeff Gilligan has been very active in the Oregon birding community. He authored and edited the book *Birds of Oregon: Status and Distribution*, was an editor for the periodicals *Oregon Birds* and *North American Birds* (formerly *American Birds*) and has been a member of the Oregon Bird Records Committee since its inception in the 1970s. He has lived in Oregon his entire life but has traveled extensively on birding trips throughout North America, Europe, Latin America, Oceania, Australia, Asia and Africa. He enjoys bird identification, looking for rarities, understanding the status, distribution and migrations of Oregon birds and the relaxation of looking at even common species.

Least Bittern